ANNUAL EDITIONS

Social Psychology

Seventh Edition

D0025849

CO-EDITORS

Karen G. Duffy
SUNY at Geneseo (Emerita)

Karen G. Duffy holds a doctorate in psychology from Michigan State University, and she is an emerita Distinguished Service Professor of State University of New York at Geneseo. Dr. Duffy continues to work on her books and research, and she is also involved in several community service projects both in the United States and Russia.

Gary E. Krolikowski
SUNY Empire State College

Gary Krolikowski is a faculty mentor at Suny Empire State College and also on the faculty of Rochester Institute of Technology, SUNY Brockport and SUNY Geneseo. A doctoral candidate at Northcentral University with Master's work at Saint Lawrence University and a BA from SUNY Potsdam, he is active in reviewing textbooks and involved in community organizations both in the United States and in Poland.

MONTCALM COMMUNITY
COLLEGE LIBRARY

2460 Kerper Blvd., Dubuque, IA 52001

Visit us on the Internet
http://www.mhcls.com

Credits

1. **Research Issues**
   Unit photo—BrandX/Jupiter Images/Getty Images
2. **The Self**
   Unit photo—BananaStock/PunchStock
3. **Social Cognition and Social Perception**
   Unit photo—image 100/PunchStock
4. **Attitudes**
   Unit photo—The McGraw-Hill Companies, Inc./John Flournoy, photographer
5. **Social Influence**
   Unit photo—Getty Images/SW Productions
6. **Social Relationships**
   Unit photo—Suza Scalara/Getty Images
7. **Social Biases**
   Unit photo—CORBIS/Royalty-Free
8. **Violence and Aggression**
   Unit photo—Ingram Publishing/Fotosearch
9. **Altruism, Helping and Cooperation**
   Unit photo—The McGraw-Hill Companies, Inc./Christopher Kerrigan, photographer
10. **Group Processes**
    Unit photo—Corbis Images/Jupiter Images

Copyright

Cataloging in Publication Data
Main entry under title: Annual Editions: Social Psychology 2007/2008.
1. Psychology—Periodicals. I. Duffy, Karen; Krolikowski, Gary E., *comp.* II. Title: Social psychology.
ISBN-13: 978–0–07–339739–9   ISBN-10: 0–07–339739–3   302'.05   ISSN 0730–6962

© 2008 by McGraw-Hill/Contemporary Learning Series, Dubuque, IA 52001, A Division of The McGraw-Hill Companies.

Copyright law prohibits the reproduction, storage, or transmission in any form by any means of any portion of this publication without the express written permission of McGraw-Hill/Contemporary Learning Series, and of the copyright holder (if different) of the part of the publication to be reproduced. The Guidelines for Classroom Copying endorsed by Congress explicitly state that unauthorized copying may not be used to create, to replace, or to substitute for anthologies, compilations, or collective works. Inquiries concerning publishing rights to the articles herein can be directed to the Permission Department at Contemporary Learning Series Publishing. 800.243.6532

Annual Editions® is a Registered Trademark of McGraw-Hill/Contemporary Learning Series, A Division of The McGraw-Hill Companies.

Seventh Edition

Cover image © Photos.com
Printed in the United States of America   1234567890QPDQPD987   Printed on Recycled Paper

Editors/Advisory Board

Members of the Advisory Board are instrumental in the final selection of articles for each edition of ANNUAL EDITIONS. Their review of articles for content, level, currentness, and appropriateness provides critical direction to the editor and staff. We think that you will find their careful consideration well reflected in this volume.

CO-EDITORS

Karen G. Duffy
SUNY at Geneseo (Emerita)

Gary E. Krolikowski
Suny Empire State College

ADVISORY BOARD

Anita P. Barbee
University of Louisville

Thomas Blass
University of Maryland, Baltimore County

Bernardo J. Carducci
Indiana University–Southeast

Marilyn N. Carroll
Rockhurst College

Susan E. Cross
Iowa State University

Joseph Davis
San Diego State University-San Diego

Stephen L. Franzoi
Marquette University

Malcolm J. Grant
Memorial University of Newfoundland

Curtis Haugtvedt
Ohio State University

Martin Heesacker
University of Florida–Gainesville

Mary Lee Meiners
Miramar College

Joann M. Montepare
Emerson College

Robert J. Pellegrini
San Jose State University

Ronald E. Riggio
Claremont McKenna College

Jonathan Springer
Kean University

Charles G. Stangor
University of Maryland, College Park

Abraham Tesser
University of Georgia

Shelley A. Theno
University of Alaska–Southeast

Fred W. Whitford
Montana State University

Staff

EDITORIAL STAFF

Larry Loeppke, Managing Editor
Jay Oberbroeckling, Developmental Editor
Jade Benedict, Developmental Editor
Nancy Meissner, Editorial Assistant

PERMISSIONS STAFF

Lenny J. Behnke, Permissions Coordinator
Lori Church, Permissions Coordinator
Shirley Lanners, Permissions Coordinator

TECHNOLOGY STAFF

Luke David, eContent Coordinator

MARKETING STAFF

Julie Keck, Senior Marketing Manager
Mary Klein, Marketing Communications Specialist
Alice Link, Marketing Coordinator
Tracie Kammerude, Senior Marketing Assistant

PRODUCTION STAFF

Beth Kundert, Production Manager
Trish Mish, Production Assistant
Kari Voss, Lead Typesetter
Jean Smith, Typesetter
Karen Spring, Typesetter
Sandy Wille, Typesetter
Tara McDermott, Designer
Maggie Lytle, Cover Graphics

Preface

In publishing ANNUAL EDITIONS we recognize the enormous role played by the magazines, newspapers, and journals of the public press in providing current, first-rate educational information in a broad spectrum of interest areas. Many of these articles are appropriate for students, researchers, and professionals seeking accurate, current material to help bridge the gap between principles and theories and the real world. These articles, however, become more useful for study when those of lasting value are carefully collected, organized, and reproduced in a low-cost format, which provides easy and permanent access when the material is needed. That is the role played by ANNUAL EDITIONS.

Social psychology is one of the most fascinating fields in all of psychology. Its rapid and continued strong growth attest to its interest level, contributions to science, and applicability.

Just what is social psychology? There are as many different definitions as there are authors. Most definitions of social psychology are similar to the following—*social psychology is the scientific study of how others affect our thoughts and behaviors*. In other words, individual "action" (behavior) may be the domain of all of psychology, but social interaction is the province of social psychology.

What does this definition mean for you? First, as stated in the definition, other people's actions and thoughts have an impact on you. You, however, have just as important an influence on them. If someone else is angry with you, you will certainly feel the effects—direct or indirect. On the other hand, if you are angry with someone, that person may also experience the repercussions.

All types of groups—large and small—are of interest to social psychologists. Loving couples, angry friends, and mothers and infants make up some of the smallest groups social psychologists study. Medium sized groups also fall under the scrutiny of social psychologists, including but not limited to work groups, committees, and even a gang of bank robbers. Large groups and sometimes whole organizations also captivate the attention of social psychologists. Such groups as students in a classroom, whole corporations, crowds at a sporting event, and chat room participants are within a social psychologist's purview.

On the other hand, there are some marked similarities between social psychologists and other psychologists. All psychologists base their knowledge and practices on science. Most research psychologists call upon the scientific method in their investigations. As in other fields of psychology, the inspiration for research in social psychology is a theory—to be supported or not. Finally, most all psychologists hope that their theories and research can be employed to help improve the human condition.

This anthology is designed to focus your attention on issues in social psychology. Some articles draw your attention to details while others pertain to major themes in social psychology. The first unit, *Research Issues*, is new to this edition. Social psychologists are more likely to utilize deception than are many other types of psychologists. Thus, they greatly worry about research ethics, research design, and protection of human participants.

Unit 2 pertains to the self-concept. Self-concept, most psychologists would argue, originates because of social interactions with significant others (namely parents). Culture also plays a key role in determining who we think we are and what we think of ourselves. Unit 3 relates to social cognition and social perception. It is divided into a subunit on each topic. Your interpretation of others' behaviors, motives, feelings, and attitudes is as important as their construal of yours. Misperception can sometimes spell disaster, especially at the international level.

Children appear to be born without attitudinal biases. Attitudes form during childhood from exchanges with others. If Mom and Dad practice a particular religion, join a certain political party, and root for a specific team, chances are their child will soon hold the same attitudes, beliefs, and values. Attitudes, attitude formation, and attitude change, then, are important aspects of social psychology and are covered in Unit 4—Attitudes.

There exist myriad methods to influence or persuade others, known as social influence. The three main techniques are conformity, compliance, and obedience—in order of the intensity of influence. These topics are covered in Unit 5. Unit 6 is equally important because it contains articles on social relationships. There are two subunits once again, one on interpersonal relationships such as friendships and another on more intimate relationships such as marriage.

Unit 6 on prejudice affords you the opportunity to examine social biases in detail. Prejudice is an attitude that can cause discrimination as well as stereotypes. Each of these topics is explored in its own subunit. Additionally, any social psychology text would be incomplete without a presentation of on the matter of violence—societal, within and between groups, or inter-individual. Several articles explore a variety of issues related to conflict, hostility, and aggressiveness in Unit 8. A more positive side of human nature is considered in the following section, Unit 9. Humans can also use their energy to benefit others. This part of the anthology includes articles on altruism and helping.

This collection ends with Unit 10—Group Processes. Because this subject is last does not mean it is least important. In fact, group (and leader) dynamics is one of the oldest areas of social psychology, in part spawned by army brigades in World War II and further nurtured by the need to know about groups and leaders, such as managers and their employees.

Annual Editions: Social Psychology 07/08 will challenge and interest you in a variety of topics. It will provide you with many answers and also stimulate many questions. As has been true in the past, your feedback on this edition would be valuable for future revisions. Please take a moment to fill out and return the postage-paid article rating form on the last page. Thank you.

Karen Grover Duffy
Co-Editor

Gary Krolikowski
Co-Editor

Contents

UNIT 1
Research Issues

UNIT 2
The Self

The concepts in bold italics are developed in the article. For further expansion, please refer to the Topic Guide and the Index.

UNIT 3
Social Cognition and Social Perception

UNIT 4
Attitudes

The concepts in bold italics are developed in the article. For further expansion, please refer to the Topic Guide and the Index.

UNIT 5
Social Influence

UNIT 6
Social Relationships

The concepts in bold italics are developed in the article. For further expansion, please refer to the Topic Guide and the Index.

UNIT 7
Social Biases

The concepts in bold italics are developed in the article. For further expansion, please refer to the Topic Guide and the Index.

UNIT 8
Violence and Aggression

UNIT 9
Altruism, Helping and Cooperation

The concepts in bold italics are developed in the article. For further expansion, please refer to the Topic Guide and the Index.

UNIT 10
Group Processes

The concepts in bold italics are developed in the article. For further expansion, please refer to the Topic Guide and the Index.

Topic Guide

This topic guide suggests how the selections in this book relate to the subjects covered in your course. You may want to use the topics listed on these pages to search the Web more easily.

On the following pages a number of Web sites have been gathered specifically for this book. They are arranged to reflect the units of this *Annual Edition*. You can link to these sites by going to the student online support site at *http://www.mhcls.com/online/*.

ALL THE ARTICLES THAT RELATE TO EACH TOPIC ARE LISTED BELOW THE BOLD-FACED TERM.

Aggression

27. Anger on the Road

Altruism

30. The Compassionate Instinct
31. Gift Giving's Hidden Strings

Anger management

27. Anger on the Road

Attitudes

12. The Science and Practice of Persuasion
13. In Search of Pro Americanism

Authority

33. Seven Transformations of Leadership
35. To Err Is Human

Bargaining

11. Implicit Discrimination

Behavior

6. How Social Perception Can Automatically Influence Behavior
8. Culture Affects Reasoning, Categorization
15. Abu Ghraib Brings A Cruel Reawakening
27. Anger on the Road
28. Bullying: It Isn't What It Used To Be

Bystander apathy

35. To Err Is Human

Cognition

6. How Social Perception Can Automatically Influence Behavior
8. Culture Affects Reasoning, Categorization
17. Contagious Behavior
26. A Bicultural Perspective on Worldviews
35. To Err Is Human

Cohort group

13. In Search of Pro Americanism

Compassion

31. Gift Giving's Hidden Strings

Cooperation

2. Ethnic and Racial Health Disparities Research: Issues and Problems
4. Self-Concordance and Subjective Well-Being in Four Cultures
8. Culture Affects Reasoning, Categorization

18. Competent Jerks, Lovable Fools, and the Formation of Social Networks
26. A Bicultural Perspective on Worldviews
30. The Compassionate Instinct
32. Trends in the Social Psychological Study of Justice

Decision making

11. Implicit Discrimination

Demographics

13. In Search of Pro Americanism

Discrimination

11. Implicit Discrimination

Ecological models

17. Contagious Behavior

Education

23. Leaving Race Behind
24. Lowered Expectations

Ethnicity

2. Ethnic and Racial Health Disparities Research: Issues and Problems
23. Leaving Race Behind

Evolutionary psychology

30. The Compassionate Instinct

Explicit attitudes

11. Implicit Discrimination

Faces and bodies (perception)

10. Perception of Faces and Bodies

False memory

7. Flashbulb Memories: How Psychological Research Shows That Our Most Powerful Memories May Be Untrustworthy

First impressions

14. "Thin Slices" of Life

Gender

13. In Search of Pro Americanism

Groups and group dynamics

34. When Followers Become Toxic
35. To Err Is Human

Self-concept

Self-esteem

Shyness

Significant others

Upward mobility

Internet References

The following Internet sites have been carefully researched and selected to support the articles found in this reader. The easiest way to access these selected sites is to go to our student online support site at *http://www.mhcls.com/online/*.

AE: Social Psychology, 7/e

The following sites were available at the time of publication. Visit our Web site—we update our student online support site regularly to reflect any changes.

General Sources

Journals Related to Social Psychology
http://www.socialpsychology.org/journals.htm

Maintained by Wesleyan University, this site is a link to journals related to the study of psychology, social psychology, and sociology.

Social Psychology Network
http://www.socialpsychology.org

The Social Psychology Network is the most comprehensive source of social psychology information on the Internet, including resources, programs, and research.

Society of Experimental Social Psychology
http://www.sesp.org

SESP is a scientific organization dedicated to the advancement of social psychology.

UNIT 1: Research Issues

American Educational Research Association (AERA)
http://www.aera.net/

AERA is concerned with improving the educational process by encouraging scholarly inquiry related to education and by promoting the dissemination and practical application of research results.

Office of Science and Technology Policy (OSTP)
http://www.ostp.gov/

The National Science and Technology Council's Committee on Science provides advice and assistance to the National Science and Technology Council on significant science policy matters that cross federal agencies.

UNIT 2: The Self

FreudNet
http://www.psychoanalysis.org

FreudNet is part of the Abraham A. Brill Library of the New York Psychoanalytic Institute. This site provides information on mental health, Sigmund Freud, and psychoanalysis.

UNIT 3: Social Cognition and Social Perception

Nonverbal Behavior and Nonverbal Communication
http://www3.usal.es/~nonverbal/

This fascinating site has a detailed listing of nonverbal behavior and nonverbal communication sites on the Web, including the work of historical and current researchers.

UNIT 4: Attitudes

Psychological Warfare Links
http://www.psywar.org/links.php

This Web site provides links to sites that use propaganda to influence and change attitudes. At this site, you can link to contemporary fascist, political, religious, and Holocaust revisionist propaganda.

The Psychology of Cyberspace
http://www.rider.edu/users/suler/psycyber/psycyber.html

This site studies the psychological dimensions of environments created by computers and online networks.

UNIT 5: Social Influence

AFF Cult Group Information
http://www.csj.org

AFF's mission is to study psychological manipulation and cult groups, to assist those who have been adversely affected by a cult experience, and to educate.

Center for Leadership Studies
http://www.situational.com

The Center for Leadership Studies (CLS) is organized for the research and development of the full range of leadership in individuals, teams, organizations, and communities.

Social Influence Website
http://www.influenceatwork.com/

This Web site is devoted to social influence—the modern scientific study of persuasion, compliance, and propaganda.

UNIT 6: Social Relationships

American Association of University Women
http://www.aauw.org

The AAUW is a national organization that promotes education and equity for all women and girls.

Coalition for Marriage, Family, and Couples Education
http://www.smartmarriages.com

CMFCE is dedicated to bringing information about and directories of skill-based marriage education courses to the public. It hopes to lower the rate of family breakdown through couple-empowering preventive education.

GLAAD: Gay and Lesbian Alliance Against Defamation
http://www.glaad.org

GLAAD was formed in New York in 1985. Its mission is to improve the public's attitudes toward homosexuality and put an end to discrimination against lesbians and gay men.

The Kinsey Institute for Research in Sex, Gender, and Reproduction
http://www.indiana.edu/~kinsey/

The purpose of the Kinsey Institute's Web site is to support interdisciplinary research and the study of human sexuality. The institute was founded by Dr. Alfred Kinsey, 1894–1956.

www.mhcls.com/online/

Marriage and Family Therapy
http://www.aamft.org/index_nm.asp

This site has links to numerous marriage and family therapy topics. Online directories, books and articles are also available.

The National Organization for Women (NOW) Home Page
http://www.now.org

NOW is the largest organization of feminist activists in the United States. It has 250,000 members and 600 chapters in all 50 states and the District of Columbia. NOW's goal has been "to take action" to bring about equality for all women.

The Society for the Scientific Study of Sexuality
http://www.ssc.wisc.edu/ssss/

The Society for the Scientific Study of Sexuality is an international organization dedicated to the advancement of knowledge about sexuality.

UNIT 7: Social Biases

NAACP Online: National Association for the Advancement of Colored People
http://www.naacp.org

The principal objective of the NAACP is to ensure the political, educational, social, and economic equality of minority group citizens in the United States.

National Civil Rights Museum
http://www.civilrightsmuseum.org

The National Civil Rights Museum, located at the Lorraine Motel, where Dr. Martin Luther King Jr. was assassinated April 4, 1968, is the world's first and only comprehensive overview of the civil rights movement in exhibit form.

United States Holocaust Memorial Museum
http://www.ushmm.org/

The United States Holocaust Memorial Museum is America's national institution for the documentation, study, and interpretation of Holocaust history, and serves as this country's memorial to the millions of people murdered during the Holocaust.

Yahoo—Social Psychology
http://www.yahoo.com/Social_Science/Psychology/disciplines/social_psychology/

This link takes you to Yahoo!'s social psychology Web sites. Explore prejudice, discrimination, and stereotyping from this site.

UNIT 8: Violence and Aggression

MINCAVA: Minnesota Center Against Violence and Abuse
http://www.mincava.umn.edu

The Minnesota Center Against Violence and Abuse operates an electronic clearinghouse via the World Wide Web with access to thousands of Gopher servers, interactive discussion groups, newsgroups, and Web sites around the world. Its goal is to provide quick, user-friendly access to the extensive electronic resources on the topic of violence and abuse.

National Consortium on Violence Research
http://www.nicic.org/Library/020733

The National Consortium on Violence Research is a newly established research and training institute that is dedicated to the scientific and advanced study of the factors contributing to interpersonal violence.

UNIT 9: Altruism, Helping and Cooperation

Americans With Disabilities Act Document Center
http://www.jan.wvu.edu/links/adalinks.htm

This Web site contains copies of the Americans With Disabilities Act of 1990 (ADA) and ADA regulations. This site also provides you with links to other Internet sources of information concerning disability issues.

Give Five
http://www.independentsector.org/give5/givefive.html

The Give Five Web site is a project of Independent Sector, a national coalition of foundations, voluntary organizations, and corporate giving programs working to encourage giving, volunteering, not-for-profit initiatives, and citizen action.

University of Maryland Diversity Database
http://www.inform.umd.edu/EdRes/Topic/Diversity/

The University of Maryland's Diversity Database is sponsored by the Diversity Initiative Program. It contains campus, local, national, and international academic material relating to age, class, disability, ethnicity, gender, national origin, race, religion, and sexual orientation.

UNIT 10: Group Processes

Center for the Study of Group Processes
http://www.uiowa.edu/~grpproc/

The mission of the Center for the Study of Group Processes includes promoting basic research in the field of group processes and enhancing the professional development of faculty and students in that field.

Collaborative Organizations
http://www.workteams.unt.edu

The Center for Collaborative Organizations is a nonprofit organization whose vision is to become the premier center for research on collaborative work systems to create learning partnerships that support the design, implementation, and development of collaborative work systems.

We highly recommend that you review our Web site for expanded information and our other product lines. We are continually updating and adding links to our Web site in order to offer you the most usable and useful information that will support and expand the value of your Annual Editions. You can reach us at: *http://www.mhcls.com/annualeditions/*.

UNIT 1

Research Issues

Unit Selections

1. **How to Be a Wise Consumer of Psychological Research**, *American Psychological Association*
2. **Ethnic and Racial Health Disparities Research: Issues and Problems**, Stanley Sue and Meenu K. Dhindsa

Key Points to Consider

- How does an individual evaluate the validity and reliability of information?

- Is total objectivity possible?

- How has androcentrism affected the validity of social psychology research in the past?

- What ethnic/racial groups do you feel are under represented and over represented in social psychology research?

- Would you be willing to volunteer as a participant in social psychological research? What concerns would you have?

- How do both culture and gender affect social psychological research?

Student Web Site

www.mhcls.com/online

Internet References

Further information regarding these Web sites may be found in this book's preface or online.

American Educational Research Association (AERA)
http://www.aera.net/

Office of Science and Technology Policy (OSTP)
http://www.ostp.gov/

Social psychologists believe firmly in the scientific method. Interestingly, because of social psychology's breadth, the arsenal of research methods available to social psychologists is very broad, although controlled experiments remain highly respected. Interviews, questionnaires, observations, and analysis of historical data are just a few of the research techniques from which social psychologists choose. You should recognize, though, that these alternate methods are borrowed from a variety of related fields, including but not limited to anthropology, education, sociology, political science, and others. As you can see, social psychologists have many intellectual brothers and sisters outside their own field. Likewise, many of these siblings share a huge interest in the results and applications of social psychological research.

Research in social psychology has one or two primary purposes. One purpose is to confirm or disconfirm a theory and related hypotheses. The second purpose is eventually to apply results to practical solutions, especially for compelling social problems, be they school the military situation in Iraq, gang violence, student-teacher conflict, or marital strife.

In their scientific endeavors, social psychologists regularly collide with a multitude of problems, not the least of which is sheer human vagary. For example, some people do not wish to participate in psychological research. Others participate but are not especially cooperative when they do. Yet others are too young, too inexperienced, or too inarticulate to contribute. Finally, some participants may be busy guessing the researcher's hypothesis, which can drastically alter research results and subsequent interpretations. There may be a tendency for the person to offer responses that skew data due to the social desirability effect wherein participants give what they believe to be the socially correct and appropriate responses (which may very well differ from the truth).

Even the investigator can alter his or her own results. If a researcher knows in advance the hypothesis or theory, holds biases against certain groups, or possesses some unusual attribute (e.g. extraordinarily tall), the results might be compromised. In fact, research on research processes has demonstrated that the mere presence of a white lab coat or of ominous looking electrical equipment can skew results.

In addition, social psychologists eventually have to move from their laboratories to the "real" world, the world of everyday social interaction. Once any researcher heads outside the lab, she or he inevitably loses some essential control over events as well as participants. Such control is valued because by containing the influence of some factors (i.e. variables), the researcher can be more certain that other factors, and only those factors, account for the results. A rainy day in the park has ruined many an observational study due to lack of park attendees, while gaps in public records have spoiled many an archival study.

While the research design is of crucial importance, another pressing issue for social psychologists is to do no harm to those they investigate. Reviewing of research proposals by an institutional review board, obtaining a participant's *informed* consent, and debriefing them are part of the ethical principles of conducting human research.

Compared to other scientists, social psychologists frequently include deception in their research. Justifying the deception and ultimately revealing it to participants are paramount pieces of our ethical principles. In order to justify deception, researchers need to be able to demonstrate that the information gleaned far outweighs the damage any deception might generate.

It is, therefore, important that students become informed consumers of the research. The methodologies and nomenclature may sometimes be misleading. In the first article "How to Be a Wise Consumer of Psychological Research," the American Psychological Association offers means by which to successfully navigate through social science research. Various methods are described in a straightforward manner to assist the student of social sciences

In the second article "Ethnic and Racial Health Disparities Research: Issues and Problems," Stanley Sue and Meenu K. Dhindsa discuss research issues central to such things as culture, disparity, ethnicity and race. In social psychology, sometimes the nature(s) of the group(s) studied impose unique and complex challenges.

How to Be A Wise Consumer of Psychological Research

It is difficult to turn the pages of a newspaper without coming across a story that makes an important claim about human nature. News stories report the latest findings regarding what causes divorce, how men and women differ psychologically, or how work-related stress influences physical illness. Other stories summarize the results of surveys designed to tell us how people will vote in an upcoming election or what proportion of Americans routinely wear seat belts. Flip to the advertisements and you will be exposed to claims about everything from how to improve your memory by listening to subliminal tapes to how to become more popular. Being able to evaluate research claims objectively is an important skill. Separating the scientific wheat from the chaff can influence how you vote, whether you adopt a new diet, or whether you decide to get professional help for a child with a learning disorder. With this in mind, this short essay is devoted to the topic of being a wise consumer of psychological research. As consumers of both products and ideas, we all need to know the difference between carefully conducted and poorly conducted research. **This essay can help you evaluate research-based claims and make you a better consumer of many of the products and services that shape your daily life.**

Show Me the Data!
Looking at Evidence

Perhaps the most important lesson about being a wise consumer of psychological research is that, from a scientific perspective, all claims require **evidence,** not just opinions. Scientists who evaluate research claims behave like ideal jury members who are asked to evaluate claims made by prosecuting attorneys. They begin with the skeptical assumption that all claims are false (the defendant is innocent until proven guilty; the diet plan is ineffective; testosterone plays no role in aggression). Only after considering the strengths and weaknesses of the evidence relevant to a claim do jurors and scientists decide whether to accept the claims of those doing the claiming (for example, prosecuting attorneys, advertisers, scientists). This decision to accept or reject a claim is best made by paying careful attention to the methods that served as the basis for a specific claim. Behavioral scientists have hundreds of tools in their methodological toolboxes, but as it turns out, two of these tools turn out to

be much more important than any others. Understanding the nature and purpose of these two tools is thus the first step to becoming an educated consumer of psychological research. In short, sound research methods lead to more valid research conclusions. The two tools that lie at the heart of sound research methods are random sampling and experimental manipulation based on random assignment.

Says Who? Random Sampling

When behavioral scientists want to assess the attitudes or preferences of very large groups of people (e.g., American voters, Asian-American college students, human beings), they face a seemingly insurmountable problem. It is usually impossible to ask every member of a very large group what he or she thinks, feels, or does. However, behavioral scientists have solved this tricky problem by developing a technique called **random sampling.** When survey researchers use random sampling, they select a very small proportion of the people from within a very large sample (e.g., 1,000 out of 50 million registered voters). They then **estimate** what the entire population is like on the basis of the responses of those sampled. The key to getting an accurate estimate is the use of random sampling. Random sampling refers to selecting people from a population so that everyone in the entire population (e.g., all registered voters in the U.S.) has an equal chance of being selected. This turns out to be an incredibly powerful technique. If every person in a group of 50 million voters really does have an equal chance of being selected into a national survey, then the results of the survey based on 1,000 people will almost always prove to resemble the results for the total population.

An excellent example of the importance of random sampling can be found in the 1936 U.S. Presidential election. Prior to that election, the *Literary Digest* sent postcards to more than 10 million Americans, asking them to report who they planned to vote for in the upcoming election. Among the 2 million Americans who returned the postcards, Alf Landon was the overwhelming favorite. In contrast, a much smaller survey conducted by the recently-formed Gallup group yielded very different results. Based on the responses of only a few thousand likely voters, the Gallup poll suggested that Franklin D. Roosevelt would be the winner. If you pull a dime out of your pocket, and look to see who's face is there, you'll see that the Gallup pollsters were correct. FDR won in a landslide, and Alf Landon faded into obscurity. How did the Gallup poll, based on many fewer people outperform the enormous *Literary Digest* poll? The Gallup pollsters came very close to performing a true random sample of likely voters. In contrast, the *Literary Digest* sampled people by taking names from automobile registrations and telephone listings. In 1936, people who owned cars and phones were usually pretty wealthy—and wealthy people overwhelmingly preferred Alf Landon.

The lesson of the *Literary Digest* error is that whenever you hear the results of any survey, you should ask yourself how the surveyed people were sampled. Were those sampled really like the pool of people (e.g., American voters, African American children) whose attitudes and behavior the researcher would like to describe?

Even when a researcher makes careful use of random sampling, it is also useful to pay attention to a different form of sampling bias, known as **non-response bias.** If only a small percentage of randomly sampled people agree to respond to a survey, it is quite likely that those who did respond will be different than those who refused. Modern pollsters have long mastered the science of random sampling. These days, most of the error in most scientific polls is based on the fact that it can be hard to get very high response rates (or hard to know who to sample in the first place). For example, if you randomly sampled all those eligible to vote in a state gubernatorial race, and you only got a 30% response rate, you would have to worry about whether those who refused to be surveyed would vote the same way as the eager 30% who agreed. Moreover, even if everyone agreed to be surveyed, you'd have to worry about whether the sub sample of all eligible voters who actually showed up at the polls on election day had the same preferences as those who either didn't bother to vote or were unable to do so.

It is also important to note that random sampling helps you describe only the population of people from whom you sampled (and not other populations). For example, if researchers randomly sampled registered voters, but only did so in North Carolina, they might get a great idea of what North Carolinians believe, but it would be very risky to generalize these results to other Americans. This is why people sometimes criticize the results of surveys taken of college students, who differ markedly from older adults. On the other hand, if surveyors wanted to know the opinions of college students, it would make little sense to sample anyone else. The key issue might be exactly which college students. A random sample of 1,000 American college students would tell us much more than a random sample of 1,000 students at Vassar College. Of course, if we cared only about Vassar College students, we would want to sample Vassarians at random. The key issue in sampling is to pay careful attention to who was sampled and to make certain that those sampled are the same kind of people about whom a researcher has made a claim (a claim about what the evidence shows).

How to Ask Why: Experimental Manipulations and Random Assignment

When a researcher moves from descriptive research to experimental research, random sampling is still important, but it begins to take a back seat to a second major technique. This second technique is random assignment, and it is the cornerstone of the experimental method. Unlike random sampling, which is a technique for deciding who to study, **random assignment** can take place only after people have already been selected into a study. Random assignment is a technique for assigning people to different specific conditions in an experiment, and random assignment occurs only when everyone in the study has an equal chance of serving in any specific condition. In the same way that random sampling guarantees that the people sampled in a study will be as similar as possible to those who were not sampled, random assignment guarantees that those assigned to one experimental condition will be as similar as possible to those assigned to a different condition. This is crucial because the whole idea of an experiment is to identify two identical groups of people and then to **manipulate** something. One group gets an experimental treatment, and one does not. If the group that gets the treatment (e.g., a drug, exposure to a violent videogame) behaves differently than the control group that did not get the treatment, we can attribute the difference to the treatment—but only if we can rest assured that the two groups were similar prior to the treatment.

Another way to put this is that if we wish to identify the causes of human behavior, we must usually perform experiments in which we manipulate one thing, or a few factors, at a time. We can only do this by making use of random assignment. Suppose a researcher at Cornell University developed a new technique for teaching foreign language. If the researcher could do so, he might persuade all of his colleagues in the Spanish department to start using this new technique. After a year of instruction using the new technique, suppose that the professor documented that the average student who completed one year of Spanish at Cornell performed well above the national average in a test of Spanish fluency (relative to students at other universities who had also completed a year of Spanish). Can we attribute this performance advantage to the new instruction technique? Given how difficult it is to get admitted to Cornell in the first place, it is likely that students at Cornell would have performed well above the national norm even if they had been taught using a new technique. If the researcher really wanted to know if his teaching technique was superior, he would have needed to randomly assign some Cornell students to receive the new form of instruction while randomly assigning others to receive a traditional form of instruction (this would be hard to do, but that is a detail).

Consider a more important question. Do seatbelts save lives? One way to find out would be to obtain records of thousands of serious automobile accidents. To simplify things, suppose a researcher focused exclusively on drivers (rather than passengers) and found an accurate way to determine whether drivers were wearing their seatbelts at the time of each crash. The researcher then obtained accurate records of whether the driver in each crash survived. Imagine that drivers wearing seatbelts were much more likely to have survived. Can we safely assume that seatbelts are the reason? Not on the basis of this study alone. The problem is that, for ethical reasons, the people in this hypothetical study were not randomly assigned to different seatbelt conditions. As it turns out, those who do and do not routinely wear seatbelts differ in many important ways. Compared with habitual non-users of seatbelts, habitual users are older, more educated, and less likely to speed or drink and drive. These additional factors are also likely to influence survival in a serious accident, and they are all confounded with seatbelt use. On the basis of this study and this study alone, we cannot tell whether it is seatbelts or other safe driving practices that are responsible for the greater survival rates among seatbelt users.

If we were to conduct a large-scale experiment on seatbelt use (by determining habitual seatbelt use on the basis of coin flips), we could completely eliminate all of these confounds in one simple step. Random assignment would create two identical groups of people, exactly half of whom were forced to use seatbelts at all times, and exactly half of whom were forbidden from doing so during the experimental period. Of course, this hypothetical experiment would be unethical. Thus, researchers interested in seatbelt use have had to do a lot of other things to document the important role that seatbelts play in saving people's lives (including laboratory crash tests and studies that used sophistical statistical techniques to separate the effects of seatbelt use from other effects). The point is not that seatbelts don't save lives. They clearly do. The point is that it has taken a lot of time and effort to document this fact because of the impossibility of conducting an experiment on this topic. If you want to conduct a single study to figure out what causes something, you will almost always need to conduct an experiment in which you make use of random assignment. As a consumer of psychological research, you must thus ask yourself whether a research claim was based on the results of a careful experiment, or whether a researcher may have compared two groups of people who differed in more than one way at the beginning of the study.

Longitudinal Research

Sometimes a researcher can bypass the use of random assignment by comparing people with themselves—by conducting a **longitudinal study** or a study with a **pretest** and a **post-test.** Although such studies can be very informative, these studies often come with their own special kinds of confounds. Many of these confounds boil down to the fact that people can and do change over time, for many reasons. For example, consider GRE prep courses. When a student who scores poorly on the GRE takes a preparation course and then takes the GRE again, such a student will often do better the second time around, sometimes a lot better! This would seem to show that the prep course is effective. However, another very effective way to improve the performance of a group of students who have recently performed poorly on a test is to give them the test again without any intervention. In most cases, such students will do better on the test the second time around (including a different version of the same test). (The reason why low scorers tend to improve in the absence of training is known as "regression toward the mean", but its details are beyond the scope of this short essay.) The key issue is that it is always important to have a control group if you want to assess the impact of a treatment.

Some Final Thoughts

There are many other ways in which research can go astray. Did Dr. Snittle word his survey questions fairly? Were participants reporting their attitudes honestly? Did those carrying out the research bias answers by subtly communicating to participants what they hoped to find? Was the size of the sample large enough to draw meaningful comparisons? For example, if you read that 4 out of 5 doctors use Brand X, were only five doctors surveyed? Were those who conducted the research strongly motivated to produce a specific result? For example, if those studying the effects of a drug were paid by a pharmaceutical company to do the research, could this conflict of interest distort the way they collect or interpret their data? The list continues. Specific issues such as these aside, however, the two concerns that should come to mind first when evaluating any research claim have to do with proper sampling and proper experimental control. First, were those studied truly representative of the people about whom we would like to draw conclusions? Second, did the researchers isolate the variables they studied by disentangling them from other confounded variables? It is not always easy to get answers to these questions, but if you get in the habit of asking them you will gradually become a better shopper for psychological truths.

From *psychologymatters.org*, 2006. Copyright © 2006 by the Office of Public Communications, American Psychological Association. Reprinted by permission.

Ethnic and Racial Health Disparities Research: Issues and Problems

Racial and ethnic disparities in health and health care are pervasive. A number of research and policy issues have been raised in the examination of disparities. This article analyzes some methodological, conceptual, and political issues that underlie disparities research. Specifically examined are the research challenges posed by the different ways of defining disparities, heterogeneity within racial or ethnic groups, measurement issues, conceptual levels of analyses, and financial/political factors. It is suggested that research funding for disparities research be substantially supported and encouraged and that researchers more adequately address methodological and conceptual difficulties that are associated with disparities research.

STANLEY SUE, PHD AND MEENU K. DHINDSA, MS

Ethnic and racial disparities in health conditions and in the quality of health services have increasingly been the topic of national reports and investigations. In general, many disparities have been found. As researchers and policy makers examine disparities more and more, a number of important issues have been uncovered. This article reviews some of the important issues that pertain to disparities research. These issues include challenges related to differing definitions of disparities, sampling, heterogeneity within racial or ethnic groups, measurement of disparities, varying conceptual levels of analysis, and financial/political considerations in research. Although we detail some examples from the field of mental health, the lessons learned from these examples are applicable to other areas of health.

Existence of Disparities in Health Status and in Receiving Quality Health Care

In the United States, African American, American Indians/Alaska Natives, Asian Americans, Hispanics, and Native Hawaiian/Pacific Islanders bear a disproportionate burden of disease, premature death, or disability. For example, compared to other ethnic or racial groups, African Americans have the highest rates of mortality from heart disease, cancer, cerebrovascular disease, and HIV/AIDS; Hispanic Americans have a high rate of mortality from diabetes; and Asian Americans experience relatively high rates of stomach, liver, and cervical cancers (Smedley, Stith, & Nelson, 2003). The prevalence of cigarette smoking and cardiovascular disease is high in American Indian communities, and American Indian men are more likely to suffer from poor health compared with men in the general population (Indian Health Service, 2001). These are but a few examples of the disparities that exist.

In addition to the health burden, research has also consistently shown that ethnic minorities tend to receive poorer health care. African Americans and Hispanics experience a lower quality of health services across a wide range of disease areas including cancer, cardiovascular disease, diabetes, and other chronic and infectious diseases (Smedley et al., 2003). The problem is pervasive (Agency for Healthcare Research and Quality [AHRQ], 2004; Smedley et al., 2003). Disparities are found even when clinical factors, such as stage of disease presentation, comorbidities, age, and severity of disease are taken into account. They exist across a range of clinical settings, including public and private hospitals, teaching and nonteaching hospitals, and so on. Even when controlling for socioeconomic class and insurance status among patients, disparities in health care exist.

Research and Policy Issues

In attempts to investigate disparities and to find solutions, several issues and dilemmas have been raised. These issues include the following:

1. How should disparities be defined?
2. Why is there a paucity of research on ethnic minority populations?
3. What kinds of problems exist in sampling and in finding appropriate assessment measures in the study of disparities with racial and ethnic minorities?
4. How can the experiences of ethnic and racial groups be conceptualized?

Definition of Disparities

As a country that is believed to have one of the best health care systems in the world (AHRQ, 2004), it is disconcerting to learn that it may also be a system replete with disparities. Although the word *disparity* is defined as "markedly distinct in quality or character" (*Merriam-Webster OnLine Dictionary*), an operational definition for the term has varied. Two widely used definitions are supplied by AHRQ and the Institute of Medicine (IOM); the former takes into account any and all group differences in health and health care, whereas the latter chooses to identify disparities as group differences that remain after precluding individual factors (AHRQ, 2004). The IOM uses a narrower conceptualization of disparities that involve racial or ethnic differences that are not due to access-related factors or clinical needs, preferences, and appropriateness of intervention. The AHRQ approach is inclusive (Smedley et al., 2003). The reasons for the disparities are not considered, nor are the types of disparity (e.g., indicators of positive health or negative health). On the other hand, the IOM definition primarily restricts disparities to those involving the operation and practices of health care systems, discrimination, and biases.

How the definition is applied in an operational manner can lead to different conclusions about the problem. One definition may maximize the disparity, whereas the other may minimize it. For example, when examining maternity care and the percentage of pregnant women receiving prenatal care in the first trimester, the AHRQ (2004) definition considers only the number of women who sought and received care. In examining ethnic group disparities, differences may be large because other factors associated with ethnicity may affect maternity care such as not having the proper education about such services or personally electing not to seek needed care. Controlling for these factors may reduce the size of statistical figures found for ethnic disparity in maternal care. Furthermore, AHRQ reported in the National Healthcare Disparities Report in 2004 that African Americans received poorer quality care compared with their Caucasian counterparts. However, rather than solely explaining this outcome in terms of racial discrimination or bias in the health care system, another viable explanation applicable to this group may be African Americans' lack of trust in the medical profession. That is to say, the AHRQ definition is very inclusive so that many different variables associated with race and ethnicity may be affecting the extent of disparities that are found. With the AHRQ definition, differences in cultural beliefs in seeking medical attention, trust in the health care providers, affordability of health care, among other variables, may affect the size of discrepancies.

Just as a broad and inclusive definition may allow for confounds to maximize the extent of disparities, a restrictive or exclusive definition may reduce the size of disparities. Because of the charge given to IOM by the U.S. Congress, its definition of disparities excluded those racial or ethnic differences associated with access-related factors or clinical needs, preferences, and appropriateness of intervention (Smedley et al., 2003). In doing so, factors known to influence health care and to be correlated with race and ethnicity, such as health insurance coverage, were not considered. Although acknowledging the importance of these other factors, IOM intentionally wanted to focus on the operation of health care systems and the legal and regulatory climate of these systems, as well as discrimination at the level of providers and patients. In practice, it is often not possible to neatly separate the effects of excluded factors from the factors of interest. For example, the operation of the health care system (of interest to IOM) may be affected by the cultural appropriateness of interventions for ethnic minority populations (not of interest to IOM).

By comparing these two methods of evaluating our health care system, it becomes evident that each renders a different picture or focus on the disparities that exist within the system. Although both definitions offer useful methods of assessing the discrepancies, it is important to reconcile the differences to gain an exact idea of the problems pervading our health care system.

It should be noted that despite the differing definitions, both the AHRQ (2004) and IOM (Smedley et al., 2003) have identified health disparities as major problems experienced by ethnic minority groups. To understand what disparities are and what processes may be involved in the disparities, researchers should clearly specify how they are defining disparities and how factors may be included or excluded from their analysis. For the purposes of our discussion, we use the broad and inclusive definition of disparities.

Lack of Research

There has been a lack of adequate and rigorous research on health and health care disparities for members of racial and ethnic minority groups (AHRQ, 2004). For example, in mental health care, the U.S. Surgeon General (2001) noted that

> controlled clinical trials used to generate professional treatment guidelines did not conduct specific analyses for any minority group.... Controlled clinical trials offer the highest level of scientific rigor for establishing that a given treatment works.... Since 1986, nearly 10,000 participants have been included in randomized clinical trials evaluating the efficacy of treatments for bipolar disorder, major depression, schizophrenia, and attention deficit/hyperactivity disorder. However, for nearly half of these participants (4,991), no information on race or ethnicity is available. For another 7 percent of participants ($N = 656$), studies only reported the designation "non-white," without indicating a specific minority group. For the remaining 47 percent of participants ($N = 4,335$) ... very few minorities were included and not a single study analyzed the efficacy of the treatment by ethnicity or race. (p. 35)

We believe that the lack of more research pertinent to racial and ethnic groups is largely attributable to the fact that such research is difficult to conduct and often requires substantial funding.

Research Difficult to Conduct

Ethnic research in general and disparities research in particular are not easy to conduct. The research is often difficult because (a) ethnic minority populations are small in number, (b) research funding and the adequacy of funding are problematic, (c) cross-culturally valid measures and diagnostic procedures may not be readily available (e.g., dealing with cultural differences in symptom presentation), (d) an adequate baseline of knowledge and theory is frequently missing, and (e) disparities research often proves to be controversial for researchers (Sue & Sue, 2003). Perhaps one of the most problematic obstacles to disparities research is the relatively small size of ethnic/racial populations. Given the relatively small size of ethnic minority populations, it is frequently difficult to find representative samples and adequate sample sizes. This is especially true if the ethnic group is small in number and the focus of the study is a health condition that has a relatively low base rate. For example, if a researcher wanted to study the prevalence of diseases and disorders among different ethnic populations, it may be difficult to find sufficient data on Hawaiian Americans with stomach cancer. Not only is the number of Hawaiian Americans relatively small, but the prevalence of stomach cancer is relatively low. Investigators who do not have large enough sample sizes cannot meaningfully analyze correlates or predictor variables (social class, cultural practices, health habits, etc.) to ethnicity or race.

In an attempt to overcome sample size problems, some researchers (a) aggregate different groups into one, (b) use convenience samples, or (c) over sample ethnic groups when possible. Aggregation of some kind is always used. Even the category of non-Hispanic Whites, often used as the comparison group for examining disparities, is composed of many subgroups (people whose heritage is from England, Canada, Germany, Spain, France, etc. or a combination). The Asian American designation is used in the AHRQ and IOM reports, even though it encompasses heterogeneous groups such as Chinese, Filipinos, Koreans, Japanese, Vietnamese, and so forth. Although such aggregation increases sample size, its meaningfulness must be subjected to scrutiny. If different groups are combined, the rationale for the combination needs to be explained. For instance, if Mexican Americans, Puerto Rican Americans, and Cuban Americans are aggregated as "Hispanics" and then compared with other ethnic groups, the basis for the aggregation should be made explicit. The groups may or may not share cultural values, language patterns, circumstances, and such that make the categorization meaningful. Obviously, collected data may not have included detailed information on ethnicity, so that it is not possible to provide disaggregated information. This means that in the planning of research, collected demographic information on ethnicity should be more specific, or the use of aggregated information should be justified.

Because of the difficulties in collecting data on enough ethnic minorities, researchers may have to resort to convenience sampling in which persons are chosen for research because they are readily available. In the previous example of a researcher who wanted to analyze Hawaiian Americans with stomach cancer, the researcher could limit the analysis to patients at certain hospitals in communities with a large Hawaiian American population. However, such a strategy might well produce a biased and unrepresentative sample of Hawaiian Americans. Finally, over-sampling ethnic minority groups is fruitful only if data on ethnic minorities are already available (and the researcher simply needs to include more of them in the analysis) or the data can be readily collected on a larger number of ethnics. Neither may be true. Given these problems, research findings for some smaller groups may be unavailable, or the extent of knowledge regarding certain ethnic minority groups may be quite limited.

Difficulties are often found in finding valid measures of symptoms, self-reported illness, attitudes and values, health practices, help-seeking patterns, and self-reported treatment outcomes. Misunderstanding of the measures or questionnaire items, cultural response sets, limitations in English proficiency, and physician-patient relations may bias assessment measures or instruments (U.S. Surgeon General, 2001). Thus, it is important to validate measures and to make sure the measures demonstrate invariance across different racial and ethnic groups.

Because of sampling problems and measurement, disparities research involving ethnic minority groups may be very costly and difficult to initiate. For example, in one of our projects to conduct a survey of the prevalence of mental disorders among Chinese Americans in Los Angeles, we had to train bilingual researchers, find and develop a valid survey questionnaire, and approach nearly 20,000 households in order to find 1,700 Chinese respondents (see Takeuchi et al., 1998). The project was funded by the National Institute of Mental Health for $1.5 million, which appears to be unreasonably expensive unless one understands the costs involved in ethnic research.

Disparities research has been controversial and reflects the kinds of tensions that exist when dealing with ethnic and racial issues. Some Americans prefer to see America as the land of opportunity, freedom, justice, and democracy. Others see and experience discrimination, prejudice, and oppression. Health disparities based on race or ethnicity are reminders that large segments of the population do not have adequate health care and that somehow the health system and society are implicated in the reasons for the disparities. Researchers may be reluctant to study disparities because of possible controversies over the work. For example, a debate over health care disparities arose in the National Health Care Disparities Report (see United States House of Representatives Committee on Government Reform, 2004). In March 2002, the IOM found overwhelming evidence that racial and ethnic minorities suffer disparities in health care and concluded that the real challenge lies not in arguing whether disparities exist but in developing and implementing strategies to reduce and eliminate them.

On December 23, 2003, under the Bush administration, Health and Human Services (HHS) released its own National Healthcare Disparities Report. However, in contrast to the IOM, HHS did not describe health care disparities as a national problem. The final version of the National Healthcare Disparities Report deleted most uses of the word *disparity*.

This action led to a number of protests (see Press Release, 2004): "Just like a tumor cannot be healed by covering it with a bandage, healthcare disparities cannot be eliminated with misrepresented facts," said Representative Elijah E. Cummings, chair of the Congressional Black Caucus. "I urge the Bush Administration to stand by its commitment to eliminating racially-defined healthcare disparities by 2010." "Instead of leading the fight against healthcare disparities, HHS is downplaying the serious inequities faced by racial and ethnic minorities," said Representative Michael M. Honda, chair of the Congressional Asian Pacific American Caucus. "By tampering with the conclusions of its own scientists, HHS is placing politics before social justice."

HHS Secretary Tommy Thompson later announced that the report would not be modified and that "disparities" would be kept in the report (Pear, 2004).

Researchers must be prepared for controversies that may develop over their work and interpretation of data. If controversies are unavoidable, they must be careful to use data and evidence to support conclusions and to discuss alternative explanations.

The Heterogeneity Issue

Disparities research has been essential in demonstrating the inequities in health and health care. The goal has been to improve health and health care for everyone, especially those who are receiving a lower quality of care. Ethnic minority populations have been ignored or have inappropriately served as demonstrated by disparities research. Compared to non-Hispanic Whites, the five racial/ethnic minority populations exhibit differences in socioeconomic status (SES) and other social and psychological factors and general health status; however, substantial variations exist within and among the minority populations and in how these social factors are associated with disease prevalence. Some variations raise important issues. As more research has emerged on disparities, striking differences are found that sometimes point to favorable health among some ethnic minority groups. In California, almost one in every three residents is Latino. Although it is true that Latinos have lower incomes, education levels, and access to care than non-Hispanic Whites, they have an overall age-adjusted mortality rate that is 26.0% lower than the non-Hispanic White rate and about 52.1% lower than the African American rate (Hayes-Bautista, 2003). Asian/Pacific Islander Americans also have mortality rates that are 36.4% lower than those of non-Hispanic Whites. A similar pattern emerges in infant mortality. Hispanics and Asian Americans/Pacific Islanders have infant mortalities equivalent to those of non-Hispanic Whites and also have 5 to 7 years longer life expectancy at birth than non-Hispanic Whites (Hayes-Bautista, 2003). In contrast, African Americans had the highest age-adjusted death rate in the United States (Woolf, Johnson, Fryer, Rust, & Satcher, 2004), and life expectancy for American Indians is significantly shorter than for Whites (Indian Health Service, 2001).

The nature of this heterogeneity raises questions. How do we handle group differences? Should attention be focused on the neediest? In areas where certain ethnics are faring well, should we devote less attention and effort? To address these questions, several considerations should be kept in mind. First, the health of ethnic minority group populations has long been ignored. Major disparities in many health conditions exist for ethnic minority groups, and substantial evidence has demonstrated that all of these populations receive poorer quality of, or access to, health services compared to non-Hispanic whites. Special efforts to improve services and prevent disease and disability are needed. Second, for the most part, disparities research is relatively recent, and much of it is descriptive. More research is needed to discover the magnitude of problems, causes of poor health, effects of preventive and treatment interventions, and so on. Third, findings of group differences in mortality, morbidity, and disease prevalence must be carefully interpreted. Complicating factors such as social class, cultural differences in reporting health conditions, and ability to identify one's race or ethnicity may affect group comparisons. Fourth, a greater understanding of the reasons for positive health including mortality and longevity is critical. Findings that Hispanics live longer, despite lower socioeconomic status and educational achievements, are puzzling. Are the findings valid? If so, what is it about Latino (and Asian American) cultures or circumstances that may influence well-being? Interestingly, convergent research findings show an inverse relationship between acculturation and mental health for Mexican Americans. That is, the longer Mexican Americans live in this country, the poorer their mental health. Mexicans living in Mexico have better mental health than Mexicans living in the United States. As noted by Hayes-Bautista (2003), perhaps Latino culture, behavior, health, the foods Latinos eat, the families they form, the spiritual communities they create, their very definitions of health and illness, and the like should be studied. Understanding of these cultural elements may provide means to improve well-being.

Ethnic as Distinct from Minority Status

In the identification of causes of the disparities, there is often confusion about explanations that rely on culture and those that are based on racial/ethnic prejudice and discrimination. This distinction is embodied in our use of the term *ethnic minority*. Although some individuals feel the term is inaccurate in that all populations are minority in one situation or another, we use the term purposefully. Ethnicity refers to one's group identity and culture. On the other hand, minority group status is used as a general concept to convey ethnic relationships in which groups often encounter prejudice and discrimination. Thus, the health status of African Americans, American Indians, Asian Americans, and Latinos is not solely a function of their own cultures or cultural patterns of behaving. Rather, historical and contemporary forms of prejudice and discrimination have also been experienced that shape health status. For example, alcohol abuse among American Indians cannot be fully understood by references to cultural differences. Patterns of exploitation have also accompanied their history that affects consumption. In other words, to fully understand these groups, culture and minority group status must both be analyzed. It is this status that distinguishes cross-cultural research, in which different cultural groups are examined, from ethnic minority and disparities research, in which cultural differences and ethnic relations are critical to consider.

Therefore, disparities can be conceptualized as a result of ethnic/cultural differences as well as racial/ethnic relations. Examples of the former would be ethnic attitudes and values toward health and health interventions, help-seeking patterns, illness behaviors, symptom expressions, interactions with health providers, compliance with treatments, health and dietary practices, folk medicine, cultural practices, and so on. The latter would include institutionalized practices based on majority-minority or mainstream-ethnic relations, stereotypes, prejudice and discrimination, correlates of majority/minority relations such as social class and poverty, access and availability of care, quality of care, and so forth. In some cases, cultural differences and minority status are both pertinent. Such is the case when providers are not familiar with a patient's background or life circumstances, which can occur because of provider-patient differences in culture or group status (e.g., social class). Obviously, the effects of culture and minority status can be easily confounded. Moreover, both can interact and have joint effects on interactions with health providers, compliance with treatments, and health practices.

Proximal or Distal Causes of Disparities

Another conceptual issue in disparities research is the level of analysis. Why do disparities exist? In attempts to explain and overcome disparities, two levels of analysis have been used. The first is at the level of proximal, specific, or concrete factors; the second involves more distal, general, or contextual phenomena. Attributing treatment disparities to interpersonal factors is an example of a proximal explanation. Service providers may render care that is inferior because they are prejudiced and discriminatory, insensitive, or unfamiliar with ethnic clients. Or, ethnic clients may have increased prevalence rates for certain health problems because they are more likely to suffer from poor nutrition. Finding links between quality of care and provider biases or between prevalence and nutrition are important. They suggest that provider characteristics are important to consider in selection and training, and that education and increased nutritional resources are needed to lower the prevalence of certain health problems. However, at a more distal level, we can ask why providers are discriminatory or unfamiliar with clients' cultural backgrounds and why ethnic clients suffer from poor nutrition. The level of analysis in addressing these questions may be much broader or contextual in nature. Issues of racism

and cultural boundedness of providers, as well as institutional practices, history, and societal inequities in wealth and power, may be raised.

Addressing disparities at the proximal rather than distal level is often less complex. Its outcomes can be readily seen. An example of a proximal solution is a health clinic that provides nutritional supplements and education on healthy practices to an ethnic minority family, which has poor nutritional practices. Outcomes for the family can be easily monitored. To critics, proximate solutions are too little, too late. Although this clinic can directly help some families to improve their nutritional practices, other families not associated with the clinic are not helped. For these critics, meaningful interventions must occur at the broader, contextual level in order to affect the lives of many more families. The elimination of poverty, ethnic/racial inequities, and racism is the ultimate method to deal with disparities. In contrast to proximate solutions, intervention at this level, although less directly linked to nutritional issues and more difficult to achieve, has the potential to accomplish much more.

Our programmatic research on treatment outcomes for mental health patients illustrate a range of analysis: (a) Do ethnic clients achieve better treatment outcomes when they are provided with services in an ethnic specific treatment setting? (b) Is ethnic similarity (versus dissimilarity) between therapist and client a predictor of treatment outcomes? (c) Finally, at a proximal level involving cognitive fit, do clients fare better when clients and therapists are similar in their perceptions of the presenting problem, coping orientation, and expectations about treatment goals? That is, regardless of ethnic group, do similarities between therapists and clients in cultural values and beliefs affect treatment outcomes? Therefore, our research questions ranged from a broad agency level to a narrower interpersonal level. We addressed (a) and (b) by using a large data set with more than 600,000 clients from the Los Angeles County Mental Health System. The cognitive fit study was conducted in a mental health clinic. In general, we found some support for the match hypothesis (see Sue, 1998; Zane et al., 2005).

Specifically, we investigated services received, length of treatment, and outcomes of thousands of African American, Asian American, Mexican American, and White clients using outpatient services in the Los Angeles County mental health system. To examine the relationship between ethnic specific treatment programs and outcomes, we compared the return rates, length of treatment, and treatment outcome of ethnic minority adults who used 1 of 36 predominantly White (mainstream) or 18 ethnic-specific mental health centers in Los Angeles County over a 6-year period. Predictor variables included type of program (ethnic-specific vs. mainstream), disorder, ethnic match (whether or not clients had a therapist of the same ethnicity), gender, age, and Medi-Cal eligibility. The criterion variables were return after one session, total number of sessions, and treatment outcome. The results generally indicated that ethnic clients who attend ethnic-specific programs stay in the programs longer than those using mainstream services (in mental health research, a greater number of sessions is related to better treatment outcomes; Sue, 1998). Finally, there was some evidence that clients at ethnic-specific services fared better than those at mainstream services. However, the results were not clear-cut, and clients had not been randomly assigned to programs.

At a more specific level, examination was made of ethnic match between therapist and client. We generally found that ethnic match was related to length of treatment for all groups and was associated with treatment outcomes for Mexican Americans. Among clients who did not speak English as a primary language, ethnic and language match was a predictor of length and outcome of treatment. That is, ethnic match between provider and client was helpful especially if the client was not well acculturated and had limited English proficiency. Finally, we designed a study at a community mental health center in San Francisco and collected data on the cultural and mental health beliefs and attitudes of therapists and clients and followed the clients from beginning to the end of treatment. The purpose of the study was to see if attitudinal and belief similarities between clients and therapists in terms of goals for treatment and coping are related to client outcomes. The results indicated that similarity in perceptions is directly related to treatment outcomes.

These studies illustrate a range in the level of analysis from health agency (ethnic-specific services) to demographic (ethnicity) to individual variables (clients' perceptions and attitudes). Because of the pervasiveness of ethnic/racial disparities, attention must be directed to all levels from proximal to distal factors.

Recommendations

A number of important steps can be taken to address ethnic and racial health and health care disparities research.

1. Researchers have used different definitions of disparities, and the extent of identified disparities varies according to the definition used. Therefore, researchers should clearly specify the criteria they use to determine disparities.
2. Research on ethnic and racial groups is difficult to conduct. One persistent problem in the research is to find adequate sample sizes of these groups. In trying to overcome the sample size problem, researchers have resorted to over-sampling of ethnic minorities, finding convenience samples, or aggregating various ethnic groups in order to achieve a larger empirical base. The strengths and weaknesses of, and justification for, using these strategies must be made explicit. For instance, if different groups are combined (e.g., Chinese, Filipino, Koreans, South Asians, etc.) to achieve a larger aggregate group (e.g., Asian Americans), a justification for the aggregation should be given (e.g., the groups share cultural variables that are of interest).
3. In studying different ethnic and racial groups, measures used to assess symptoms, illness, health practices, cultural attitudes, and so on need to be cross-culturally validated. Otherwise, ethnic comparisons can yield misleading information disparities.
4. Political intrusions that deny the extent of disparities and that run counter to research findings should be deemed

unacceptable. Although political considerations are a fact of life in making funding decisions, setting priorities, and addressing problems, the political process cannot be allowed to alter research findings and conclusions.

5. In approaching disparities research, both proximal (e.g., interpersonal factors) and distal (e.g., institutional practices) levels of analysis are needed. Furthermore, in studying the causes of disparities, both ethnicity/culture and minority group status are important to examine.

References

Agency for Healthcare Research and Quality. (2004). *National healthcare disparities report.* Rockville, MD: U.S. Department of Health and Human Services.

Hayes-Bautista, D. E. (2003). Research on culturally competent healthcare systems: Less sensitivity, more statistics. *American Journal of Preventive Medicine, 24,* 8–9.

Indian Health Service. (2001*). Trends in Indian health 1998–1999.* Rockville, MD: U.S. Department of Health and Human Services, Indian Health Service.

Pear, R. (2004, February 22). Taking spin out of report that made bad into good health. *New York Times,* p. 16.

Press Release concerning letter to Tommy G. Thompson, U.S. Secretary of Health and Human Services, January 13, 2004 from Henry A. Waxman, Rep. Elijah E. Cummings, Rep. Ciro D. Rodriguez, Rep. Michael M. Honda, Del. Donna M. Christensen, Rep. Hilda L. Solis, Rep. Danny K. Davis, and Rep. Dale E. Kildee.

Smedley, B. D., Stith, A. Y., & Nelson, A. R. (2003). *Unequal treatment: Confronting racial & ethnic disparities in health.* Washington, DC: National Academy Press.

Sue, S. (1998). In search of cultural competence in psychotherapy and counseling. *American Psychologist, 53,* 440–448.

Sue, S., & Sue, L. (2003). Ethnic research is good science. In G. Bernal, J. E. Trimble, A. K. Burlew, & F. T. L. Leong (Eds.), *Handbook of racial and ethnic minority psychology* (pp. 198–207). Newbury Park, CA: Sage.

Takeuchi, D. T., Chung, R. C., Lin, K. M., Shen, H., Kurasaki, K., Chun, C., et al. (1998). Lifetime and twelve-month prevalence rates of major depressive episodes and dysthymia among Chinese Americans in Los Angeles. *American Journal of Psychiatry, 155,* 1407–1414.

United States House of Representatives Committee on Government Reform. (2004). *A case study in politics and science: Changes to the national healthcare disparities report.* Washington, DC: Author.

U.S. Surgeon General. (2001). *Mental health: Culture, race, and ethnicity. A supplement to mental health: A report of the surgeon general.* Rockville, MD: U.S. Department of Health and Human Services.

Woolf, S. H., Johnson, R. E., Fryer, G. E., Rust, G., & Satcher, D. (2004).The health impact of resolving racial disparities: An analysis of US mortality data. *American Journal of Public Health, 94,* 2078–2081.

Zane, N., Sue, S., Chang, J., Huang, L., Huang, J., Lowe, S., et al. (2005). Beyond ethnic match: Effects of client-therapist cognitive match in problem perception, coping orientation, and therapy goals on treatment outcomes. *Journal of Community Psychology, 33*, 569–585.

STANLEY SUE and **MEENU K. DHINDSA**, Department of Psychology, University of California, Davis.

Address reprint requests to Stanley Sue, Department of Psychology, University of California, Davis, One Shields Ave., Davis, CA 95616-8686; phone: (530) 754-6173; e-mail: ssue@ucdavis.edu.

This article was based on a presentation at the Society for Public Health Education (SOPHE) Health Disparities Summit in August 2005.

From *Health, Education, and Behavior*, Vol. 34, no. 4, 2006, pp. 459-469. Copyright © 2006 by Society for Public Health Education. Reprinted by permission of Sage Publications. www.sagepub.com

UNIT 2
The Self

Unit Selections

3. **Self-Esteem Development Across the Lifespan**, Richard W. Robins and Kali H. Trzesniewski
4. **Self-Concordance and Subjective Well-Being in Four Cultures**, Kennon M. Sheldon et. al.
5. **Mirror, Mirror: Seeing Yourself As Others See You**, Carlin Flora

Key Points to Consider

- Do you feel that your understanding of your self concept is constant or evolving based upon your social experiences?

- Do you think that other people perceive you as you view yourself?

- How do our social experiences affect our self-concept?

- What role does culture play in self-concept?

- How does one's self-concept affect one's interpersonal and intrapersonal relationships?

Student Web Site

www.mhcls.com/online

Internet References

Further information regarding these Web sites may be found in this book's preface or online.

FreudNet
http://www.psychoanalysis.org

Joaquin looks at himself in the mirror. He is 14 years old. His parents were divorced when he was a baby. As he stares into the mirror, he wonders if he is handsome, will he ever marry, and will he make a good father? He assures himself that his new girlfriend really likes him, although they are both young.

Have you ever pondered yourself in the mirror? Do you wonder how you stack up compared to other college students? Are you smarter? Better looking? More successful? Babies cannot and do not ask themselves these questions.

Philosophizing about oneself appears to be quintessentially human. Other animals high on the evolutionary scale may recognize their own self-images and be able to communicate with others of their own specie. They do not appear, however, to experience existential crises and self-doubts as do humans. Neither are they egotistical nor are their psyches as fragile as ours.

From where do our questions about ourselves come? Better yet, where does self-concept, itself, originate? Both psychologists and sociologists have examined these issues and have pronounced that our sense of self—our self-concept—develops by means of interaction with others. Our parents and significant others, such as teachers, play an especially important role in this development.

Scientists believe that it is through *reflected appraisal* from others that we form our own self-impressions. Reflected appraisal means that we detect others' reactions to us in their faces, mannerisms and comments and, thus, begin to incorporate these mirrored evaluations into our own self-concepts. Here's an example: if as a child Joaquin repeatedly spilled his milk and his mother frequently labeled him "clumsy", Joaquin would probably think of himself as clumsy, in spite of his gracefulness and athleticism on the basketball court.

Self-concept, then, is probably established at an early age, but as many social psychologists hypothesize, the perception of the self can be modified by experience. Suppose that in late adolescence Joaquin is accepted to college, participates in intramural basketball, and the head coach seated in the grandstand takes notice. After Joaquin tries out for the varsity team and is accepted and becomes the team's star in his senior year, Joaquin may well begin to think of himself as anything but clumsy.

Besides significant others, the culture in which we are reared also plays a powerful role in the promulgation of self-concept. For example, some individuals live in collective cultures, where the goals of others take precedence over the advancement of the individual. On the other hand, in individualistic societies, individual achievement regularly occurs at the expense of others or at least ahead of others' wants and needs. Individualism versus collectivism is but one way in which cultures differ and hence affect the development of self-concept.

There are many aspects or components of self-concept, including but not limited to *ideal self* (the self we'd like to be), the *real self* (the self we think we are), and the *negative self* (as-

pects of the self which you would like to change) The Johari window provides insight into self-concept as well as self-disclosure as one view the varying selves perceived by both ourselves and others. Perhaps the most important facet of self-concept, though, is *self-esteem*. Self-esteem, briefly, is your feeling of self-worth. Some individuals have high esteem, now and then to the point of overconfidence; others have low self-esteem, which can lead to depression, even suicide. The articles in the second unit offer varying views of the self.

In "Self-Concordance and Subjective Well-Being in Four Cultures," the authors investigate how committed to one's personal values and interests individuals in various cultures are. (Some of these cultures are collective and others are individualistic as described above.) Despite a few assorted differences, the authors conclude that self-concordance ("be true to thyself") must be a universal human value.

In "Self-Esteem Development Across the Lifespan," Richard Robins and Kali Trzesniewski offer the opportunity to view identity not only in its formation but also rather in its remarkable continuity throughout the lifespan. This continuity truly impacts the life lived by the individual.

Carlin Flora ("Mirror, Mirror: Seeing Yourself as Others See you") explores the influence that others may play in how we view ourselves. By considering the varying perceptions that others may have about you as an individual, one might conclude that identity of self is affected by social influences.

Self-Esteem Development Across the Life Span

After decades of debate, a consensus is emerging about the way self-esteem develops across the lifespan. On average, self-esteem is relatively high in childhood, drops during adolescence (particularly for girls), rises gradually throughout adulthood, and then declines sharply in old age. Despite these general age differences, individuals tend to maintain their ordering relative to one another: Individuals who have relatively high self-esteem at one point in time tend to have relatively high self-esteem years later. This type of stability (i.e., rank-order stability) is somewhat lower during childhood and old age than during adulthood, but the overall level of stability is comparable to that found for other personality characteristics. Directions for further research include (a) replication of the basic trajectory using more sophisticated longitudinal designs, (b) identification of the mediating mechanisms underlying self-esteem change, (c) the development of an integrative theoretical model of the life-course trajectory of self-esteem.

RICHARD W. ROBINS AND KALI H. TRZESNIEWSKI
Department of Psychology, University of California, Davis, and Institute of Psychiatry, King's College, London, United Kingdom

As he was nearing the end of his life, Michelangelo began working on what many people believe to be his most important work, the Florentine Pietà. After working intensely for almost a decade, he entered his studio one day and took a sledgehammer to the sculpture. He broke away the hands and legs and nearly shattered the work before his assistants dragged him away. Why did Michelangelo attempt to destroy one of his greatest creations, a statue that has been described as among the finest works of the Renaissance? Disillusioned and isolated in the last decades of his life, Michelangelo had a heightened sense of perfectionism that was exacerbated by his failure to live up to the expectations of his father, who viewed being a sculptor as akin to being a manual laborer. Michelangelo, it seems, had self-esteem issues. Was Michelangelo's low self-esteem normative for someone his age? Was he likely to have been plagued by self-doubts throughout his life? An emerging body of evidence about self-esteem is beginning to offer answers to these kinds of questions.

In this article, we review the current state of scientific evidence regarding the development of self-esteem across the lifespan.[1] After decades of debate, a consensus is emerging about the way self-esteem changes from childhood to old age. We focus here on two forms of change: (a) normative changes in self-esteem, which reflect whether individuals, on average, increase or decrease over time (assessed by mean differences in self-esteem across age groups); and (b) the stability of individual differences in self-esteem, which reflect the degree to which the relative ordering of individuals is maintained over time (assessed by correlations between self-esteem scores across two time points, i.e., test–retest correlations).[2]

The Normative Trajectory of Self-Esteem Across the Lifespan

As we go through life, our self-esteem inevitably waxes and wanes. These fluctuations in self-esteem reflect changes in our social environment as well as maturational changes such as puberty and cognitive declines in old age. When these changes are experienced by most individuals at about the same age and influence individuals in a similar manner, they will produce normative shifts in self-esteem across developmental periods.

The findings from three recent studies—a meta-analysis of 86 published articles (Trzesniewski, Donnellan, & Robins, 2001; see also Twenge & Campbell, 2001); a large, cross-sectional study of individuals aged 9 to 90 (Robins, Trzesniewski, Tracy, Gosling, & Potter, 2002); and a cohort-sequential longitudinal study of individuals aged 25 to 96 (Trzesniewski & Robins, 2004)—paint a portrait of the normative trajectory of self-esteem across the lifespan (see Fig. 1). Below, we summarize the major changes that occur from childhood to old age.

Childhood

Young children have relatively high self-esteem, which gradually declines over the course of childhood. Researchers have speculated that children have high self-esteem because their self-views are unrealistically positive. As children develop cognitively, they begin to base their self-evaluations on external feedback and social comparisons, and thus form a more balanced and accurate appraisal of their academic competence, social skills, attractiveness, and other personal characteristics. For

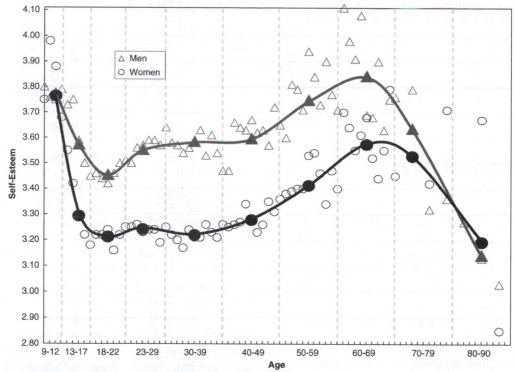

Fig. 1. Mean level of self-esteem for males and females across the lifespan (Robins et al., 2002). Also plotted are year-by-year means, separately for males (open triangles) and females (open circles).

example, as children move from preschool to elementary school they receive more negative feedback from teachers, parents, and peers, and their self-evaluations correspondingly become more negative.

Adolescence

Self-esteem continues to decline during adolescence. Researchers have attributed the adolescent decline to body image and other problems associated with puberty, the emerging capacity to think abstractly about one's self and one's future and therefore to acknowledge missed opportunities and failed expectations, and the transition from grade school to the more academically challenging and socially complex context of junior high school.

Adulthood

Self-esteem increases gradually throughout adulthood, peaking sometime around the late 60s. Over the course of adulthood, individuals increasingly occupy positions of power and status, which might promote feelings of self-worth. Many lifespan theorists have suggested that midlife is characterized by peaks in achievement, mastery, and control over self and environment (e.g., Erikson, 1985). Consistent with these theoretical speculations, the personality changes that occur during adulthood tend to reflect increasing levels of maturity and adjustment, as indicated by higher levels of conscientiousness and emotional stability (Trzesniewski, Robins, Roberts, & Caspi, 2004).

Old Age

Self-esteem declines in old age. The few studies of self-esteem in old age suggest that self-esteem begins to drop around age 70 (about the age when Michelangelo began working on the Florentine Pietà). This decline may be due to the dramatic confluence of changes that occur in old age, including changes in roles (e.g., retirement), relationships (e.g., the loss of a spouse), and physical functioning (e.g., health problems), as well as a drop in socioeconomic status. The old-age decline may also reflect a shift toward a more modest, humble, and balanced view of the self in old age (Erikson, 1985). That is, older individuals may maintain a deep-seated sense of their own worth, but their self-esteem scores drop because they are increasingly willing to acknowledge their faults and limitations and have a diminished need to present themselves in a positive light to others. Consistent with this interpretation, narcissism tends to decline with age (Foster, Campbell, & Twenge, 2003).

Gender Differences

Overall, males and females follow essentially the same trajectory: For both genders, self-esteem is relatively high in childhood, drops during adolescence, rises gradually throughout adulthood, and then declines in old age. Nonetheless, there are some interesting gender divergences. Although boys and girls report similar levels of self-esteem during childhood, a gender gap emerges by adolescence, such that adolescent boys have higher self-esteem than adolescent girls (Kling, Hyde, Showers, & Buswell, 1999; Robins et al., 2002). This gender gap persists throughout adulthood, and then narrows and perhaps even disappears in old age (Kling et al., 1999; Robins et al., 2002). Researchers have offered numerous explanations for the gender difference, ranging from maturational changes associated with puberty to social-contextual factors associated with the differential treatment of boys and girls in the classroom or gender differences in body image ideals. However, no generally accepted integrative theoretical model exists.

Rank-Order Stability of Self-Esteem

Over the past several decades, researchers have debated the degree to which self-esteem should be thought of as a trait-like construct that remains relatively stable over time or as a state-like process that continually fluctuates in response to environmental and situational stimuli. If self-esteem is less stable over the long term than other personality characteristics, then it may not be a useful predictor of important real-world outcomes.

The findings of a recent meta-analysis support the claim that self-esteem is a stable, trait-like construct (Trzesniewski, Donnellan, & Robins, 2003). The stability of self-esteem across all age groups, as determined by test-retest correlation, is comparable to that of the major dimensions of personality, including extraversion, agreeableness, conscientiousness, neuroticism, and openness to experience (Roberts & DelVecchio, 2000). Thus, individuals who have relatively high self-esteem at one point in time tend to have high self-esteem years later; likewise those with low self-esteem earlier in life tend to have low self-esteem later.

However, self-esteem is more stable in some periods of life than in others. Stability is relatively low during early childhood, increases throughout adolescence and early adulthood, and then declines during midlife and old age. This curvilinear trend holds for men and women, for U.S. and non-U.S. participants, and for different self-esteem scales.

The lower levels of stability found during childhood and old age may reflect the dramatic life changes, shifting social circumstances, and relatively rapid maturational changes that characterize both the beginning and end of life. For example, during old age, important life events such as retirement and becoming a grandparent may transform one's sense of self, producing higher levels of self-esteem in some individuals and lower levels in others. These life events can lead to lower levels of self-esteem stability if they are experienced at different ages (e.g., some people retire earlier than others) or differentially affect individuals (e.g., only some retirees decline in self-esteem). Moreover, Erikson (1985) noted that as individuals grow older they begin to review their lifelong accomplishments and experiences, leading in some cases to more critical self-appraisals (ego despair) and in other cases to increased self-acceptance (ego integrity). Thus, a developmental shift toward greater self reflection in old age may produce increases in self-esteem for some individuals but decreases for others.

Implications

Until recently, the self-esteem literature had been caught in a quagmire of conflicting findings and there was little agreement about the way self-esteem develops. The research reviewed in this article will hopefully move the field toward consensus, and help address questions such as: When in the lifespan is self-esteem relatively high or low? Is self-esteem more like a state (relatively transitory) or more like a trait (relatively unchanging)?

Understanding the trajectory of self-esteem may provide insights into the underlying processes that shape self-esteem development. For example, the fact that self-esteem drops during both adolescence and old age suggests that there might be something common to both periods (e.g., the confluence of multiple social and physical changes) that negatively affects self-esteem.

Knowledge about self-esteem development also has implications for the timing of interventions. For example, the normative trajectory of self-esteem across the lifespan suggests that interventions should be timed for pre- or early adolescence because by late adolescence much of the drop in self-esteem has already occurred. Moreover, developmental periods during which rank order stability is relatively low may be ideal targets of intervention programs because self-esteem may be particularly malleable during these times of relative upheaval in the self-concept.

Conclusions and Future Directions

Research accumulating over the past several years paints an increasingly clear picture of the trajectory of self-esteem across the lifespan. Self-esteem shows remarkable continuity given the vast array of experiences that impinge upon a lived life. At the same time, self-esteem also shows systematic changes that are meaningfully connected to age-related life experiences and contexts. These normative changes illustrate the role of the self as an organizing psychological construct that influences how individuals orient their behavior to meet new demands in their environment and new developmental challenges.

Several difficult but tractable issues remain. First, some of the findings reported here require further replication and exploration. In particular, relatively few studies have documented the decline in self-esteem during old age. Establishing the robustness of this effect is important given inconsistent findings in the literature about whether emotional well-being and other aspects of adjustment drop during old age (Mroczek, 2001). In addition, a more fine-grained analysis of age trends might reveal important fluctuations (e.g., changes from early to late adulthood) that were obscured in the present studies.

Second, although the methodological quality of self-esteem research has improved dramatically over the past decade, there is still room for improvement. Greater attention should be paid to measurement issues, including analyses of whether self-esteem scales show different forms of measurement invariance (e.g., does the meaning of self-esteem items vary across age groups?). The use of more representative samples would increase the generalizability of the findings and allow for a deeper exploration into the potential moderating effects of gender, race, ethnicity, and social class. Sophisticated statistical models should be used to better understand dynamic, reciprocal causal influences (e.g., is self-esteem a cause or consequence of important life experiences) (e.g., Ferrer & McArdle, 2003). Cohort sequential longitudinal studies, in which individuals from different age groups are followed over time, are needed to tease apart aging and cohort effects (e.g., will all older individuals develop lower self-esteem or just the particular cohort of individuals who experienced the Great Depression and other life events unique to that cohort?). Finally, genetically informed designs are needed to explore the mutual influence of nature and nurture on self-esteem development; researchers have yet to appreciate the profound implications of the finding that global self-esteem, like most traits, has a genetic basis (e.g., McGuire et al., 1999).

Third, research is needed on the mediating mechanisms underlying self-esteem change. Chronological age has no causal force per se. We need to understand what else changes with age that might produce changes in self-esteem at different developmental periods. One approach is to document the social-contextual factors associated with chronological age, such as the key social roles and events that define and shape one's position in the life course. However, it is important to recognize that such factors can only influence self-esteem through intrapsychic mechanisms, such as perceptions of control and agency and feelings of pride and shame, which shape the way people react to, and therefore internalize, the events that occur in their lives. In our view, the best way to understand self-esteem development is to understand the self-evaluative mechanisms that drive the self system—that is, the cognitive and affective processes presumed to play a role in how self-evaluations are formed, maintained, and changed. Although experimental studies have linked a number of self-evaluative processes to short-term changes in self-evaluation, we know little about the influence of such processes on selfesteem change over long periods of time. Lifespan research on the self should draw on this experimental work to develop hypotheses about long-term change in self-esteem and explore how self evaluative processes documented in the lab play out in real-world contexts.

Finally, the literature on self-esteem development lacks an overarching theoretical framework. Most past theoretical work has focused on particular developmental periods (e.g., the transition to adolescence) and particular life domains (e.g., work). Consequently, although the literature has generated a laundry list of possible reasons why self-esteem might drop during adolescence (and why this might be particularly true for girls), there is no integrative model of how the various proposed processes work together to shape self-esteem development. We also do not know whether these same processes can be invoked to account for the drop in self-esteem during old age. Given the complexity of self-esteem development, such a model would necessarily incorporate biological, social, and psychological factors; account for reciprocal and dynamic causal influences; and include mechanisms of continuity as well as change (e.g., various forms of person–environment interaction). Our hope is that, by examining patterns of findings across developmental

contexts (childhood to old age) and across life domains (work, relationships, health), the field will move toward an overarching theory of the life-course trajectory of self-esteem.

Recommended Reading

Harter, S. (1998). The development of self-representations. In W. Damon & N. Eisenberg (Eds.), *Handbook of child psychology* (pp. 553–617). New York: Wiley.

Robins, R.W., Trzesniewski, K.H., Tracy, J.L., Gosling, S.D., & Potter, J. (2002). (See References)

Trzesniewski, K.H., Donnellan, M.B., & Robins, R.W. (2003). (See References)

Acknowledgments

This research was supported by Grant AG022057 from the National Institute of Aging.

References

Erikson, E.H. (1985). *The life cycle completed: A review.* New York: W. W. Norton.

Ferrer, E., & McArdle, J.J. (2003). Alternative structural models for multivariate longitudinal data analysis. *Structural Equation Modeling, 10,* 493–524.

Foster, J.D., Campbell, W.K., & Twenge, J.M. (2003). Individual differences in narcissism: Inflated self-views across the lifespan and around the world. *Journal of Research in Personality, 37,* 469–486.

Kling, K.C., Hyde, J.S., Showers, C.J., & Buswell, B.N. (1999). Gender differences in self-esteem: A meta-analysis. *Psychological Bulletin, 125,* 470–500.

McGuire, S., Manke, B., Saudino, K., Reiss, D., Hetherington, E.M., & Plomin, R. (1999). Perceived competence and self-worth during adolescence: A longitudinal behavioral genetic study. *Child Development, 70,* 1283–1296.

Mroczek, D.K. (2001). Age and emotion in adulthood. Current *Directions in Psychological Science, 10,* 87–90.

Roberts, B.W., & DelVecchio, W.F. (2000). The rank-order consistency of personality from childhood to old age: A quantitative review of longitudinal studies. *Psychological Bulletin, 126,* 3–25.

Robins, R.W., Trzesniewski, K.H., Tracy, J.L., Gosling, S.D., & Potter, J. (2002). Global self-esteem across the lifespan. *Psychology and Aging, 17,* 423–434.

Trzesniewski, K.H., Donnellan, M.B., & Robins, R.W. (2001, April). *Self-esteem across the life span: A meta-analysis.* Poster session presented at the biennial meeting of the Society for Research on Child Development, Minneapolis, MN.

Trzesniewski, K.H., Donnellan, M.B., & Robins, R.W. (2003). Stability of self-esteem across the lifespan. *Journal of Personality and Social Psychology, 84,* 205–220.

Trzesniewski, K.H., & Robins, R.W. (2004). *A cohort-sequential study of self-esteem from age 25 to 96.* Poster presented at the Society for Personality and Social Psychology. Austin, Texas.

Trzesniewski, K.H., Robins, R.W., Roberts, B.W., & Caspi, A. (2004). Personality and self-esteem development across the lifespan. In P.T. Costa, Jr. & I.C. Siegler (Eds), *Recent advances in psychology and aging* (pp. 163–185). Amsterdam, the Netherlands: Elsevier.

Twenge, J.M., & Campbell, W.K. (2001). Age and birth cohort differences in self-esteem: A cross-temporal meta-analysis. *Personality and Social Psychology Review, 5,* 321–344.

Notes

1. The focus of this article is on explicit (i.e., conscious) global evaluations of self-worth, not implicit (i.e., unconscious) or domain-specific (e.g., math ability) self-evaluations.

2. These two forms of change are conceptually and statistically distinct. Individuals in a sample could increase substantially in self-esteem but the rank ordering of individuals would be maintained if everyone increased by the same amount. Similarly, the rank ordering of individuals could change substantially over time without producing any aggregate increases or decreases (e.g., if the number of people who decreased offset the number of people who increased).

RICHARD W. ROBINS and **K. H. TRZESNIEWSKI**, "Self-esteem development across the lifespan" (2005). Current Directions in Psychological Science. 14 (3), pp. 158-162. Postprint available free at: http://repositories.cdlib.org/postprints/865

Posted at the eScholarship Repository, University of California. http://repositories.cdlib.org/postprints/865

From *Current Directions in Psychological Science*, Vol. 14 (3), no. 865, 2005, pp. 158-162. Copyright © 2005 by the Association for Psychological Science. Reprinted by permission of Blackwell Publishing, Ltd.

Self-Concordance and Subjective Well-Being in Four Cultures

Sheldon and colleagues have recently focused research attention on the concept of self-concordance, in which people feel that they pursue their goals because the goals fit with their underlying interests and values rather than because others say they should pursue them. Self-concordant individuals typically evidence higher subjective well-being (SWB). But is this also true in non-Western cultures, which emphasize people's duty to conform to societal expectations and group-centered norms? To address this question, this study assessed goal self-concordance and SWB in four different cultures. U.S., Chinese, and South Korean samples evidenced equal levels of self-concordance, whereas a Taiwanese sample evidenced somewhat less self-concordance. More importantly, self-concordance predicted SWB within every culture. It appears that "owning one's actions"—that is, feeling that one's goals are consistent with the self—may be important for most if not all humans.

KENNON M. SHELDON, ANDREW J. ELLIOT, RICHARD M. RYAN, VALERY CHIRKOV, YOUNGMEE KIM, CINDY WU, MELIKSAH DEMIR, AND ZHIGANG SUN

Recently, Sheldon and colleagues (Sheldon, 2002; Sheldon & Elliot, 1999; Sheldon & Houser-Marko, 2001) have proposed the idea of *self-concordance* as a way of conceptualizing optimal goal-striving. Self-concordant individuals are people who pursue life goals with a sense that they express their authentic choices rather than with a sense that they are controlled by external forces over which they have little say. Thus, self-concordant goals are ones that represent people's actual interests and passions as well as their central values and beliefs. In contrast, nonconcordant goals are ones that are pursued with a sense of "having to," as the person does not really enjoy or believe in the goals. For example, a student's goal of learning to play the piano may be self-concordant; that is, the student has an interest in music and a genuine desire to master the instrument. Or, it may be non-self-concordant; that is, the student has little natural inclination or interest for the piano and practices only because his or her parents insist.

To measure self-concordance, Sheldon (2002) has drawn from self-determination theory (SDT; Deci & Ryan, 1985, 1991, 2000) and its concept of the "perceived locus of causality continuum" (PLOC). The question is, does a person engage in goal-pursuits with a sense that "I" chose them (an internal perceived locus of causality, or I-PLOC)? Or does a person pursue goals with a sense that his or her situation is the source of the goals (an external perceived locus of causality, or E-PLOC)? Research focusing on Western samples has shown that self-concordance (i.e., greater I-PLOC than E-PLOC) is associated with concurrent subjective well-being (SWB; Sheldon & Kasser, 1995). In addition, self-concordance also predicts longitudinal increases in SWB by way of the greater goal-attainment inspired by self-

concordance (Sheldon & Elliot, 1999; Sheldon & Houser-Marko, 2001; Sheldon & Kasser, 1998). In terms of the aforementioned example, the student who practices piano with a sense of interest and conviction is typically a happier person than the student who practices with a sense of pressure and obligation, and this student would also tend to improve his or her playing more rapidly, perhaps becoming an even happier person. Based on such findings, Sheldon (2002) suggested that self-concordance—that is, the sense of "owning" one's personal goals—might be a culturally invariant need or benefit for human beings. However, Sheldon reported no cross-cultural goal data to support this idea.

Relevant to Sheldon's claim, researchers working within the SDT tradition have now published considerable data demonstrating the importance of internal motivation within non-Western samples. For example, Chirkov, Ryan, Kim, and Kaplan (2003) showed that although different types of social behaviors were differently internalized within four different cultures, having an I-PLOC regarding behavior predicted SWB in every culture. Hayamizu (1997) found that in a sample of Japanese high school students, internal motivation was related to positive coping, whereas external or "controlled" motivation was associated with maladaptive coping. Yamaguchi and Tanaka (1998) recently reported more adaptive learning styles and positive experiences in Japanese students with an I-PLOC for academic behavior. In addition, Deci et al. (2001) found in a sample of Bulgarian adults that I-PLOC on the job predicted work engagement, job performance, and psychological wellbeing (see Deci & Ryan, 2000, for a more comprehensive consideration of this emerging literature).

In the current work, we sought to generalize these cross-cultural results to the case of self-generated personal goals. Indeed, there is reason to suspect that the above-cited effects may not generalize to personal goal constructs. Idiographic goals represent people's self-generated initiatives for positive change and life improvement, and it may be that not all cultures support such proactive initiatives. For example, Markus and Kitayama (1994) suggested that in interdependent or collectivist cultures (Triandis, 1997), goals undertaken to "fit in" and have harmonious relationships with others should be most conducive to SWB, whereas goals undertaken to advance self-interests or achievements may actually be harmful to SWB. Similarly, Oishi (2000) has also argued that goals associated with independence and self-expression may be less beneficial within collectivist cultures than in individualist cultures. In this vein, Oishi and Diener (2001) reported that relative to European American college students, Asian college students did not benefit as much emotionally by attaining goals pursued "for fun and enjoyment," whereas achieving goals undertaken to "please friends and parents" resulted in greater emotional benefits for participants within collectivist cultures.

In sum, although some theoretical perspectives and cross-cultural data suggest that pursuing self-concordant personal goals should be beneficial within any cultural context, other perspectives and data suggest that it may always not be the case (Markus, Kitayama, & Heiman, 1996).[1] The current research sought to shed new light on these issues by assessing personal goals, self-concordance, and SWB within four different cultures: the United States, China, Taiwan, and South Korea. Based on past findings concerning the current measure of self-concordance, our primary hypothesis was that self-concordance would be positively associated with SWB in many, if not all, of these cultures. However, we also believed that the effects of self-concordance might to some extent be moderated by culture; we sought to uncover any such cultural differences. In addition, we wished to examine cultural mean differences in self-concordance. However, we had no theoretical reasons for making hypotheses concerning mean differences.

Secondary Issues

Below, we briefly consider each of the four types of motivation that together constitute the self-concordance concept and measure; we will also present data regarding each type separately. According to SDT, motivations can be located on a continuum of internalization, ranging from external motivation (the person acts with a feeling of being controlled by external pressures or contingencies) to introjected motivation (the person acts with a feeling of being controlled by his or her own internal processes) to identified motivation (the person acts with a sense of choice and volition, even if he or she does not enjoy the action) to intrinsic motivation (the person acts because the activity is inherently interesting and challenging). External and introjected motivations are classified as nonconcordant and potentially problematic motivations because the person does not fully assent to his or her own behavior. In contrast, identified and intrinsic motivations are classified as concordant and more

beneficial motivations (Deci & Ryan, 2000; Ryan & Connell, 1989) because the person fully accepts them and because these motivations typically represent more central and stable aspects of the person.

According to SDT, intrinsic motivation is the prototypical self-concordant motivation as it represents the organism's self-initiated attempts to learn about the world and master new skills. We believed it might be very illuminating to examine this motivation by itself as some cross-cultural research calls into question the invariant association of intrinsic motivation with positive outcomes (Iyengar & Lepper, 1999; Oishi & Diener, 2001). Nevertheless, we hypothesized that intrinsic goal motivation, defined in terms of people's sense of interest and engagement in their personal goals as well as the enjoyment associated with those goals, should tend to be beneficial in every culture. We ventured no hypotheses concerning cultural differences in intrinsic motivation as we believe that people can find ways to be intrinsically motivated in almost any context.

Identified motivation, the second form of self-concordant motivation, may be a particularly important motivation to examine in a cross-cultural context because it represents the extent to which external prescriptions have been internalized into the self. In fact, SDT maintains that people can follow tradition, obey rules, and defer to others to no harmful effect as long as they identify with the behavior and enact it willingly—indeed, in this case, pursuing externally-mandated goals may even be positive (Chirkov et al., 2003). Based on this reasoning, we hypothesized that identified motivation should tend to be beneficial in every culture. We ventured no hypotheses concerning cultural differences in mean levels of identified motivation.

Introjected motivation, the sense that "I must force myself" to do a behavior, is also an important motivation to examine in a cross-cultural context, given likely cultural differences in the strength of social pressures, obligations, and expectations. Although one might expect greater introjection in more traditional or collectivist cultures, it is also possible that prosocial norms in such cultures help people to more fully internalize imposed motivations, leading to less introjection overall. Thus, although we expected introjection to be associated with lower SWB in most if not all cultures, we ventured no hypotheses regarding cultural mean differences in introjection.

Finally, external motivation is also worthy of examination in its own right. Although Oishi and Diener (2001) assumed that "striving to please my parents" is an external motivation, again, we believe it depends on the person's PLOC for the behavior. According to SDT, one might strive to please one's parents with a sense of being controlled by unassimilated forces or with a sense of wholeheartedly wanting to please them; as noted earlier, positive relations with SWB are expected to the extent that the latter is true. Again, because the internalization process might actually be better supported in non-Western than in Western cultures, we ventured no hypotheses regarding cultural mean differences in external motivation. However, we did expect that external motivation would be associated with lower SWB in most if not all cultures.

Finally, as an additional measure, in each culture we also asked participants to rate the extent their goals are self-focused (undertaken primarily to serve the needs and preferences of the self) versus other-focused (undertaken primarily to serve the needs and preferences of social groups, such as family, team, club, or friends). This allowed us to directly assess the extent to which goals are perceived as addressing individual interests and achievements, relative to collective interests and achievements—an important distinction according to Markus and Kitayama (1994) and many other cultural theorists. Notably, however, selfdetermination theorists have argued that the individualism/collectivism distinction is largely independent of the concordance/nonconcordance distinction (Chirkov et al., 2003; Deci & Ryan, 2000). In other words, one might engage in either collectivist or individualist behaviors with either a sense of self-ownership or with a sense of being controlled by nonassimilated forces. Thus, we expected few or weak correlations of self-focus with self-concordance. If a positive association emerged, we intended to control for self-focused goals in the self-concordance-to-SWB analyses to ensure that self-concordance effects involve more than a tendency to pursue primarily self-interests.

Summary of Hypotheses

Again, our primary hypothesis was that self-concordant motivation would be associated with SWB in most, if not all, of the cultural groups studied. In terms of the four constituent dimensions of self-concordance, external and introjected motivation should tend to be negatively associated with SWB, and intrinsic and identified motivation should tend to be positively associated with SWB. We ventured no a priori hypotheses regarding cultural mean differences for either the aggregate self-concordance measure or for the four individual motivation measures.

Methods

Participants and Procedure

Five hundred and fifty-one college undergraduates participated in the study, all of them students at large universities. There were 194 South Korean students from Hanyang University in Seoul, South Korea;[2] 153 U.S. students from the University of Missouri in Columbia, Missouri); 163 Taiwanese students from the National SunYat-Sen University, in Kaohsiung, Taiwan; and 41 Chinese students from the Guangdon Commercial College in Guangzhou, South China).[3] Participants were drawn from a variety of majors and courses of study. All participants were volunteers, although Missouri participants received credit toward their introductory psychology experimental requirement for participating. The data collections occurred between November 1999 and December 2001. Participants attended small group questionnaire sessions. During these sessions participants first completed SWB measures, then goal measures, then demographic measures.

An English version of the questionnaire was created for use with the U.S. sample. Chinese, Taiwanese, and South Korean versions were created by a process in which a bilingual psychologist/native to the country translated the questionnaire into the appropriate language, after which it was translated back by a second individual proficient in both English and the language in question. The equivalence of the original and the back-translated versions of the questionnaire was evaluated, and minor revisions were made to arrive at the final versions of the questionnaire.

Measures

Personal goals. All participants completed a standard personal-strivings assessment (Emmons, 1989) in which they were first told, "We are interested in the things that you typically or characteristically are trying to do in your everyday behavior. Think about the objectives that you are typically trying to accomplish or attain. We call these personal strivings." Participants were given examples of strivings and were then asked to list eight personal strivings of their own.

Next, we asked participants to rate the extent to which they pursue each striving for external, introjected, identified, and intrinsic reasons, using a Likert-type scale from 1 (*not at all for this reason*) to 7 (*completely for this reason*; Ryan & Connell, 1989; Sheldon & Elliot, 1999, 2000; Sheldon & Houser-Marko, 2001; Sheldon & Kasser, 1995, 1998). Again, the former two reasons are conceptualized as nonconcordant forms of motivation, and the latter two reasons are conceptualized as self-concordant forms of motivation (see Table 1 for the specific item wordings). As in prior research, we computed an aggregate self-concordance score for each participant by summing the eight identified and the eight intrinsic ratings and then subtracting the eight external and the eight introjected ratings. Cronbach's alpha coefficients for this 32-item variable ranged between .70 and .80 across the four samples. Below, we present data for this composite as well as for the four individual motivation dimensions.

In addition, participants were asked to rate the extent to which their goals were self-focused versus other-focused. The following wording was used:

> Goals can be adopted primarily to serve the needs and preferences of the *self* ("self-focused" goals), or to serve the needs and preferences of *social groups*, such as family, team, club, or friends ("group-focused" goals). For example, one might pursue the goal "get very high grades" because this is what one wants for oneself or because this is what one's family deems important. As another example, one might pursue the goal "get into good physical condition" because this is what one wants for oneself or because this is what one's sports team needs. Of course, a goal may also represent both at the same time. Please rate the extent to which each goal represents your own needs and preferences or the needs/preferences of important social groups.

A Likert-type scale was used in which 1 = *primarily group needs*, 3 = *represents both equally*, and 5 = *primarily personal needs*. Cronbach's alpha coefficients for the self-focus variable ranged between .50 and .66 across the four samples. These coefficients are rather low, suggesting that participants viewed their eight goals as varying considerably on their degree of self versus group focus.

Table 1 Item Wordings for the Four Motivation Dimensions

Wording	Dimension
External (nonconcordant)	You are pursuing this striving because somebody else wants you to or because your situation seems to demand it. Stated differently, you probably wouldn't have this striving if you didn't get some kind of reward, praise, or approval for it (or avoid some kind of punishment, criticism, or disapproval). For example, you might try to "go to church more regularly" because others might criticize you if you didn't, or because you need to be seen at church for your job.
Introjected (nonconcordant)	You are pursuing this striving because you would feel ashamed, guilty, or anxious if you didn't. Rather than having this striving just because someone else thinks you should, you feel that you "ought" to strive for that something. For example, you might try to "go to church more regularly" because you would feel bad about yourself if you didn't.
Identified (concordant)	You are pursuing this striving because you really believe that its an important goal to have. Although others may have urged you to pursue this striving in the past, now you endorse it freely and value it for personal reasons. For example, you might try to "go to church more regularly" because you genuinely feel this is the right thing to do, even if you don't really enjoy it.
Intrinsic (concordant)	You are pursuing this striving because of the fun and enjoyment which the striving provides you. While there may be many good reasons for the striving, the primary "reason" is simply your interest in the experience itself. For example, you might try to "go to church more regularly" because being at church is inherently interesting and enjoyable to you.

Subjective well-being. In addition, all participants rated the 20 mood adjectives of the Positive Affect Negative Affect Schedule (Watson, Tellegen, & Clark, 1988), indicating how much they have felt each emotion "in the past month or so." A Likert-type scale from 1 (*very slightly or not all*) to 5 (*extremely*) was employed, and positive affect and negative affect scores were derived by averaging the appropriate items. Participants also completed the five items of the Satisfaction With Life Scale (Diener, Emmons, Larsen, & Griffin, 1985), also with reference to the past month or so, using a Likert-type scale from 1 (*strongly disagree*) to 5 (*strongly agree*). These items were averaged to create a life-satisfaction score. Alpha coefficients ranged between .60 and .82 across the four samples for positive affect, between .63 and .83 for negative affect, and between .75 and .81 for life satisfaction. As in other recent studies (Bettencourt & Sheldon, 2001; Elliot, Sheldon, & Church, 1997; Sheldon & Elliot, 1999), we also computed an aggregate measure of SWB by first standardizing all scores and then subtracting negative affect from the sum of positive affect and life satisfaction (Diener, 1994).

Demographics. At the end of the questionnaire participants rated their family income, using a 5-point Likert-type scale adjusted to each nation's currency and range of income levels. In addition, they rated their mother's level of education and their father's level of education from 1 (*some high school or less*) to 5 (*postgraduate degree*). We intended to control for these variables to ensure that they could not account for the primary results.

Results

Sample-wide Means in SWB and Self-concordance

Table 2 presents the overall sample mean for the SWB and motivation variables. The mean for aggregate self-concordance was positive, indicating that on the whole, participants felt that their personal goals were more internally than externally caused. Also, participants seemed generally happy, with means on life satisfaction and positive affect above the mid-point of the scale and the negative affect mean falling below the mid-point (Myers, 2000).

Mean Differences Between Cultures in SWB and Self-concordance

Table 2 also presents means for the 10 variables and separately for each sample. We conducted one-way ANOVAs on each of the 10 variables, with cultural group as a four-level factor. Significant omnibus effects emerged in nine cases (*F*s ranging from 6.02 to 193.1, all *p*s < .01; external motivation was the exception). For these nine variables, we then conducted a series of *t* tests to compare each sample to each other sample. Because so many tests were conducted, we employed a .01 alpha level. Table 2 contains the results.

Consistent with earlier studies of national well-being (i.e., Diener, Diener, & Diener, 1995), the U.S. sample evidenced significantly higher levels of all three first-order SWB measures, the only exception being that Chinese participants did not report lower positive affect than the U.S. sample. Also consistent with past results, the U.S. participants evidenced significantly higher aggregate SWB than the other three samples. In addition, the South Korean and Chinese samples evidenced significantly more SWB than the Taiwanese sample.

Table 2   Variable Means for the Entire Sample and for Each Subsample

Variables	Sample				
	Total Sample	United States	South Korea	Taiwan	China
Aggregate SWB	3.51	4.73_a	3.16_b	2.78_c	3.41_b
Positive affect	3.12	3.49_a	2.99_b	2.90_b	3.29_a
Negative affect	2.44	2.10_a	2.56_b	2.56_b	2.64_b
Life satisfaction	2.82	3.34_a	2.73_b	2.44_b	2.77_b
Self-concordance	3.04	3.57_a	3.43_a	2.39_b	3.41_a
External motivation	2.93	2.88	2.82	3.03	3.17
Introjected motivation	3.86	3.82_a	3.39_b	4.35_c	4.22_{ac}
Identified motivation	5.35	5.61_a	5.31_b	5.20_b	5.19_{ab}
Intrinsic motivation	4.59	4.66_a	4.34_a	4.57_a	5.60_b

NOTE: SWB = subjective well-being. Subsample means not sharing subscripts are significantly different from each other at the .01 level.

Next, we turned to the self-concordance variable. One-sample t tests revealed that self-concordance was significantly greater than zero in every sample (all $ps < .01$). This indicates that in every cultural group, people felt more I-PLOC than E-PLOC with respect to their personal goals. There were no significant differences in self-concordance between cultures, with the exception that the Taiwanese sample was lower than the other three samples. Considering the four individual motivation dimensions, no significant differences emerged for external motivation. The South Korean sample reported the least introjected motivation, and the Taiwanese and Chinese samples reported the most, with the U.S. sample in the middle. The U.S. sample reported the most identified motivation, with the other three samples reporting lower levels of identified motivation. Finally, the Chinese sample reported the most intrinsic motivation for goals, with the U.S., South Korean, and Taiwanese samples reporting less intrinsic motivation.

Sample-wide Associations of Self-Concordance with SWB

Turning to our primary hypotheses, we next examined the associations between the motivation measures and the SWB measures. Table 3 presents these correlations collapsed across the four samples ($N = 551$; all measures were standardized within sample prior to this analysis). Consistent with prior findings (Sheldon, 2002), aggregate self-concordance was significantly positively correlated with positive affect, life-satisfaction, and aggregate SWB, and it was significantly negatively correlated with negative affect. Table 3 also provides the correlations between the individual motivation dimensions and SWB. As expected, external and introjected motivation correlated negatively with aggregate SWB, and identified and intrinsic motivation correlated positively with aggregate SWB. The same basic pattern emerged for the four motivation variables in relation to the three first-order SWB variables, although not all of the correlations reached significance.

Next, we turned to the control variables—namely, family income, mother's education, father's education, and self-focused goals. Would the association of self-concordance and SWB in the Asian samples be reducible to the effect of these variables? This was a possibility, given that self-concordance correlated positively with both father's and mother's education ($rs = .16$ and $.14$, respectively, $ps < .05$) and with self-focused goals ($r = .07$, $p < .10$); SWB also correlated positively with father's and mother's education ($rs = .11$ and $.15$, respectively, both $ps < .01$) and with self-focused goals ($r = -.25$, $p < .01$).

To ensure that self-concordance has effects on SWB that are independent of these associations, we conducted a hierarchical regression in which the control variables were entered at the first step and self-concordance was entered at the second step. At Step 1, income and mother's education were both significant predictors of SWB ($\beta s = .12$ and $.13$, both $ps < .05$). At Step 2, self-concordance accounted for significant incremental variance (R^2 change $= .104$, $p < .01$; $\beta = .33$). In short, it appears the associations of self-concordance with SWB represent more than the effects of family education, family income, or individualist goal contents.

Variations in the Self-concordance to SWB Association Across Samples

Table 4 presents the correlation of aggregate self-concordance with each SWB measure, split by sample. As can be seen, self-concordance correlated significantly and positively with aggregate SWB in every sample and, as expected, was significantly associated with the first-order well-being variables in 9 out of 12 cases. Also as expected, external and introjected motivation were negatively correlated with aggregate SWB in every sample, and intrinsic and identified motivation were positively correlated with SWB in every sample (although 7 of the 16 correlations involving individual motivation dimensions did not reach significance). Notably, none of the 80 correlations presented in Table 4 were significant in the direction opposite from that predicted.

Table 3 Correlations of Goal-Motivation Measures with SWB Measures, Collapsed Across Cultures (N = 551)

Predictors	SWB Measures			
	Positive Affect	Negative Affect	Life-Satisfaction	Aggregate SWB
Self-concordance	.20***	−.31***	.18***	.33***
External	−.15***	.26***	−.11***	−.24***
Introjected	−.06	.21***	−.06	−.16***
Identified	.05	−.09**	.02	.08**
Intrinsic	.16***	−.09**	.18***	.21***

NOTE: SWB = subjective well-being.
**p < .05. ***p < .01.

Table 4 Correlations of Goal-Motivation Measures with SWB Measures

Culture	SWB Measures			
	Positive Affect	Negative Affect	Life-Satisfaction	Aggregate SWB
United States				
Self-concordance	.26***	−.42***	.12	.33***
External	−.29***	.43***	−.21***	−.39***
Introjected	−.04	.17**	.02	−.07
Identified	.07	−.15*	−.01	.08
Intrinsic	.20**	−.17**	.09	.19**
South Korea				
Self-concordance	.14**	−.20***	.22***	.27***
External	−.09	.11	−.11	−.14**
Introjected	−.04	.27***	−.17**	−.23***
Identified	.06	−.01	.04	.05
Intrinsic	.11	−.01	.15**	.13*
Taiwan				
Self-concordance	.19**	−.35***	.21***	.40***
External	−.10	.29***	−.10	−.27***
Introjected	−.12	.19**	−.04	−.18**
Identified	.00	−.11	.00	.06
Intrinsic	.13*	−.06	.28***	.25***
China				
Self-concordance	.24	−.30**	.05	.33**
External	−.15	.18	.16	−.07
Introjected	.01	.13	.05	−.04
Identified	.18	−.16	.12	.26
Intrinsic	.31**	−.27*	.23	.46***

NOTE: SWB = subjective well-being.
*p < .10. **p < .05. ***p < .01.

Next, we conducted a hierarchical regression analysis to examine a further question; that is, does self-concordance interact with the sample to predict SWB? To simplify the presentation, we analyzed only the aggregate SWB variable, regressing it on self-concordance at Step 1, three dummy variables representing the three Asian samples at Step 2, and three Dummy × Self-Concordance product terms at Step 3 to represent the interactions between sample and self-concordance. At

Step 1, self-concordance was significant (R^2 change = .114, $p < .01$; $\beta = .33$); at Step 2, the three dummy variables were significant as a set (R^2 change = .204, $p < .01$), and each was significant individually (βs = −.46, −.50, and −.21 for Korea, Taiwan, and China, respectively; all three ps < .01). At Step 3, the three product terms were nonsignificant as a set (R^2 change = .002, $p > .50$), and none were significant individually (βs = −.07, .00, and −.06, respectively; all three ps > .30). The lack of interactions further supports the hypothesis that self-concordance may have universal benefits.

Discussion

Summary of Results

In this research, we tried to compare members of an individualist and three collectivist cultures in their levels of goal self-concordance and SWB. We wished to examine both the cultural mean differences in self-concordance and SWB and the cultural differences in patterns of association between self-concordance and SWB. We reasoned that if self-concordance was correlated with SWB in every sample, this would provide important new support for our assumption that self-concordance is beneficial regardless of one's cultural membership.

Analyses of mean differences revealed that Asian participants were much lower than U.S. participants in SWB, a finding that is consistent with earlier work (Diener et al., 1995; Diener & Suh, 1999). However, there was no strong tendency for the Asians to report less concordant motivation than the U.S. participants. For example, there were no cultural differences in external motivation. Also, the South Korean sample reported less introjected motivation than the U.S. participants, and the Chinese sample reported more intrinsic motivation than the U.S. participants. On the other hand, all three Asian samples reported lesser identification with their strivings compared to the U.S. sample. Perhaps most importantly, Asians experienced equal levels of aggregate self-concordance in their personal goals (except in the Taiwanese sample, discussed below). Furthermore, mean levels of self-concordance were positive in every sample, indicating that people feel more autonomous than controlled in every culture. Finally, self-concordance correlated only weakly with demographic variables and with a measure of the self-focused (versus group-focused) content of individuals' goals. Taken together, these findings suggest that it is possible for people to "own their goals" everywhere, regardless of their cultural membership, their income, family education, and the concrete focus of the goals.

Directly supporting our primary SWB-related hypotheses, self-concordance was predictive of every measure of SWB in the aggregate sample and was also predictive of SWB separately within every cultural sample by itself. In no culture did self-concordance correlate negatively with SWB as a cultural relativist perspective might predict based on the assumption that self-possessed individuals do not "fit" within collectivist societies. Furthermore, the associations of self-concordance with SWB remained significant when the effects of self-focused

goals were partialed out and also remained significant when the effects of demographic characteristics were controlled.

One less consistent finding concerned the Taiwanese sample. Although self-concordance correlated positively with SWB in this sample as in the other samples, Taiwanese participants reported significantly less self-concordance than the other samples as well as reporting significantly less SWB than the other samples. We believe this difference may have emerged because the Taiwanese University (National Sun Yat-Sen) and its city of location (Kaohsiung) are fairly traditional and perhaps more collectivistic. In contrast, the other Asian universities in the sample (Hanyang and Guangdon) are located in more Westernized or cosmopolitan cities (Seoul and Guangzhou). However, future research will be required to establish whether Taiwanese samples from less traditional settings might evidence equal self-concordance as South Korean or Chinese samples and, conversely, whether Korean or Chinese students from less urbanized parts of these countries might evidence lower self-concordance.

Overall, these findings are quite consistent with our hypothesis that self-concordant goal pursuit is important in all cultures. Returning to the ongoing example, students (piano or otherwise) in every culture may benefit more when they strive because they enjoy and identify with the process of learning, rather than because they feel they must or should. In other words, when one goes along with strong social forces, it is likely better to reach a state of agreement with them than to resist or resent them. Indeed, this conclusion is consistent with humanistic, existential, organismic, psychosocial, and psychodynamic perspectives regarding optimal human functioning (Ryff & Singer, 1998; Sheldon & Kasser, 2001), which stress the importance of individuals' ability to assimilate and accommodate sociocultural norms, expectations, and constraints.

One positive feature of the current work is that it examined several non-Western cultures rather than just one, as occurs in many cross-cultural studies. Also, several different exemplars of collectivist culture were examined, varying on dimensions such as modern/traditional and democratic/socialist. As noted earlier, the fact that we found the same basic pattern of results across these different cultural contexts lends added confidence to our study conclusions. Yet another innovation of this research is that it employed a mixed idiographicnomothetic methodology, which allowed participants to voice their unique concerns while allowing us to directly compare participants based on their ratings of those concerns (Elliot, Chirkov, Kim, & Sheldon, 2001; Emmons, 1989). This may be especially desirable in cross-cultural studies where the content of people's goals and activities may vary more than the underlying meanings and purposes they represent.

Limitations and Unanswered Questions

Limitations of this study include the fact that only college student samples were employed. It will be important to replicate the findings using older adults as college students may represent the most Westernized segment of many traditional cultures. Also, only self-report data were collected. It will also be important to perhaps eliminate method variance confounds by solic-iting observer- as well as self-reports regarding participants' apparent self-concordance and/or SWB. In addition, it will be important to measure and control for stable trait variables such as neuroticism or extraversion as these might account for the self-concordance to SWB effects (but see Elliot & Sheldon, 1998, for evidence that self-concordance effects are not reduc-ible to neuroticism or behavioral inhibition). Future cross-cul-tural goal research should also examine longitudinal changes in SWB as a function of participants' level of goal attainment during the period of study as such studies might yield different results than those reported here (Oishi & Diener, 2001). Finally, future research should also study self-concordance and SWB in other cultures besides U.S. and Asian cultures as there are many types and styles of collectivism and individualism.

Conclusion

At the broadest level, the results of this study suggest a need for greater differentiation and phenomenological specificity in characterizations of autonomy, individualism, and agency. In particular, our results support a view in which humans function more optimally and have more positive experiences when they do what they enjoy and believe in, no matter what their cultural membership. Indeed, one might question the health or sustain-ability of a culture that did not tolerate this basic expression of human rights (Diener & Suh, 1999).

Notes

1. Notably, some might view personal goals as an inherently individ-ualistic construct, given that goals, by definition, concern people's proactive personal initiatives (Markus & Kitayama. 1994). Howev-er, along with other contemporary goal theorists, we assert that goals are actually among the most important means by which indi-viduals adapt to social contexts and enhance their connectivity with others (Cantor & Sanderson, 1999; Salmela-Aro & Nurmi, 1996). That is, rather than being inherently self-centered, many goals, in-stead, concern the external world, especially the world of social roles and interpersonal concerns (Ryff & Singer. 1998; Salmela-Aro, Pennanen, & Nurmi, 2001; Sheldon & Elliot, 2000). The fact that many personal goals address social tasks is only logical, giv-en that perhaps the primary adaptive environment for Homo sapi-ens throughout history has been the social environment (Caporael, 1997).

2. Data from the South Korean sample were used earlier to examine a different set of research questions (Elliot, Chirkov, Kim, & Sheldon, 2001; Sheldon, Elliot, Kim, & Kassel; 2001).

3. One hundred and sixty-one Chinese participants completed ques-tionnaires. Unfortunately, we were able to match up subjective well-being (SWB) data and goal-data for only 41 of these respon-dents because of an error of questionnaire administration. Provid-ing some assurance that this subsample was equivalent to the main sample, we found no differences between the 41 final par-ticipants and the 120 excluded participants on any of the four SWB measures (all $ps > .50$). Thus, we decided to include the Chinese data in this article.

References

Bettencourt, B., & Sheldon, K. M. (2001). Social roles as vehicles for psychological need satisfaction within groups. *Journal of Personality and Social Psychology, 81*, 1131–1143.

Cantor, N., & Sanderson, C. (1999). Life-task participation and well-being: The importance of taking part in daily life. In D. Kahneman, E. Diener, & N. Schwarz (Eds.), *Well-being: The foundations of hedonic psychology* (pp. 230–243). New York: Russell Sage Foundation.

Caporael, L. R. (1997). The evolution of truly social cognition: The core configurations model. *Personality and Social Psychology Review, 1*, 276–298.

Chirkov, V. I., Ryan, R. M., Kim, Y., & Kaplan, R. (2003). Differentiating autonomy from individualism and independence: A self-determination theory perspective on internalization of cultural orientations and well-being. *Journal of Personality and Social Psychology, 84*, 97–109.

Deci, E. L., & Ryan, R. M. (1985). *Intrinsic motivation and self-determination in human behavior*. New York: Plenum.

Deci, E. L., & Ryan, R. M. (2000). The "what" and "why" of goal pursuits: Human needs and the self-determination of behavior. *Psychological1nquiry, 4*, 227–268.

Deci, E. L., Ryan, R. M., Gagne, M., Leone, D. R., Usunov, J., & Kornazheva, B. P. (2001). Need satisfaction, motivation, and well-being in the work organizations of a former Eastern Bloc country. *Personality and Social Psychology Bulletin, 27*, 930–942.

Diener, E. (1994). Assessing subjective well-being: Progress and opportunities. *Social Indicators Research, 31*, 103–157.

Diener, E., Diener, M., & Diener, C. (1995). Factors predicting the subjective well-being of nations. *Journal of Personality and Social Psychology, 69*, 851–864.

Diener, E., Emmons, R., Larsen, R., & Griffin, S. (1985). The Satisfaction with Life Scale. *Journal of Personality Assessment, 47*, 1105–1117.

Diener, E., & Suh, E. M. (1999). National differences in subjective well-being. In D. Kahneman, E. Diener, & N. Schwarz (Eds.), *Well-being: The foundations of hedonic psychology* (pp. 434–452). New York: Russell Sage Foundation.

Elliot, A. J., Chirkov, V., Kim, Y., & Sheldon, K. M. (2001). A cross-cultural analysis of avoidance (relative to approach) personal goals. *Psychological Science, 12*, 505–510.

Elliot, A. J., & Sheldon, K. M. (1998). Avoidance personal goals and the personality-illness relationship. *Journal of Personality and Social Psychology, 75*, 1282–1299.

Elliot, A. J., Sheldon, K. M., & Church, M. (1997). Avoidance personals goals and subjective well-being. *Personality and Social Psychology Bulletin, 23*, 915–927.

Emmons, R. A. (1989). The personal strivings approach to personality. In L. A. Pervin (Ed), *Goal concepts in personality and social psychology*. Hillsdale, NJ: Lawrence Erlbaum.

Hayarnizu, T. (1997). Between intrinsic and extrinsic motivation: Examination of reasons for academic study based on the theory of internalization. *Japanese Psychological Research, 39*, 98–108.

Iyengar, S. S., & Lepper, M. R. (1999). Rethinking the value of choice: A cultural perspective on intrinsic motivation. *Journal of Personality and Social Psychology, 76*, 349–366.

Markus, H., Kitayama, S., & Heiman, R. (1996). Culture and basic psychological principles. In E. T. Higgins & W. Kruglanski (Eds.), *Social psychology: Handbook of basic principles* (pp. 857–913). New York: Guilford.

Markus, H. R., & Kitayama, S. (1994). The cultural construction of self and emotion: Implications for social behavior. In S. Kitayama &

H. R. Markus (Eds.), *Emotion and culture: Empirical studies of mutual influence* (pp. 89–130). Washington, DC: American Psychological Association.

Myers, D. (2000). The funds, friends, and faith of happy people. *American Psychologist, 55*, 56–67.

Oishi, S. (2000). Goals as cornerstones of subjective well-being: linking individuals and cultures. In E. Diener & E. Suh (Eds), *Culture and subjective well-being* (pp. 87–112). Cambridge, MA: MIT Press.

Oishi, S., & Diener, E. (2001). Goals, culture, and subjective well-being. Personality and Social Psychology Bulletin, 27, 1674–1682.

Ryan, R. M., & Connell, J. P. (1989). Perceived locus of causality and internalization: Examining reasons for acting in two domains. *Journal of Personality and Social Psychology, 57*, 749–761.

Ryff, C. D., & Singer, B. (1998). The role of purpose in life and personal growth in positive human health. In P. T. P. Wong & P. S. Fry (Eds.), *The human quest for meaning: A handbook of psychological research and clinical applications* (pp. 213–235). Mahwah, NJ: Lawrence Erlbaum.

Salmela-Am, K., & Nurmi, J. (1996). Uncertainty and confidence in interpersonal projects: Consequences for social relationships and well-being. *Journal of Social and Personal Relationships, 13*, 109–122.

Salmela-Am, K., Pennanen, R., & Nurmi, J. (2001). Self-focused goals: What they are, how they function, and how they relate to well-being. In P. Schmuck & K. Sheldon (Eds.), *Life goals and well-being: Towards a positive psychology of human striving* (pp. 148–166). London: Hogrefe.

Sheldon, K. M. (2002). The self-concordance model of healthy goal-striving: When personal goals correctly represent the person. In E. L. Deci & R. M. Ryan (Eds.), *Handbook of self-determination research* (pp. 65–86). Rochester, NY: University of Rochester Press.

Sheldon, K. M., & Elliot, A. J. (1999). Goal striving, need satisfaction, and longitudinal well-being: The Self-Concordance Model. *Journal of Personality and Social Psychology, 76*, 546–557.

Sheldon, K. M., & Elliot, A. J. (2000). Personal goals in social roles: Divergences and convergences across roles and levels of analysis. *Journal of Personality, 68*, 51–84.

Sheldon, K. M., Elliot, A. J., Kim, Y., & Kasser, T. (2001). What's satisfying about satisfying events? Comparing ten candidate psychological needs. *Journal of Personality and Social Psychology, 80*, 325–339.

Sheldon, K. M., & Houser-Marko, L. (2001). Self-concordance, goal-attainment, and the pursuit of happiness: Can there be an upward spiral? *Journal of Personality and Social Psychology, 80*, 152–165.

Sheldon, K. M., & Kasser, T. (1995). Coherence and congruence: Two aspects of personality integration. *Journal of Personality and Social Psychology, 68*, 531–543.

Sheldon. K. M., & Kasser, T. (1998). Pursuing personal goals: Skills enable progress but not all progress is beneficial. *Personality and Social Psychology Bulletin, 24*, 1319–1331.

Triandis, H. C. (1997). Cross-cultural perspectives on personality. In R. Hogan, J. Johnson, & S. Briggs (Eds.), *Handbook of personality psychology* (pp. 439–464). San Diego, CA: Academic Press.

Watson, D., Tellegen, A., & Clark, L. (1988). Development and validation of brief measures of positive and negative affect: The PANAS scales. *Journal of Personality and Social Psychology, 54*, 1063–1070.

Yamauchi, H., & Thnaka, K. (1998). Relations of autonomy, self-referenced beliefs and self-regulated learning among Japanese children. *Psychological Reports, 82*, 803–816.

KENNON M. SHELDON received his Ph.D. in social-personality psychology from the University of California at Davis in 1992. He is an associate professor of psychology at the University of Missouri. He studies goals, motivation, and psychological well-being. Much of his work is summarized in his 2003 book with Williams and Joiner, *Self-Determination Theory in the Clinic: Motivating Physical and Mental Health (Yale University Press)*.

ANDREW J. ELLIOT is a professor of psychology at the University of Rochester. He received his Ph.D. from the University of Wisconsin–Madison. His research focuses on approach-avoidance motivation and personality—in particular, within the achievement domain.

RICHARD M. RYAN is a professor of psychology and psychiatry at the University of Rochester, where he has been on the faculty since 1981. As a researcher, he is best known for his work on human motivation, particularly his investigations of intrinsic motivation and internalization processes. He is the author of numerous research articles in both theoretical and applied areas, including the topics of motivation in health care, the development of self-regulation, psychopathology, education, work, sport and exercise, and parenting, among other foci.

VALERY CHIRKOV received a Ph.D. in industrial psychology from Leningrad State University in Russia and came to the United States in 1995 for further training. He received his Ph.D. in social psychology at the University of Rochester in 2001 and is currently an assistant professor of psychology at the University of Saskatchewan. His research focuses on the problem of the internalization of cultural practices and values, the role of parents and teachers in the transmission of cultural values, and the psychological aspects of immigration, acculturation, and cultural adjustment.

YOUNGMEE KIM, PH.D., is a director of family studies at the Behavioral Research Center at the National Home Office of the American Cancer Society. She received her B.A. and M.A. from Yonsei University and her M.A. and Ph.D. in social and personality psychology from the University of Rochester. Her research focuses on the physical and psychological effect of cancer in the family.

CINDY WU is an assistant professor in the Hankamer School of Business at Baylor University. She received her Ph.D. from the University of Illinois at Urbana-Champaign. Her research focuses on employee motivation, training, leadership, and cross-cultural management.

MELIKSAH DEMIR got his B.A. from the Middle East Technical University, Ankara, Turkey. He is currently a Ph.D. student at Wayne State University, Detroit, Michigan. His research interests are friendship and subjective well-being.

ZHIGANG SUN is the director of the Center for Advanced Social Research of the University of Missouri's School of Journalism. His research interests include the effects of mass communication on social capital and civic norms, health communication, political communication, and the application of research design and methodology in social attitudinal and behavioral studies.

From *Journal of Cross-Cultural Psychology*, March 2004, pp. 209-223. Copyright © 2004 by International Association for Cross-Cultural Psychology. Reprinted by permission of Sage Publications. www.sagepub.com

Mirror Mirror: Seeing Yourself as Others See You

To navigate the social universe, you need to know what others think of you— although the clearest view depends on how you see yourself.

CARLIN FLORA

I gave a toast at my best friend's wedding last summer, a speech I carefully crafted and practiced delivering. And it went well: The bride and groom beamed; the guests paid attention and reacted in the right spots; a waiter gave me a thumbs-up. I was relieved and pleased with myself. Until months later—when I saw the cold, hard video documentation of the event. * As I watched myself getting ready to make the toast, a funny thing happened. I got butterflies in my stomach all over again. I was nervous for myself, even though I knew the outcome would be just fine. Except maybe the jitters were warranted. The triumph of that speech in my mind's eye morphed into the duller reality unfolding on the TV screen. My body language was awkward. My voice was grating. My facial expressions, odd. My timing, not quite right. Is this how people saw me? * It's a terrifying thought: What if I possess a glaring flaw that everyone notices but me? Or, fears aside, what if there are a few curious chasms between how I view myself and how others view me? What if I think I'm efficient but I'm seen as disorganized? Critical, but perceived as accepting?

While many profess not to care what others think, we are, in the end, creatures who want and need to fit into a social universe. Humans are psychologically suited to interdependence. Social anxiety is really just an innate response to the threat of exclusion; feeling that we're not accepted by a group leaves us agitated and depressed.

Others always rate you one point higher than you rate yourself on a scale of physical attractiveness.

The ability to intuit how people see us is what enables us to authentically connect to others and to reap the deep satisfaction that comes with those ties. We can never be a fly on the wall to our own personality dissections, watching as people pick us apart after meeting us. Hence we are left to rely on the accuracy of what psychologists call our "metaperceptions"—the ideas we have about *others'* ideas about us.

The Bottom Line: It Comes Down to What You Think About Yourself

Your ideas about what others think of you hinge on your self-concept—your own beliefs about who you are. "You filter the cues that you get from others through your self-concept," explains Mark Leary, professor of psychology at Wake Forest University in Winston-Salem, North Carolina.

Our self-concept is fundamentally shaped by one person in particular: Mama. How our mother (or primary caregiver) responded to our first cries and gestures heavily influences how we expect to be seen by others. "Children behave in ways that perpetuate what they have experienced," says Martha Farrell Erickson, senior fellow with the Children, Youth and Family Consortium at the University of Minnesota. "A child who had an unresponsive mother will act obnoxious or withdrawn so that people will want to keep their distance. Those with consistently responsive mothers are confident and connect well with their peers."

As an infant scans his mother's face he absorbs clues to who he is; as adults we continue to search for our reflections in others' eyes. While the parent-child bond is not necessarily destiny, it does take quite a bit to alter self-concepts forged in childhood, whether good or bad. People rely on others' impressions to nurture their views about themselves, says William Swann, professor of psychology at the University of Texas, Austin. His research shows that people with negative self-concepts goad others to evaluate them harshly, especially if they suspect the person likes them—they would rather be right than be admired.

The Top Line: You Probably Do Know What People Think of You

But it's likely you don't know any one person's assessment. "We have a fairly stable view of ourselves," says Bella DePaulo, visiting professor of psychology at the University of California at Santa Barbara. "We expect other people to see that same view immediately." And they do. On average there is consensus about how you come off. But you can't apply that knowledge to any one individual, for a variety of reasons.

For starters, each person has an idiosyncratic way of sizing up others that (like metaperceptions themselves) is governed by her own self-concept. A person you meet will assess you through her unique lens, which lends consistency to her views on others. Some people, for example, are "likers" who perceive nearly everyone as good-natured and smart.

Furthermore, if a particular person doesn't care for you, it won't always be apparent. "People are generally not direct in everyday interactions," says DePaulo. Classic work by psychologist Paul Ekman has shown that most people can't tell when others are faking expressions. Who knows how many interactions you've walked away from thinking you were a hit while your new friend was actually faking agreeability?

And there's just a whole lot going on when you meet someone. You're talking, listening and planning what you're going to say next, as well as adjusting your nonverbal behavior and unconsciously responding to the other person's. DePaulo calls it "cognitive busyness."

Because of all we have to contend with, she says, we are unable to effectively interpret someone else's reactions. "We take things at face value and don't really have the means to infer others' judgments." Until afterward, of course, when you mull over the interaction, mining your memory for clues.

Context is Key

While our personalities (and self-concepts) are fairly consistent across time and place, some situations, by their very structure, can change or even altogether wipe out your personality. You might feel like the same old you wherever you are, but the setting and role you happen to be playing affect what people think of you. Suppose you describe yourself as lighthearted and talkative. Well, no one could possibly agree if they meet you at your brother's funeral.

What Type of Person Can Handle Feedback …

Are you open to experience? Are you, say, perennially taking up new musical instruments or scouting out-of-the-way neighborhoods? If so, your curiosity will drive you to learn new things about the world and yourself. You'll be inclined to ask people how you're doing as you embark on new challenges, and you will gather a clearer idea of how you come off to others, says David Funder, professor of psychology at the University of California at Riverside.

How to Solicit a Character Critique (Yours!)

Muster your courage and set up an "exit interview" if you're left wondering why a relationship went south, in a spirit of fact-finding—that is, without hostility—contact your ex and ask for an honest and kind discussion of how things went awry. You're not looking to get your ex back (or get back at your ex) but to gather information to prevent lightning from striking twice. Ask questions ("What could I have done better?") and listen. Be sure you don't use the conversation to justify your old behavior.

People endowed with the trait of physical awareness have a keen sense of how they present themselves. If you are concerned with the observable parts of personality—voice, posture, clothes and walk—as an actor would be, says Funder, "you will control the impression you give, and your self-perception will be more accurate." If, for example, you slouch but don't know it, your droopy posture registers in the minds of those you meet and enters into how they see you—unbeknownst to you.

If you are someone who craves approval, you will tend to think you make a positive impression on other people. And generally, you will, says DePaulo.

People who have learned to regulate their emotions are in a much better position to know what others think of them, says Carroll Izard, professor of psychology at the University of Delaware: "They are able to detect emotions on others' faces and to feel empathy." If you are either overwhelmed with feelings or unable to express them at all, it becomes difficult to interpret someone else's response to you. Learning to give concrete expression to your feelings and to calm yourself in highly charged moments will give you a much better grip on your own and others' internal states.

Those with personalities that feed the accuracy of their metaperceptions are handsomely rewarded. "The more accurate you are about how others perceive you, the better you fare socially," says Leary. "Think of a person who thinks he's really funny but isn't. He interprets polite laughter as genuine laughter, but everyone is on to him and annoyed by him."

… And What Kind of Person Rejects Feedback

There are people who behave in ways that prevent them from getting direct feedback from others, which renders them less able to know how they come off'. Maybe you're a boss who is prickly and hostile in the face of criticism. Or a student who bursts into tears over a bad evaluation. Either way, coworkers and teachers will start leaving you in the dark to fumble over your own missteps.

Such demeanor may even encourage others to lie to you, says DePaulo. You may project a fragility that makes others afraid they will break you by offering honest criticism.

Too much concern about what others think of you can only constrict behavior and stifle the spirit.

Narcissism also blocks metaperception. Instead of wincing, as "normal" subjects do, when forced to see themselves on-screen, narcissists become even more self-biased, finds Oliver John, professor of psychology at the University of California at Berkeley. When he and his team videotaped people diagnosed as pathological narcissists, a group absorbed with themselves, their subjects loved watching the footage and uniformly thought they came off beautifully! The finding underscores how fiercely we defend our self-concepts, even if they reflect psychological instability.

Shyness: A Double Whammy

If you are socially anxious (otherwise known as shy), you likely fret that you don't come off well. Unfortunately, you're probably right. Shy people convey unflattering impressions of themselves, says DePaulo. But not for the reasons they think. People don't see them as lacking in smarts, wit or attractiveness but as haughty and detached. When you're anxious, you fail to ask others about themselves or put them at ease in any way, which can be seen as rude and self-centered.

In a way, many shy people are self-centered, points out Bernie Carducci, psychologist at Indiana University Southeast and author of *Shyness: A Bold New Approach*. They imagine that everyone is watching and evaluating their every move. They think they are the center of any social interaction, and because they can't stand that, they shut down (unlike an exhibitionist, who would relish it). Socially anxious people are so busy tracking what others think that they can't act spontaneously. Still, many people find them endearing, precisely because they don't hog attention.

The Powerful and the Beautiful

Neither group gets accurate feedback. "People are too dazzled or intimidated to react honestly to them," says Funder. Michael Levine, the head of a Hollywood public relations agency, has run up against many such people, who end up with a deluded sense of self thanks to a coterie of sycophants. If you are among the bold and the beautiful, he says, you must invite feedback by playing on the fact that people want desperately to be liked by you. "You must let them know that your approval is conditional upon their honesty with you."

Don't Worry—You're Not See-Through

The traits others judge us on fall roughly into two categories—visible and invisible. Funder has found that others notice our visible traits more than we ourselves do (the eye, after all, can't

see its own lashes, as the Chinese proverb goes). You would rate yourself higher on the characteristic of "daydreams" than others would—simply because they cannot easily discern whether or not you're a daydreamer. They'll tend to assume you're not.

There's always a trade-off between how good you want to feel—and what you want to know.

The good news, however, is that on a scale of physical attractiveness, others always rate you about one point higher than you rate yourself. This applies to "charm," too—another characteristic you can't easily convey to yourself, one that others naturally have a better window onto. "Imagine trying to be charming while alone on a desert island," Funder observes.

One common concern is that internal states are evident for all to see. In a study where subjects did some public speaking and then rated their own performances, the anxious ones in the group gave themselves a low rating, thinking that their inner churning was apparent to all. But audiences reported that they did just fine.

"Invisible" traits aren't entirely invisible—at least not to close friends. But an anxious friend would still rate herself higher on worry than we would.

The invisible/visible trait divide helps explain why people agree more on your positive attributes than your negative ones, says Eric Turkheimer, professor of psychology at the University of Virginia.

"First of all, people are less honest about their own negative traits," he says, "and many of these are 'stealth' traits. You'd have to know someone really well to have any thoughts on whether or not he 'feels empty inside,' for example."

Self-Awareness: A Blessing and a Curse

There is one sure way to see yourself from others' perspective—on videotape (as I did post-toast). But remember, the image is still filtered through your self-concept—it's still you watching you. Paul Silvia, assistant professor of psychology at the University of North Carolina at Greensboro, points to an experiment in which psychologically healthy adults watched tapes of themselves giving group presentations. They described it as quite sobering. They cued into their faults and judged themselves much more harshly than they would have had they relied on their own impressions of the experience. You evaluate yourself much more critically when you are self-aware, because you are focused on your failure to meet internal standards.

If I watch myself on tape, I'm not only viewing with my self-concept in mind, I'm comparing "me" to my "possible selves," the "me's" I wish to become. Here is where an unbridgeable gap opens up between people: I will never have a sense of anyone else's possible selves, nor they mine.

So, should we just rely on our memories of events, protective of self-esteem as they are, and eschew concrete documentation of ourselves? Not necessarily, says Silvia. But the dilemma reveals how self-awareness is a double-edged sword. Self-awareness furnishes a deep, rich self-concept—but it also can be paralyzing, warns Leary, author of *The Curse of the Self." Self-Awareness, Egotism and the Quality of Human Life*. "It leads you to overanalyze others' reactions to you and misinterpret them."

Many of the most unpleasant shades on our emotional palettes—embarrassment, shame, envy—exist solely in the interpersonal realm. We cannot feel them until we are self-aware enough to worry what others think about us. These emotions are supposed to motivate us to cut out potentially self-destructive behaviors. But, Leary points out, given the brain's natural bias toward false alarms, people feel overly embarrassed. Too much concern about what others think can only constrict behavior and stifle the spirit.

Do You Really Want to Know How You Come Off?

Report cards and annual reviews give you information on your performance in school and at work. But you'll rarely be treated to a straightforward critique of your character—unless someone blurts one out in a heated argument or you solicit it directly. "You could always ask a family member or someone else who knows you are stuck with them to tell you honestly what they think of you," says Funder. Publicist Levine took this approach a bit further when he asked several ex-girlfriends to each list three positive and three negative aspects of being in a relationship with him. "There was some consistency in their answers," he says. "It was challenging to take it in, but really helpful."

"There's always a trade-off between how you want to feel and what you want to know," says DePaulo. If ignorance is bliss, maybe it's best to trust someone's instinct to protect you. "But there are times when you really need accurate feedback," she says, "such as when you are trying to decide if you would be good in a certain career."

Perhaps the delicate balance between feeling good about yourself and knowing exactly how you come off is best maintained not by all those elusive "others." Maybe it's maintained by your most significant ones, the people who will keep you in line but appreciate you for who you are, not just for the impressions you leave behind.

Reprinted with permission from *Psychology Today Magazine*, May–June 2005, pp. 54-57. Copyright © 2005 by Sussex Publishers, Inc.

UNIT 3

Social Cognition and Social Perception

Unit Selections

Key Points to Consider

- What is social cognition and social perception? How do they differ from other forms of cognition and perception as studied by psychologists?

- Are most social behaviors and interpersonal interactions planned or automatic?

- How can our memories warp or alter our interactions with memories of other people or social situations? What are false memories?

- Culture is very relevant to social cognition. What are the various ways that culture influences our social cognitions and perceptions?

- Why do psychologists insist on utilizing undergraduates as research participants? What are the problems with doing so?

- Just how "social" are our perceptions and actions? What are joint actions? Why and how do they occur?

- What role does the face and the body play in social relationships? Are both equally useful to person perception accuracy?

Student Web Site

www.mhcls.com/online

Internet References

Further information regarding these Web sites may be found in this book's preface or online.

Nonverbal Behavior and Nonverbal Communication
http://www3.usal.es/~nonverbal/

One neighbor called the police about another neighbor. The first did not know the second, but when she heard slapping sounds and painful grunts emanating from the neighbor's apartment, she thought child or spousal abuse was occurring. During the investigation, the police determined that there was no abuse. Upon further inquiry, the police realized that the first neighbor was highly sensitized to slapping sounds because she herself had been abused as a child. "What," you ask, "was the second neighbor doing?" He was watching professional wrestling on television!

How we perceive and interpret others' behaviors, sentiments, and emotions is very important. Without such insights we would not accomplish much in our social interactions. You should remember that others are observing you and scrutinizing your actions in an effort to better understand you. Try to imagine a world where we do not feel competent to predict others' actions or to understand their moods and motives.

In this third unit, we move from self-perception to social perception and social cognition. Most theories of social perception and social cognition assume that we are fairly rational and methodical in our assessments of others. But, is this really the case? Do we instead make snap judgments of others? Research on cognitive misers (lazy perceivers of social information) suggests that we characteristically prefer quick appraisals and use shortcuts in our assessments.

Social *cognition* involves the way people think about others, represent others in memory, and strategize to understand oth-

ers. Processes such as learning and remembering are important to social cognition. And, once again, culture plays an active role in how we proceed to understand others. Besides the story about wrestling, another astonishing example of social cognition gone awry is the inaccuracy of eyewitnesses. Despite the witness's confidence, research demonstrates that most eyewitnesses are inaccurate, including professional witnesses such as the police.

Social *perception* or person perception entails how we form overall impressions of others. Another example is in order. Suppose someone you hardly know steals a valued possession from you. You might jump to the conclusion that this individual is just plain bad. Social psychologists would say that you attribute (ascribe or assign) a description of or form an opinion about this other person on the basis of just one behavior. Your attribution is most probably inaccurate. Why? All humans display both positive and negative qualities. What if later you are attending synagogue, and the rabbi announces that this same person made a sizeable donation for an addition to the building? Would you agree that your appraisal of the individual might merit modification? Would you be willing to adjust your characterization of the person?

Besides misattribution, our impressions of others (and the impressions we in turn leave on others) are muddied by a variety of additional processes that consequently make our interpersonal tasks more difficult. For example, some individuals actively manipulate the perceptions others form of them. One such individual is known as a *self-monitor* or someone who is chameleon-like. The individual feigns friendliness, likes to attract attention at parties, appears studious and intellectual in class while at the same time gives the impression of somberness and devotion at church. While all of us are culpable of manipulation from time to time, the self-monitor is the champion impression manager.

Let us further examine some of these issues in two subunits—the first on social cognition and the other on social perception.

In "How Social Perception Can Automatically Influence Behavior," Ferguson and Bargh argue that our memories can unintentionally and unknowingly alter our impressions of someone else. The memory might even be colored by the memory of a similar person. The authors claim that such reminiscences are automatic and outside of our awareness. In sum, the authors provide yet another reason to question the accuracy of our evaluations of others.

The article that follows details some of the fascinating works on social memory alluded to above. We now have years of research on this issue and on the memory errors we make. The overarching conclusion of this research—as presented by Daniel Greenberg in the second article—is that many social memories as well as other memories are indeed mistaken.

The subunit on social cognition would be incomplete without commentary on the role culture plays in fashioning our assumptions about others. Author Zak Stambor discusses the notion that cultures differ in how their members behave and also construe the actions of others. Stambor questions that, with the many subcultures in America, why do American social psychologists utilize mainly white undergraduate participants in their research of social phenomena?

The subunit on social perception commences with a general article on the nature of social perception. The review of the literature by Gunther Knoblich and Natalie Sebanz offers an overview of how higher mental processes affect the way we engage with other people and even share joint social behaviors with them.

The final selection for this unit is "Perception of Faces and Bodies." The human form, whether it is the face or our bodily postures and gestures, offers cues to others about our inner life. While the face has received the most attention in social psychology, body cues are now attracting the attention of researchers, because they, too, reveal much about us to others. Some scientists, however, argue that they operate in ways that differ from the facial cues.

How Social Perception Can Automatically Influence Behavior

Do we always know the reasons for our actions? Or is our behavior sometimes unknowingly and unintentionally influenced by what we have recently perceived? It has been traditionally assumed that the automatic influence of knowledge in memory is limited to people's interpretation of the world, and stops short of shaping their actual behavior. Researchers in experimental social psychology have begun to challenge this assumption by documenting how people's behaviors can be unknowingly influenced by knowledge that is incidentally activated in memory during social perception. We review findings that suggest that the social knowledge that is incidentally activated while reading words or imagining events subsequently affects participants' behaviors across a range of ostensibly unrelated domains.

MELISSA J. FERGUSON[1] AND JOHN A. BARGH[2]

Experimental social psychologists have amassed a large body of findings over the past three decades suggesting that social knowledge is automatically activated in memory during the natural course of perception. That is, while people are seeing and listening to the world around them, social knowledge that corresponds to perceived stimuli is spontaneously and immediately activated in memory without people's awareness or intention. This research has also shown that automatically activated information then shapes and guides people's impressions, judgments, feelings and intentions without people being aware that such influence is occurring.[1,2,3]

Although there is now a general consensus that people's understanding of the world is automatically shaped by previous experiences and knowledge, many people assume that complex behaviors are untainted by such influences. Instead, behaviors are often presumed to result solely from conscious, intentional thought. Recent research in social psychology has placed this long-standing assumption under scrutiny by showing that complex behaviors can also be automatically initiated and guided. This represents a significant shift in the kind of effects automatic social knowledge activation has, from subjective impressions of the world to actual behaviors in the world. Such a shift is crucial for developing theories, not only about how behavioral information is represented in memory, but also about the determinants of everyday behaviors. Just as previous research has informed us that our impressions of the world are inevitably shaped by factors outside of our awareness, the current work suggests that we might not always be aware of how we are behaving—or perhaps more importantly, why. This article first briefly describes the research on how incidental knowledge activation influences judgments and impressions, and then reviews recent findings concerning automatic effects on social behavior.

Perception Automatically Activates Social Knowledge

Social psychological research about how social knowledge is automatically activated during perception was inspired by research in cognitive psychology a quarter of a century ago.[4,5] Cognitive psychologists showed that the perception of a stimulus in the environment (e.g. a bird) activates in memory a vast array of semantically and lexically related information (e.g. robin, wings, trees, etc.). This was discovered using priming paradigms, which demonstrated that people inevitably 'go beyond the information given', inferring more information from a perceived stimulus than is physically present.[6] Furthermore, this work showed that the activation of such knowledge does not require the perceiver's intention.[4,5]

Inspired by these findings, social psychologists demonstrated that *social* information is also activated in an automatic fashion (see Box 1).[1,2,3] Using a variety of priming methodologies, researchers established that when a person perceives a member of a social group, such as an elderly person, information about that group is instantly activated, including attitudes, exemplars (i.e. memories of individual group members), and social stereotypes (beliefs and expectancies about the group; *e.g. elderly people are slow and forgetful*).[7,8,9] The perception

[1]Department of Psychology, Cornell University, Ithaca, NY 14853, USA
[2]Department of Psychology, Yale University, New Haven, CT 06520, USA

Box 1

Automaticity in Contemporary Social Psychology

What constitutes an automatic effect of knowledge activation on judgment or behavior? Historically, efficient processes that occur without the person's awareness, intention or control have been considered automatic[3,4,5,56,57,58]. Research that addresses whether a given process meets these criteria for automaticity, as well as speculation about how the concept of automaticity should be conceptualized, is prevalent within social psychology[1,2,3,56,57,59,60,61,62,63,64]. Much contemporary work on automatic processes, however, has focused on the criterion of awareness (although see research on efficient social processes[10,11]). In particular, given the well-established finding that people are unaware of the vast amount of social knowledge that becomes activated during social perception, researchers have tested the degree to which people's judgments and behavior are unknowingly influenced by such incidental knowledge activation. If participants are unaware that their behavior has been influenced by recently perceived information, they necessarily did not intend such an influence, nor could they have controlled the influence. Although this kind of operationalization of automaticity is regularly being scrutinized and refined, it does effectively capture the unintentional and non-conscious aspects of many social behaviors, the determinants of which have traditionally been assumed to be completely conscious and deliberate.

How do researchers ensure that participants are unaware of the impact of a priming episode on their judgment or behavior? The critical requirement is that participants do not suspect any influence of the priming on their subsequent behavior[65], and this can be accomplished even when participants are consciously processing the priming stimuli, as long as the cover story obscures the relation between the two. Accordingly, many researchers present priming stimuli in tasks that are ostensibly unrelated to subsequent dependent measures[66]. One common method is to use a scrambled sentence task in which prime words are embedded in sentences that participants have to unscramble as part of a 'linguistic task'[67].

At the end of an experiment, researchers carefully assess participants' suspicion by administering a 'funnel debriefing'[66]. This procedure consists of increasingly specific questions aimed at probing participants' awareness and suspicion. For example, the first question asks participants to speculate in general about the purpose of the experiment, whereas the later questions ask whether they noticed any connection between certain words in the first part of the experiment, and their answers or behaviors in the latter part of the experiment[66]. Although this type of measure might not capture those participants who were actually suspicious but do not want to admit to 'spoiling' the experimenter's plans[68], it could encourage those participants who actually were not suspicious to report nevertheless their awareness to avoid appearing gullible. Because there are possible ways in which a funnel debriefing might be either a conservative or liberal proxy of awareness, researchers are continually striving for more sensitive ways to measure the degree to which behavioral effects occur non-consciously.

of behaviors themselves also leads to the activation of social knowledge. When people read about an actor performing a behavior, trait knowledge that corresponds to that behavior is spontaneously and unintentionally activated.[10,11,12] Taken together, this research suggests that the perception of any social stimulus will inevitably activate in memory a diverse array of related knowledge.

Incidentally Activated Knowledge Affects Social Judgment

Knowledge that is incidentally activated during perception can influence people's judgments because it can guide the categorization of judgment-relevant stimuli. Social stimuli are often inherently ambiguous in that they are multiply categorizable.[13] For instance, people can be judged according to their membership in any of numerous groups (e.g. race, sex, age, etc.), and social behaviors can usually be interpreted in multiple ways (e.g. is he acting in a conceited or shy manner?). Because there are always many categories into which a person or event can be placed, the ultimate classification of a stimulus will depend on the relative accessibility of the relevant categories [14].

This is when incidentally activated knowledge can determine the categorization of a stimulus, and therefore influence later judgments and interpretations. A particular category can become accessible because of the recent perception of an event, and then capture a subsequently encountered stimulus, even if the only relation between the perceived event and the subsequent stimulus is a semantic one. For instance, a particular social category, such as African-Americans, might become activated naturally and incidentally when perceiving a member of that group in the street (or on television or in a newspaper); but that category will remain activated ('primed') for some time thereafter, even after the original stimulus is no longer present in the environment. During the time it remains active and accessible, it can influence the categorization of other, race-ambiguous people. But perhaps more importantly, because any categorization carries with it a unique set of social stereotypes, attitudes and knowledge, all of this associated knowledge (e.g. stereotypic traits, such as hostility) also remains accessible and likely to be used in the interpretation of other people's behavior. This well-established research suggests that people are not only unaware of the information that is activated during the normal course of perception, but also of the way in which such information guides their judgments and impressions of the world around them.

Incidentally Activated Knowledge Affects Behavior

Until recently, it has been largely assumed that although judgments and feelings can be shaped by factors outside of people's awareness, complex social behavior is determined by people's conscious and deliberately made choices. This assumption is part of a rich tradition of rational-choice theories of behavior as well as the humanistic tradition within psychology, both of which assume that people more or less carefully and intentionally weigh their behavioral options and then choose the optimal one.[1,2]

In contrast to this assumption, researchers in social psychology have begun to demonstrate that complex behavior is also automatically shaped and guided by the knowledge that is incidentally activated during perception. Their argument builds on previous theory and research suggesting that behavioral representations can be automatically activated in memory during perception, and, once activated, can guide actual behavior.

Perception Activates Behavioral Representations

Numerous theorists have argued that behavior is mentally represented in a similar way to other social information such as judgments and attitudes. In particular, theorists have asserted that behavioral and perceptual representations are closely interconnected in memory[15,16,17,18,19,20,21,22,23,24], and recent research supports this claim. For instance, researchers have found, in both Macaque monkeys[25] and humans[26], that the same area of the pre-motor cortex is active both when monkeys and humans perceive an action and when they perform that action themselves.

On the assumption that behavioral responses are mentally represented and associated with perceptual representations, behavioral responses might be among the forms of knowledge that are automatically activated in response to perceiving a social stimulus. For instance, just as a stereotype presumably becomes associated with a group after repeated group-stereotype pairings, a behavior that a person repeatedly performs in a particular situation, or in response to a particular other person, might become associated in memory with the features of that situation or person. In both cases, the mere perception of the group member, or situation, might automatically activate the respective stereotype or behavior.

Activated Behavioral Information Affects Behavior

Assuming that behavioral responses are represented mentally and can be automatically activated during the normal course of perception, can they influence how a person behaves? There is a long history of theories arguing for this very possibility. For

example, William Carpenter in the 1860s developed the principle of 'ideomotor action', in which simply thinking about an action is sufficient to lead to the performance of that action[27,28]. William James elaborated on this notion in the 1890s by asserting that the occurrence of thoughts about actions leads to the performance of those actions unless the person consciously intervenes to prevent it[29].

Much contemporary work on human mimicry suggests that in fact the perception of certain actions can lead to the performance of those actions. There is abundant evidence that people exhibit imitative behavior from an early age onwards, mimicking everything from facial expressions to the speech of their conversation partners[30,31,32,33]. This research suggests that the knowledge that is activated in response to perceiving a given action can also lead to the performance of that same action, at least for simple behaviors such as facial expressions and the use of syntax.

Recent Research on Automatic Social Behavior

Social psychologists have recently explored whether more complex social behavior is influenced by incidental knowledge activation. For example, although research has suggested that people will adopt the accent of a conversation partner[32], will a person act more aggressively if she or he perceives the trait *hostility*? As an initial attempt to test this possibility, Bargh, Chen and Burrows[16] covertly primed participants with trait knowledge about *rudeness* (Study 1), stereotypes of the elderly (and thus the trait *slowness*; Study 2), and stereotypes of African-Americans (and thus the trait *hostility*; Study 3).

Those participants primed with trait information were significantly more likely than non-primed participants to show behavior relevant to the primed trait: specifically, to interrupt another person (Study 1), walk slowly down the hallway (Study 2), or express hostility after being provoked (Study 3). Crucially, none of the participants reported any awareness of a connection between the priming episode and their behavior (see Box 1). Thus, when participants faced a situation that could be responded to with either rudeness or politeness, slow or fast walking, hostility or calmness, they acted in accordance with trait information covertly primed only minutes before in an unrelated context.

This first set of studies laid the groundwork for research that has since examined how various behaviors can be automatically guided by information that is incidentally activated from the environment. The studies over the past five years differ in terms of the source of social knowledge activation (e.g. traits, stereotypes, behavior, contexts) as well as the nature of the behavioral effects (e.g. simple, complex).

Trait Knowledge Influences Behavior

Dijksterhuis and van Knippenberg[21] addressed whether social behavior that is more complex than walking speed or hostility can be primed. They subtly primed participants with the trait 'intelligence' or 'stupidity', and then asked them to complete an ostensibly unrelated knowledge test that included questions such as 'Who painted *La Guernica*?' (a. Dali, b. Miro, c. Picasso, d. Velasquez), and 'What is the capital of Bangladesh?' (a. Dhaka, b. Hanoi, c. Yangon, d. Bangkok).

Dijksterhuis and van Knippenberg expected that priming participants with intelligence or stupidity would lead to the increased accessibility of related knowledge, including behavioral responses associated with the corresponding concept. This activated knowledge would then affect their performance on the test, relative to non-primed participants. As expected, those primed with '*intelligence*' significantly outperformed non-primed participants whereas those primed with '*stupidity*' significantly underperformed non-primed participants. None of the participants reported any awareness of a connection between the priming episode and the test. These results suggest that incidentally activated knowledge can influence even complex behavior, such as performance on a knowledge test.

Behavioral Information Influences Behavior

Researchers have also explored whether knowledge other than trait information might influence people's behavior in an automatic fashion. Given the evidence that people tend to adopt the tone and speech of their conversation partners, researchers have examined whether people might also unknowingly mimic the actions of their conversation partners.[34,35,36,37,38] Several recent articles provide support for this hypothesis, and show, for example, that people are significantly more likely to shake their foot or rub their face unconsciously if their conversation partner is doing so than if their partner is not.[19] In all of these studies, participants were carefully questioned after the experiment to assess their awareness of their own and their partner's behaviors. Participants did not report any awareness of their own behavior, their partner's behavior, or any relation between the two. This research suggests that the mere perception of actions automatically increases the likelihood of the performance of those same actions, without the person's intention or awareness.

Recent work has expanded upon this topic by showing that the perception of behaviors does not always increase the likelihood of performing those same behaviors. Tiedens and Fragale[39] hypothesized that the perception of behaviors that connote high or low status might non-consciously lead to the adoption of the opposite (i.e. low or high status, respectively) behaviors. The findings suggest that when participants interacted with a partner whose posture suggested dominance (i.e. an expansive posture), the participants themselves non-consciously adopted submissive postures (i.e. restricted). A sensitive probing process at the end of these experiments indicated that participants were not aware of their own posture, their partner's posture, or any connection between the two. Thus, the perception of another's behavior can unintentionally and unknowingly lead to the performance of either that same behavior, or one that is diametrically opposed in terms of the socially relevant dimension of status.

Goal-Relevant Information Influences Behavior

In addition to investigating the kinds of information that can influence social behavior, researchers have also explored the type of behavior that can result from such an influence[40,41,42,43]. Recent research by Bargh *et al.*[42] suggests that incidental social perception also activates goal knowledge that can automatically influence actual goal-pursuit—that is, behavior that is directed towards an objective, persists over time, and resumes after an interruption.

Across several studies, participants were covertly primed with words related to *achievement*, and then completed a series of word-search puzzles. Not only did primed participants perform significantly better than non-primed participants during the same time period, they were more likely than non-primed participants to maximize their performance by disobeying experimenter instructions to stop working on the task. Primed participants were also significantly more likely than non-primed participants to choose to continue working on the puzzles after an interruption rather than begin a cartoon-assessment task that had been rated in another study as more enjoyable. As in other experiments in this area of research, none of the participants in any of the studies reported any awareness of a connection between the priming tasks and the dependent measures. This type of research can potentially extend the effects of incidental knowledge activation on behavior from relatively static displays of a trait-consistent action, to complex, feedback-dependent sequences of behaviors.

Context Information Influences Behavior

Researchers have also investigated whether the perception of social settings might also influence behavior in a similar fashion. Aarts and Dijksterhuis[44] used as priming stimuli locations that were associated with situational norms (i.e. prescriptions for acceptable behavior within a certain situation). For example, some participants were primed with stimuli related to libraries, a location for which the norm is quiet behavior. Those who were primed with the location and who had the goal to visit the location later behaved in ways that were consistent with the norm for that location. For instance, those primed with library subsequently recited a text passage in a significantly softer voice than non-primed participants. Again, none of the participants reported any awareness of a connection between the priming procedure and the subsequent dependent measures.

As another example of research that shows how context information inadvertently influences behavior, researchers have examined whether participants who are primed with crowded group-settings display different amounts of helping behavior compared with non-primed participants. Given the well-established finding in social psychology that people in a crowd exhibit less helping behavior than people who are alone,[45] Garcia *et al.*[46] tested whether the incidental activation of knowledge about being in a large group might automatically influence later, ostensibly unrelated helping behavior. They asked participants either to imagine themselves in a group, or alone (e.g. in a crowded or empty movie theater) and then measured their willingness in a variety of helping behaviors, such as donating money to charity. Those who imagined themselves in a group context later exhibited significantly less helping behavior than control participants. Great care was taken across five studies to ensure that participants did not suspect any connection between the priming task and the helping measure, and indeed, none of the participants reported any suspicion. These studies suggest that behavioral information can be activated from the mere perception of social settings or contexts (such as a library, or a crowded movie theater) and subsequently influence actual behavior in the absence of people's intentions and awareness.

Parameters of the Effect of Social Perception on Behavior

A crucial question concerns the mechanisms that might underlie such automatic effects on behavior, and researchers have identified both some boundary conditions as well as some potential mechanisms[15,47,48,49,50]. For example, Dijksterhuis and colleagues[49,50] have explored how the concreteness of the priming stimuli influences the nature of the effect, by priming participants with trait information either via social groups (e.g. the group *professors* activates the trait *intelligence*) or via exemplars of those social groups (e.g. *Albert Einstein* also primes the trait *intelligence*). In line with findings from the social judgment literature[51,52,53], those participants primed with a social group (i.e. abstract information) exhibited behavior in line with traits associated with the group (i.e. assimilative effects), but those primed with exemplars from the group (i.e. relatively more concrete information) exhibited behavior in contrast with the associated trait (i.e. contrast effects; see Figure 1).

Researchers have argued that whereas the perception of an abstract prime activates an interpretive frame that is used to interpret subsequent stimuli, the perception of concrete exemplars invokes comparative processes whereby the exemplar anchors the dimension of judgment along which subsequent stimuli are judged. When the exemplars are extreme, most subsequently perceived (or in this case, performed) behaviors will be positioned away from the exemplar. Dijksterhuis and colleagues[49] argued that contrast effects emerge in behavior because participants implicitly compare themselves with the primed exemplar and then act accordingly.

As one might expect, the magnitude of the priming effect on behavior has been found to depend upon the strength of association in memory between the prime material (e.g. the social group, context, trait, stereotype) and the particular behavior. Dijksterhuis and colleagues[54] predicted that the effect of priming participants with '*elderly people*' on later memory performance would be contingent on how much contact participants previously had with the elderly. As expected, those participants with lots of previous contact with the elderly performed significantly worse on a memory test after being covertly primed with the group (this was expected because poor memory is part of the elderly stereotype). However, those with little previous contact did not show any priming effect, suggesting that the degree to which incidental knowledge activation increases the likelihood of performing an associated behavior depends on the presence and strength of that association in memory. Presumably, the be-

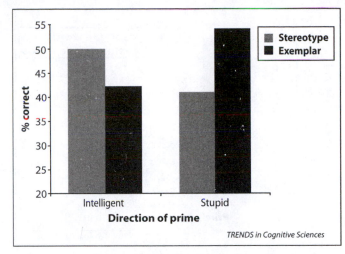

Figure 1. Percentage correct on a general knowledge test as a function of the type (stereotype or exemplar) and direction (intelligence or stupidity) of the primes. Participants were covertly primed with a stereotype indicating intelligence (*professors*) versus stupidity (*supermodels*), or an exemplar indicating intelligence (Albert Einstein) versus stupidity (*Claudia Schiffer*). A significant interaction between the type and direction of primes on percentage correct emerged, such that whereas stereotype primes led to assimilation effects (participants' behavior was in accord with the direction of the prime), exemplar primes led to contrast effects (participants' behavior was in contrast with the direction of the prime). In other words, whereas those primed with professors significantly outperformed those primed with supermodels, those primed with Albert Einstein significantly underperformed those primed with Claudia Schiffer. Adapted from.50

lief about the elderly having poor memory was reinforced in those who interacted frequently with members of the group.

Researchers have also recently examined whether the effect on later behavior of being primed with a social group is mediated by the activation of traits associated with that group. Kawakami et al.[55] tested whether the effect of being primed with *elderly* on response speed in a lexical-decision task depended on the activation of the trait *slow* (see Figure 2). The findings showed a priming effect on behavior, as primed participants exhibited a significantly slower response speed overall compared with non-primed participants. In addition, primed participants responded significantly faster to stereotype-consistent (e.g. *slow*) than to inconsistent traits, compared with non-primed participants, who showed no difference, suggesting that the stereotyped traits were activated in memory, as expected. Most importantly, however, the effect of priming on behavior (overall slowness of responses) was independent of the effect of priming on stereotype trait activation. This suggests that the perception of a stimulus activates a diverse array of knowledge (e.g. behaviors, traits, exemplars), and that types of knowledge can have independent effects on subsequent behavior.

Conclusions

Over the past five years, researchers in experimental social psychology have demonstrated not only that people's judgments and attitudes are sometimes automatically influenced by factors

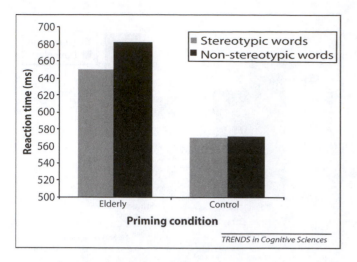

Figure 2. Reaction time to words in a lexical-decision task as a function of priming condition (elderly vs. non-primed control) and type of target words (stereotypic of the elderly vs. non-stereotypic of the elderly). The results suggest a priming effect on behavior such that primed participants responded significantly more slowly overall than non-primed participants. They also suggest a priming effect on stereotype activation such that primed participants responded significantly faster to stereotypic than to non-stereotypic words, whereas non-primed participants showed no difference. Importantly, a mediational analysis demonstrated that the effect of priming on overall response speed was independent of the effect on stereotype activation, suggesting that behavioral effects are not necessarily mediated by the activation of group-relevant traits. Adapted from.55

outside of their awareness, but that their actual behaviors are as well. Given the inherent ambiguity in social stimuli and situations, and thus the range of behavioral responses that might be appropriate for any given situation, it seems likely that people's behavior is often shaped and guided in part by knowledge that has become accessible through incidental means, such as unrelated recent experiences. This suggests that, in contrast to the assumption that we always consciously decide how to behave, we might routinely be unaware of some or even many of the determinants of our behavior.

Future research in this area will increasingly focus on the mechanisms that underlie the apparent potential independence of conscious intention and actual behavior (see Box 2). Not only will this research identify boundary conditions and mediators of such effects, it is likely to uncover a variety of neural substrates that underlie or enable the effects. For example, there is emerging evidence from cognitive neuroscience that points to fundamental dissociations in the human brain between those structures that are responsible for guiding complex motor behavior, and those that afford conscious access to our current intentions and purposes[15]. As researchers gather more information about the nature of these non-conscious effects, we may begin to understand more fully the phenomenon of behavior without intention.

Box 2

Questions for Future Research

- What types of activated knowledge mediate effects on behavior? For example, assuming that the mere perception of a stimulus activates trait, context, goal, affective and behavioral information, which types of knowledge mediate the variety of effects shown in this recent research?
- To what degree do priming effects on complex behavior meet the traditional four criteria for automaticity? For example, to what extent does participant suspicion of a relation between the priming episode and the dependent measures qualify as an 'automatic' priming effect on behavior? What cognitive capacity is required for these effects to occur?
- What are the necessary preconditions for incidental acts of social perception to influence relatively static displays of behavior (e.g. walking slowly), and how do these differ (if at all) from the conditions needed to influence more complex and feedback-dependent sequences of behavior (e.g. the attempt to achieve across multiple tasks and interruptions)?
- What is the magnitude and duration of these types of priming effects, and what factors moderate these variables?
- What sources of knowledge affect behavior in an automatic fashion, beyond those that have been studied so far?
- To what extent do priming effects on various sorts of complex behavior occur in real-life situations (i.e. outside the laboratory)?

References

1. J.A. Bargh and T. Chartrand, The unbearable automaticity of being. *Am. Psychol.* 54 (1999), pp. 462–479.
2. J.A. Bargh and M.J. Ferguson, Beyond behaviorism: on the automaticity of higher mental processes. P*sychol. Bull.* 126 (2000), pp. 925–945.
3. M.S. Gazzaniga and T.F. Heatherton, *The Psychological Science: Mind, Brain, and Behavior,* W.W. Norton (2003).
4. J.H. Neely, Semantic priming and retrieval from lexical memory: rules of inhibitionless spreading activation and limited-capacity attention. *J. Exp. Psychol. Gen.* 106 (1977), pp. 226–254.
5. M.I. Posner and C.R.R. Snyder, Attention and cognitive control. In: R.L. Solso, Editor, *Information Processing and Cognition: The Loyola Symposium,* Erlbaum (1975).
6. J.S. Bruner, On perceptual readiness. *Psychol. Rev.* 64 (1957), pp. 123–152.
7. R.H. Fazio et al., Variability in automatic activation as an unobtrusive measure of racial attitudes: a *bona fide* pipeline?. *J. Pers. Soc. Psychol.* 69 (1995), pp. 1013–1027.
8. E.R. Smith and M.A. Zarate, Exemplar-based model of social judgment. *Psychol. Rev.* 99 (1992), pp. 3–21.
9. I. Blair and M. Banaji, Automatic and controlled processes in stereotype priming. *J. Pers. Soc. Psychol.* 70 (1996), pp. 1142–1163.
10. A. Todorov, and J.S. Uleman, The automaticity of binding spontaneous trait inferences to actors' faces. *J. Exp. Soc. Psychol.* (in press).

11. A. Todorov and J.S. Uleman, Spontaneous trait inferences are bound to actors' faces: evidence from a false recognition paradigm. *J. Pers. Soc. Psychol.* 83 (2002), pp. 1051–1065.

12. J.S. Uleman, Spontaneous versus intentional inferences in impression formation. In: S. Chaiken and Y. Trope, Editors, *Dual-Process Theories in Social Psychology,* Guilford Press (1999), pp. 141–160.

13. G.V. Bodenhausen and C.N. Macrae, Stereotype activation and inhibition. In: R.S. Wyer, Editor, *Advances in Social Cognition* Vol. 11, Erlbaum (1998), pp. 1–52.

14. E.T. Higgins, Knowledge activation: accessibility, applicability, and salience. In: E.T. Higgins and A.W. Kruglanski, Editors, *Social Psychology: Handbook of Basic Principles,* Guilford Press (1996), pp. 133–168.

15. Bargh, J.A. (2003) Bypassing the will: towards demystifying the nonconscious control of social behavior. In *The New Unconscious* (Hassin, R. *et al.,* eds), pp. 111–222, Oxford University Press (in press).

16. J.A. Bargh *et al.,* Automaticity of social behavior: direct effects of trait construct and stereotype priming on action. *J. Pers. Soc. Psychol.* 71 (1996), pp. 230–244.

17. L. Berkowitz, Some effects of thoughts on anti- and prosocial influences of media events: A cognitive-neoassociation analysis. *Psychol. Bull.* 95 (1984), pp. 410–427.

18. L. Berkowitz, Some thoughts extending Bargh's argument. In: R.S. Wyer, Editor, *Advances in Social Cognition* Vol. 10, Erlbaum (1997), pp. 83–94.

19. T.L. Chartrand and J.A. Bargh, The chameleon effect: the perception-behavior link and social interaction. *J. Pers. Soc. Psychol.* 76 (1999), pp. 893–910.

20. A. Dijksterhuis and J.A. Bargh, The perception-behavior expressway: automatic effects of social perception on social behavior. In: M.P. Zanna, Editor, Advances in Experimental Social Psychology Vol. 33, Academic Press (2001), pp. 1–40.

21. A. Dijksterhuis and A. van Knippenberg, Automatic social behavior or how to win a game of trivial pursuit. *J. Pers. Soc. Psychol.* 74 (1998), pp. 865–877.

22. W. Prinz, A common coding approach to perception and action. In: O. Neumann and W. Prinz, Editors, *Relationships Between Perception and Action,* Springer-Verlag (1990), pp. 167–201.

23. R.R. Vallacher, Mental calibration: forging a working relationship between mind and action. In: D.M. Wegner and J.W. Pennebaker, Editors, *Handbook of Mental Control,* Englewood Cliffs, Prentice Hall (1993), pp. 443–472.

24. E. Woody and P. Sadler, On reintegrating dissociated theories: comment on Kirsch and Lynn (1998). *Psychol. Bull.* 123 (1998), pp. 192–197.

25. G. Rizzolatti and M.A. Arbib, Language within our grasp. *Trends Neurosci.* 21 (1998), pp. 188–194.

26. G. Buccino *et al.,* Action observation activates premotor and parietal areas in somatotopic manner: an fMRI study. *Eur. J. Neurosci.* 13 (2001), pp. 400–404.

27. Carpenter, W.B. (1888) *Principles of Mental Physiology,* Appleton.

28. Wegner, D.M. (2002) *The Illusion of Conscious Will,* MIT Press.

29. James, W. (1890) *The Principles of Psychology* (Vol. 2), Holt.

30. J.K. Bock, Syntactic persistence in language production. *Cogn. Psychol.* 18 (1986), pp. 355–387.

31. J.K. Bock, Closed-class immanence in sentence production. *Cognition* 31 (1989), pp. 163–186.

32. G.S. Dell, A spreading activation theory of retrieval in sentence production. *Psychol. Rev.* 93 (1986), pp. 283–321.

33. J.B.J. Smeets and E. Brenner, Perception and action are based on the same visual information: distinction between position and velocity. *J. Exp. Psychol. Hum. Percept. Perform.* 21 (1995), pp. 19–31.

34. Chartrand, T.L. *et al.* (2003) Beyond the perception-behavior link: the ubiquitous utility and motivational moderators of nonconscious mimicry. In *Unintended Thought II: The New Unconscious,* (Hassin, R. *et al.,* eds), Oxford University Press (in press).

35. Cheng, C.M. and Chartrand, T.L. Self-monitoring without awareness: using mimicry as a nonconscious affiliation strategy. *J. Pers. Soc. Psychol.* (in press).

36. van Baaren, R.B. *et al.* Mimicry for money: behavioral consequences of imitation. *J. Exp. Soc.* Psychol. (in press).

37. van Baaren, R.B. *et al.* Mimicry and pro-social behavior. *Psychol. Sci.* (in press).

38. van Baaren, R. *et al.* The forest, the trees, and the chameleon: context dependency and nonconscious mimicry. *J. Pers. Soc. Psychol.* (in press).

39. L.Z. Tiedens and A.R. Fragale, Power moves: complementarity in dominant and submissive noverbal behavior. *J. Pers. Soc. Psychol.* 84 (2003), pp. 558–568.

40. H. Aarts and A. Dijksterhuis, Habits as knowledge structures: automaticity in goal-directed behavior. *J. Pers. Soc. Psychol.* 78 (2000), pp. 53–63.

41. J.A. Bargh, Auto-motives: preconscious determinants of social thought and behavior. In: E.T. Higgins and R.M. Sorrentino, Editors, *Handbook of Motivation and Cognition* Vol. 2, Guilford Press (1990), pp. 93–130.

42. J.A. Bargh *et al.,* The automated will: nonconscious activation and pursuit of behavioral goals. *J. Pers. Soc. Psychol.* 81 (2001), pp. 1014–1027.

43. G.M. Fitzsimons and J.A. Bargh, Thinking of you: nonconscious pursuit of interpersonal goals associated with relationship partners. *J. Pers. Soc. Psychol.* 84 (2003), pp. 148–163.

44. H. Aarts and A. Dijksterhuis, The silence of the library: environment, situational norm, and social behavior. *J. Pers. Soc. Psychol.* 84 (2003), pp. 18–28.

45. B. Latane and J.M. Darley, Group inhibition of bystander intervention. *J. Pers. Soc. Psychol.* 10 (1968), pp. 215–221.

46. S.M. Garcia *et al.,* Crowded minds: the implicit bystander effect. *J. Pers. Soc. Psychol.* 83 (2002), pp. 843–853.

47. A. Dijksterhuis *et al.,* Of men and mackerels: attention, subjective experience, and automatic social behavior. In: H. Bless and J.P. Forgas, Editors, The *Message Within: The Role of Subjective Experience in Social Cognition and Behavior,* Psychology Press (2000), pp. 37–51.

48. A. Dijksterhuis and J.A. Bargh, The perception-behavior expressway: automatic effects of social perception on social behavior. In: M. Zanna, Editor, *Advances in Experimental Social Psychology* Vol. 33, Academic Press (2001), pp. 1–40.

49. A. Dijksterhuis *et al.,* Seeing one thing and doing another: contrast effects in automatic behavior. *J. Pers. Soc. Psychol.* 75 (1999), pp. 862–871.

50. A. Dijksterhuis *et al.,* Reflecting and deflecting stereotypes: assimilation and contrast in impression formation and automatic behavior. *J. Exp. Soc. Psychol.* 37 (2001), pp. 286–299.

51. G.B. Moskowitz and I.W. Skurnik, Contrast effects as determined by the type of prime: trait versus exemplar primes initiate processing strategies that differ in how accessible constructs are used. *J. Pers. Soc. Psychol.* 76 (1999), pp. 911–927.

52. D.A. Stapel and W. Koomen, The impact of interpretation versus comparison mindsets on knowledge accessibility effects. *J. Exp. Soc. Psychol.* 37 (2001), pp. 134–149.

53. D.A. Stapel and W. Koomen, How far do we go beyond the information given? The impact of knowledge activation on interpretation and inference. *J. Pers. Soc. Psychol.* 78 (2000), pp. 19–37.

54. A. Dijksterhuis *et al.,* On the relation between associative strength and automatic behavior. *J. Exp. Soc. Psychol.* 36 (2000), pp. 531–544.

55. K. Kawakami *et al.,* Automatic stereotyping: category, trait, and behavioral activations. *Pers. Soc. Psychol. Bull.* 28 (2002), pp. 3–15.

56. J.A. Bargh, Conditional automaticity: varieties of automatic influence in social perception and cognition. In: J.S. Uleman and J.A. Bargh, Editors, *Unintended Thought*, Guilford Press (1989), pp. 3–51.

57. J.A. Bargh, The four horsemen of automaticity: awareness, intention, efficiency, and control in social cognition. In: R.S. Wyer and T.K. Srull, Editors, *Handbook of Social Cognition* Vol. 1, Erlbaum (1994), pp. 1–40.

58. L.W. Barsalou, Cognitive Psychology: *An Overview for Cognitive Scientists,* Erlbaum (1992).

59. J.A. Bargh, Automaticity in social psychology. In: E.T. Higgins and A.W. Kruglanski, Editors, *Social Psychology: Handbook of Basic Principles,* Guilford Press (1996), pp. 169–183.

60. J.A. Bargh, The automaticity of everyday life. In: R.S. Wyer, Editor, *Advances in Social Cognition* Vol. 10, Erlbaum (1997), pp. 1–61.

61. S. Chaiken and Y. Trope, *Dual-Process Theories in Social Psychology,* Guilford Press (1999).

62. Hassin, R. *et al. The New Unconscious*, Oxford University Press (in press).

63. D. Wegner and J.A. Bargh, Control and automaticity in social life. In: D.T. Gilbert and S.T. Fiske, Editors, *The Handbook of Social Psychology* Vol. 1, McGraw-Hill (1998), pp. 446–496.

64. D.M. Wegner, Ironic processes of mental control. *Psychol. Rev.* 101 (1994), pp. 34–52.

65. J.A. Bargh, Does subliminality matter to social psychology? Awareness of the stimulus versus awareness of its influence. In: R.F. Bornstein and T.S. Pittman, Editors, *Perception Without Awareness: Cognitive, Clinical, and Social Perspectives,* Guilford Press (1992), pp. 236–255.

66. J.A. Bargh and T.L. Chartrand, The mind in the middle: a practical guide to priming and automaticity research. In: H.T. Reis and C.M. Judd, Editors, *Handbook of Research Methods in Social and Personality Psychology,* Cambridge University Press (2000), pp. 253–285.

67. T.K. Srull and R.S. Wyer, Jr, The role of category accessibility in the interpretation of information about persons: some determinants and implications. *J. Pers. Soc. Psychol.* 37 (1979), pp. 1660–1672.

68. M.T. Orne, On the social psychology of the psychological experiment: with particular reference to demand characteristics and their implications. *Am. Psychol.* 17 (1962), pp. 776–783.

From *Trends in Cognitive Sciences* by Melissa J. Ferguson and John A. Bargh, pp. 33-39. Copyright © 2004 by Elsevier Science, Ltd. Reprinted by permission.

Flashbulb Memories: How Psychological Research Shows That Our Most Powerful Memories May Be Untrustworthy. (False Memories)

DANIEL GREENBERG

On arrival in New York we caught a cab and headed for the city. The cab had no radio on. As fate would have it, the cabby missed a turn somewhere and we were off the highway, somewhere in Astoria, Queens, I think. We were stopped for a red light when a woman came out of her house screaming and crying. I rolled down the cab window to ask what the matter was.... She told me that John Kennedy had just been shot in Dallas. We drove the rest of the way in silence.

—Richard Nixon's memory of
the Kennedy assassination[1]

Although I was but four and a half years old when [the President] died, I distinctly remember the day when I found on our two white gateposts American flags companioned with black. I tumbled down on the harsh gravel walk in my eager rush into the house to inquire what they were "there for." To my amazement I found my father in tears, something that I had never seen before, having assumed, as all children do, that grown-up people never cried. The two flags, my father's tears, and his impressive statement that the greatest man in the world had died constituted my initiation ... [into] a world lying quite outside the two white gateposts.

—Jane Addams's memory of
the Lincoln assassination[2]

Most of us can tell stories like these. Shocking events seem to etch themselves in our minds; we recall them with a clarity and emotional intensity that few other memories can match. We remember more than just the basic facts of the event; we know our personal stories as well—where we were, who told us, and what we were doing when we heard

the news. Even trivial details seem to fix themselves in our memories: on the day of the Kennedy assassination, for example, Julia Child remembers that she and her husband were eating fish soup. Some people notice strange and compelling coincidences: Arthur Sulzberger was discussing presidential security when Kennedy's death was announced; Billy Graham had a sense of foreboding a week before; Bob Hope had just received a signed photograph of himself with Kennedy, which was sitting atop the television on which he heard the news. All of these features are unusual and intriguing, but the long life of these memories stands out above all else. Few of us can remember what we did on the day before a shocking event; as for the day itself, we feel that we can see it in our minds, that we can remember it as though it were yesterday, and we feel that that we cannot possibly forget it.

The vividness and apparent durability of these memories has fascinated psychologists for over a century. In 1899, a psychologist named F. W. Colegrove investigated people's 34-year old memories of the Lincoln assassination. He found that over two-thirds of the people he interviewed could remember what they had been doing when they heard the news, a result he considered a testament to "the abiding character of vivid experiences."[3] Decades later, when Roger Brown and James Kulik of Harvard University studed memories of shocking events of the 1960s and 1970s they proposed the term "flashbulb memory" to capture what they described as "the primary, 'live' quality [of the memories] that is ... very like a photograph."[4] As Brown and Kulik noted, the metaphor is not perfect, as some details are not preserved, but on the whole it aptly describes the strength and clarity of the memories as well as the rapidity with which they are originally stored.

We may have flashbulb memories for private events as well, such as a first kiss or the birth of a child, but the most compelling flashbulbs—the ones that we find ourselves relating over and over—tend to involve shocking historic events. Thus, people have reported **flashbulb memories** for many occasions, including the Lincoln assassination, the attack on Pearl Harbor, the assassinations of John F. Kennedy and Martin Luther King, the attempted assassination of President Reagan, the 1989 San Francisco earthquake, the Challenger explosion—and, most recently, the September 11th attacks.[5]

The Strange Case of the President's Memory

Shortly after 9/11, one particular person's memories attracted the attention of the Internet's conspiracy theorists. That person was President George W. Bush, and the controversy arose over apparent changes in his story. The fuss began on December 4, 2001, when the President told a crowd of people how he heard the news about the attacks:

> I was in Florida. And my chief of staff, Andy Card— actually I was in a classroom talking about a reading program that works. And I was sitting outside the classroom waiting to go in, and I saw an airplane hit the tower—the TV was obviously on, and I use[d] to fly myself, and I said, "There's one terrible pilot." And I said, "It must have been a horrible accident." But I was whisked off there—I didn't have much time to think about it, and I was sitting in the classroom, and Andy Card, my chief who was sitting over here walked in and said, "A second plane has hit the tower. America's under attack."[6]

Just over two weeks later, on December 20, the President told a different story during an interview with the Washington Post:

> Bush remembers senior adviser Karl Rove bringing him the news, saying it appeared to be an accident involving a small, twin-engine plane. In fact it was American Airlines Flight 11, a Boeing 767 out of Boston's Logan International Airport. Based on what he was told, Bush assumed it was an accident. "This is pilot error," the president recalled saying. "It's unbelievable that somebody would do this." Conferring with Andrew H. Card Jr., his White House chief of staff, Bush said, "The guy must have had a heart attack".... At 9:05 a.m., United Airlines Flight 175, also a Boeing 767, smashed into the South Tower of the trade center. Bush was seated on a stool in the classroom when Card whispered the news: "A second plane hit the second tower. America is under attack."[7]

Then on January 5, 2002, the President's story changed again:

> I was sitting there, and my Chief of Staff—well, last of all, when we walked into the classroom, I had seen this plane fly into the first building. There was a TV set on. And you know, I thought it was pilot error and I was amazed that anybody could make such a terrible mistake. And something was wrong with the plane, or—

anyway, I'm sitting there, listening to the briefing, and Andy Card came and said, "America is under attack."[8]

Clearly, something is wrong here. In the second memory, the President claims that Karl Rove told him about the last crash, but in the first and third memories, he claims that he saw the news on television. Stranger still, the first and third memories seem impossible: there was no footage of the first plane, at least not at that hour of the morning.[9] What could the explanation be? Conspiracy theorists had plenty of suggestions. Sites across the Web erupted with accusations of dishonesty and calls for impeachment. "Bush slip reveals total 9/11 complicity," screamed freeworldalliance.com:

> Complicit factions of the U.S. federal government, including virtually ALL upper-level members of the BushMob, actually FILMED their own attack on New York's World Trade Center—and Bush has admitted that he WATCHED IT!!!! And there is only one POSSIBLE way such footage COULD have existed: the perpetrators of the WTC attack HAD THEIR OWN CAMERAS IN PLACE TO FILM IT [emphasis in the original].[10]

The website bushwatch.com took a somewhat more moderate view, noting that "the most benign conclusion, then, is that Bush was not telling the truth when he told Jordan that he saw the first plane hit the first tower prior to his going into the classroom."[11] Even the Guardian, a British newspaper, found Bush's statements worthy of comment, noting that "the story that he was watching TV contradicts reports from correspondents at the time that he got the news in a phone call."[12]

What are we to make of this? Are we obliged to believe that the President is smart enough to carry out a horrific conspiracy to attack America, but dumb enough to reveal it—twice? Should we instead believe that the President lied about what happened—twice but not three times—even though he had much to lose and nothing to gain from such a lie? Or should we believe something else entirely?

Fortunately, scientific studies of memory can offer a more benign explanation. We don't need to posit irrational lies or a massive conspiracy imperfectly hidden from the eyes of everyday citizens. Instead, we need only consider the frailties of human memory.

The False Memory Phenomenon

All of us know that our memory can fail us—we forget the location of our car keys, the name of our second-grade teacher, or the kind of drink we had with lunch three days ago. But memory can betray us in another way, too: we may also experience false memories—putative "memories" for events that never took place. While forgetting is easy to notice, false memories are much harder to detect because they can seem just like normal memories. Nevertheless, over the last century, hundreds of studies have shown just how common false memories can be.

Consider one of the most straightforward demonstrations of false memory—originally proposed by James Deese—which has been used in introductory psychology classrooms as well as experimental research. An experimenter reads a list of about a dozen words ("bed, rest, awake, tired, dream," etc.), all of which are related to one particular word, known as the lure (in this case, "sleep"). The listeners are then asked to recall as many words as they can. In one sense, people perform quite well—they can remember most of the words on the list. Yet in one particular way, they perform quite poorly: many people falsely recall hearing the lure, even though the experimenter never read it. This is not just a vague impression or a guess; people will often express great confidence in their memory of the lure, saying that they can "hear" the experimenter's voice in their minds, or that they remember exactly when in the list it was presented. (In fact, their confidence can be so strong as to be unshakable. When I first watched an instructor try this on her class, a few students simply refused to believe that she never read the lure, instead asserting that she must be lying!)

In another classic experiment, Elizabeth Loftus and John Palmer showed people a videotape of a car accident. They then asked participants a series of questions about what they had seen. One of the questions had two forms: half of the participants estimated how fast the cars had been going when they hit each other; the other half estimated how fast the cars were going when they smashed. This simple one-word difference produced a startling effect: while most people got the question right, participants who received the "smashed" question were more likely to claim that they had seen broken glass, even though there was no broken glass in the original video. In short, our memory of an event can be altered by the way in which someone asks us about it—a problem that proves particularly vexing to police officers and lawyers.

In some cases, people can even have entirely fictitious memories for full-fledged, specific events. In one study, Ira Hyman and Joel Pentland of Western Washington University tried to "implant" a false memory in the minds of their participants. They started by obtaining a list of childhood events from each participant's parents, and then interviewed each participant about the memories that his or her parents had provided. They also asked each participant about one fictitious memory—a memory of spilling a punchbowl on a bride during a wedding reception—but told participants that all memories, including the punchbowl memory, had been provided by the participant's parents. If they didn't "recall" the punchbowl memory during the original interview (and most participants didn't) they were asked to think about the event or to visualize it in their minds as best they could. When tested several days later, almost 25% of the participants in the experiment claimed to have some memory of spilling the punchbowl. These people didn't just remember that the experimenter had told them about it, nor did they just claim that they knew that it happened. Rather, they claimed to have a detailed memory of the event itself—and some of them even elaborated on the memory, providing details that the experimenter had never mentioned. This straightforward experimental design—which simply involves asking people to imagine an event they'd never experienced—was enough to create a false memory. Overall, somewhere between 15 to 25% of adults can be induced to create false memories in this way.[13] A similar phenomenon may explain False Memory Syndrome, in which fictitious memories of sexual abuse are inadvertently implanted in patients' minds by therapists who use guided-visualization and other suggestive techniques.[14]

False Flashbulb Memories

This research provides important and comprehensive demonstrations of the ease with which we can be induced to remember events that never happened. Skeptics, however, might argue that each of these studies leaves out a vital component of the flashbulb memory experience.[15] After all, most people find word lists rather dull, while flashbulb memories record some of the most shocking and horrifying events of our lives. Videotapes of car accidents may be more exciting, but they still lack the immediacy and emotional impact of a surprising historic event. As for full-blown false memories of the sort that Hyman and colleagues created, they generally arise after substantial coaxing by an experimenter or a therapist; flashbulb memories need no such help, as they seem fixed in our minds from the start. Moreover, we know that the original flashbulb experience really happened—we know that we heard about the news somehow. Can memories like these really be wrong?

As a matter of fact, yes. The flashbulb metaphor and our own intuition suggest that these memories are accurate and permanent, but experiment after experiment shows that they too can mutate over time. For example, Ulric Neisser and Nicole Harsch developed a questionnaire to assess the consistency of memories for the space shuttle Challenger disaster. The questionnaire asked people to remember the basic facts of their experience, such as where they were, what they were doing, how they heard the news, and so on. They first tested people 24 hours after the explosion; 2.5 years later, some of the participants filled out the questionnaire again. Overall, people performed quite poorly—the average score was just under 3 out of a possible 7. Other studies of Challenger memories yielded similar remits: one study by Michael McCloskey and colleagues found that 25% of participants gave at least one inconsistent response after a 9-month delay; John Bohannon and Victoria Symons found that after a 3-year delay, 33% of participants told inconsistent stories. Memories for September 11th also suffer from inconsistencies: studies by Peter Lee and Norman Brown as well as Marilyn Smith and colleagues showed that on average, only 65% of memory details remained consistent between the first test and the second. In fact, Neisser himself has a false memory for the announcement of the bombing of Pearl Harbor. He has always remembered that he was listening to a baseball game on the radio when it was interrupted by an announcement of the Pearl Harbor attack—but the attack occurred on December 7, 1941, and no baseball is played in December. Thus, numerous studies have shown that people experience false flashbulb memories for a wide variety of events.

In spite of all this, people feel quite confident in their memories for shocking events. Neisser and Harsch showed their participants the stories they had written during the first session. Even when their stories had changed considerably, people still expressed surprise at the difference and didn't revert to their first memory:

> No one who had given an incorrect account in the interview even pretended that they now recalled what was stated on the original record. On the contrary, they kept saying "I mean, like I told you, I have no recollection of it at all" or "I still think of it as the other way around." As far as we can tell, the original memories are just gone.[16]

In a recent study, Jennifer Talarico and David Rubin, two of my colleagues at Duke University, conducted a detailed examination of this phenomenon. On September 12, 2001, they asked people to provide two memories: one for September 11th and another for an everyday event that happened a few days before the attacks. When they tested the participants a second time (1, 6, or 32 weeks later), they found that both memories contained a similar number of inaccuracies. Nevertheless, confidence in the everyday memory declined over time, while confidence in flashbulb memories remained high. While we may think that our flashbulb memories are as permanent as a photograph, they decay just as quickly as memories for everyday events.[17]

But can the inconsistencies be as substantial as those in the President's stories? In fact, they can. Consider the stories told by one of the people in Neisser and Harsch's study:

Memory 1 (24 hours after the event): I was in my religion class and some people walked in and started talking about it…. Then after class I went to my room and watched the TV program talking about it …

Memory 2 (2.5 years later): When I first heard about the explosion I was sitting in my freshman dorm room with my roommate and we were watching TV. It came on a news flash….[18]

This person's memories, along with the memories of nine other people in the study, changed in the same way. They originally remembered hearing the news from another person, but later came to remember that they saw it on TV—exactly the change that happened between President Bush's second and third recollections. There are even more examples: In a study by Hans Crombag and colleagues, 60% of participants reported seeing footage of the crash of an El A1 jet in Amsterdam, even though no such footage exists. And, in Kathy Pezdek's study of memories for September 11th, 73% of participants made precisely the mistake that the President made, claiming to have seen the footage of the first plane crash on September 11th itself.[19]

The scientific evidence is clear. People frequently experience false flashbulb memories. Further, people can experience false flashbulb memories for nonexistent footage of a plane crash. This kind of memory error is not just possible, but commonplace.

The Source of False Memories

What makes these memories change over time? We can't know for certain, because we don't know how the person really heard about the event and we don't know for certain what he or she experienced between the first test and the second. Still, studies of everyday memory offer some insights. For example, Bill Brewer of the University of Illinois showed that people make similar errors with everyday memories, not just flashbulbs. In one of his studies, he asked people to record daily events in diaries; in a later test, he asked them to relate what had happened to them at a particular point in time. When he checked their answers against the diaries, he found that people often responded with a fairly accurate story about something that happened at a completely different time—a mistake he called the "wrong time slice" error. As Neisser showed, John Dean suffered from a similar problem during his Watergate testimony; while his memory for conversations often seemed quite vivid and detailed, later reviews of the Watergate tapes showed that he tended to combine statements from separate conversations that had occurred on different days.

In the case of **flashbulb memories**, we can safely assume that Neisser and Harsch's participants, Pezdek's participants, and George W. Bush himself all saw footage of the event on television, since it was shown again and again in the weeks and months following the attacks. Then, when they were asked to tell their story again, they did just what the people in Brewer's study did; they accurately remembered what they saw, but misjudged when they first saw it.

Why do people falsely recall that time slice instead of the correct one? Part of the answer lies in the power of a picture. Flashbulb events generally involve strong and vivid images, which is what led Brown and Kulik to propose the flashbulb metaphor in the first place. We have known for millennia that images like these are highly memorable, which is why many memory-improvement techniques make use of them; it makes sense, then, that people would remember these images particularly clearly. Moreover, a strong mental image affects judgments about memory. For example, when people retrieve a mental image, they generally feel more confident that the memory is accurate. If you're wondering whether you turned off the stove, you're likely to conclude that you did if you can conjure up a mental picture of yourself doing it. But while images affect confidence in memory, they can also be misleading. They can bring about memory errors precisely because they are easy to generate, easy to modify, and easy to remember. When people reflect on an event that they have not seen, for example, they may imagine how it must have looked. These images are memorable as well, and can easily be mistaken for real memories—which is just what happened in Hyman and Pentland's study. In other words, it comes as no surprise that people remember visual images more than anything else—but it also comes as no surprise that these images can be modified, fabricated, or attributed to the wrong time.

The organization of the memory may also play a role. People often relate memories in the form of stories, giving them a logical flow as well as a beginning, middle, and end. Gaps in the story can be reconstructed based on a script, a general idea of what usually happens in such a situation. Neisser and Harsch, for example, propose that the participants in the Challenger study retrieved a vivid visual image, and knew it was quite reasonable that they would have heard about the explosion from TV; then, over time, they developed the erroneous belief that the TV had been the source of the news.

These phenomena provide a simple, uncontroversial explanation of the President Bush's changing story. In particular, they show how Memory 2 can be related to the implausible Memories 1 and 3. According to Memory 2, his advisor Karl Rove told the President about the first crash, but, as in many such situations, the early information was inaccurate. The President was not told that it was an attack involving a passenger jet, but rather that it was a small twin-engine plane—a surprising and disturbing event, to be sure, but not on the level of a national emergency, and nowhere near as shocking as what was to come. In any case, the President, like most Americans, presumably saw the footage many times in the subsequent months, including footage of the last crash when it became available. Then, when the President tried to remember how he heard about the first attack, he did just what so many other people have done, retrieving information from the wrong time slice and recalling a vivid, memorable visual image instead of the more mundane statements of Karl Rove.

The President may also have worked this image into a complete narrative. According to one report, footage of the aftermath of the first crash (but not the crash itself) was shown at the school, as people sought out televisions to find out what was going on. In other words, the President may have seen the end of this sequence of events, but not the beginning. After seeing the footage of the crash, he may have incorporated it into the video he saw at the school, completing the story by adding cause to effect. In the few seconds or so it took him to formulate an answer to the question, this story may have seemed reasonable enough; there was footage, after all; people do tend to learn these things from TV; and he was watching TV that morning. It is worth noting that the President sounded a bit tentative when relating Memories 1 and 3: both times, he started by discussing the second attack, only to interrupt himself and talk about the first; when he does talk about the first crash, he backtracked, making statements like "the TV was obviously on." Such hesitations and revisions create the impression that the President was reasoning it out—perhaps reconstructing it—as he went along.

The President's shifting memory does differ in one important respect from the memories of Neisser and Harsch's participants. In that study, memory errors were irreversible once they had been established. Even when participants were confronted with their original memories—which they themselves had written down—they did not change their stories; they did not suddenly remember the event as they originally had. The President's memory does not fit this pattern, though: he first reported an implausible memory, then switched to a plausible one, then changed back to the implausible version. (The disparity in delay intervals may account for this difference: the President's recollections all took place within the space of a month, but Neisser and Harsch's participants were retested after three years.)

That aside, we should give the President some credit: although his memory of the first crash changed from one point to the next, his memory of the second was quite consistent. On all three occasions, he remembered that he was sitting in the classroom when Andy Card walked in and told him about it (a memory perhaps bolstered by a widely-published photograph of Card whispering in the President's ear). Moreover, his memory of Card's statement remained the same from one point in time to the next, with the President using almost the same words every time.

All of the available scientific evidence suggests that we don't need to resort to any wild conspiracy theories. Instead, the studies on false memory suggest that a simple and commonplace mistake best explains the changes and implausibilities in the President Bush's story. And they suggest that our own memories—no matter how vivid and realistic they may seem—must be regarded with skepticism too.

Portions of this essay originally appeared in Greenberg, D. L. (2004). President Bush's false 'flashbulb' memory of 9/11//01. Applied Cognitive Psychology. Copyright John Wiley & Sons Limited. Reproduced with permission.

References

1. Berendt, J. 1973. "Where Were You?" Esquire. November.
2. Addams, J. 1992. From J. K. Conway (Ed.), Written by herself. New York: Vintage, 506–525.
3. Colegrove, F. W. 1899. American Journal of Psychology, 10, 255.
4. Brown, R. and J. Kulik. 1977. Cognition, 5, 74.
5. Of course, the phenomenon is not limited to the United States. Many UK residents experienced **flashbulb memories** of the resignation of Margaret Thatcher, the Hillsborough football disaster, and the death of Princess Diana; Scandinavians often have flashbulbs of the assassinations of Olaf Palme and Anna Lindh; and residents of Turkey have flashbulbs of the death of Ataturk or the major earthquake in 1999.
6. "President Holds Town Meeting." 2001. www.cnn.com/ TRANSCRIPTS/0112/04/se.04.html.
7. Balz, D. and B. Woodward. 2002. The Washington Post, January 27, A1, A11.
8. "President Holds Town Hall Forum." 2002. www.whitehouse.gov/news/releases/2002/01 /20020105-3.html.
9. Later on, it turned out that a camera crew had accidentally caught the first impact into the World Trade Center on tape while filming an unrelated program. As best I can determine, this footage was not made available until September 12th. There is nothing to suggest that it was broadcast "live" in time for the President to see it early that morning.
10. "Bush Slip Reveals Total 9/11 Complicity." 2001. www.freewoddalliance.com/news-flash/pre_2002/news flash1100.htm
11. "Potitex's Bush Watch for Bush Lies." 2001. www.bushnews.com/bushlies.june.htm
12. Engel, M. 2001. The Guardian. December. www.guardian.co.uk/ september11/story/0,11 209,612354,00.html.
13. There are far too many studies on false memory to discuss here; for a review, see: Bjorklund, D. (Ed.) 2000. False Memory Creation in Children and Adults. Mahwah, NJ: Lawrence Erlbaum Associates.
14. For more on False Memory Syndrome, see SKEPTIC Vol. 2, No. 3, 58–61 and SKEPTIC Vol. 3, No. 4, 3641.
15. This assertion should not be construed as a slight against the experimenters; it would obviously be unethical to replicate the horror of flashbulb memory experiences in the laboratory.
16. Neisser, U., and Harsch, N. 1992. From U. Neisser and D. Winograd (Eds.), Affect and Accuracy in Recall. New York: Cambridge University Press, 21.
17. A few research projects have documented strikingly consistent flashbulb memories, including a study of the Thatcher resignation by Conway and colleagues as well as a study of Turkish memories for September 11th by Tekcan and colleagues. On the

whole, though, most studies show that **flashbulb memories** accumulate errors over time—far more errors than one would expect, given how confident people claim to be.

18. Neisser and Harsch, op. cit., 9.

19. For more studies of flashbulbs, see: Conway, Martin. 1995. Flashbulb Memory. Hillsdale, NJ: Lawrence Erlbaum Associates.

From *Skeptic*, vol. 11, no. 3, Winter 2005, pp. 74-80. Copyright © 2005 by Skeptics Society. Reprinted by permission.

Culture Affects Reasoning, Categorization

A Northwestern University professor finds that people's culturally shaped perceptions have profound effects on cross-cultural research.

ZAK STAMBOR
Monitor Staff

Most children of the Menominee American Indian tribe begin school with a precocious understanding of biology, whether they live on or off the reservation. From the time they enter school through the fourth grade, they consistently score above the national average in science—their best subject—on standardized tests. But by the eighth grade, the same tests show science as their worst subject, with scores below the national average.

The Reason?

Conflicting world views between Menominee culture and the way biology is taught in the classroom may be to blame, suggested Northwestern University psychology professor Douglas Medin, PhD, at APA's 2005 Annual Convention.

"There is a clash between the Menominee concept of nature and the typical European-American view," said Medin. "Indian parents want their children to understand that they are a part of nature, not to understand how to dominate or care for it."

The dissonance between the way science is taught in school and Menominee cultural views grows as the material becomes more advanced, and Menominee children grow increasingly disinterested because they fail to see their values, experiences and worldview reflected in the curriculum, Medin said.

Although researchers shouldn't think of culture as an independent variable, Medin said, those who are selecting populations for cross-cultural studies can find a necessary and important starting point when they understand differing cultural perceptions and viewpoints, such as the schism between Menominee culture and science taught through a Euro-American cultural lens. Medin's point is echoed in a study he recently co-authored with lead author Scott Atran, PhD, of the University of Michigan, and Norbert Ross, PhD, of Vanderbilt University, in the November issue of APA's *Psychological Review* (Vol. 112, No. 4).

Undergraduate Knowledge

Another situation in which Medin said researchers should consider their study populations is research using college students as reference populations. Researchers need to ask themselves how well undergraduates' responses in cross-cultural studies carry over to the broader world, he said.

Medin noted how in one study he handed Northwestern University students a list of 80 tree names. He told them to circle any names they had heard of before, regardless of whether they knew anything about them. He found that fewer than half of the students had any familiarity with trees such as alder, buckeye or tulip—all of which are common on the university's campus.

The results indicate that undergraduates may not work well as a comparison population in, for example, research on nature-knowledgeable Itza' Mayan elders because they may not be a valid "standard" when it comes to biology.

"We've long treated undergraduate students as 'the standard' and treated anyone who knows more about nature as an expert," he said. "But when one takes the knowledge of the typical member of a nonindustrialized society as the standard, undergraduate knowledge would be considered much below average."

More valid might be a population that relates more directly to nature, such as landscapers, taxonomists or park-maintenance employees.

Traditional lab studies with undergraduates may only allow researchers to see abstract or default notions that come into play when one has little or no relevant knowledge, he said.

Resolving Cultural Problems

Medin is currently working on research with Menominee and European-Americans to test aspects of cultural compatibility to determine what is behind such problems as the Menominee students' difficulties in science.

Because Medin does not think there is an "insurmountable cultural divide" between the two groups, he believes that systematically identifying and bridging barriers between the two notions of nature could benefit both cultures. As a result, he's working in a research partnership that includes the American Indian Center of Chicago and a tribal college on a Menominee reservation to develop a culturally based educational framework to use in an after-school program. Similar projects with Native Hawaiian populations have helped students' school adjustment and academic achievement, he said.

Moreover, by shining light on the cultural differences, Medin also aims to improve the validity of researchers' reference population data.

"Even if researchers don't care about culture, they need to understand how it affects their work," he said.

From *Monitor on Psychology*, Vol. 36 (10), November 2005, pp. 44-45. Copyright © 2005 by American Psychological Association. Reprinted by permission. No further distribution without permission from the American Psychological Association.

The Social Nature of Perception and Action

Humans engage in a wide range of social activities. Previous research has focused on the role of higher cognitive functions, such as mentalizing (the ability to infer others' mental states) and language processing, in social exchange. This article reviews recent studies on action perception and joint action suggesting that basic perception-action links are crucial for many social interactions. Mapping perceived actions to one's own action repertoire enables direct understanding of others' actions and supports action identification. Joint action relies on shared action representations and involves modeling of others' performance in relation to one's own. Taking the social nature of perception and action seriously not only contributes to the understanding of dedicated social processes but has the potential to create a new perspective on the individual mind and brain.

GÜNTHER KNOBLICH AND NATALIE SEBANZ
Rutgers University

Cognitive scientists have long believed that perception and action are two servants of the mind, residing in opposite wings of the mental mansion. According to this view, perception delivers messages from the outside world to keep the mind informed, and action executes what the mind commands. Recent research in the cognitive sciences and neurosciences suggests that the mind is actually more like a kibbutz than a mansion: Perception, action, and cognition seem to form a collective community. Perception and action are intimately linked, and cognition is firmly grounded in both of them.

This new perspective has important implications for understanding the functional and brain mechanisms that support people's ability to interact with others. Individuals do not just infer intentions, emotions, and attitudes from others' behavior (Fiske, 1992); rather, researchers have postulated a more immediate way of social understanding and social interaction, based on the close link between perception and action. For example, when one observes another individual performing a particular action, this activates the representations in one's own action system that one uses to perform the observed action. Taking the social functions of perception and action seriously might help to better understand disorders of social functions, including autism and certain symptoms of schizophrenia such as delusions of control.

In this article, we discuss recent findings from two research domains that shed new light on the social nature of perception and action. Research on action perception demonstrates that individuals rely on their bodies and the action system moving their bodies to understand others' actions and to identify their own actions. Research on joint action has revealed how individuals share representations, predict each other's actions, and learn to jointly plan ahead.

Bodily and Motor Contributions to Action Perception

Understanding

When people watch sports games like basketball or soccer, they often find their limbs twitching as though they are taking part in the game. This indicates that observing actions can directly activate the motor system. The common-coding hypothesis provides a functional principle that can explain such phenomena. According to this hypothesis, perceiving and performing an action results in the activation of the same representations—i.e., "common codes." Evidence for common coding has been found at the level of single neurons, the so-called minor neurons. The same neurons in the premotor cortex of a macaque monkey fire both when the monkey grasps an object and when it observes an experimenter grasping the same object. The implication of this striking finding is that brain areas that were thought to be purely motor areas also support action perception. This creates a new perspective on how individuals make sense of others' actions. Rather than understanding observed actions by mapping them onto abstract concepts, people "relive" them by mapping them onto their own action knowledge. This leads to an immediate recognition of the goals underlying observed actions. Numerous brain-imaging studies have demonstrated that the mirror system supports action understanding.

Identification

But how do observed actions get mapped onto action representations? According to the common-coding principle, the more similar an observed action is to the way the observer would perform the action, the higher the activation of action representations. This was recently demonstrated in a study by Calvo-Merino and colleagues (Calvo-Merino, Glaser, Grezes, Passingham, & Haggard, 2005), in which ballet dancers and capoeira dancers watched videos of ballet dancing and capoeira dancing. Activation of the mirror system was stronger when the dancers watched the type of dancing they were experts in. The mirror system should become even more strongly activated when persons perceive recordings of actions that they themselves have previously performed, such as when seeing videos of themselves dancing or hearing recordings of their own piano playing. The higher level of activation during the perception of self-produced actions might allow individuals to distinguish their own actions from those of others (Repp & Knoblich, 2004).

Several studies have shown that people are indeed able to distinguish between their own and others' actions even when there are no cues with respect to the actor's identity besides dynamic information about body movements or the effects they result in. For instance, when people see point-light displays of themselves and their best friend dancing, jumping, or boxing, they can identify themselves better than they can identify their friend (Loula, Prasad, Harber, & Shiffrar, 2005). If visual familiarity were the main factor, the opposite result should be observed, because one sees one's friend's movements much more often than one's own from a third-person perspective. In a similar vein, people can identify their own handwriting from a single moving dot (Knoblich & Flach, 2003).

One is also able to identify the results of one's earlier performed actions in the auditory domain. It was found that nonmusicians were able to identify their own clapping (Flach, Knoblich, & Prinz, 2004). Expert piano players could distinguish a recording of a piece they had played for the first time from recordings of the same piece performed by other pianists (Repp & Knoblich, 2004). Whereas experts use subtle timing deviations from the score, known as expressive timing, to identify their playing, nonmusicians rely on tempo and salient rhythmic idiosyncrasies to identify their clapping. Thus there is converging evidence that the similarity between observed actions and the way one would perform them oneself leads to a higher activation of common codes. This, in turn, allows people to identify their own previous actions.

Simulation

In addition to action understanding and action identification, the mirror system seems to support the prediction of future action outcomes (action simulation). In particular, matching observed actions to one's own action repertoire allows one to exploit mechanisms in the motor system that are normally used to predict the outcomes of one's own actions. This solution is more parsimonious than predicting the results of others' actions based on a separate perceptual-anticipation mechanism. In support of simulation, it was found that people observing someone throwing a dart could quite accurately predict where the dart would land. Importantly, the predictions of the landing position were most accurate when participants observed videos of themselves throwing the dart, although recording session and recognition session were at least 1 week apart. This makes it very unlikely that the higher accuracy for self was due to memories for the outcome of particular throws (Knoblich & Flach, 2003). The higher degree of similarity between a perceived action and the way one would perform it oneself led to the higher prediction accuracy for oneself than for others.

There is also reason to believe that proprioceptive signals (sensing position of body parts) and tactile signals from one's own body contribute to action simulation. A recent study showed that lacking these signals impairs action understanding (Bosbach, Cole, Prinz, & Knoblich, 2005). In this study, two de-afferented individuals were tested. De-afferentation refers to the loss of body sense due to a degeneration of all nerve fibers that normally transmit sensory information to the brain. The two individuals observed videos of an actor lifting a box. Prior to lifting the box, the actor had sometimes been told the correct weight of the box and had sometimes been deceived about its weight. Both individuals had difficulties telling whether the actor lifting the box had the right or wrong expectation about its weight. In contrast, healthy participants had no problems making these judgments. They could tell from the actor's body posture and body movements whether or not the actor had been deceived, suggesting that action simulation in healthy individuals is supported by peripheral bodily signals. The lack of peripheral bodily signals in the de-afferented patients resulted in faulty simulations.

Engaging in Joint Action with Others

Acknowledging the close links between perception and action also has implications for theorizing about joint action-social interactions wherein two or more individuals coordinate their actions in space and time to bring about a change in the environment. Some examples are doing the dishes together, rowing a canoe together, or playing a piano duet. Joint action involves sharing action representations and coordinating one's actions with those of others to achieve common goals (Clark, 1996).

Shared Representations

While previous research has focused on the role of language and theory of mind for successful social interaction, more immediate interpersonal links may exist in the form of a common coding system for perception and action. If the actions one performs and actions one observes in others are represented in a functionally equivalent way, this would provide an optimal integration platform for performing tasks together. An implication that follows from this view is that sharing a task should be quite similar to performing it on one's own, at least when two complementary actions are distributed across two persons. In

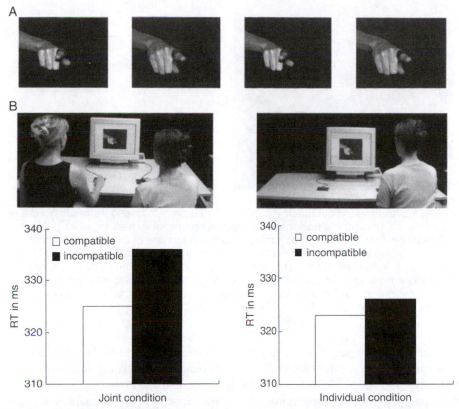

Fig. 1. Spatial-compatibility task used to test whether action representations are shared. Participants observed pictures of a hand pointing left or right (A), and were instructed to respond to the color of the ring on the index finger, ignoring the direction in which the finger was pointing. In the group condition (B, left panel), each participant responded to one color. In the individual condition (B, right panel) participants performed the same task alone, responding to one color and not responding to the other color. On compatible trials, the irrelevant pointing stimulus corresponded to the location of the required action. On incompatible trials, the pointing stimulus referred to the other's action (joint condition) or to no action (individual condition). Response time (RT) on incompatible trials in the joint condition (left graph) were slowed because the pointing stimulus activated a representation of the action at the other's command.

particular, the way actions are represented should not depend on whether one has all possible actions at one's own command or whether a part of the possible actions are at somebody else's command.

A simple spatial compatibility task was used to test this prediction (Sebanz, Knoblich, & Prinz, 2003). In the baseline condition, individual participants responded to a stimulus color with a left or right button press (e.g., red–left, green–right). Each stimulus also carried spatial information that had to be ignored (the stimulus, a colored ring, was on a finger that pointed either left or right, see Fig. 1A). A standard spatial-compatibility effect was observed: Participants responded slower when the irrelevant spatial dimension did not correspond to the location of the required action (e.g., red stimulus pointing right, when a left button press was required). Surprisingly, when the two action alternatives were distributed across two participants so that each participant performed a go/no-go task (responding to one stimulus and not responding to the other stimulus—e.g., Person A, red stimulus and left button press; Person B, green stimulus and right button press), the same pattern of results was observed

(see Fig. 1B). However, there was no spatial-compatibility effect when individual participants performed the same go/no-go task alone (e.g., Person A, red stimulus and left button press; no Person B). Together, these results confirm that actions at another person's command are represented just as if they were at one's own command. Action representations are shared even if that leads to a decline in one's own performance. It seems that people cannot help representing what other people do.

Further evidence for the tendency to form shared action representations was obtained by measuring event-related potentials (ERPs; brain electrical activity following a stimulus) while participants performed our go/no-go task together and alone (Sebanz, Knoblich, Prinz, & Wascher, in press). This method allows one to determine what happens on trials in which participants need to refrain from responding because it is the other participant's turn (no-go trials). In particular, the amplitude of the no-go P3 component (a late-appearing positive voltage potential occurring roughly 400–600 milliseconds after the stimulus appears) indicates to what extent an action tendency needs to be inhibited. Analysis of this component revealed stronger in-

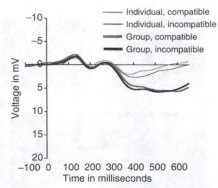

Fig. 2. Event-related potentials (brain electrical activity following a stimulus) were recorded while particapnts performed the spatial-compatibility task together (left panel) and alone; in both cases a participant responded to just one of the two color stimuli and not the other (no-go task). The right panel shows the amplitude of the no-go P3 component at a frontal electrode. This is a measure of how much inhibition is needed to suppress a response. The amplitude of the no-go P3 was significantly larger on no-go trials in the group condition, in which the other person acted, than it was in no-go trials in the individual condition, in which no one acted.

hibition when participants were required not to act because it was the other's turn than when they were required not to act but were alone (see Fig. 2). The additional need for inhibition when with another person further supports the assumption that one represents actions at the other's command in the same way as one's own actions. Representing the other's action leads to an action tendency on no-go trials that needs to be suppressed.

Surprisingly, the tendency to form shared action representations is present even in individuals who have difficulties understanding others' mental states. When high-functioning individuals with autism performed our go/no-go task either alone or together with a healthy participant, they showed the same tendency to form shared action representations that the healthy control participants did (Sebanz, Knoblich, Stumpf, & Prinz, 2005). This contrasts with the assumption of a common-coding (mirror-system) deficit in autism and raises the possibility that high-functioning individuals with autism have a specific deficit understanding that others' beliefs can differ from their own while more basic perception–action links supporting social interaction are intact.

Coordination

How do individuals adjust their actions to those of other people to achieve common goals (Clark, 1996)? Clearly, sharing action representations is not sufficient for successful interpersonal coordination. Whereas shared action representations allow individuals to simulate and predict others' actions, successful joint action often requires choosing appropriate complementary actions at an appropriate time. Take rowing a canoe as an example: When rowing a canoe alone, one can coordinate the timing of left and right paddle strokes quite easily because both actions are at one's own command. In contrast, two people rowing a canoe together must adjust to each other, because each partner has just the left or the right paddle strokes at his or her command. Knowing whether the other performs left or right

paddle strokes will not be sufficient for successful coordination. Instead, to avoid going around in circles, each rower also needs to attend to the timing of the other rower's strokes when timing his or her own. The coordination will be smoothest if each rower acquires an internal model that allows predicting the timing of the other rower's actions in relation to his or her own.

Knoblich and Jordan (2003) investigated the mechanisms underlying such anticipatory coordination, using a simple computer game that posed coordination challenges similar to rowing a canoe together. The main question was whether receiving an unambiguous signal about the timing of the other person's action would allow two individuals to achieve the same degree of coordination as a single individual playing the game alone. Although, initially, group performance was much worse than individual performance, groups who received timing feedback gradually became as effective as individuals in coordinating the two actions. Groups that were only given information about the joint outcome of their actions never reached the level of individual performance. Feedback led partners to develop a model of each other, allowing them to anticipate each other's action timing.

These results seem to suggest that one has to start from scratch when modeling the actions of unfamiliar people. However, the action-simulation account described in the last section opens up an alternative: Initial predictions about others' actions could take one's own action parameters as the default. In other words, one initially assumes that other people act just like one would act oneself if one were to perform their actions. In the course of joint action, this initial model is adjusted to match others' actual performance. This implies that coordination should be best when coordinating with people whose performance is very similar to one's own. Thus one should be one's own optimal partner, for instance when playing a piano duet. This idea was tested in a study in which expert pianists played one part of a piano duet in synchrony with a recording of the other part that they themselves had played or that had been played by another pianist (Keller, Knoblich, & Repp, in press). The temporal synchronization error between the two parts of the duet was significantly smaller when pianists synchronized with their own playing. This supports the assumption that predictions about others' action timing are initially based on one's own simulated performance.

Concluding Thoughts

Our review of some new findings on action perception and joint action suggests that basic perception–action links are crucial building blocks for social understanding and social interaction. It seems that a comprehensive understanding of social interaction can only be achieved if we continue to investigate how "lower-level" processes related to action understanding and action coordination enable and complement "higher-level" functions involved in thinking about and communicating with others (Smith & Semin, 2004).

What else can be learned from the finding that perception and action are social in nature? The obvious conclusion is that specific perceptual, cognitive, and motor processes are dedicated to social interaction. This seems to be the currently dominant view in the new field of social cognitive neuroscience. This approach has led to important progress, because it is now possible to map social behavior to particular cognitive and brain functions. However, we suggest that a deeper understanding of the processes supporting social interaction might be achieved if one takes the more radical stance that the demands of social interaction have shaped perception, action, and cognition (Fiske, 1992) through and through (Smith & Semin, 2004).

In particular, reassessing perception, action planning, and motor control in the light of their potential social roots might reveal that functions traditionally considered hallmarks of individual cognition originated through the need to interact with others. For instance, humans' ability to perform two tasks at the same time could be supported by processes that originally enabled individuals to perform one task while monitoring another individual's task performance. Along these lines, Roepstorff and Frith (2004) have speculated that the homunculus who has plagued psychology from its beginnings might be exorcized through a social exegesis. The hidden controller of our actions might be nothing more than an internalized other giving commands. Further exploration of how perception, action, and cognition are grounded in social interaction might have the potential to turn social cognitive neuroscience into a coherent framework that is more than the sum of its parts.

Recommended Reading

Barsalou, L.W, Simmons, W.K., Barbey, A., & Wilson, C.D. (2003). Grounding conceptual knowledge in modality-specific systems. *Trends in Cognitive Sciences, 7,* 84–9l.

Gallese, V., Keysers, C., & Rizzolatti, G. (2004). A unifying view of the basis of social cognition. *Trends in Cognitive Sciences, 8,* 396–403.

Jackson, P.L., & Decety, I. (2004). Motor cognition: A new paradigm to investigate social interactions. *Current Opinion in Neurobiology, 14,* 259–263.

Sebanz, N., Bekkering, H., & Knoblich, G. (2006). Joint action: Bodies and minds moving together. *Trends in Cognitive Sciences, 10,* 70–76.

Wilson, M., & Knoblich, G. (2005). The case for motor involvement in perceiving conspecifics. *Psychological Bulletin, 131,* 460–473.

References

Bosbach, S., Cole, J., Prinz, W., & Knoblich, G. (2005). Understanding another's expectation from action: The role of peripheral sensation. *Nature Neuroscience, 8,* 1295–1297.

Calvo-Merino, B., Glaser, D.E., Grezes, I., Passingham, R.E., & Haggard, P. (2005). Action observation and acquired motor skills. *Cerebral Cortex, 15,* 1243–1249.

Clark, H. (1996). *Using language.* Cambridge, England: Cambridge University Press.

Fiske, S.T. (1992). Thinking is for doing: Portraits of social cognition from daguerrotype to laser photo. *Journal of Personality and Social Psychology, 63,* 877–889.

Flach, R., Knoblich, G., & Prinz, W. (2004). Recognizing one's own clapping: The role of temporal cues in self-recognition. *Psychological Research, 11,* 147–156.

Keller, P., Knoblich, G., & Repp, B.H. (in press). Pianists duet better when they play with themselves. *Consciousness & Cognition.*

Knoblich, G., & Flach, R. (2003). Action identity: Evidence from self- recognition, prediction, and coordination. *Consciousness and Cognition, 12,* 620–632.

Knoblich, G., & Jordan, S. (2003). Action coordination in individuals and groups: Learning anticipatory control. *Journal of Experimental Psychology: Learning, Memory, & Cognition, 29,* 1006–1016.

Loula, F., Prasad, S., Harber, K., & Shiffrar, M. (2005). Recognizing people from their movement. *Journal of Experimental Psychology: Human Perception and Performance, 31,* 210–220.

Repp, B.H., & Knoblich, G. (2004). Perceiving action identity: How pianists recognize their own performances. *Psychological Science, 15,* 604–609.

Roepstorff, A., & Frith, C. (2004). What's at the top in the top-down control of action? *Psychological Research, 68,* 189–198.

Sebanz, N., Knoblich, G., & Prinz, W. (2003). Representing others' actions: Just like one's own? *Cognition, 88,* B11–B21.

Sebanz, N., Knoblich, G., Prinz, W., & Wascher, E. (in press). Twin Peaks: An ERP study of action planning and control in co-acting individuals. *Journal of Cognitive Neuroscience.*

Sebanz, N., Knoblich, G., Stumpf, I., & Prinz, W. (2005). Far from action blind: Representation of others' actions in individuals with autism. *Cognitive Neuropsychology, 22,* 433–454.

Smith, E.R., & Semin, G.R. (2004). Socially situated cognition: Cognition in its social context. *Advances in Experimental Social Psychology, 36,* 53–117.

Acknowledgments—This work was supported by the research initiative "Embodied Communication" at the Center of Interdisciplinary Research (ZIF) at the University of Bielefeld, Germany.

Address correspondence to **GÜNTHER KNOBLICH**, Psychology Department, Rutgers University, Smith Hall, 101 Warren Street, Newark, NJ 07102; e-mail: knoblich@psychology.rutgers.edu.

From *Current Directions in Psychological Science*, Vol. 15, no. 3, June 2006, pp. 99-104. Copyright © 2006 by the Association for Psychological Science. Reprinted by permission of Blackwell Publishing, Ltd.

Perception of Faces and Bodies

Similar or Different?

Human faces and bodies are both complex and interesting perceptual objects, and both convey important social information. Given these similarities between faces and bodies, we can ask how similar are the visual processing mechanisms used to recognize them. It has long been argued that faces are subject to dedicated and unique perceptual processes, but until recently, relatively little research has focused on how we perceive the human body. Some recent paradigms indicate that faces and bodies are processed differently; others show similarities in face and body perception. These similarities and differences depend on the type of perceptual task and the level of processing involved. Future research should take these issues into account.

VIRGINIA SLAUGHTER, VALERIE E. STONE, AND CATHERINE REED
Early Cognitive Development Unit and Cognitive Neuroscience, School of Psychology, University of Queensland, Brisbane, Australia, and Developmental Cognitive Neuroscience Program, Psychology Department, University of Denver

Probably the most important and complex objects we perceive are other humans. From the time we are born, other humans capture our attention and elicit complex behaviors from us. We can identify other humans as humans because they possess both a human face and a human body. Further, we identify specific individuals not only on the basis of their unique faces and body shapes, but also on the basis of their characteristic expressions, postures, and movements. Given these functional similarities between faces and bodies, how similar are the visual processing mechanisms used to recognize them?

Faces as Special Objects

It has long been argued that the visual system uses special perceptual processing for faces that is different from the processing used for other objects. The rationale is that faces are such significant social stimuli that natural selection acted to create dedicated face-processing mechanisms in the brain. There is evidence consistent with the idea that faces are special: From early in development, infants are biased to look at faces more than other complex objects (Johnson & Morton, 1991). Also, adult perception of faces reveals unique effects, including the inversion effect (upside-down faces are more difficult to recognize than other complex inverted stimuli) and the caricature effect (a face with its distinctive features exaggerated is easier to recognize than the original face). Event-related potential studies, which measure the timing of the brain's electrical responses to stimuli, show that the brain responds differently to faces than to other objects within 170 ms after they are presented. Functional magnetic resonance imaging (fMRI) research, showing activity in the brain while participants are actively performing perceptual or cognitive tasks, further suggests that distinct brain areas respond to faces compared with other objects.

However, not all researchers agree that these apparently face-specific phenomena genuinely reflect unique processing of faces. Some authors suggest that responses to faces are driven by the abstract perceptual features of faces, such as symmetry or high contrast, rather than their face-ness per se (Turati, Simion, Milani, & Umilta, 2002). Others argue that the apparently special processing faces receive simply reflects the ubiquity and importance of faces, and that the perceptual effects adults exhibit when viewing faces will be evident for any objects that they are highly practiced at perceiving (e.g., cars for car enthusiasts or dogs for dog breeders; Tanaka & Gauthier, 1997). These authors propose that visual expertise changes the way that objects are processed: Within a given domain, novices recognize objects by focusing on their distinctive parts, but experts rely on configural processing, focusing on the spatial relationships between parts. The argument is that configural processing in general can explain perceptual effects that appear to distinguish faces.

Bodies Are Special, Too

Another class of objects that may be subject to special processing is human bodies. Although there has been relatively little research on perception of the human body compared with that of faces, several similarities between faces and bodies suggest that they may be processed similarly. First, bodies and faces share a number of abstract configural properties that may make the perceptual system treat them similarly. All faces share the same set of parts (eyes, nose, mouth, etc.), as do all bodies (arms, legs, torso, etc.). As a result, for both faces and bodies, perceptual distinctions depend on the exact shape and position of component parts. Also, from the front, both faces and bodies are symmetrical along the vertical axis. Further, the spatial relationships between parts of faces and between parts of bodies are relatively fixed. Across individuals, the configural arrangement of the eyes, nose, and mouth of the face is relatively unchanging, as is the arrangement of the head, torso, and limbs.

Second, faces and bodies are both salient conveyors of social information. Both provide information about other individuals' attentional and emotional states, and inform basic social categorizations, including attributions of age, gender, and attractiveness. Faces and bodies are both used for communication.

Finally, our embodied internal experience of both faces and bodies could distinguish them as special object classes. Our ability to move and functionally use our faces and bodies could influence the visual recognition of other faces and bodies. Recent neurophysiological studies with monkeys have revealed a class of *mirror* neurons, so called because the same neurons are active whether a given motor action is performed or observed. There is some indirect evidence that similar motor-mirroring structures exist in humans (see Gallese & Goldman, 1998, for a review), suggesting that visual and motor representations interact. The ability both to see faces and bodies and to move our own faces and bodies may make them similarly unique compared with other perceptual objects.

Despite these arguments for special perceptual processing of bodies, there are also reasons to suppose that faces and bodies may be treated differently by the visual system. The nature of the information conveyed by faces and bodies is arguably different. Faces, although often moving, are perceptually informative even while still. We can make judgments about another person's gender, identity, emotion, attractiveness, and direction of attention (conveyed most saliently in eye gaze) from a still photograph of the face. Bodies, in contrast, are typically moving, and much of the information that bodies convey is in dynamic movement. We can identify another person's gender, emotion, and direction of attention from that person's body most easily if it is in motion.

Thus, it remains an open question whether the visual system applies similar or different perceptual processes to faces and bodies. Insight into this question may be gained by considering two factors. First, the various ways that scientists measure face and body perception may place more or less difficult demands on the visual system. Second, patterns in the development of face perception and of body perception may give insight into how and when faces are treated similarly by the visual system.

Levels of Perceptual Processing of Faces and Bodies

Perception of faces or bodies is a multistage process. The extent to which faces and bodies are treated similarly by the perceptual system depends on the stage of processing, and thus the type of perceptual task participants are asked to perform. It may be useful to distinguish two stages of perceptual processing and two types of perceptual tasks: detection versus recognition. Face or body *detection* refers to the ability to determine whether a particular stimulus is a face or a body rather than something else, and is an early stage of visual processing. Paradigms that compare participants' responses to faces or bodies with their responses to other types of objects are measuring detection.

Face or body *recognition* is a later stage of visual processing and involves making distinctions between individuals within a category. Recognition is often tested by asking participants to distinguish individual faces or bodies. Recognition processes are invoked not only for identifying individual persons, but also for identifying specific body postures (e.g., sitting vs. running) and specific facial expressions (e.g., happy vs. angry).

Detection of Faces and Bodies

Recent work has shown that the developmental time courses for detecting human faces and bodies are different. When young infants are presented with a typical human face image and a scrambled human face image in which the eyes, nose, and mouth are moved to noncanonicallocations, they prefer to look at the typical face (Johnson & Morton, 1991). Thus, in this task, infants detect the presence of a face (as opposed to a scrambled nonface). A recent study used a similar experimental procedure to investigate development of human body perception (Slaughter, Heron, & Sim, 2002). Infants between the ages of 12 and 18 months were shown typical and scrambled images of human bodies (see Fig. 1) as well as face-like stimuli, and their looking preferences were measured. The data indicated differences in the way infants responded to faces and bodies. Infants younger than 18 months of age did not show a preference for typical or scrambled body pictures, suggesting that they did not notice the differences between them, yet these young infants clearly preferred the typical face to the scrambled face. By 18 months of age, infants looked longer at the scrambled than at the typical body pictures, presumably because they found the scrambled images novel or surprising. These developmental data indicate that infants' perceptual expectations about typical human faces develop much earlier than their expectations about human bodies.

Adults also show a dissociation between face and body detection. In recent fMRI studies, distinct brain regions were activated when participants viewed pictures of faces, bodies, or body parts. Detection of faces consistently correlated with activation in the fusiform face area, located in the ventral temporal lobe (the underneath surface of the brain toward the back; Kanwisher, McDermott, & Chun, 1997). In contrast, the extra-striate body area, located in the lateral occipitotemporal cortex (the lower left or right outside surface of the brain toward the back), was active

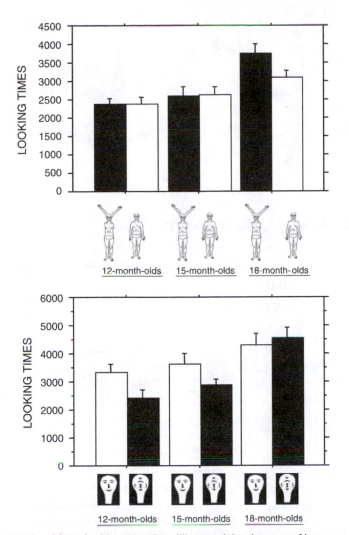

Fig. 1. Mean looking time (in milliseconds) to images of human bodies (top) and facelike stimuli (bottom) with typical (white bars) and scrambled (black bars) arrangements of parts. Results are presented separately for 12-, 15-, and 18-month-olds. From Slaughter, Heron, and Sim (2202).

would be most easily recognized by the spatial arrangement of their component parts. The inversion effect, in which recognition of objects is disrupted by turning them upside down, is traditionally considered an indicator of configural processing because inverting a familiar object makes it more difficult to recognize relations between the parts. The inversion effect has been demonstrated for faces and also for other objects when viewed by experts (e.g., dog breeders, car experts). A recent study (Reed, Stone, Bozova, & Tanaka, 2003) demonstrated that adults show similar inversion effects for faces and body postures: Both faces and bodies are more difficult to recognize when presented upside down than when presented right side up, but the same is not true of other complex stimuli, such as houses (see Fig. 2). It appears that both face and body-posture recognition depend on mentally representing the spatial configuration of stimulus parts.

Despite this similarity in the recognition of faces and bodies, there are suggestions of differences in recognition processes as well. Evidence from neuropsychological patients indicates a dissociation between face and body recognition. In prosopagnosia, patients are unable to recognize individual faces—a recognition problem that can be independent from difficulties with recognition of other objects. This pattern of visual recognition problems suggests that these patients have damage to a specialized face-processing area in the brain. The disorder autotopagnosia (or somatotopagnosia) affects patients' ability to recognize, point to, or name specific body parts within the context of a whole body, although these patients have no difficulty naming parts of other complex objects (e.g., Ogden, 1985). Though each of these disorders is distinct from general object recognition problems, prosopagnosia and autotopagnosia do not typically occur together. The existence of these two distinct neuropsychological disorders, one affecting face recognition and the other body-part recognition, suggests that recognition of faces and recognition of bodies involve some distinct processes.

Conclusions

The studies reviewed here provide evidence for both similarities and differences in the way we perceive faces and bodies. Detection tasks have demonstrated mostly differences: developmental differences in responses to typical and scrambled faces versus bodies, and activation of different brain areas for face versus body processing in adults. Recognition tasks have shown similarity between perception of faces and perception of bodies, in the effects of expertise and inversion. But there are also some differences in face and body recognition: Prosopagnosia and autotopagnosia reveal independent deficits for recognition of faces and bodies and do not co-occur.

This complex pattern may be explained in terms of the levels of processing involved. Detection tasks appear to tap into relatively basic visual categorization processes, possibly processes depending on simple spatial properties. Thus, the evidence from such tasks suggests the initial identification of faces and bodies as such occurs in distinct areas of the brain. Recognition tasks, in contrast, may recruit several different complex processes that

only when participants were shown images of the human body or body parts (Downing, Jiang, Shuman, & Kanwisher, 2001). The extrastriate body area does not respond to images of faces.

Thus, both in infancy and in adulthood, there are demonstrated differences in basic perceptual detection of human faces and bodies.

Recognition of Faces and Bodies

In contrast to the data on detection, data on face and body recognition reveal some similarity in how adults process faces and bodies. Without explicit training, people should be experts at recognizing both individual faces and individual body postures, because of their ubiquity in everyday life. If perceptual expertise means that visual recognition relies on configural processing, then one would expect that both faces and bodies

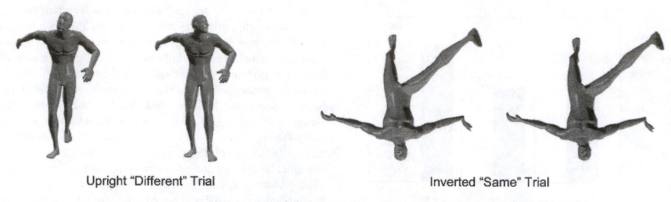

Upright "Different" Trial   Inverted "Same" Trial

Orientation X Object Interactions: Bodies, Houses and Faces

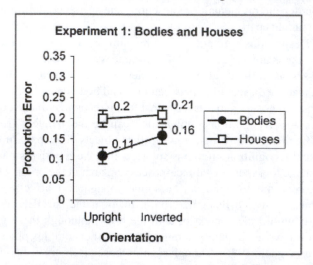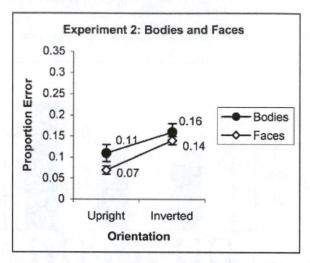

Fig. 2. Examples of stimuli and results from a study on ability to recognize upright and inverted stimuli. On each trial, two stimuli, which could be either the same or different, were presented in either upright or inverted orientation. The task was to indicate whether the stimuli were identical. The graphs show the percentage of trials on which participants responded incorrectly. From Reed, Stone, Bozova, and Tanaka (2003).

analyze configural properties, identify individuals, and assign meaning. Some processing, such as the configural processing affected by expertise, may operate similarly for faces and bodies. Other recognition processing (e.g., how parts are represented relative to the whole or how the motion of parts is represented) may operate differently for faces and bodies.

Directions for Future Research

Understanding the extent to which faces and bodies are treated similarly in visual processing will require more work that explicitly contrasts responses to faces, bodies, and other complex objects. Furthermore, it will be important for such work to define carefully the level of processing being tested. Detection paradigms involve differentiating faces and bodies from other objects or scrambled stimuli. The developmental work to date has focused on body detection, but can be expanded to explore the development of body recognition. At what stage of development would infants recognize individual, meaningful body postures?

Recognition encompasses a variety of processes, depending on what about the face or body is being represented in the mind.

Inversion and discrimination studies, for example, test whether participants are sensitive to relatively small changes in configuration, and performance in these studies thus may not depend on representing the whole object. Paradigms that test how well parts are recognized within the whole or individually (e.g., tests used with autotopagnosics) may tap into a different level of processing, at which the structure of the whole object and the relationship of parts to that whole are represented. Processing of bodies and processing of faces may therefore be similar in some recognition tasks, but different in others, depending on the level of processing involved. Detailed work testing recognition at different levels of processing can help clarify the levels at which bodies and faces share processing and mental representations and the levels at which they do not.

Finally, further work on this topic should consider the importance of motion. The studies reviewed here all involved detection or recognition of static human faces and bodies. However, static and dynamic information are arguably weighted differently in face and body processing; as noted, static information is more meaningful in faces, whereas dynamic information is more crucial to body perception. For example, static images easily afford recognition of individual faces, but recognition of individual bodies probably has less to do with body shape than with characteristic motion patterns. Prosopagnosics report using motion patterns to recognize familiar people. Recent evidence suggests that facial information is processed by two distinct cognitive streams: a ventral stream (through the lower parts of the temporal lobes, corresponding to brain areas below the ears) that recognizes individuals by static features and a dorsal stream (through the upper parts of the parietal lobes, corresponding to brain areas above the ears) that processes dynamic information (O'Toole, Roark, & Abdi, 2002). Different brain areas are activated by static versus dynamic displays of facial expressions. The brain also responds differently to displays of the biomechanical motion of human bodies than to static human bodies, but this may not be a dorsal-ventral differentiation (Vaina, Solomon, Chowdhury, Sinha, & Belliveau, 2001). Thus, perhaps one of the most important future directions for research in this area is the exploration of how visual processes involved in the perception of faces and bodies depend on dynamic information.

Recommended Reading

Bentin, S., Allison, T., Puce, A., Perez, E., & McCarthy, G. (1996). Electrophysiological studies of face perception in humans. *Journal of Cognitive Neuroscience, 8,* 551–565.

Downing, P., Jiang, Y., Shuman, M., & Kanwisher, N. (2001). (See References)

Kanwisher, N., & Moscovitch, M. (2000). The cognitive neuroscience of face processing: An introduction. *Cognitive Neuropsychology, 17,* 1–11.

Reed, C.L., Stone, V.E., Bozova, S., & Tanaka, J. (2003). (See References)

Slaughter, V., Heron, M., & Sim, S. (2002). (See References)

References

Downing, P., Jiang, Y., Shuman, M., & Kanwisher, N. (2001). A cortical area selective for visual processing of the human body. *Science, 293,* 23–26.

Gallese, V., & Goldman, A. (1998). Mirror neurons and the simulation theory of mind-reading. *Trends in Cognitive Sciences, 2,* 493–501.

Johnson, M.H., & Morton, J. (1991). *Biology and cognitive development: The case of face recognition.* Oxford, England: Basil Blackwell.

Kanwisher, N., McDermott, J., & Chun, M. (1997). The fusiform face area: A module in human extrastriate cortex specialized for face perception. *The Journal of Neuroscience, 17,* 4302–4311.

Ogden, J. (1985). Autotopagnosia: Occurrence in a patient with nominal aphasia and with an intact ability to point to parts of animals and objects. *Brain, 108,* 1009–1022.

O'Toole, A., Roark, D., & Abdi, H. (2002). Recognizing moving faces: A psychological and neural synthesis. *Trends in Cognitive Sciences, 6,* 261–266.

Reed, C. L., Stone, V.E., Bozova, S., & Tanaka, J. (2003). The body inversion effect. *Psychological Science, 14,* 302–308.

Slaughter, V., Heron, M., & Sim, S. (2002). Development of preferences for the human body shape in infancy. *Cognition,* 85(3), B71–B81.

Tanaka, J., & Gauthier, I. (1997). Expertise in object and face recognition. In R. Goldstone, P. Schyns, & D. Medin (Eds.), *Psychology of learning and motivation: Vol. 36. Perceptual mechanisms of learning* (pp. 83–125). San Diego, CA: Academic Press.

Turati, C., Simion, F., Milani, I., & Umilta, C. (2002). Newborns' preference for faces: What is crucial? *DeveloPmRntal Psychology, 38,* 875–882.

Vaina, L., Solomon, J., Chowdhury, S., Sinha, P., & Belliveau, W. (2001). Functional neuroanatomy of biological motion perception in humans. *Proceedings of the National Academy of Sciences, USA, 98,* 11656–11661.

Acknowledgments—We thank Derek Moore for his insightful comments on an early version of this article.

Address correspondence to **VIRGINIA SLAUGHTER**, School of Psychology, University of Queensland, Brisbane, 4072 Australia; e-mail: vps@psy.uq.edu.au.

From *Current Directions in Psychological Science*, Vol. 13, no. 6, December 2004, pp. 219-223. Copyright © 2004 by the Association for Psychological Science. Reprinted by permission of Blackwell Publishing, Ltd.

UNIT 4
Attitudes

Unit Selections

Key Points to Consider

- What are explicit attitudes? Implicit attitudes? Do they function differently? Which do you think are the most important in shaping social interactions? How are implicit attitudes related to racial prejudice?

- What are some of the ways to persuade others to adopt a certain attitude? Can you think of examples of each method from your own life or from advertising?

- Why are Americans so reviled? Or are they? What types of people are our friends? Why do individuals from certain societies dislike us? Are there individual differences even within a society?

Student Web Site
www.mhcls.com/online

Internet References
Further information regarding these Web sites may be found in this book's preface or online.

Psychological Warfare Links
http://www.psywar.org/links.php

The Psychology of Cyberspace
http://www.rider.edu/users/suler/psycyber/psycyber.html

Several new college graduates formed a company on the basis of a single idea. What was the idea? A small circular refrigerator that could be used as an end table. The shelves inside rotated so that the consumer wouldn't have to arise to reach refreshments in the back. The refrigerator would make cold refreshments available in offices, for television viewers, and in employee break rooms. The young women and men who established the company believed their idea was 'a quick sell", "a sure thing", something that would make them millionaires. After considerable marketing research, the company began making and selling the small refrigerators disguised as furniture. Appliance and furniture stores were the company's main targets, but sales in college bookstores were also pursued. In no time, the meager savings of the graduates were exhausted; large loans were called in by banks, and bankruptcy was filed. What went wrong?

Despite the best-laid plans and hard work of most manufactures, most new products fail. Why? In the case of the circular refrigerator-end table, the young entrepreneurs forgot that most homes already contain a refrigerator not too far from the television, and many businesses already offer some form of refrigeration in employee break rooms. Frankly, there was little need for this stubby, superfluous appliance. Consumers had never developed a need for the refrigerator, so they held the opinion that it was an unnecessary expense.

This case is fictional but helps to highlight the importance of attitudes. *Attitudes* are learned tendencies to evaluate some-

thing as positive or negative. Apparently, consumers held negative attitudes (e.g. it just isn't necessary) toward the little refrigerator.

Social psychologists are extremely interested in how attitudes are formed, why they are so staunchly maintained, and how to persuade individuals to change attitudes. Attitudes appear to be formed by interaction with others. Generally speaking, many attitudes are learned from significant others, such as our parents. Other attitudes are acquired as a result of being exposed to certain environments, such as educational institutions.

Research in social psychology indicates that a specific attitude is not held by an individual in a vacuum. That is, one attitude is typically connected to another which is connected to still another. Thus, an attitudinal network is formed. For example, suppose you assume that the moon is made of bleu cheese, you hate bleu cheese and therefore would never, ever want to go to the moon. Moreover, you might also maintain that the moon is too close to the sun, the sun causes skin cancer, your family is prone to skin cancer, and, again, there is little reason for you to go to the moon.

This tongue-in-cheek example of an attitudinal network also demonstrates how attitudes and behaviors usually are connected. Many people act on their attitudes. And some social psychologists suggest that our behaviors help in turn to establish our attitudes.

63

Once attitudes become intertwined, they are hard to change. Most theoreticians assume that people prefer consistency among their various attitudes. People feel uncomfortable or experience dissonance when attitudes are inconsistent or when attitudes and behaviors are disparate.

Some attitudes, however, are not always expressed—either verbally or behaviorally. A few business owners, for instance, harbor strong negative prejudices (a type of attitude) against certain groups. They know that by law they cannot act on their prejudices; in other words, they cannot keep the groups out of their place of business. They still embrace prejudice, though.

Research on the attitudinal network also suggests that attitude change is difficult. Persuasion has long been a fertile area for social psychological research. There are many important applications of attitude change research. Here are but a few: advertisements, presentations to juries, editorials in the newspaper, psychotherapy, and international diplomacy.

Social psychologists have broken attitudinal messages into three major research areas. One area involves the *content of the message*, for example the use of threat (e.g. if you don't brush your teeth with new White-Bright, your teeth will rot"). Another heavily researched aspect is the *role of the messenger*, for instance a celebrity endorser who claims to use White-Bright. *The audience* is another a vital ingredient in any attempt to change attitudes. Some audiences are initially hostile to the message (e.g. "My teeth are too sensitive for regular toothpastes"), others

are open-minded (e.g. "Gee, I would try that if there were a coupon"), while yet others are neutral to the communication ("Was that a toothpaste ad?"). Finally, *the situation* surrounding the persuasive message is important. Whether the message is accompanied by music and on what medium (e.g. television, radio, or newspaper) also influence persuasive efforts.

In this unit we will explore several aspects of attitudes and attitude change. The first article, "Implicit Discrimination," reveals that there are two types of attitudes: *explicit attitudes* of which we are aware and *implicit attitudes* which affect us but of which we are often unaware. How these two types of attitudes function, especially implicit attitudes, provide the crux of the information in this article. Implicit attitudes, the authors conclude, may well be responsible for much of the racial discrimination witnessed in American society.

The second article is authored by Robert Cialdini, a leading social psychologist ready to "give psychology away" to the public. In this second article, Cialdini with coauthor Noah Goldstein offers six tried and true strategies to enhance persuasive messages.

The final selection of this unit presents a timely, global issue—anti-Americanism. Anne Applebaum reviews who likes the U.S., who doesn't and, most importantly, why. She considers several factors in the international community such as gender and cohort group membership that dictate how much citizens of other countries admire or despise everything American.

Article 11

New Approaches to Discrimination[†]

Implicit Discrimination

MARIANNE BERTRAND, DOLLY CHUGH, AND SENDHIL MULLAINATHAN[*]

What drives people to discriminate? Economists focus on two main reasons: "taste-based" and "statistical" discrimination. Under both models, individuals *consciously* discriminate, either for a variety of personal reasons or because group membership provides information about a relevant characteristic, such as productivity. Motivated by a growing body of psychological evidence, we put forward a third interpretation: implicit discrimination. Sometimes, we argue, discrimination may be *unintentional* and outside of the discriminator's awareness.

I. Psychology of Implicit Attitudes

Most modern social psychologists believe that attitudes occur in both implicit and explicit modes, suggesting that people can think, feel, and behave in ways that oppose their explicitly expressed views, and even, explicitly known self-interests.[1] The preferences and beliefs that economists typically describe as an individual's "attitudes" are what psychologists would specify as "explicit attitudes," which may or may not align with the same individual's "implicit attitudes," defined as *unconscious* mental associations between a target (such as an African-American) and a given attribute.

One of the most important recent research insights is that implicit attitudes can be measured. A widely used measure of implicit mental processes is the Implicit Association Test (IAT) (Anthony G. Greenwald et al., 1998). The IAT relies on test-takers' speed of response to represent the strength of their unconscious mental associations.[2] IATs are used to measure a wide range of implicit attitudes about social groups, products, or self-identity. We illustrate this with a race IAT.

The race IAT is typically taken on a computer. The test-taker must quickly categorize words and pictures of faces that appear in the center of the screen. Faces are to be categorized as African-American or white and words (such as happiness or tragedy) as good or bad. Pairs of categories appear on either side of the screen. If the stimulus belongs to categories on the right (left), the test-taker hits a key on the right (left) side of the keyboard. Each test-taker completes two versions of the task, categorizing as many as 60 different stimuli. In one, the "compatible" version, the two categories on one side are paired according to a stereotype, such as "African-American" with "bad" in one corner, and "White" with "good" in the other corner. In the "incompatible" version, the categories are paired counter-stereotypically, such as "African-American" with "good," and "white" with "bad." The key insight of the race IAT is that an implicit bias against African-Americans shows up as a response time differential. Most people respond more quickly in the compatible pairing, when African-American is paired with bad rather than good, demonstrating a stronger mental response.

Because people may misrepresent their explicit attitudes, perhaps the IAT is simply a less "fakable" measure. However, recent neuroscientific studies demonstrate that conscious processing activates different regions in the brain than does unconscious processing, thus these are distinctive mental processes. One study showed greater brain activity associated with control and regulation when supraliminally processing black faces, in contrast with greater brain activity associated with emotion and fear when subliminally processing black faces. Another showed a correlation between the IAT and amygdala activation (fear response) in response to black faces. In addition, the divergence of implicit and explicit attitudes is not limited to socially sensitive domains. For example, the social demands to conceal one's preferences about a Mac versus PC computer, or Coke versus Pepsi seem minimal. Yet, implicit and explicit attitudes in these domains are imperfectly correlated, with both having predictive power.

Can implicit attitudes influence behavior in meaningful ways? Evidence to date suggests yes. A meta-analysis of 61 studies found an average correlation of 0.27 between the IAT and outcome measures such as judgments, choices, and physiological responses. Most importantly, the IAT outperformed explicit attitude measures for less-controllable behavioral

[†]*Discussants:* Dan Black, Syracuse University; David Neumark, Public Policy Institute of California and Michigan State University; Shelly Lundberg, University of Washington; Kerwin Charles, University of Michigan.

[*]Bertrand: Graduate School of Business, University of Chicago, 5807 South Woodlawn Avenue, Chicago, IL 60603; Chugh: Harvard Business School, Soldiers Field Road, Boston, MA 02163; Mullainathan: Department of Economics, Harvard University, Littauer Center, Cambridge, MA 02138. This paper is based on work supported by the National Science Foundation under grant no. 0351184.

outcomes. In one study, white participants interacted with both a white and African-American experimenter, and also took the IAT. Participants' implicit attitudes favoring whites predicted more smiling, speaking time, extemporaneous social comments, and general friendliness, as well as fewer speech errors and speech hesitation, toward the white experimenter.

These findings suggest that controllability may be an important behavioral dimension. But could any relevant economic behavior, such as a hiring decision, truly be characterized as "hard-to-control"? In fact, social psychologists argue that even theoretically controllable behaviors may operate with greater automaticity under certain situational conditions. Chugh (2004) described the "messy, pressured, and distracting" conditions of managerial work as conducive to implicit mental processes. Time pressure and stress are two situational influences likely to first generate an acceleration of the mental process, and then an attempt to reduce the amount of information needing processing. This type of "cognitive load," also occurs in the form of conflicting yet simultaneous task demands and excessive attentional demands.

In addition, social psychologists argue that many seemingly controllable behaviors may be prone to implicit attitudes under conditions of ambiguity, and have demonstrated that implicit discrimination is more likely to occur in situations where multiple, non-racist explanations for the behavior might exist. Thus, some conditions under which implicit attitudes may arise are threefold: inattentiveness to task, time pressure or other cognitive load, and ambiguity.

II. Can Implicit Attitudes Be "Manipulated"?

One intriguing feature of implicit attitudes is their potential manipulability. In one study, white participants were told they would be working with a black individual, who would either be their subordinate or their superior. Those anticipating a black superior showed more positive implicit attitudes toward blacks than those anticipating a black subordinate, suggesting that positive and powerful black exemplars are important cues. In another, exposure to photographs of admired African-Americans (e.g., Bill Cosby) led to a decrease in anti-black implicit attitudes, an effect that persisted for 24 hours. In another, reducing attention to race cues (e.g., by increasing attention required by the task) moderated implicit attitudes. This work certainly does not imply that implicit attitudes can be reversed with simple manipulations of the situation or task. However, the work suggests malleability in implicit attitudes and associated behaviors.

III. Interpreting Existing Audit Studies in the Light of Implicit Discrimination

Obviously, implicit attitudes cannot explain all forms of racial discrimination. Explicit discrimination in employment ads prior to the Civil Rights Act of 1964 had little to do with implicit at-

titudes. However, we find it reasonable to hypothesize that several other documented forms of differential treatments may, in part, reflect such implicit attitudes.

The Bertrand and Mullainathan (2004) résumé task, for example, theoretically satisfies several criteria thought to be important for implicit discrimination to arise. First, the task is typically performed under important time pressure, as the screeners have to make their way through a thick pile of résumés, often juggling this task with multiple other administrative loads. The task is also involves considerable ambiguity: in the search for a "good" job applicant, there is no such thing as a simple formula to be followed to determine which candidates are above the "fit line." Also, the typical task is a nonverbal automatic process consisting in placing a given résumé either on the "yes" pile or on the "no" pile, with little commentary on each résumé.

Several other field experiments may fit the implicit discrimination model. Consider Ian Ayres et al.'s (2004) finding of African-American cab drivers receiving lower tips than white cab drivers. A tipping decision is often made quickly, just as the passenger is stepping out of the cab, and when the passenger's mind is preoccupied with an upcoming destination or event. Finally, ambiguity exists in how to interpret subtle cues about friendliness and honesty.

Bargaining is another relevant context, as in John List's (2004) study of discrimination in the sports-card market. When a prospective buyer expresses interest in a card, the seller makes a quick first offer. Very often, this first offer is made as the seller's attention is split between the current buyer and other prospective buyers nearby.

Also, consider the housing audit studies documenting differential treatment of equally qualified African-American and white home buyers in realtors' showing of additional units, both in terms of numbers and quality (see e.g., Jan Ondrich et al., 2003). The realtor faces a subtle, complex, and ambiguous task in forecasting a client's idiosyncratic tastes.

A police officer's decision of whether or not to shoot a potentially armed target is taken in an ambiguous split second. Joshua Correll et al. (2002) used a videogame to show that subjects were quicker at deciding not to shoot an unarmed white target versus an unarmed black target, even though both targets were armed at equal rates in the context of this game. Most interestingly, the authors showed that this difference was not related to cross-subjects differences in explicit racial prejudice.

IV. Testing for Implicit Discrimination

Hence, implicit discrimination could potentially explain some economic phenomena, with sufficient testing. We suggest several potential directions for future research.

A first approach would be to perform more correlation exercises in the field between economic behavior and IAT. One could contact the realtors after a fair-housing audit took place and ask them to take an IAT, or contact sports-card traders studied by List (2004). Alternatively, with some creativity, one might integrate a field element within a lab study. For example, if taxicabs pick up subjects to bring to the lab for an IAT, one could correlate subjects' IAT scores with their tipping behavior.

Second, one could perform additional tests by empirically varying situational factors shown to be important for implicit attitudes to affect behavior. For example, one could schedule an appointment with a realtor either when s/he is quite busy or less busy. Or one could vary the level of ambiguity of the realtor's task with a more-specific or less-specific description of the client's desired home.

One could also reduce attention to the social cues in the context of the résumé study by modifying the location of the names on résumés. Bertrand and Mullainathan (with Abhijit Banerjee) are currently carrying out such a manipulation in India in the context of caste-based discrimination. In India, it is possible for a given individual to have a caste-neutral name but for his or her father to have a lower-caste name. It is also common for an individual to report the father's name at the *bottom* of the resume. One can therefore compare callback rates for lower-caste people whose caste affiliation is communicated through their names versus through their father's names.

Another testing possibility is to attempt to mimic natural situations in the laboratory itself. We have started exploring this possibility in the context of the résumé study. Specifically, we recruited 115 subjects for a study on information-processing and attention. The task was to screen 50 résumés for a company filling an administrative assistant position (job description provided). Their task was to select the 15 best candidates. Each participant received a unique set of résumés in that, following Bertrand and Mullainathan (2004), each résumé was randomly assigned either a white-sounding or African-American sounding first name. After completing this task, the participants took several IATs, answered explicit attitude measures about African-Americans, and completed a debriefing survey ("how rushed did you feel …?"). Anonymity on all measures was fully guaranteed to all participants.

While our pilot testing findings are preliminary, some encouraging results have emerged. First, participants who reported feeling rushed picked a significantly lower fraction of résumés with African-American names. We also found a negative correlation between the number of African-American résumés selected by a given subject and that subject's implicit attitude about intelligence in blacks and whites (where negative scores indicate an association between African-American and dumb). Most interestingly, this negative correlation was concentrated among those subjects who *ex post* reported feeling most rushed during the task. In contrast, we found no apparent correlation between the number of African-American résumés picked and the self-reported explicit attitudes towards African-Americans.

Obviously, such a lab exercise lacks external validity and faces implementation problems. In this regard, the subjects' background (mostly undergrads) and the difficulty of providing naturalistic incentives may explain one major issue with our pilot study so far: we did not find discrimination, on average, in the lab and only those subjects who felt rushed picked a lower than base-rate fraction of African-American résumés. In the future, we hope to implement a similar exercise within a firm.

Also, once the design is perfected, we could test de-biasing remedies that emerge naturally from the psychological evidence. First, and most obvious, one might simply inform human resource managers about the existence of the implicit bias. Second, small changes in the situational context of résumé screening could have potential large positive effects. Simply leaving more time to the screeners to assess the merit of each résumé may limit the role for unconscious responses while performing this task. Also, having an African-American person in the interview room, or even in mind, may operate as a positive exemplar (not a monitor) which could mute the importance of unconscious reactions. Also, a more structured review process that draws attention to the task cues rather than social cues (such as highlighting the positive and negative aspects of each résumé, or evaluation along highly specific job criteria, rather than a general "fit" comparison to a broad job description).

V. Conclusion

However we test for it, implicit discrimination is not useful simply as a subtle alternative interpretation. If it is a powerful driver of discriminatory behavior, it should reshape the way we understand discrimination and alter our available spectrum of remedies. A key differential feature of potential remedies to implicit discrimination is that they could limit the amount of discrimination without forcing agents to take decisions against their will. In fact, because people may be engaging in injurious behavior without realizing it, the remedies may bring their decisions closer in line with what they (explicitly) think or favor for their organization. Another important feature of these remedies is that, unlike most affirmative-action policies, they can be implemented at low cost and without making race salient, greatly increasing political feasibility.

References

Ayres, Ian; Vars, Fred and Zakariya, Nasser. "Racial Disparities in Taxicab Tipping." Working paper, Yale Law School, 2004.

Bertrand, Marianne; Chugh, Dolly and Mullainathan, Sendhil. "Implicit Discrimination." Working paper, Graduate School of Business, University of Chicago, 2005.

Bertrand, Marianne and Mullainathan, Sendhil. "Are Emily and Greg More Employable Than Lakisha and Jamal?" American Economic Review, 2004, 94(4), pp. 991–1013.

Chugh, Dolly. "Why Milliseconds Matter: Societal and Managerial Implications of Implicit Social Cognition." Social Justice Research, 2004, 17(2), pp. 203–22.

Correll, Joshua; Park, Bernadette; Judd, Charles M. and Wittenbrink, Bernd. "The Police Officer's Dilemma: Using Ethnicity to Disambiguate Potentially Threatening Individuals." Journal of Personality and Social Psychology, 2002, 83(6), pp. 1314–29.

Greenwald, Anthony G.; McGhee, Debbie E. and Schwartz, Jordan L. K. "Measuring Individual Differences in Implicit Cognition: The Implicit Association Test." Journal of Personality and Social Psychology, 1998, 74(6), pp. 1464–80.

List, John. "The Nature and Extent of Discrimination in the Marketplace: Evidence from the Field." Quarterly Journal of Economics, 2004, 119(1), pp. 49–89.

Ondrich, Jan; Ross, Stephen and Yinger, John. "Now You See It, Now You Don't: Why Do Real Estate Agents Withhold Available Houses from Black Customers?" Review of Economics and Statistics, 2003, 85(4), pp. 854–73.

Notes

1. Due to space constraints, we omit many references. See Bertrand et al. (2005) for full references to the relevant papers.

2. A demonstration of the test is available online: <http://implicit.harvard.edu>.

From *American Economic Review*, Vol. 95, no. 2, May 2005, pp. 94-98. Copyright © 2005 by American Economic Association. Reprinted by permission of AEA and the authors.

The Science and Practice of Persuasion

From business owners to busboys, the ability to harness the power of persuasion is often an essential component of success in the hospitality industry.

ROBERT B. CIALDINI AND NOAH J. GOLDSTEIN

Research reveals that there are six basic principles that govern how one person might influence another. Those principles can be labeled as: liking, reciprocation, consistency, scarcity, social validation, and authority.[1] In the pages that follow we elaborate on each of those six principles and highlight some of their applications in the hospitality industry—for instance, how a restaurant manager might reduce the reservation no-show rate by two-thirds; how to influence the size of the gratuity patrons leave for their servers; how to encourage customers to order additional food when they do not really want it; and how to get customers to comply with employees' reasonable requests.

Simply put, in general people are inclined to favor and to comply with those whom they like. A good illustration of this fundamental principle of influence in action is the Tupperware party, in which salespeople invite their friends and neighbors to their homes to pitch useful household plastic products. A study done by Frenzen and Davis confirmed what the Tupperware Corporation knew all along: guests' liking for their hostess was twice as important as was their opinion of the products in influencing their purchase decisions.[2]

In the case of the Tupperware party, the seller is not just a likeable person, but is probably a friend and respected community member as well. The power of the "liking" principle is so pervasive, however, that even perfect strangers can recognize whether there is any affinity between them within a relatively short time. Researchers have identified four primary determinants of our fondness for another person: physical attractiveness, similarity, cooperation, and the extent to which we feel the person likes us.

Looking good. Most of us acknowledge that those who are physically attractive have a social advantage held by few others, but evidence suggests that we have grossly underestimated the degree to which that is true. For example, good-looking candidates received more than two-and-a-half times as many votes as did unattractive candidates in the 1974 Canadian federal elections, despite the fact that most voters adamantly denied that attractiveness had any influence on their decisions.[3]

One possible explanation for such findings is that we tend to view attractive individuals as possessing numerous other positive qualities that would be considered relevant to our liking them—such as talent, kindness, honesty, and intelligence.[4] One practical (and unfortunate) result of the "attractiveness" principle is that less-attractive individuals who rely heavily on tips for income may have to work especially hard to gain customers' affection, approval, and cash.[5]

The social and monetary rewards that beautiful people garner extend far beyond those benefits; they are also more successful at eliciting compliance with their requests. Reingen and Kernen found that an attractive fundraiser for the American Heart Association collected almost twice as many donations as did less-attractive individuals.[6] That finding suggests that training programs in the hospitality industry could increase the effectiveness of trainees by including, for instance, grooming tips.

Simpatico. Similarity is another important factor that affects our liking for others. The effects of similarity—however superficial—can be quite astounding because of the instant bond that similarity can create between two people. Consider that in one study a fundraiser on a college campus more than doubled the contributions received by simply adding the phrase "I'm a student, too" to the request.[7] Just as salespeople are trained to find or even manufacture links between themselves and their prospective clients, individuals whose livelihoods depend on quick-forming rapport with their customers—such as food servers or valets—may enhance their earnings simply by pointing out a connection between themselves and their guests. "Hold the mayonnaise? Yeah, I don't eat it very often myself," and "Wow, you're from Chicago? My wife is from just south of there. She sure doesn't miss the winters" are examples of commonplace attempts to create such a bond.

Similarities need not be overtly called to the other individual's attention to obtain the desired compliance. Researchers found that a person was significantly more likely to receive a requested dime from a stranger when the two were dressed similarly than when they were not.[8] Since the majority of workers in the restaurant and hospitality industry wear uniforms, this subtle form of persuasion may be rare. As a notable exception, however, many waiters and waitresses at one popular restaurant chain wear a myriad of buttons pertaining to their interests on their uniforms, at least some of which are likely to match the backgrounds and interests of their guests.

Allies. Cooperation has also been shown to engender feelings of liking, even between parties that previously exhibited mutual animosity. Muzafer Sherif and his colleagues found that preexisting disdain between two groups of children at a camp was transformed into affection after they worked together to accomplish a necessary, mutual goal.[9] Wane would hope that food servers would start off on a better footing with their guests than the children in Sherifs study had with one another, so an air of cooperation should already exist. However, just as car salespeople "go to war" with their managers on behalf of their clients, some food servers benefit by making themselves seem particularly cooperative with their guests: "You want more chips and salsa, sir? Well, the manager normally asks us to charge extra for that, but I'll see whether I can get you some at no charge."

Our fondness for another person also depends on the extent to which we believe the other person likes us. Just ask Joe Girard, the world's greatest car salesman for 12 years in a row (according to the Guinness Book of World Records). One secret to his success may lie in a simple greeting card that he sent to all 13,000 of his former customers every single month. Although the holiday theme of each month's card differed, the text never varied. Other than his name, the only words written on the card were, "I like you."[10]

As a general rule we tend to like and to be more willing to comply with the requests of those who show they are partial to us.[11] Interestingly, one study revealed that a flatterer's laudatory comments engendered just as much liking for the sweet-talker when the remarks were false as when they were correct.[12] Thus, praise is one way for food servers to show their fondness for their clientel—and thereby to increase their tips. Having pointed that out, however, servers would be wise to proceed with caution—or better yet, with honesty—because the "praise" tactic runs the risk of backfiring if guests perceive servers' comments to be a duplicitous attempt to manipulate them.

Researchers have established that there are a number of fairly basic strategies servers can use to increase the average gratuity they receive by at least 20 percent. Many of those strategies use the simplicity of the liking principle. Squatting, smiling, and occasional touching, for example, help to build a friendly rapport, while writing "thank you" and drawing a happy face on the bill are presumably signals to patrons that they are liked and that their waiter or waitress was especially happy to serve them.[13]

It is important to note that these techniques are not necessarily additive and that the appropriateness of each strategy varies depending on a number of factors, including the type of eating establishment, the disposition of each guest, and even the gender of the food server.[14] For example, waitresses who drew smiling faces on their customers' checks significantly increased average tip size by 18 percent.[15] No significant difference was found for their male counterparts, however. If anything, the smiley-face strategy actually backfired when used by waiters. Due to perceived violations of gender-based expectations, it appears that for males, drawing a smiling face on the check may very well draw out a frowning face from the guests.

Reciprocation

A Chinese proverb states, "Favors from others should be remembered for a thousand years." The maxim succinctly emphasizes the importance of the norm of reciprocity—that we are obligated to repay others for what we have received from them—in all human societies. The norm pushes us toward fairness and equity in our everyday social interactions, our business dealings, and our close relationships, while it helps us build trust with others. At the same time, however, it also leaves us susceptible to the manipulations of those who wish to exploit our tendencies to achieve inequitable personal gains.

An informative study of the reciprocity principle and its potential to be exploited was conducted by Dennis Regan in 1971.[16] In the experiment, individuals who received a small, unsolicited favor from a stranger ("Joe") in the form of a can of Coca-Cola purchased twice as many raffle tickets from Joe as those who received no favor at all. This occurred even though the favor and the request took place one-half hour apart, and that Joe made neither implicit nor explicit reference to the original favor when he made his pitch about the raffle tickets. Interestingly, despite all that we have stated about the strong association between liking and compliance, Regan found that individuals who received a Coke from Joe made their purchase decisions completely irrespective of the extent to which they liked him. That is, those who didn't like Joe purchased just as many raffle tickets as those who did like him if they were the recipients of the gift earlier on. Thus, we see that the feelings of indebtedness caused by the power of the reciprocity manipulation are capable of trumping the effects of the liking principle.

While we have so far established that the norm of reciprocity is powerful, the principle's true power comes from its ability to create situations in which unequal exchanges take place. Regan found that on average, the Coke-bearing stranger had a 500-percent return on his investment, hardly an equal exchange at all!

Corporations and fundraisers alike have been aware of the power of reciprocity for many years, and have attempted to use those principles with the public. The Disabled American Veterans organization, a charitable group that seeks donations via fundraising letters, for example, increased its average response rate from 18 percent to 35 percent simply by enclosing a small gift in the envelope.[17] The new addition—a set of personalized address labels—caused the recipients to feel an immediate sense of obligation to repay the organization, despite the fact that the gift was inexpensive to produce and the recipients never asked for it in the first place.

Individuals in the hospitality, travel, and tourism industries are also in an appropriate position to harness the power of the reciprocity principle. After all, tipping in the U.S. service industry is supposed to be based on a reciprocity-related quid pro quo system, in which it is tacitly acknowledged that the consumer will make a more generous payment in exchange for better-than-average service. Although the strength of the actual relationship between service and tipping has been challenged,[18] it is clear that food-service workers and others who rely heavily on tips stand to benefit substantially by providing better overall service; specifically, the server should make "additional" efforts that at least slightly exceed customer expectations. For example, Lynn and Gregor showed that a bellman nearly doubled his tip earnings by adding three simple and seemingly inconsequential steps to his standard duties: He showed the guests how to operate the television and thermostat, opened the drapes to expose the room's view, and offered to bring the guests ice from the machine down the hall.[19]

Tip Tips.

The above example illustrates the success of an individual who essentially made a low-risk investment that often paid big dividends. Food servers can take advantage of the reciprocity principle, too.[20] In one study it was shown that tips were higher when the servers allowed each guest to select a fancy piece of chocolate at the end of the meal than when no offer was made. Given that finding, we can see that the proprietor of the first dine-in Chinese restaurant to serve fortune cookies at the end of the meal made a clever and profitable decision. Unfortunately for the wait staff in Chinese restaurants today, patrons have come to see a fortune cookie at the end of a meal as part of the experience—that is, as more of a right than a privilege or extra treat.

A second study by the same researchers showed that allowing the guests to select two relatively inexpensive pieces of chocolate proved even more fruitful than when the server offered just one.[21] More revealing, the server who offered two pieces was most successful when she first offered each guest one piece of candy, gestured as if she was about to leave the table, and then let each guest choose one more piece of chocolate, as opposed to when she simply allowed the guests to choose both pieces at once. It seems likely that the guests in the "1 + 1" condition assumed that the waitress was making an extra effort beyond what was normally required of her by the managers, possibly because she liked these diners more than she did most of her guests. These findings suggest that hotel housekeepers who leave mints on pillows may be the recipients of larger tips than those who do not, but that they may be even more successful by placing several extra mints on top of a personal thank you note the day before their guests check out.

Hotel managers might find the use of the reciprocity norm especially helpful when appealing to guests to reuse towels and linens in an effort to conserve energy and resources. Currently, most pleas rake approaches that either educate the guests regarding the total amount of energy necessary to clean those items daily for a year, or invoke the guests' sense of social responsibility. Some hotels emphasize the benefit to themselves in their appeals; few guests, however, will be motivated to give up their clean sheets in exchange for a clean getaway by the hotel owner with the profits gained from such compliance. Perhaps in addition to one of the other two appeals mentioned, hotel managers may achieve a higher rate of participation by extending a reciprocation-based approach in the form of a promise to donate a portion of the money saved to an environmental-conservation organization or any other cause deemed worthy. For example, the Windows of Hope Family Relief Fund, an organization that provides aid to the families of those in the food-service profession who were victims

of the World Trade Center tragedy, successfully used this principle in an event dubbed DineOut, which took place on the day exactly one month after the attack. More than 4,000 restaurants throughout the world participated and agreed to donate at least 10 percent of that evening's sales to the fund, which both raised millions of dollars for the charity and dramatically increased many of the participating restaurants' business for that night and potential beyond.

Bargaining.

While the rule of reciprocity most often takes the form of gifts or favors, a specific application of the principle is frequently used in the negotiation process, which involves reciprocal concessions. That is, if Person A rebuffs a large request from Person B, and Person B then concedes by making a smaller request, Person A will feel obligated to reciprocate this concession with a concession of his or her own by agreeing to this lesser plea.

The first author and his colleagues conducted a study to examine this phenomenon in the mid-1970s.[22] Half of the students in the experiment were approached on a college campus walkway and asked if they would agree to chaperone juvenile-detention-center inmates on a day trip to the local zoo; relatively few (17 percent) responded in the affirmative. The other half of the students were asked a different question first; a plea was made for them to volunteer as a counselor for these inmates for two hours per week for the next two years. Not surprisingly, everyone who heard this appeal refused to participate. But when this same group was then asked if they would agree to chaperone the inmates at the onetime-only day trip to the zoo, the compliance rate for this smaller request was nearly triple that of the half who were never approached with the larger plea.

Some hotel managers make use of this approach when negotiating deals for conventions and banquets by holding back in their initial offer so that they can later appear to concede to the client a number of amenities nor present in the original proposal. The assumption in this case is that the client will feel the need to reciprocate this concession by accepting the deal without making any more demands. Similarly, many managers start off the bargaining process with higher-than-desired price quotes in anticipation of having to shave off from the total charge during negotiations.

Consistency

Prior to 1998, Gordon Sinclair, the owner of a prominent Chicago eatery; was too often the victim of a common occurrence in the restaurant business: the dreaded reservation no-show. On average, approximately 30 percent of all would-be patrons who called for reservations failed to appear and never bothered to notify the restaurant with a statement of cancellation. One day, Sinclair thought of a way that might minimize the problem, so he asked his receptionists to make a few slight modifications in the reservation-taking procedure. Instead of ending their phone calls with "Please call if you have to change your plans," Sinclair instructed the receptionists to ask, "Will you please call if you have a change to your plans?" and then to pause for a moment to allow the caller to respond. Once the new strategy was implemented, the no-show-no-call rate dropped from 30 to 10 percent.

Sinclair's technique was successful because it took advantage of a fundamental human tendency to be and to appear consistent with ones actions, statements, and beliefs. This principle was illustrated in a study that found that residents who accepted and agreed to wear a small lapel pin supporting a local charity were significantly more likely to make donations to that charity during a fundraiser at a later date than those who had not been approached before the donation drive took place.[23] Those who had previously been induced to make public commitments to that charity felt compelled to act consistently with these commitments and to support it later on. Similarly, those who called for reservations and made a public commitment regarding their future actions felt obligated to be consistent with their statements and to live up to their pledges.

Dessert first.

Some shrewd servers benefit from their keen understanding of this principle by drawing out commitments from their guests regarding potential dessert purchases when the patrons (and their stomachs) are at their most vulnerable. At one restaurant in particular, immediately following the introduction, some food servers enthusiastically ask, "Who here is getting cheesecake tonight?" After each person gives an affirmative response—an action that originates not from the brain, but the belly—the server then goes through the standard procedures. Once everyone at the table is feeling full and bloated after completing the main course, their server comes back, reminds the guests of their earlier commitments in a non- threatening, jovial manner, and begins to make dessert suggestions. In the end, despite initial urges to decline—tendencies that now originate from a full belly, the brain, and the wallet—many patrons still feel obligated to say yes.

Scarcity

In the early 1970s Stephen West discovered that undergraduates' ratings of a University of Wisconsin campus cafeteria rose significantly within a nine-day span of time.[24] Surprisingly, the difference in opinion had nothing to do with a change in the quality of the eatery's food or service, but rather with its availability. Before the second set of ratings were assessed, students learned that due to a fire they would not be able to eat there for the next two weeks.

Whether it's an unavailable eating establishment, the last piece of apple pie, the only remaining convertible in a rental company's lot, the last lobster in the tank, the only hotel room with a balcony that's still vacant, or the final unclaimed blanket on an airplane, items and opportunities that are in short supply or unavailable tend to be more desirable to us than those that are plentiful and more accessible.[25] This often adaptive mental shortcut is one that naturally develops, since we learn early on in our lives that things existing in limited quantities are hard to get, and that things that are hard to get are typically better than those that are easy to get.[26]

Act now! Marketing strategists and compliance practitioners take advantage of the scarcity principle by emphasizing that their products are in limited supply, available for a limited time only, or are one-of-a-kind—often without regard to the veracity of those claims. Although assertions regarding availability status are in many cases spurious, businesses frequently employ scarcity-based marketing strategies legitimately in a genuine effort to make their offers more attractive. Lower rates for plane flights, hotel rooms, cruises, tours, and vacation packages are especially likely to be justifiably advertised as "limited time only" and "in limited supply" because such offers tend to be made for the small pockets of time when business would otherwise be slower.

Proprietors of nightclubs and restaurants can also make use of those principles by artificially limiting the availability of space. Nightclub owners, for example, commonly restrict the number of people allowed inside even though there is plenty of space for more, not due to concerns regarding maximum occupancy laws, but because the apparent inaccessibility of the clubs makes these establishments seem more desirable. Similarly, some restaurant managers limit the actual number of seats available to use the power of scarcity.

The domains in which the scarcity principle operates are not just limited to products and opportunities, but to information, as well. Research has shown that information that is exclusive is seen as more valuable and more persuasive. For instance, a former doctoral student of the first author showed that wholesale beef buyers more than doubled their orders when they were informed that a shortage of Australian beef was likely due to weather conditions overseas.[27] When those purchasers were told that the information came from an exclusive source at the Australian National Weather Service, however, they increased their orders by an astounding 600 percent. In this case the information regarding the upcoming shortages was true, but one can imagine the potential for abuse of this principle, given its dramatic effectiveness. Thus, we should question any situation in which an individual claims that he or she is supplying us—and only us—with a certain piece of information.

Up to this point we have explained the scarcity principle in terms of the mental shortcut it provides between something's availability and its quality. There is another factor at work here as well, and it is related to the idea that as opportunities become less available, we lose freedoms. According to Jack Brehm's well-supported theory of psychological reactance, whenever our freedoms are threatened or restricted, we vigorously attempt to reassert our free choice, with a specific focus on retaining or regaining exactly what was being limited in the first place.[28]

A study conducted by Reich and Robertson suggests that a sign posted next to the hotel pool that reads, "Don't You Dare Litter" or even just "Don't Litter" is likely to backfire, especially with regard to young, unsupervised children. Instead, a less-strongly phrased message that emphasizes the social norm, such as "Keeping the Pool Clean Depends on You," stands the greatest chance of success.[29] Similar results were found in another study that showed that high-threat anti-graffiti placards placed in restroom stalls were defaced to a greater extent than were the low-threat placards,[30] Thus, some proprietors of bars—whose restrooms are particularly susceptible to such vandalism—stand to benefit by replacing messages that may be perceived as hostile or threatening with more moderate pleas.

Social Validation

Earlier we described how some nightclub owners make their businesses appear more desirable by restricting the number of individuals allowed in at anyone time. The secret of the success of this policy lies not only in its manipulation of scarcity, but also in its use of the principle of social validation, which asserts that we frequently look to others for cues on how to think, feel, and behave, particularly when we are in a state of uncertainty.

Before returning to the example of a nightclub, an examination of a study done by Peter Reingen should prove informative.[31] In the experiment, a group of researchers posing as fundraisers went door-to-door to solicit donations for a local charity. As part of their request, the purported fundraisers showed homeowners a list of neighbors who had already agreed to donate to that particular cause. The experiment revealed that the likelihood of donation was positively correlated with the length of the list of names.

Just as many of those in the Reingen study decided how they would act based on the number of people they thought were engaging in the same behavior, individuals selecting where they would like to spend their time and money for an evening often use the number of others participating in a particular activity to gauge the popularity—and thus, the worthiness of that activity. Since club operators limit the rate at which the inbound traffic moves, a figurative gridlock occurs, producing long lines of people waiting for their turn to move forward and into the club. As a result, passersby view the large crowd of individuals waiting to get in as evidence of the club's value. In this case, quantity is believed to be a true indicator of quality: If that many people are willing to endure the wait to get in, it must really be worth it.

In like manner, bartenders and live entertainers sometimes seed their tip jars with a number of bills in an attempt to manipulate patrons' perceptions of the ripping norm. Consider the difference in the messages conveyed by a jar filled three-fourths of the way to the top with one- and five-dollar bills, versus a jar completely devoid of anything, except a nickel and seven pennies, a ticket stub from the movie Ishtar, and an East German Deutschmark. The former indicates that tipping—specifically, with bills—is the norm and creates a pressure for others to be consistent with this rule, while the latter suggests that tipping hasn't been the norm since the fall of the Berlin Wall.

Most companies have long understood the ability of social validation to sway our opinions and our wallets in their direction, which is why marketers spend much of their time thinking of ways to spin their products as the leading, the largest-selling, or the most popular ones out there. A common strategy is to make nebulous, lawsuit-proof claims to convey the product's popularity among the public such as, "We're the number-one cruise line in North America," even if not true by any reasonable statistical standard. Still others attempt to quantify their success, such as the McDonald's Corporation, which claims "Billions and Billions Served."

The outcomes of social validation at work are often the result of deliberate planning by businesses to harness this principle's power, but sometimes the effects of the principle fortuitously appear in unplanned and unintended domains. For example, some restaurants that are located inside malls (and airports) give pagers to their patrons and encourage them to walk around while they wait for a table to become available. Since the pagers are in most cases too large to place in one's pocket, the guests usually hold them in their hands as they stroll around the complex. Although clearly not intended to work in such a fashion, the beepers—which are being carried around by a multitude of individuals—act as a signal to others that the restaurant is a popular and worthwhile place to eat a meal. This suggests that if a mall contains more than one eating establishment with this policy, then each restaurant would make the greatest use of the principle of social validation if its pagers were both large and distinctive enough in colors, patterns, or design so that a potential customer could easily identify the restaurant to which it belonged.

Supplying individuals with specific descriptive norms—essentially, information about what other people are doing[32]—to elicit comparable behavior has proven to be successful in a number of different domains, including neighborhood household recycling.[33] Similarly, another way that hotel managers may attain greater results with their pleas for resource conservation is to inform their guests that a large number of people have already participated in the program since its inception.

Authority

On the bitterly cold afternoon of January 13, 1982, Air Florida Flight 90 sat on the tarmac of National Airport in Washington, D.C. Following a series of delays, the plane was finally cleared to take off. As the captain and the first officer were completing their last round of pre-flight checks, the following exchange took place regarding one of the systems:

First officer: God, look at that thing. That don't seem right, does it? Uh, that's not right.

Captain: Yes it is, there's eighty

First officer: Naw, I don't think that's right. Ah, maybe it is.[34]

Shortly after this conversation transpired, the plane took off. Less than one minute later. Flight 90 crashed into the icy waters of the Potomac River.

This tragedy is an example of a troubling and all-too-pervasive problem in aviation that officials in the airline industry have referred to as "Captainitis."[35] This occurs when crew members fail to correct an obvious error made by the plane's captain, resulting in a crash. In this case—and many others like it—the copilot made the calamitous decision to defer to the captain's authority. This is a clear example of the power of the principle of authority; that is, we tend to defer to the counsel of authority figures and experts to help us decide how to behave, especially when we are feeling ambivalent about a decision or when we are in an ambiguous situation. Experts also have a hand in helping us decide what we should think. For example, one study found that when an acknowledged expert's opinion on an issue was aired just once on national television, public opinion shifted in the direction of the expert's view by as much as 4 percent.[36]

Although we have seen how the principle of authority has the potential to steer us wrong, more often than not experts provide reliable information that we use as shortcuts to make good decisions. In an increasingly complex world, deferring to individuals with highly specialized knowledge in their fields is often an essential part of smart decision making.

Some research shows that we are more swayed by experts who seem impartial than those who have something to gain by convincing us.[37] For instance, we tend to believe a laminated copy of a restaurant review from a local newspaper posted in that particular restaurant's front window or entryway because we have reason to believe that food critics have no vested interest in the outcome. Our confidence in a particular expert wanes, however, when we believe that he or she is biased in some way. Although many people see a "Chefs Choice" label next to an entree listed on the menu as more appetizing because it is coming from a credible authority on the restaurant's food—the one who cooks it—a number of others would be less convinced. After all, a label like this might be subject to the biases and motivations of the restaurant managers, who could be trying to boost the sales of a less-popular choice or increase net earnings by choosing dishes with high profit margins.

Food Experts.

Some crafty servers are careful to keep these principles in mind when taking their guests orders. Their general approach is as follows: A guest asks about or orders a particular dish from the menu, to which the food server replies, as if it were a secret, "I'm afraid that is not as good [or fresh] tonight as it normally is. May I recommend instead [the names of two slightly less-expensive dishes]?" Notice that the food server accomplishes two important objectives. First, the server establishes him- or herself as an authority regarding the quality of the restaurant's food. Second, by suggesting two less-expensive entrees, the server seems to be making recommendations against the restaurant's and his or her own interests, since it could theoretically lead to a smaller bill and, subsequently, to a smaller tip. The server knows that, in actuality, the tip will probably be larger because the guests will like the server more and want to reciprocate the favor by leaving a generous gratuity. In addition, because the server now appears to be a trustworthy authority on the restaurant's food, the guests are more likely to take any other advice offered throughout the course of the meal, such as suggestions to order expensive desserts and wine that they would not have ordered otherwise.

Car-rental agencies may use a derivative of this approach, even inadvertently, when their employees offer customers extra insurance options. In many cases a customer won't be completely aware of his or her own insurance policy's car-rental coverage, so the rental agent makes some recommendations. The staff member, who is seen as the authority on car-rental insurance, says something like, "Well, you are going to have the car for only two

days, so you'd probably be wasting your money with personal-accident insurance, the personal-effects coverage, or the supplemental liability insurance. However, I would recommend that you get the partial damage waiver, which is what most people go for." (Notice the additional use of social validation.)

Knowledge of the power of the tactic used in the above two examples goes back many centuries. Francois Duc de La Rochefoucauld, a seventeenth-century French writer and moralist, wrote, "We only confess our little faults to persuade people that we have no big ones." Many companies today have implemented such a strategy in marketing. By mentioning a shortcoming of their product, they hope to appear more honest and trustworthy to their potential customers, meaning that prospective consumers will assume that the product is likely to be of high quality in all other respects. For instance, one well-known company slogan is "Avis: We're number two, but we try harder."

We have thus far examined the role of impartiality and trust in how we perceive experts and the advice they dispense. In all of the examples above, those serving their customers could be considered—at least to some degree—legitimate authorities. To what extent can people be led astray by someone who is no more an authority than they are? A study sought to answer this question by examining the connection between perceived authority and the way an individual is dressed.[38] The researchers had a 31-year-old man illegally cross the street on a number of different occasions, while they surreptitiously observed the number of pedestrians who followed him across each time. Three times more people followed the jaywalking man into traffic and across the street when he wore formal business attire than when he was dressed in a more casual work outfit. Clearly, there are dangers of various kinds inherent in allowing non-authority figures to make decisions for us—some of which could be potentially hazardous.

Some Final Considerations

It is important to emphasize that although we discussed each of the six tendencies separately for the sake of clarity, these principles often work in conjunction with one another to produce a more potent persuasive effect. For example, we mentioned earlier how some sly waiters and waitresses use their authority to gain larger tips by preventing their patrons from making an ostensibly poor entree choice. Since most customers would view this action as a favor done for them by an amicable individual, the servers also commission the power of the liking and reciprocation principles.

Be Honest.

We also feel that it is imperative to stress that knowledge of the fundamental principles of social influence does not carry with it the right to use this information unscrupulously. In trying to persuade others, one can ethically point to genuine expertise, accurate social validation, real similarities, truly useful favors, legitimate scarcity, and existing commitments. Those who do attempt to dupe or to trap others into compliance are setting themselves up for a double-barreled whammy—by breaking the code of ethics and by risking getting caught—that can produce the disagreeable consequences of diminished self-concept and diminished future profit.

References

1. See also: Harsha E. Chacko, "Upward Influence: How Administrators Get Their Way," *Cornell Hotel and Restaurant Administration Quarterly,* Vol. 29, No. 2 (August 1988). pp. 48–50.

2. Jonathan K. Frenzen and Harry L. Davis, "Purchasing Behavior in Embedded Markets," *Journal of Consumer Research,* Vol. 17 (1990), pp. 1–12.

3. M.G. Efran and E.W.J. Patterson, "The Politics of Appearance," unpublished paper, University of Toronto, 1976.

4. For a review, see: Alice H. Eagly, Wendy Wood, and Shelly Chaiken, "Causal Inferences about Communicators and Their Effect on Opinion Change," *Journal of Personality and Social Psychology,* Vol. 36 (1978), pp. 424–435.

5. For evidence of the pervasiveness of this discrepancy in the salaries of North Americans, see Daniel S. Hammermersh and Jeff E. Biddle, "Beauty and the Labor Market," *The American Economic Review.* Vol. 84 (1994), pp. 1174–1194.

6. Peter H. Reingen and Jerome B. Kernen, "Social Perception and Interpersonal Influence: Some Consequences of the Physical Attractiveness Stereotype in a Personal Selling Setting," *Journal of Consumer Psychology,* Vol. 2, No. 1 (1993), pp. 25–38.

7. Kelly R. Aune and Michael D. Basil, "A Relational Obligations Approach to the Foot-in-the mouth Effect," *Journal of Applied Social Psychology,* Vol. 24, No. 6 (1994), pp. 546–556.

8. Tim Emswiller, Kay Deaux, and Jerry B. Willits, "Similarity, Sex, and Requests for Small Favors," *Journal of Applied Social Psychology.* Vol. 1 (1971), pp. 284–291.

9. Muzafer Sherif, O.J. Harvey, B.J. White, W.R. Hood, and C.W. Sherif, Intergroup Conflict and Cooperation: The Robbers' Cave Experiment (Norman, OK: University of Oklahoma Institute of Intergroup Relations, 1961).

10. Robert B. Cialdini, *Influence: Science and Practice,* fourth edition (Boston, MA: Allyn & Bacon, 2001).

11. Ellen Berscheid and Elaine Hatfield Walster, *Interpersonal Attraction* (Reading, MA: Addison Wesley, 1978).

12. See: David Drachman, Andre deCarufel, and Chester A. Insko, "The Extra-credit Effect in Interpersonal Attraction," *Journal of Experimental Social Psychology,* Vol. 14 (1978), pp. 458–467; and Donn Byrne, Lois Rasche, and Kathryn Kelley, "When 'I Like You' Indicates Disagreement," *Journal of Research in Personality,* Vol. 8 (1974), pp. 207–217.

13. For a review, see Michael Lynn, "Seven Ways to Increase Servers' Tips," *Cornell Hotel and Restaurant Administration Quarterly,* Vol. 37, No. 3 (1996), pp. 24–29.

14. Ibid.

15. Bruce Rind and Prashant Bordia, "Effect of Restaurant Tipping of Male and Female Servers Drawing a Happy, Smiling Face on the Backs of Customers' Checks," *Journal of Applied Social Psychology* Vol. 26, No. 3 (1996), pp. 218–225.

16. Dennis T. Regan, "Effects of a Favor and Liking on Compliance," *Journal of Experimental Social Psychology.* Vol. 7 (1971), pp. 627–639.

17. Jill Smolowe, "Read This!!!!!!!!," *Time,* Vol. 136, No. 23 (November 26, 1990), pp. 62–70.

18. See: Michael Lynn, "Restaurant Tipping and Service Quality: A Tenuous Relationship," *Cornell Hotel and Restaurant Administration Quarterly.* Vol. 42, No. 1 (February 2001), pp. 14–20.

19. Michael Lynn and Robert Gregor, "Tipping and Service: The Case of the Hotel Bellman," *Hospitality Management,* Vol. 20 (2001), pp. 299–303.

20. David B. Strohmetz, Bruce Rind, Reed Fisher, and Michael Lynn, "Sweetening the Till—The Use of Candy to Increase Restaurant Tipping," *Journal of Applied Social Psychology,* Vol. 32, No. 2 (2002), pp. 300–309.

21. Ibid.

22. Robert B. Cialdini, Joyce E. Vincent, Stephen K. Lewis, Jose Catalan, Diane Wheeler, and Betty Lee Darby, "Reciprocal Concessions Procedure for Inducing Compliance: The Door-in-the-Face Technique," *Journal of Personality and Social Psychology* Vol. 31 (1975), pp. 206–215.

23. Patricia Pliner, Heather Hart, Joanne Kohl, and Dory Saari, "Compliance without Pressure—Some Further Data on the Foot-in-the-door Technique," *Journal of Experimental Social Psychology* Vol. 10 (1974), PP. 17–22.

24. Stephen G. West, "Increasing the Attractiveness of College Cafeteria Food: A Reactance Theory Perspective," *Journal of Applied Psychology,* Vol. 60 (1975), pp. 656–658.

25. Michael Lynn, "Scarcity Effects on Value," *Psychology and Marketing,* Vol. 8 (1991), pp. 43–57.

26. Michael Lynn, "Scarcity Effect on Value: Mediated by Assumed Expensiveness," *Journal of Economic Psychology,* Vol. 10 (1989), pp. 257–274.

27. Amram Knishinsky, "The Effects of Scarcity of Material and Exclusivity of Information on Industrial Buyer-perceived Risk in Provoking a Purchase Decision," Ph.D. dissertation, Arizona State University, 1982.

28. Jack W. Brehm, *A Theory of Psychological Reactance* (New York: Academic Press, 1966).

29. John W. Reich and Jerie L. Robertson, "Reactance and Norm Appeal in Anti-littering Messages," *Journal of Applied Social Psychology.* Vol. 9, No. 1 (1979), pp. 91–101.

30. James W. Pennebaker and Deborah Y. Sanders, "American Graffiti: Effects of Authority and Reactance Arousal," *Personality and Social Psychology Bulletin,* Vol. 2, No. 3 (1976), pp. 264–267.

31. Peter H. Reingen, "Test of a List Procedure for Inducing Compliance with a Request to Donate Money," *Journal of Applied Psychology.* Vol. 67 (1982), pp. 110–118.

32. Robert B. Cialdini, Raymond R Reno, and Carl A. Kallgrem, "A Focus Theory of Normative Conduct: A Theoretical Refmement and Reevaluation of the Role of Norms in Human Behavior," *Advances in Experimental Social Psychology,* Vol. 21 (1990), pp. 201–234.

33. P. Wesley Schultz, "Changing Behavior with Normative Feedback Interventions: A Field Experiment on Curbside Recycling," *Basic and Applied Social Psychology,* Vol. 21, No. 1 (1999), pp. 25–36.

34. www.avweb.com/articles/bogusepr/cvr.html. (as viewed on May 9, 2002).

35. Clayton M. Foushee, "Dyads at 35,000 Feet: Factors Affecting Group Processes and Aircraft Performance," American Psychologist, Vol. 39 (1984), pp. 885–893.

36. Benjamin Page, Robert Y. Shapiro, and Glenn R. Dempsey,

From *Cornell Hotel & Restaurant Administration Quarterly,* April 2002. Copyright © 2002 by Cornell University School of Hotel Administration. Reprinted by permission of Sage Publications.

In Search of Pro-Americanism

There has never been a more popular time to be anti-American. From Beijing to Berlin, from Sydney to São Paulo, America's detractors have become legion. But not everyone has chosen to get on the anti-American bandwagon. Where— and among whom—is America still admired, and why? Meet the pro-Americans.

ANNE APPLEBAUM

I was in London on the afternoon of Sept. 11, 2001, a day when strangers in shops, hearing my American accent, offered their cell phones in case I wanted to call home. That evening, parties were cancelled. The next day, political events were called off. An American friend who lives in London received a condolence card from his neighbors, whom he'd never met—and he was not alone. Overwhelmingly, the first British reaction to the terrorist attacks on Washington and New York was deeply sympathetic, and profoundly pro-American.

But so were the reactions of many others, across Europe and around the world. Several days after September 11, I left London and returned to Poland, where I was then living. That evening I attended a concert in a provincial city. In the foyer of the symphony hall, someone had put up a large American flag and surrounded it with candles. At the start of the concert, the conductor announced that there would be a change: Instead of the planned program, the orchestra would play only Mozart's *Requiem*, in honor of the 9/11 victims. These decisions were completely spontaneous and utterly apolitical: No one had reason to think that there would be even a single American in the audience. Within a few days, of course, a second reaction had set in. In London, a television studio audience attacked the former American ambassador on the air, accusing the United States of provoking international hatred and therefore bearing responsibility for the attacks. *The New Statesman*, an influential British left-wing magazine, ran a cover story, saying more or less the same thing. "American bond traders, you may say, are as innocent and undeserving of terror as Vietnamese or Iraqi peasants," the editors wrote. "Well, yes and no.... If America seems a greedy and overweening power, that is partly because its people have willed it. They preferred George Bush to both Al Gore and Ralph Nader." Elsewhere in Europe, then French Prime Minister Lionel Jospin had already urged the United States to be "reasonable in its response," and German Chancellor Gerhard Schröder took it upon himself to remind the United States that "we are not at war."

Since then, that initial trickle of post-9/11 anti-Americanism has grown to a flood. A Pew Research Center poll taken in February 2004, showed that 49 percent of French, 28 percent of Germans, and 12 percent of Britons had a "very" or "somewhat" unfavorable opinion of the United States. In January 2005, a poll published by the BBC showed that 54 percent of French, 64 percent of Germans, and 50 percent of Britons consider the United States a "negative influence" in the world. These numbers and others like them have spawned a mini-industry. Front-page news stories, television documentaries, and entire books have been devoted to the phenomenon of anti-Americanism, and there is no sign that interest is flagging. Earlier this year, *Newsweek International* once again put the subject on its cover, under the headline "America Leads … But Is Anyone Following?"

Given all of the attention that has been lavished upon anti-Americanism in the past four years, however, it is surprising how little analysis has been applied to that first, spontaneous pro-American reaction to 9/11, and to pro-Americanism in general. After all, the population of some countries continues to show approval of the United States, of the American president, and of U.S. foreign policy, even now. Even the most damning evidence, such as the BBC poll quoted above, also reveals that some percentage of the population of even the most anti-American countries in Europe and Latin America remains pro-American. Some 38 percent of the French, 27 percent of Germans, 40 percent of Chinese, and 42 percent of Brazilians remain convinced that the United States exerts a "positive influence on the world." Who are they?

America's Best Behavior

Anecdotally, it isn't hard to come up with examples of famous pro-Americans, even on the generally anti-American continents of Europe and Latin America. There are political reformers such as Vaclav Havel, who have spoken of how the U.S. Declaration of Independence inspired his own country's founding fathers.

There are economic reformers such as José Piñera, the man who created the Chilean pension system, who admire American economic liberty. There are thinkers, such as the Iraqi intellectual Kanan Makiya, who openly identify the United States with the spread of political freedom. At a recent event in his honor in Washington, Makiya publicly thanked the Americans who had helped his country defeat Saddam Hussein. (He received applause, which was made notably warmer by the palpable sense of relief: At least someone over there likes us.) All of these are people with very clear, liberal, democratic philosophies, people who either identify part of their ideology as somehow "American," or who are grateful for American support at some point in their countries' history.

There are also countries that contain not only individuals but whole groups of people with similar ideological or nostalgic attachments to the United States. I am thinking here of British Thatcherites—from whom Prime Minister Tony Blair is in some sense descended—and of former associates of the Polish Solidarity movement. Although Lady Thatcher (who was herself stridently pro-American) is no longer in office, her political heirs, and those who associate her with positive economic and political changes in Britain, are still likely to think well of the United States. Their influence is reflected in the fact that the British, on the whole, are more likely to think positively of the United States than other Europeans. Polish anticommunists, who still remember the support that President Ronald Reagan gave their movement in the 1980s, have the same impact in their country, which remains more pro-American than even the rest of Central Europe.

In the Philippines, 88 percent of the population has a "mainly positive" view of the United States.

In some countries, even larger chunks of the population have such associations. In the Philippines, for example, the BBC poll shows that 88 percent of the population has a "mainly positive" view of the United States, an unusually high number anywhere. In India, that number is 54 percent, and in South Africa, it's 56 percent, particularly high numbers for the developing world. In the case of the first two countries, geopolitics could be part of the explanation: India and the Philippines are both fighting Islamist terrorist insurgencies, and they see the United States as an ally in their struggles. (Perhaps for this reason, both of these countries are also among the few who perceived the reelection of U.S. President George W. Bush as "mainly positive" for the world as well.) But it is also true that all three of these countries have experienced, in the last 20 years, political or economic change that has made them richer, freer, or both. And in all three cases, it's clear that people would have reasons to associate new prosperity and new freedom with the actions of the United States.

These associations are not just vague, general sentiments either. New polling data from the international polling firm GlobeScan and the Program on International Policy Attitudes at the University of Maryland break down pro- and anti-American

sentiments by age, income, and gender. Looking closely at notably pro-American countries, it emerges that this pro-Americanism can sometimes be extraordinarily concrete. It turns out, for example, that in Poland, which is generally pro-American, people between the ages of 30 and 44 years old are even more likely to support America than their compatriots. In that age group, 58.5 percent say they feel the United States has a "mainly positive" influence in the world. But perhaps that is not surprising: This is the group whose lives would have been most directly affected by the experience of the Solidarity movement and martial law—events that occurred when they were in their teens and 20s—and they would have the clearest memories of American support for the Polish underground movement.

Younger Poles, by contrast, show significantly less support: In the 15–29-year-old group, only 45.3 percent say they feel the United States has a "mainly positive" influence in the world—a drop of more than 13 percent. But perhaps that is not surprising either. This generation has only narrow memories of communism, and no recollection of Reagan's support for Solidarity. The United States, to them, is best known as a country for which it is difficult to get visas—and younger Poles have a very high refusal rate. Now that Poland is a member of the European Union, by contrast, they have greater opportunities to travel and study in Europe, where they no longer need visas at all. In their growing skepticism of the United States, young Poles may also be starting to follow the more general European pattern.

Looking at age patterns in other generally anti-American countries can be equally revealing. In Canada, Britain, Italy, and Australia, for example, all countries with generally high or very high anti-American sentiments, people older than 60 have relatively much more positive feelings about the United States than their children and grandchildren. When people older than 60 are surveyed, 63.5 percent of Britons, 59.6 percent of Italians, 50.2 percent of Australians, and 46.8 percent of Canadians feel that the United States is a "mainly positive" influence on the world. For those between the ages of 15 and 29, the numbers are far lower: 31.9 percent (Britain), 37.4 percent (Italy), 27 percent (Australia), and 19.9 percent (Canada). Again, that isn't surprising: All of these countries had positive experiences of American cooperation during or after the Second World War. The British of that generation have direct memories, or share their parents' memories, of Winston Churchill's meetings with Franklin Roosevelt; the Canadians and Australians fought alongside American G.I.s; and many Italians remember that those same G.I.s evicted the Nazis from their country, too.

These differences in age groups are significant, not only in themselves, but because they carry a basic but easily forgotten lesson for American foreign policymakers: At least some of the time, U.S. foreign policy has a direct impact on foreigners' perceptions of the United States. That may sound like a rather obvious principle, but in recent years it has frequently been questioned. Because anti-Americanism is so often described as if it were mere fashion, or some sort of unavoidable, contagious virus, some commentators have made it seem as if the phenomenon bore no relationship whatsoever to the United States' actions abroad. But America's behavior overseas, whether support for anticommunist movements or visa policy, does matter. Here, looking at the problem from the opposite perspective is proof: People feel more positive about the United States when their personal experience leads them to feel more positive.

An Inspiration—To Some

Direct political experience is not, however, the only factor that shapes foreigners' perceptions of the United States. Around the world, there are millions of people who associate the United States not merely with a concrete political ideal, or even a particular economic theory, but with more general notions of upward mobility, of economic progress, and of a classless society (not all of which exist in the United States anymore, but that's another matter). Advertising executives understand very well the phenomenon of ordinary women who read magazines filled with photographs of clothes they could not possibly afford. They call such women "aspirational." Looking around the world, there are classes of people who are "aspirational" as well. And these aspirational classes, filled with people who are upwardly mobile or would like to be, tend to be pro-American as well.

Looking again at some relatively anti-American countries is instructional. In Britain, for example, it is absolutely clear that the greatest support for the United States comes from people in the lowest income brackets, and those with the least amount of formal education. In Britain, 57.6 percent of those whose income is very low believe the United States has a mainly positive influence. Only 37.1 percent of those whose income is very high, by contrast, believe the same. Asking the same question, but breaking down the answers by education, the same pattern holds in South Korea, where 69.2 percent of those with a low education think the United States is a positive influence, and only 45.8 percent of those with a high education agree. That trend repeats itself in many developed countries: those on their way up are pro-American, and those who have arrived are much less so.

In Europe, Asia, and South America, men are far more likely than women to have positive feelings about the United States.

In developing countries, by contrast, the pattern is sometimes reversed. It turns out, for example, that Indians are much more likely to be pro-American if they are not only younger but wealthier and better educated. And that too makes sense: Younger Indians have had the experience of working with American companies and American investors, whereas their parents did not. Only in recent decades have Indians been full members of the international economy, and only in recent years was India fully open to foreign investment. The poor in India are still untouched by globalization, but the middle and upper-middle classes—those who see for themselves a role in the English speaking, America-dominated international economy—are aspirational, and therefore pro-American. In fact, some 69 percent of Indians with very high incomes think the United States is a mainly positive influence; 43.2 percent of those with average incomes feel that way; and only 29.6 percent of those

with very low incomes are likely to think of American influence as positive.

Taking a slightly different tack, it is possible to identify countries in which the country as a whole could be described as aspirational, rather than one particular class. Here it is worth looking at Spain, Portugal, and Italy. Again, none of these countries can be described as overwhelmingly pro-American as can, for example, the Philippines. Spain in particular has registered very high opposition to the American war in Iraq and even overturned a government on those grounds. But these countries are slightly different from others in Europe, not only because, unlike France and Germany, they follow the Canadian and British pattern—the less educated and the least wealthy are relatively pro-American—but also because all three have, at some point in the past several years, elected notably pro-American leaders. Former Prime Ministers José María Aznar in Spain and Pedro Santana Lopes in Portugal as well as current Prime Minister Silvio Berlusconi in Italy made close relations with the United States a central part of their foreign policies, and all three sent troops to fight in Iraq.

True, their support for the United States following 9/11 is more directly explained by European politics: Like Britain and Denmark, the three southern European countries dislike the increasing Franco-German dominance of Europe, and see the American presence in Europe as an important counterweight. But it is also the case that Italy, Spain, and Portugal are Europe's nouveau riche: All have grown wealthier in the past generation, and all still have large numbers of "upwardly mobile" citizens. That too might help explain their politicians' fondness for the United States, a country that is, by older European standards, a true arriviste. This same phenomenon might also account for the persistence of a surprising degree of popular pro-Americanism in such places as Vietnam, Indonesia, Brazil, and, again, the Philippines: They're getting richer—like Americans—but aren't yet so rich as to feel directly competitive.

Portrait of a Pro-American Man

There is, finally, one other factor that is associated almost everywhere in the world with pro-Americanism: In Europe, Asia, and South America, men are far more likely than women to have positive feelings about the United States. In some cases, the numbers are quite striking. Asking men and women how they feel about the United States produces an 11 percent gender gap in India, a 17 percent gender gap in Poland, and even a 6 percent gap in the Philippines. This pattern probably requires more psychological analysis than I can muster, but it's possible to guess at some explanations. Perhaps the United States is associated with armies and invasions, which historically appeal more to men. Perhaps it is because the United States is also associated with muscular foreign policy, and fewer women around the world are involved in, or interested in, foreign policy at all. Perhaps it's because men are more attracted to the idea of power, entrepreneurship, or capitalism. Or it may just be that the United States appeals to men in greater numbers for the same intuitive reasons that President George W. Bush appeals to men in greater numbers, whatever those are.

Although not as surprising as some of the other numbers, this gender gap does help us come up with a clearer picture of who the typical pro-American might be. We all know the stereotypes of the anti-Americans: The angry Arab radical, demonstrating in the mythical Arab street; or the left-wing newspaper editor, fulminating at Berlin dinner parties; or the French farmer, railing against McDonald's. Now, perhaps, we should add new stereotypes: The British small businessman, son of a coal miner, who once admired Thatcher and has been to Florida on holiday. Or the Polish anticommunist intellectual, who argued about Reagan with his Parisian friends in the 1980s, and disagrees with them about the Iraqi war now. Or the Indian stockbroker, the South Korean investment banker, and the Philippine manufacturer, all of whom have excellent relations with their American clients, all of whom support a U.S. military presence in their parts of the world, and all of whom probably harbor a fondness for President Bush that they wouldn't confess to their wives. These stock figures should be as firmly a part of the columnists' and commentators' repertoire as their opponents have become.

They also matter, or should matter, to the United States. These people, and their equivalents in other countries, are America's natural constituents. They may not be a majority, either in the world or in their own countries. But neither are they insignificant. After all, pro-Americans will vote for pro-American politicians, who sometimes win, even in Europe. They can exert pressure on their governments to support U.S. foreign policy. They will also purchase American products, make deals with American companies, vacation in the United States, and watch American movies.

They are worth cultivating, in other words, because their numbers can rise or fall, depending on U.S. policies. Their opinions will change, according to how American ambassadors conduct business in their countries, according to how often the U.S. secretary of state visits their cities, and according to how their media report on American affairs. Before the United States brushes away Europe as hopelessly anti-American, Americans should therefore remember that not all Europeans dislike them. Before Americans brush off the opinion of "foreigners" as unworthy of cultivation either, they should remember that whole chunks of the world have a natural affinity for them and, if they are diligent, always will.

ANNE APPLEBAUM is a columnist and member of the editorial board of the Washington Post.

From *Foreign Policy*, Vol. 149, July-August 2005, pp. 32, 34-40. Copyright © 2005 by the Carnegie Endowment for International Peace. Reprinted with permission. www.foreignpolicy.com

UNIT 5
Social Influence

Unit Selections

Key Points to Consider

- What is social influence? What are conformity, compliance, and cooperation? What social conditions stimulate each of these?

- Do first impressions unduly influence us? How so? What does research say about the effects of first impressions? How long does it take us to form a first impression upon meeting a stranger?

- What was Zimbardo's mock prison demonstration? What did he find? How does torture of Muslim prisoners mimic Zimbardo's research? Or does it?

- What is the foot-in-the-door technique? How does it induce compliance? How is the norm of reciprocity related to compliance and social influence?

Student Web Site

www.mhcls.com/online

Internet References

Further information regarding these Web sites may be found in this book's preface or online.

AFF Cult Group Information
http://www.csj.org

Center for Leadership Studies
http://www.situational.com

Social Influence Website
http://www.influenceatwork.com/

Bob obtained an associates degree in business and achieved high honors at his community college. Upon graduation, he was immediately hired by a life insurance company. Bob's job was to sell insurance policies to clients. The policies supposedly accrued value as the client matured, leaving the buyer or beneficiary with a tidy sum of money upon the death of the insured person.

Bob considered himself very lucky; he came from a large extended family and had made many friends at the college. He even considered some of the faculty and staff at the college to be more than mere acquaintances. As Bob began his new life as a salesman, he was quite sure that he "had it made in the shade", as he told his brother, because there were so many potential customers already available.

Bob soon discovered that selling anything to friends and family is difficult. In fact, his initial sales were so low that he had to call strangers and go door-to-door in an attempt to sell more policies. "What's going wrong?", Bob wondered. "I thought this would be so easy."

In the previous unit (Unit 4, Attitudes), you learned that for a myriad of reasons persuasion is very difficult. Related to the issue of persuasion is the topic of social influence. *Social influence* is like social pressure—obvious or subtle—to make others submit to our wishes. There are three major types of social influence studied by social psychologists: conformity, compliance,

and obedience in respective order of their degree of directness, from least to most direct.

Conformity, the subtlest type of social influence, was one of the first social influence phenomena studied by social psychologists. *Conformity* is the result of subtle pressure to do or think like others. Solomon Asch in the 1940s and 1950s examined the effects of group pressure on an individual. In the prototype of his research, participants were asked to judge which line—A, B, or C—was closest in length to comparison line D. Unbeknownst to the real subject, other participants were allies of the researcher. After giving several appropriate answers, the confederates started providing the wrong answers. Asch waited to see what the real participant would do: submit to group pressure and give the wrong answer or stick to the correct answer in the face of perceived coercion. Asch discovered that many Americans are conformists, something that the average American probably might vehemently deny.

A second type of social influence is *compliance*, in which someone makes a direct request for you to do something. When Bob tried to sell his insurance policies to friends, he was really making a request that apparently his friends did not feel compelled to fulfill. There are many compliance techniques which are well-known by salespeople like Bob. Social psychologists, via their research, have also noted that public compliance sometimes occurs in the absence of private acceptance.

A third form of social influence is *obedience*. Obedience takes place when one person responds to a direct order by a second person who is usually an authority figure. Obedience is a issue that permeates many settings, including military life, laws and public policies, prisoner behaviors, and other real world phenomena. Some of the classic studies in social psychology have demonstrated all too well that many individuals follow orders without much thought. In fact, some individuals when asked to harm someone else will do so just because a powerful person asked them.

Social influence is a very important issue in the fabric of community life. We will explore it with three different articles. The first article is about impression management. Other people try to influence us with the impressions they leave on us. Lea Winerman reviews historic as well as contemporary studies on impression formation and impression management.

With this introduction, we next turn to a specific form of social influence—obedience to authority. In a shocking scandal, American soldiers were charged with prisoner abuse at Abu Ghraib Prison. Clive Cookson reviews Zimbardo's mock prison experiment and uses his review as a platform to demonstrate why such behavior is not necessarily surprising.

The final article in this unit by Michael Lovaglia describes another social influence technique known as the foot-in-the-door effect employed to gain compliance. Using this method, the requester first issues a small request, followed by a larger (and more desired request). This technique is remarkably effective, albeit quite manipulative.

'Thin Slices' of Life

Psychologists are finding that our first impressions of others can be remarkably accurate—but also can fail us.

Lea Winerman

For the past several years, bars and restaurants around the country have been hosting a new type of dating ritual. At events organized by companies like HurryDate and 8MinuteDating, dozens of eligible singles meet up for a round of lightning-quick "dates"—sometimes as short as three minutes each—with 10 or 20 other people. At the end of each date, participants mark on a card whether or not they'd like to see the other person again.

When the evening is over, event staff correlate the results and provide contact information to any mutually interested pair.

The speed-dating concept rests on a simple premise: that a few minutes can be plenty of time to size a person up and evaluate compatibility.

It's no secret that people often judge each other based on immediate intuitions. We make split-second judgments of strangers all the time: When a student decides to drop a class based on minutes of a professor's teaching or when we meet someone at a party, our first impressions count. For as long as parents have admonished their children "don't judge a book by its cover," most of us have been doing just that.

In the past 15 years, though, researchers have become interested in trying to systematically answer the questions: How much can those fleeting first impressions really tell us? How much of people's personality is it possible to intuit within a few seconds, or minutes, of meeting them?

The psychologists are finding that in some cases our social intuition is indeed amazing—we can sometimes pick up a remarkable amount of information about a person's personality or skills in just a few seconds. At other times, though, we can all be social dunces—oblivious to these nuances.

Old Questions, New Answers

Until the mid-1980s, psychologists mostly weren't interested in answering those questions at all, says Nalini Ambady, PhD, a social psychologist at Tufts University. Researchers wanted to study the processes by which people judged others, not how accurate those judgments were, she explains.

Dave Kenny, PhD, a psychologist at the University of Connecticut, was one of the first researchers to look into the accuracy of first impressions. In a 1988 study, he examined whether people's first impressions of strangers' personalities matched up with the strangers' self-ratings, scores on personality tests or other measures of personality.

Kenny based his research on a 1966 study by two University of Michigan psychologists, Warren Norman, PhD, and Lewis Goldberg, PhD. In that study, which was published in the *Journal of Personality and Social Psychology* (Vol. 4, No. 6), Norman and Goldberg asked University of Michigan students to rate their peers' personalities on the first day of class, before the students had had a chance to interact. They found that the students' ratings of one another tended to agree with their self-ratings, particularly on the traits "sociable" and "responsible."

This result was, Kenny says, overlooked for more than 20 years, until he and his colleagues picked up and extended the work in 1988.

"At the time, it was so counterintuitive and not what people expected—even Norman and Goldberg hadn't expected it—that they downplayed it," Kenny says. "That's just not where the field was at the time."

In his study, which appeared in the *Journal of Personality and Social Psychology* (Vol. 55, No. 3), Kenny divided more than 250 students in a psychology class into groups of four. After making sure none of the group members knew each other and had not had a chance to talk, the students rated all members of their group, including themselves, on five factors that each represented a personality trait. The factors were sociable (representing extroversion), good-natured (representing agreeableness), responsible (representing conscientiousness), calm (representing emotional stability) and intellectual (representing culture). Again, as in the Norman and Goldberg study, the strangers' first impressions of each other correlated significantly with self-ratings for the traits "extroversion" and "conscientiousness."

Self-ratings, however, don't necessarily provide accurate descriptions of everyone's personality.

"Look at all those movie stars who say they're really shy," Kenny points out. "Plenty of people think they're less extroverted than they really are."

With this in mind, he and colleague Maurice Levesque, PhD, conducted another study, also published in the *Journal of Personality and Social Psychology* (Vol. 65, No. 6). This time, groups of four strangers rated each other on the five personality traits. Then, the strangers met in pairs and were videotaped talking to each other. Later, judges watched the extensive videotapes and rated each subject's extroversion, based on the amount of time he or she spent talking, the number of arm movements and other factors. Again, the strangers' first-impression ratings of extroversion strongly correlated with people's rated levels of ext level extroversion as seen on the videotape.

In the 14 years since Kenny's studies, numerous researchers have replicated and expanded his results. Overall, the studies have indicated that people are good at sensing a stranger's level of extroversion or sociability. Some have suggested people can sense the other four traits as well (particularly conscientiousness and agreeableness), but those results are much more mixed, and the conclusions murky.

This makes sense, says Ambady, who analogizes personality to the layers of an onion. "The layers near the top," she says, "are the easiest to pick up."

Extroversion may be the most obvious of personality traits, but there are some researchers who think that other, more internal traits can also be visible.

Frank Bernieri, PhD, a social psychologist at Oregon State University, agrees that extroversion is the most easily visible trait. But, he notes, that fact could be partially explained by the experimental designs used by most researchers in the area.

"The contexts in which we've asked people to evaluate others are social interactions where, of course, extroversion would be the most obvious trait," he says.

In fact, Bernieri firmly believes that all aspects of personality are embedded in behavior.

To test this, he and his student Amber McLarney-Vesotski, PhD, now a psychology instructor at Alpena Community College in Michigan, devised situations in which they believed the other four aspects of a person's personality would become more apparent. In one, for example, a stranger asks the subject his or her opinion of a Rorschach-blot-like painting—a task designed to determine the subject's degree of openness. In another, the subject plays a game with an obstinate, irritating stranger—designed to determine neuroticism or calmness and emotional stability. The researchers then showed 10-second video clips of these situations to a panel of college-student judges, and the judges were able to predict all five aspects of the subjects' personalities at a better-than-chance level.

Beyond Personality

Sometimes, we aren't looking to divine someone's overall personality or intelligence based on a first impression; we simply want to know how good they will be at a particular skill or set of skills, like teaching. Tufts psychologist Nalini Ambady has found that students, for example, are surprisingly good at predicting a teacher's effectiveness based on first impressions. She creates these first impressions with silent video clips of teachers—clips she calls "thin slices."

In a 1993 study published in the *Journal of Personality and Social Psychology* (Vol. 64, No. 3), Ambady and a colleague videotaped 13 graduate teaching fellows as they taught their classes. She then took three random 10-second clips from each tape, combined them into one 30-second clip for each teacher and showed the silent clips to students who did not know the teachers. The student judges rated the teachers on 13 variables, such as "accepting," "active," "competent" and "confident." Ambady combined these individual scores into one global rating for each teacher and then correlated that rating with the teachers' end-of-semester evaluations from actual students.

"We were shocked at how high the correlation was," she says. It was 0.76. In social psychology anything above 0.6 is considered very strong.

Curious to see how thin she could make her slices before affecting the student judges' accuracy, Ambady cut the length of the silent clips to 15 seconds, and then to six. Each time, the students accurately predicted the most successful teachers.

"There was no significant difference between the results with 30-second clips and six-second clips," Ambady says.

In a later experiment in the same study, she cut out the middleman—the global variable—and simply asked students to rate, based on thin-slice video clips, the quality and performance of the teachers. Again, the ratings correlated highly with the teachers' end-of-semester evaluations. Ambady also replicated her results with high school teachers.

Of course, one could argue that the true measure of a teachers' effectiveness is not what their students say about them, but how much those students learn. Ambady, acknowledging this, has tried to measure whether students actually learn more from teachers who give a first impression of effectiveness.

In an as-yet-unpublished study, she videotaped groups of five participants, one of whom was randomly assigned to be the "teacher." The teacher spent time preparing a lesson, and then taught students a mathematical language in which combinations of letters represent different numbers, as in 10=djz or 3=vfg. The students took a test at the end of the lesson to measure their knowledge of the new language. Then, as before, strangers watched 10-second video clips of the teachers and rated them on the same variables as in the first study. The thin-slice ratings of teacher effectiveness, Ambady says, significantly predicted students' performance on the test.

"Students learned more from teachers who were seen in the thin slices as having the qualities of a better teacher," Ambady says.

A Cautionary Note

Do all of these studies, then, suggest that people should simply trust their gut instincts and, when meeting strangers, go with their first impressions? Is what you see really what you get?

Well, it's not quite that simple. First, there is the inevitable counterexample. First impressions can, sometimes, be dreadfully wrong. Serial killer Ted Bundy was a seemingly normal, attractive man who fooled not only his victims, but two women with whom he had long-term relationships, Bernieri points out.

"We can be distracted by the most visible and salient aspects of a person's personality," Bernieri says. Physical attractiveness and charisma (a large part of which is extroversion) can hide the inner layers of the onion.

"I believe that personality is truthfully encoded within the first 30 seconds of behavior," Bernieri says, "but that doesn't mean we're going to accurately get all of it all the time." Dave Kenny agrees. "People can certainly make inaccurate judgments, sometimes tragically so," he says.

It's also important to remember that all first-impression studies deal with aggregates, not individuals. "When we talk about accuracy, we're not looking at single judgments, we're looking at the average of a lot of judgments," says Kenny.

When a study indicates that people, in the aggregate, can judge whether strangers are extroverts or introverts at better-than-chance levels, it does not mean that everyone is equally good at doing so. "People do vary in their social intelligence," says Bernieri. "There are dunces among us who just never get it."

Even people with high "social intelligence" might vary in their ability to accurately judge a stranger, depending on something as simple as how they feel when they are making the judgment.

In a 2002 study published in the *Journal of Personality and Social Psychology* (Vol. 83, No. 4), Ambady found that people who were induced into a happy mood by watching a scene from a happy movie were able to more accurately predict a teacher's effectiveness from a thin-slice video clip than were people who were induced into a sad mood. Ambady thinks that this might be because people who are in a sad mood don't trust their snap judgments—they might come to the same immediate first impression as someone in a happy mood, but then doubt themselves and start second-guessing.

Making and judging first impressions is also, of course, a two-way street. The judge, the judged and the rapport and similarity between the two all affect the accuracy of a first impression. Few studies have specifically looked at cross-cultural first impressions, but research on nonverbal sensitivity has shown that people from similar cultures are better at judging each others' personalities based on nonverbal cues than people from very different cultures.

"An extroverted Chinese person might look completely different than an extroverted American," says Bernieri. "But even though they might not seem loud and talkative to us, they'll be louder and more talkative than another Chinese person. The key to judging someone accurately is that you have to be able to compare within cultures, not between cultures."

Overall, then, psychologists have accumulated a decade-and-a-half's worth of evidence that people are, collectively, better than you might think at deciphering a stranger's personality and abilities based on a first impression. But individually, it seems, we're still on our own.

"I would never give anyone a blanket statement that they should trust their first impressions, or not," says Nalini Ambady. "That's too dependent on the person, the context of the first impression, everything."

From *Monitor on Psychology*, Vol. 36 (3), March 2005, pp. 54-56. Copyright © 2005 by American Psychological Association. Reprinted by permission. No further distribution without permission from the American Psychological Association.

Abu Ghraib Brings a Cruel Reawakening

The recent revelations of abuse at the Iraqi jail have had far-reaching effects on the victims of past violence, says Clive Cookson.

CLIVE COOKSON

The shocking pictures from Abu Ghraib prison in Baghdad have come as a double blow to the doctors and therapists working with torture survivors in 170 rehabilitation centres around the world. On top of their dismay that US forces could treat prisoners so cruelly, staff have been overwhelmed with requests for help over the past few weeks, as the images and descriptions reawaken horrific memories in people who have been tortured.

"The events at Abu Ghraib have had a profound effect on the people we care for," says Allen Keller, director of the Bellevue/New York University Program for Survivors of Torture. "The pictures have been very disturbing and retraumatising for many of our patients, who have been suffering a recurrence of nightmares and other sleeping problems."

Gill Hinshelwood, senior examining doctor at the Medical Foundation for the Care of Victims of Torture in London, reports a similar surge in symptoms. "Some of my Iraqi clients (who suffered under Saddam Hussein's regime) have had a resurgence of nightmares; others are coming back with aches and pains," she says. "Many are obsessed with what is going on."

Yet staff at rehabilitation centres say some good will come out of the horror of Abu Ghraib, if it increases awareness of how to diagnose and treat torture. At present the medical community pays insufficient attention to what Prof Keller calls a global public health problem. "Around 400,000 torture survivors have come to live in the US alone," he says.

Richard Mollica, director of the Harvard Program in Refugee Trauma, agrees. "Despite routine exposure to the suffering of victims of human brutality, healthcare professionals tend to shy away from confronting this reality," he says. "Clinicians avoid addressing torture-related symptoms of illness because they are afraid of opening a Pandora's box: they believe they won't have the tools or time to help torture survivors once they've elicited their history."

Even the damage caused by physical brutality may be hard for a general practitioner to spot. For instance, falanga, in which the soles of the feet are beaten with rods, may leave no outward sign of damage even though internal damage to nerves and tendons can make walking excruciatingly painful.

Diagnosing and treating the psychological legacy of torture is even more difficult. All the attention given by psychology researchers to post-traumatic stress disorder has not necessarily helped those working with torture victims.

"This emphasis on PTSD has obscured the reality that the most common mental illness diagnosed in torture survivors is depression—often a serious and socially debilitating condition associated with serious medical consequences," says Prof Mollica. The depression caused by torture and extreme violence can be distinguished from other forms of depression by the intense and repetitive nightmares that accompany it.

Dr. Hinshelwood says this depression is best described as "a deep and long-term sense of passivity and pessimism". She adds: "People—and men in particular—are even more depressed if their torture includes rape or sexual abuse."

Sexual abuse was, of course, a prominent feature of the American mistreatment of prisoners at Abu Ghraib. Although there has been some debate about whether this amounted to torture, organisations working with torture victims, such the Medical Foundation in London, state unequivocally that it did. And they say that US interrogators have used an unacceptably harsh sort of coercion—sometimes called "stress and duress" or "torture lite"—systematically, not only in Iraq, but also at Guantanamo Bay in Cuba and Bagram air base in Afghanistan.

In response to the shock of many Americans, who asked why "seemingly normal" US soldiers could behave so sadistically in Iraq, the American Psychological Association put the professional view that "most of us could behave this way under similar circumstances".

Two famous experiments proved the point more than 30 years ago. First Stanley Milgram at Yale University showed that most normal volunteers would follow the instructions of an authority figure—a scientist in a white coat—and give other people a series of increasingly powerful electric shocks, even though they elicited agonising screams.

Then Philip Zimbardo set up a simulated prison at Stanford University, in which students were randomly selected to play the roles of prisoners and guards. Prof Zimbardo believes his experiment has striking similarities with Abu Ghraib: "I have exact, parallel pictures of naked prisoners with bags over their heads, who are being sexually humiliated by the prison guards, from the 1971 study."

According to the APA, these two classic experiments—and other psychological studies in the laboratory and in the field—go a long way to explaining what went wrong at Abu Ghraib. Any prison is an environment in which the balance of power is so unequal that normal people can become brutal and abusive, unless the institution has strong leadership and transparent oversight to prevent the abuse of power.

Abu Ghraib not only lacked such leadership, but also had another ingredient for abuse: an ethnic, cultural, linguistic and religious gulf between guards and prisoners. Robert Jay Lifton, psychiatry professor at Harvard Medical School, says people are naturally predisposed to distrust or even attack others whom they categorise as outsiders.

The Abu Ghraib guards allegedly thought they were following orders from intelligence officers. However, this sort of mistreatment is counterproductive even from the narrow viewpoint of intelligence gathering, says Vince Iacopino, research director of the Massachusetts-based group Physicians for Human Rights.

"Unfortunately, some may assume that physical and psychological coercion techniques serve to 'soften up' detainees for interrogation," says Dr Iacopino. "In our experience it is clear that physical and psychological forms of coercion or ill treatment or torture do not provide accurate and reliable information. On the contrary, by inflicting physical and/or emotional pain, perpetrators reduce their victims to a point that precludes obtaining reliable 'information'—and victims frequently falsely confess to whatever they think interrogators want to hear."

Prof Mollica points out that perpetrators can also be psychologically damaged by their experience and requests to treat them can put doctors in a difficult position.

"In medicine we have the controversial concept of 'medical neutrality', which holds that the doctor has an obligation to treat someone regardless of political situation or the circumstances that made them ill," he says. "But if a perpetrator of torture comes to you for therapy, what do you do?"

There are clearly far more victims than perpetrators of torture—and most are more seriously damaged. But there is hope, as psychologists around the world gain experience in helping torture victims to recover their mental health, first through proper diagnosis and then through a mixture of therapy and, if appropriate, treatment with antidepressants or other drugs.

"Twenty years ago there was a widespread impression that survivors of extreme violence could never really recover from the experience," says Prof Mollica. "Now we are much more optimistic."

While many of the world's torture victims suffer renewed torment through the images of Abu Ghraib, their long-term prospects may be becoming slightly brighter.

From *Financial Times*, July 2, 2004, pp. 13. Copyright © 2004 by Financial Times Syndication. Reprinted by permission.

Persuasion: What Will It Take to Convince You?

Michael J. Lovaglia
University of Iowa

Persuasion by Inches

Have you noticed that big building projects always seem to cost much more than was originally estimated? No matter how high the original estimate, the project almost always ends up costing millions, sometimes billions of dollars more. It is not that accurate estimates are too difficult to make. If accuracy were the problem, then the original estimate would be too high only about half the time and too low the rest. The error here is too one-sided to be accidental. Taxpayers, certainly, do not like having to pay additional billions of dollars for a new highway. Yet contractors continue to give low estimates then ask for increases along the way. No matter how annoyed people get, the practice continues. Social psychology explains why.

An initially low estimate is a powerful persuasive tool, whether you are buying a car or the government is buying a highway. When people are shopping for a car, they are often strongly attracted to one more expensive than they can easily afford. The salesperson's job is to persuade them to buy a car that will strain but not break their financial resources. Suppose you are shopping for a car. You have made a firm resolution to spend no more than $12,000. At one dealership, however, you are attracted to one that costs $16,000. You realize this is out of your price range and start to move on. At that point, salespeople are taught to ask, "Would you be interested if I could get the price of this car down to $10,900?"

There are two reasons for the salesperson's question. First, notice that it is a leading question. He did not say that he could get the price reduced by $5,000. He only asked if you would be interested. However, by asking the leading question, he implied that a price of $10,900 was at least possible. Second, you would probably answer yes to the question. (A good salesperson would already have found out that it was in your price range.) Once you agree that you are interested in that car at that price, you have made a commitment. We are all taught to keep our commitments. It is difficult for people to stop and reverse themselves once they have started something. By agreeing that you would be interested, you committed yourself in a small way to buying that car. If the salesperson is good at his job, then you will buy that car and be happy with it, but the price you pay will be closer to $16,000 than it will be to $10,900. Had the salesperson accurately estimated that you might be able to buy the car for

$14,900, you would not have been interested. To the salesperson's credit, you probably like your new car more than any you could have found for less than $12,000. On the other hand, your financial situation may be shaky for a while because of it.

Cialdini, Cacioppo, Bassett, and Miller (1978) investigated why giving a very low initial cost estimate is such a persuasive technique. Researchers called people on the phone to ask them to participate in a psychology study. Half of the people were told immediately that the study would take place at 7 A.M. The early hour made it unlikely that many people would agree to participate. The rest of the people were told about the study and that it would take place at a variety of times during the day. Then all of the people in the study were asked if they would like to participate first. Only after people said that they were interested in participating were they told that they would be needed at the 7 A.M. session of the study. Researchers wanted to know if getting people to agree that they were interested in the study first, before they knew how early they would have to arrive, would increase the number who eventually showed up for a 7 A.M. study.

Cialdini and colleagues (1978) showed that giving a low initial cost estimate effectively persuaded people to participate in their study. When researchers told subjects up front that the study would take place at 7 A.M., less than a third (31 percent) agreed to participate. However, when researchers got people to agree that they were interested in participating before telling them what time the study would take place, more than half (56 percent) agreed to participate. But would more people really show up for the study after having had a chance to consider their decision? Saying yes on the phone is one thing. But if people actually get out of bed in the morning to come to a study, then they really must have been persuaded. Cialdini and colleagues found that giving a low initial cost estimate was even more effective when it came to changing people's actual behavior. When researchers forthrightly told people about the 7 A.M. study time, less than a quarter (only 24 percent) actually showed up for the study. However, when researchers got people to agree that they were interested before telling them about the early starting time, more than half (53 percent) showed up on time. Almost all of those who agreed to participate actually appeared. Once we commit in even a small way to participating in a project, we are unlikely to drop out, even if the cost of continuing increases dramatically along the way.

Mentioning a Little to Get a Lot

Charitable organizations that solicit contributions face an interesting dilemma. If they ask for large amounts of money from people, then more people will say no. However, if solicitors ask for small amounts, more people will say yes, but rarely will large amounts be given. How can solicitors convince as many people as possible to contribute without decreasing the average amount that each person gives?

Cialdini and Schroeder (1976) found a solution to the problem faced by charitable organizations that required adding only five words to the end of a request for a contribution: "Even a penny will help." In their study, research assistants solicited funds for the American Cancer Society. All used a standard request for funds: "Would you be willing to help by giving a donation?" However, half the research assistants added the sentence "Even a penny will help." Almost twice as many people contributed when they were told that even a penny would help. More surprisingly, their contributions were no smaller than the contributions given by those who were not told that a penny would help. Researchers concluded that mentioning the penny legitimized a small donation, making it more difficult for people to say no. However, because the amount suggested—a penny—was so small, people did not use it to estimate the size of a reasonable donation.

Who Will Help You?

Most people realize that if you want people to help you, it is good to help them. The practice of giving and receiving gifts is universal in human culture. From a very young age, we learn to give things to people in the hope that we will get something else in return. We have no guarantee that the people we give gifts to will give us gifts in return, or give us gifts of equal value. However, we are all taught that giving gifts is a good thing and that we should not keep too close an account of who gives us what in return. The idea is that by giving gifts we start to form lasting relationships with people. For example, in my large extended family, it would not be practical for everyone to give everyone else a Christmas present. We would all be broke and spend the whole year shopping. Instead, we draw names and everyone gives one other person a gift. I give my aunt a scarf. My nephew gives me a sweater. Almost no one gets a gift from the person to whom she or he gave one. Nonetheless, gift giving works to maintain good relationships among people. Although I do not see my relatives often, I feel comfortable asking for help from my aunt or nephew when I need it. A good way to persuade people to help you is to start by giving them a gift, doing them a favor, providing some small service.

Salespeople and charitable organizations know something more surprising about giving gifts and doing favors. Another good way to persuade people to help you in the future is to get them to do you a small favor first. This is the opposite of how we are taught the social world works. We grow up thinking that we can expect about as much help from other people as we are willing to give in return. If someone does us a favor, then that person should be less likely to do us another favor right away. It is as is if we have withdrawn some of our credit in the goodwill bank account. We will not be eligible for another favor until we make a deposit by helping someone else. But there are good social psychological reasons to continue helping someone we have already helped.

Recall from a previous section that once people commit to a project, they are likely to continue with it although the cost involved inches steadily upward. We feel the same way about people, but to a greater degree. It is important to us to keep and maintain our personal relationships. So once we have committed to helping a person, we are likely to agree to help the next time we are asked. We will continue to help even though the second favor requested of us is bigger than the first. Have you noticed that if you send a small donation to a charitable organization, they will send you requests for more money every couple of months? The more money that you give, the bigger and more frequent are the requests that follow. Aren't charities worried that they will wear out donors with repeated, escalating requests for money? Apparently not.

Freedman and Fraser (1966) showed that by getting a person to do you a small favor first, you increase the chance that she will do you a bigger favor later. To test this surprising idea, researchers contacted people by telephone. Researchers wanted to find out how many people would agree to a big favor that researchers would ask of them. Researchers requested that they be allowed to enter people's homes and for several hours catalog their personal belongings. Most people would be hesitant to grant such a request over the phone. Half the people contacted were first asked for a small favor. Researchers asked people merely to answer a few questions for a consumer survey. Then, three days later, researchers called back with the big request. The rest of the people in the survey were only asked if they would agree to the big favor, allowing researchers to come to their homes and make a list of their possessions. Would more people agree to let researchers come into their houses after they had first agreed to the small favor of answering a few survey questions?

Getting people to agree to doing a small favor first had a major effect (Freedman and Fraser 1966). When people were first asked to answer a few survey questions, more than half (53 percent) later agreed to let researchers come into their homes. (Imagine how successful you would be if you called strangers and asked if you could come over and go through their stuff for a couple of hours!) In contrast, when only the large request was made, just 28 percent, a little more than a quarter, agreed to let researchers come into their homes. By asking for a small favor first, researchers nearly doubled the percentage of people who would agree to grant their major request.

The lesson is clear. If you will need someone's help in the future, get that person to help you in small ways now, thus increasing the likelihood of agreement to an important request later. Note that as with the low initial bid technique of the previous section, getting people to do you a small favor requires no pressure. Persuasion starts to occur before a request is ever made. The more people help you, the more people will want to continue helping you. They become committed to your success.

The technique of gaining people's commitment by getting them to do you a favor can work for customers as well as salespeople. The one time in my life where it seemed that I got an especially good deal on a used car is an example. I had moved back to California from Idaho. I was working, selling furniture, but I no longer needed the truck that I had used to deliver waterbeds and hot tubs. I had decided to go back to school and needed a reliable car. A few blocks from the furniture store where I worked was a car lot where a national car rental company sold the rental cars to the public after they were a couple of years old. One day, as I drove by the lot, a Mustang convertible caught my eye. What better car to drive to college in California? After driving by that car several days in a row, I wanted it badly. I stopped by the lot after work to find out more about the car. With tax and license, the total price would be a little over $9,000. The salesperson told me that I would have to get my own financing. Also, the company had a strict "one-price" policy. Car prices were not negotiable. The best price for each car was plainly marked on it. No haggling. While this seems a fair way to sell cars, it leaves the dealer firmly in control of the ultimate price that customers pay. I decided to try a little social psychology to get the price down.

I returned to the car lot prepared to buy the car. Nonetheless, I let the salesperson go through his entire sales routine. I drove the car a second time. I let him tell me at length about the company's one-price policy that was such a benefit for customers because it relieved them of the anxiety of negotiating. We practiced putting the convertible top up and down. I asked him to show me how to operate everything on the car. I asked him to help me make sure that everything worked. In social psychological terms, I was gaining his commitment to sell me that car. Every time I asked him to help me with something, to show me something, he became a little more committed to completing the sale. The only thing salespeople have to work with is their time. While he was spending time with me, he could not work with anyone else. The more time he spent with me, the more important it was to him that our meeting result in a successful sale.

Eventually he suggested that we go to his desk to "get some information" from me. He was getting impatient. At his desk, we talked about price again. He repeated the company's no-exceptions one-price policy. No negotiating. I told him that I had already arranged a loan and that the price seemed reasonable. However, $9,000 was more than I was prepared to pay. Instead, I gave him a cashier's check for $8,000 and asked him to sell me the car for that amount. He laughed a little nervously at that point. He knew I was serious—$8,000 is a lot of money and a cashier's check has more impact than a personal check. He told me that he could not do it. It was against company policy to lower the price. I paused for what seemed like a long time, then said, "OK, let's go look at the car again." More time commitment from the salesperson.

I had already noticed a small tear in the outer shell of the convertible top, perhaps half an inch long. It seemed minor but might get worse. I pointed it out to the salesperson and asked how much a new convertible top would cost. He said that he did not know. I smiled and said, "Why don't we find out?" Back at his desk, I went through the yellow pages and asked him to call convertible top repair shops. More commitment; he was doing me a favor. We eventually agreed that a new convertible top would cost about $1,200 dollars. I suggested that we subtract the price of a new top from the price of the car and complete the sale. He said that he couldn't do that. I asked him what he could do. He said he would have to find out. Would he do that for me, please? More commitment. I told him that I was taking my new girlfriend to lunch and would be back in an hour or two.

The salesperson had spent a substantial amount of his working day with me. He had nothing to show for it yet. He was commit-

ted. When my girlfriend and I got back from lunch, the salesperson agreed to drop the "nonnegotiable" price by $500. After a little more bargaining, I wrote him a personal check for about $150 to add to the cashier's check of $8,000 that I had already given him. I had saved about $1,000. By getting him to help me repeatedly in small ways, I gained his commitment to help me in a bigger way. When I asked him to help me get the price I wanted, he found it difficult to refuse. As for the tear in the convertible top, a tube of vinyl repair goo fixed it nicely. Many good things got started that day. I drove to college with the top down and made it to graduation. Then I married my girlfriend.

To Persuade Them, Let Them Persuade You

Cialdini, Green, and Rusch (1992) put an interesting twist on the idea that people want to help people who have helped them. Because people feel the need to reciprocate, researchers proposed that if someone has persuaded you to do something in the past, then that person will be easier for you to persuade to do something in the future. Salespeople experience the situation often. When I sold furniture to a person in business, I felt obligated to use their services as well. When a family that owned a dry cleaners bought both dining room and living room furniture from me, I started taking my clothes to their cleaners, although it required driving across town.

Cialdini and colleagues (1992) proposed that a person would be persuaded more easily by someone who had yielded to her arguments on some unrelated topic. That is, once a person has persuaded you of something, that person will feel the need to reciprocate, return the favor, by letting you persuade her on some other issue. Researchers first asked people to give their opinions about the minimum drinking age. For half the people in the study, a research assistant at first disagreed but then admitted to bring convinced by their arguments. For the rest of the people in the study, the research assistant remained unconvinced by their arguments. Then in the second part of the study, the research assistant's opinions about whether to require comprehensive exams in college were given to people. Researchers wanted to find out if people would agree more with the researcher after the researcher had agreed with them about the drinking age issue.

After the research assistant was persuaded by their arguments, people were more likely to be persuaded by the research assistant on a different topic. Cialdini et al. (1992) were correct. Researchers asked people to estimate how much their attitude had changed after listening to the research assistant's arguments. When the research assistant had agreed with people's opinions on the earlier topic, people reported that on average their attitudes had been changed 27 percent by the research assistant. That is, the research assistant's brief statement of her or his opinions had been highly persuasive. However, when the research assistant had been unconvinced by people's opinions on an earlier topic, people reported that on average their attitudes had been changed only 6 percent by the research assistant.

To get people to agree with you, first agree with them. The implications go well beyond any individual negotiations. These research results suggest a personal style that will increase your success in social life. Most arguments people get into are silly because the outcome doesn't matter very much. But those minor disagreements set the stage for major conflict when an important issue does arise. When I was in high school I loved to argue. I practiced and studied ways to construct a sound argument. I believed that logic would prevail. It was important for me to be right and for people to acknowledge that I was right. An implication that I had not considered was that by acknowledging I was right, people would be admitting that they were wrong. People do not like to admit that they are wrong.

For several years I argued every chance I got. It puzzled me, however, that no matter how brilliant my argument, the people I argued with never seemed to be convinced. After a particularly heated argument, I would review it in my mind for days to make sure I had been right. Yet later I would find that the person I had argued with remained unconvinced. My logic was sound enough but my social psychology was weak. I had ignored the importance of reciprocity in human relationships. To convince somebody of something, it helps to let that person convince you of something else first. And because the outcome of most arguments doesn't matter very much, it pays to agree with other people most of the time. Save your arguments for situations where the outcome is truly important to you. Agree with people unless you have a good reason not to. Let them convince you. That was exactly the opposite of the way I had approached my relationships with people. I wanted to show people that I was right. So I argued about everything. But people were not convinced. A better way to approach the people in your life is to agree with them as much as possible. Show them how right they are. Then, when an issue comes up that is very important to you, you will be more likely to convince them that on this rare but important occasion, you might be right.

Status as the Most Subtle Way to Persuade

Most of this chapter has described effective, subtle, and sometimes devious techniques that salespeople and organizations use to persuade people. You have seen how you can benefit from using similar techniques when you need to persuade someone to help you…. Some people do not seem to need such techniques to persuade others. The doctor merely tells you that an operation is necessary and you agree to let her remove part of your body. Why doesn't your doctor need the subtle techniques of persuasion commonly used by salespeople?

The answer is *status*. Your status is your standing within a group based on your prestige, the respect that other group members give you. Doctors have high status in our society. They are respected, honored. The magic of high status is that people will try to find out what it is you want them to do, and do it for you, without your ever having to make a request. I noticed myself doing this just last week. By watching my diet and starting to exercise, I recently lost most of the excess weight I had carried around for years. I have more energy and feel healthier. Then

last week it occurred to me that I should go to my doctor for the first time in years to get a physical examination. Why should I want to go to the doctor now that I feel great? I usually avoid going when I am sick. What I really wanted was my doctor's approval. I wanted the doctor to tell me what a good job I had done getting rid of that extra body fat. Her approval is important to me because of her high status. My doctor never told me I should lose weight, although she did hint last time that a little exercise would help. However, I thought my doctor would approve if I lost weight. Thus the opinion I expected her to have influenced my behavior without her having to express that opinion directly. When people have high status, their opinions count.

Techniques of persuasion can be highly effective in specific situations, but to wield real influence, a person needs high status….

Further Reading

Of General Interest

Bacharach, S. B., Lawler, E. J. (1984). *Bargaining*. San Francisco: Jossey-Bass.

Cialdini, R. B. (1993). *Influence: Science and practice*. New York: HarperCollins.

Damasio, A. R. (1994). *Descarte's error: Emotion, reason, and the human brain*. New York: Grosset/Putnam.

Pfeffer, J. (1992). *Managing with power: Politics and influence in organizations*. Boston: Harvard Business School Press.

Recent and Technical Issues

Axsom, D., Yates, S., & Chaiken, S. (1987). Audience response as a heuristic cue in persuasion. *Journal of Personality and Social Psychology, 53*, 30–40.

Fleming, J. H., Darley, J. M., Hilton, J. L., & Kojetin, B. A. (1990.) Multiple audience problem: A strategic communication perspective on social perception. *Journal of Personality and Social Psychology, 58*, 593–609.

Frey, K. P., & Eagly, A. H. (1993). Vividness can undermine the persuasiveness of messages. *Journal of Personality and Social Psychology, 65*, 32–44.

Gorassini, D. R., Olson, J. M. (1995). Does self-perception change explain the foot-in-the-door effect? *Journal of Personality and Social Psychology, 69*, 91–105.

Kruglanski, A., Webster, D. M., & Klem, A. (1993). Motivated resistance and openness to persuasion in the presence or absence of prior information. *Journal of Personality and Social Psychology, 65*, 861–876.

Petty, R. E., Schumann, D. W., Richman, S. A., & Strathman, A. J. (1993). Positive mood and persuasion: Different roles for affect under high- and low-elaboration conditions. *Journal of Personality and Social Psychology, 64*, 5–20.

Vorauer, J. D., & Miller, D. T. (1997). Failure to recognize the effect of implicit social influence on the presentation of self. *Journal of Personality and Social Psychology, 73*, 281–295.

Zarnoth, P., & Sniezek, J. A. (1997). The social influence of confidence in group decision making. *Journal of Experimental Social Psychology, 33*, 345–366.

From *Knowing People: The Personal Use of Social Psychology*, 2nd ed., chapter 6, pp. 118-125. Copyright © 2007 by Michael Lovaglia. Reprinted by permission of Rowman & Littlefield.

UNIT 6
Social Relationships

Unit Selections

Key Points to Consider

- How does one facilitate the forming of positive social relationships with others of different ethnicities and cultures?

- How has technology (e.g. the Internet) affected our social relationships with others? Has it increased or decreased our social relationships?

- What do same-sex intimate relationships have in common with heterosexual unions? How do they differ?

- How could you improve the quality of your social relationships?

- What are the differences between love and liking? What social factors play a role in your answer?

Student Web Site

www.mhcls.com/online

Internet References

Further information regarding these Web sites may be found in this book's preface or online.

American Association of University Women
http://www.aauw.org

Coalition for Marriage, Family, and Couples Education
http://www.smartmarriages.com

GLAAD: Gay and Lesbian Alliance Against Defamation
http://www.glaad.org

The Kinsey Institute for Reasearch in Sex, Gender, and Reproduction
http://www.indiana.edu/~kinsey/

Marriage and Family Therapy
http://www.aamft.org/index_nm.asp

The National Organization for Women (NOW) Home Page
http://www.now.org

The Society for the Scientific Study of Sexuality
http://www.ssc.wisc.edu/ssss/

As children, Amanda and Yolanda were attracted to each other because their names rhymed. Not only did they attend the same elementary school, but they soon discovered that their interests were the same. Both girls were tomboys. Amanda loved animals and so, too, did Yolanda.

In high school, although the girls often found themselves in different classes, they still spent much of their free time together—so much that both of their mothers teased them about being twins. The two young women agreed that they ought to attend the same college and be roommates. Other students at the high school could not help but notice their unique bond and soon referred to them as the "Anda" twins.

In their junior year of high school, Yolanda and Amanda became interested in and attracted to the same new student, a young man named Ty. At first, Ty relished in the attention that the women bestowed on him. "And why not?," he mused to himself. "I'm good-looking, smart, and athletic." Ty quickly became one of the most popular boys at the school.

Amanda and Yolanda soon found themselves skirmishing over Ty. Amanda wanted to sit next to him at lunch, but so, too, did Yolanda. Amanda claimed that Ty invited her to watch him play basketball, and Yolanda became jealous and confronted Ty. On the other hand, Yolanda waited in the library for Ty to appear, and they would sit together. Upon discovering them, Amanda would storm out of the library.

The rivalry between the girls became so intense that their grades suffered. Other students began to ridicule them. Ty soon felt the sting of other students' scorn and decided to forego his friendship with Amanda and Yolanda. Of course, Yolanda and Amanda blamed each other for Ty's disinterest. In self-defense, Ty soon started dating an entirely different young woman, Sara, who was not friends with either of the "Anda" twins.

The friendship between Amanda and Yolanda never repaired itself. Each of them applied to and was accepted at different universities so went their separate ways. Years later at their tenth high school reunion, Yolanda and Amanda were still not speaking to one another. And what of Ty? He and Sara attended the reunion as a happily married couple.

How and why do people become friends or lovers? What types of people are attracted to one another, whether the same or opposite sex? These questions and others relate to social relationships—the topic of this unit.

The unit contains two subunits—one on interpersonal relationships such as friendships and the second on intimate relationships such as marriage. We will commence with the topic of interpersonal relationships.

In "Beyond Shyness and Stage Fright: Social Anxiety Disorder," details about social anxiety disorder are revealed. Shyness is one thing; social anxiety disorder is another. *Social anxiety disorder* is more than temerity about interacting with others. It can dramatically alter the sufferer's life. Fortunately, the disorder is treatable.

In a companion article, "Linking Up Online," author Rebecca Clay discusses loneliness—a likely companion of shyness. Lonely individuals feel that their need to be with others is unmet. Some social psychologists have suggested that the Internet offers intriguing opportunities to interact with others. Social psychologists are examining communities established solely on the Internet in chat rooms and elsewhere.

Our attention next turns to intimate and romantic relationships such as dating and marriage. Three articles disclose interesting information on close relationships.

The first article is entitled "Isn't She Lovely?" by Brad Lemley. Lemley discusses the power of beauty over observers. Beautiful and handsome people tend to be perceived as superior to everyone else. What makes us perceive someone is attractive or unattractive forms the heart of this article.

As mentioned above, some individuals are using the Internet to meet others. The Internet has burgeoned with people looking not only for friendship but also for dates and mates. This web-wide universe is changing how people meet, date, and find love, according to Karen Gold, author of the next article.

This unit concludes with one additional article on intimate relationships. Marriage, or at least lifetime commitment to another, is the single most intimate relationship of all. Close relationships like marriage, however, can sour. Romantic attraction can and does elicit strong emotions – both positive and negative. In "The Marriage Savers," Richard Corliss and Sonja Steptoe present information about couples therapy and research on its effectiveness.

Contagious Behavior

SHIRLEY WANG

On a fall morning in 1998, a teacher at a Tennessee high school noticed the smell of gas in her classroom and soon felt dizzy and nauseous. Some of her students then reported feeling ill as well, and they were transported by ambulance to a nearby hospital. As concerned staff and students watched them go, some of them started feeling sick, too.

That day, 100 people showed up in the emergency room with symptoms they believed to be associated with the exposure to gas at the school. But the illnesses could not be explained by medical tests. Extensive environmental tests conducted at the school concluded that no toxic source could be the cause, according to results published in the *New England Journal of Medicine*.

What occurred was real illness, although not caused by germs or fumes, according to Timothy F. Jones, lead author of the paper and deputy state epidemiologist at the Tennessee Department of Health.

"It was not an infection, but it was certainly transmitted," Jones said.

It was a phenomenon known as *mass psychogenic illness*, in which symptoms are passed from person to person among people who are visible to one another.

"You get sick because you see someone else getting sick," said Jones.

Mass psychogenic illness is an extreme example of the more general phenomenon of contagious behavior: the unconscious transmission of actions or emotions from one individual to another.

Our everyday lives are filled with examples of how we "catch" even subtle emotions and complex behaviors, such as happiness and anger, bulimic symptoms, and depression, from other people. Psychologists, anthropologists, and neuroscientists have studied how and why such contagion occurs.

Contagion appears to involve both biological and social processes. It is pervasive, and yet we are often unaware of the influence of other's emotions and behaviors on our own—which is particularly striking because the consequences of contagious behavior can be significant.

Do You Feel Like I Feel?

The contagious quality of mood and emotion has been perhaps the most widely studied of all the different forms of contagion. People are extremely good at picking up on other people's emotions—both negative and positive—without consciously trying.

APS Fellow and Charter Member Elaine Hatfield, professor at the University of Hawaii and a pioneer in the study of emotional contagion, became interested in the topic when wondering how clinicians were being affected by their patients' moods, particularly when patients were not articulating their feelings.

In the lab, she and her colleagues studied whether people catch the emotions of others, and to what extent they pay attention to explicit, verbal descriptions of feelings compared to nonverbal facial and postural cues as their source of emotional information.

In one study, participants watched a videotape of a target person describing a positive or negative memory. The tape continued to show the target as he viewed his own taped description. The target expressed surprise at the emotion showing on his face, and he felt very different than how he appeared on tape.

The participants then assessed the target's emotion, as well as their own. Hatfield and her team found that the participants rated the target's emotion largely based on his words. That is, if the target said he felt much sadder than he looked, participants rated him as quite sad.

However, when participants rated their own emotion, they were much more similar to the emotion expressed by the target's nonverbal cues. It appeared that the participants' mood was affected by the target—but they responded to his displayed emotion, not his stated one.

This suggests that if we think we begin to feel an emotion when interacting with another individual, it's quite possible that person is also feeling the same emotion.

"We're reflecting what they feel," Hatfield said. "If we feel irritated at a client, the client is irritated at us or something else."

Thomas Joiner, professor at Florida State University, has found that not only are negative moods contagious, but depressive symptoms—such as sleep problems and thoughts about death—also appear to spread over time.

Unfortunately, Joiner said, it's not a two-way street. While it would be wonderful if an individual's nondepressed mood could ease the mood of a depressed person, the direction of contagion doesn't usually go that way.

Mood Rings

Still, the good news is that emotional contagion can be used constructively to promote behavior change.

Sigal Barsade, associate professor at the University of Pennsylvania, brought groups of participants into a lab to complete a simulated managerial exercise. The group included a research confederate who was either positive or negative, and who exerted high or low energy.

Examining both participants' self-reported mood and independent video coders' ratings, Barsade found that individuals grouped with the positive mood confederates became more positive over time, while those in the other condition became, as expected, more negative.

"We aren't emotional islands," said Barsade. "People are sort of walking mood conductors and we need to be aware of that."

The positive-emotional-contagion groups experienced increased cooperation, less conflict, and improved perceived performance compared to those in the negative condition.

In fact, the group emotional experience was so powerful that in some groups the participants ended up exchanging phone numbers after the study, according to Barsade.

"It's critical that people understand emotional contagion is not just a self-contained phenomenon that ends with the 'catching' of the emotion," she said. "This contagion then influences our cognition and behavior—and we often don't even realize the process is happening."

Mechanisms of Contagion

There are multiple paths through which contagion can occur, and several processes interact to produce the phenomenon.

On a biological level, we are built to mimic others. Recent research shows that humans, like monkeys, have certain types of neurons that fire when simply watching someone else carry out an action, even when we ourselves are not doing the same thing. Such neurons help prime us to understand and identify with other people.

Say, for instance, you are sitting at home intently watching a football game on television, and you really like the team's quarterback. When he makes a long pass, you would likely show some electrical signal in our own arm as well, according to APS Fellow and Charter Member John Cacioppo, director of the Center for Cognitive and Social Neuroscience at the University of Chicago. You've identified with that player and, as part of that, you have an actual physiological reaction to his action.

"Synchrony is necessary in social animals," said Cacioppo, a past member of the APS Board of Directors. "This synchrony is fundamental to not only having that emotional back and forth, but also to basic correspondence. One really does resonate physiologically."

Physiologic mimicking occurs with facial expressions, and is often so subtle that we ourselves don't even realize we're doing it, but it is important to our social interactions.

Laugh and the World Laughs With You

"Essentially the bottom line is that people, in almost a monkey-see monkey-do kind of way, are wired up to imitate others' faces and voices," said Hatfield.

Such seems to be the case with laughter, considered a particularly contagious behavior. Laughter is highly stereotyped—it is generally similar across people—and hard to interrupt mid-stream. Once it starts, it has a tendency to run its course to completion, according to Robert Provine, a professor at the University of Maryland-Baltimore County.

We appear to have an almost automatic laugh reaction in response to others' laughter—think laugh tracks on television shows—and it's hard to laugh while alone. His research shows that we are 30 times more likely to laugh in the presence of other people than by ourselves.

In fact, laughing alone can serve as an alert to others that a person may not be in touch with reality, according to Provine. Imagine the villain on television who laughs maniacally to himself. Generally we are much better at inhibiting laughter than producing it on command.

"Laughter is a social relationship between people," said Provine. "The essential ingredient is another person."

Imitating others' behavior is only part of what makes emotion contagious. According to one theory, we infer our emotion from our expressions and behaviors. We smile, therefore we must be happy.

Alternatively, we may use the emotions and behaviors of others as a means of social comparison, to gauge how we should be feeling and acting in a particular situation.

Matching others may also be one way to show empathy, or just "I like you," according to Hatfield.

Researchers have brought couples into the lab and observed their behavior. Those who like each other behave more similarly. Conversely, "if a couple is out of sync, they don't like each other as much," said Cacioppo.

Infection or Selection

One question that arises in conducting work on contagion among individuals who already know each other, such as roommates or couples in a romantic relationship, is whether individuals who are already more similar to each other in affect tend to seek each other out—a selection effect—rather than truly being "infected" by the other person's moods.

Both processes appear to occur: People do tend to seek out those who are more similar to them, but they are also influenced by others' emotions and actions.

"People who are similar will think and interpret the information similarly," said Thomas Sy, assistant professor at California State University Long Beach, who studies how leadership status affects group emotions and productivity. The same action, like crossing one's arms, might be interpreted very differently by people who work in a corporate setting versus a clinical one.

In Sy's studies on group behavior, he finds that not only do individuals' moods shift toward their leader, but that the variation in emotion between group members decreases over time. Individuals end up feeling not just better or worse, but more similar to each other.

"It makes a lot of sense that if I want to be part of this group, I will think and act and behave—and in this case feel—like the rest of my group members," said Sy.

Our experiences over the years also help build scripts, or routines, that we tend to then perform in a particular situation. When a script is enacted, it triggers a set of behaviors with a high degree of automaticity, according to Raymond Novaco, professor of psychology and social behavior at the University of California, Irvine, whose research focuses on anger and aggression.

In the case of road rage, repeated exposure to other people's behavior on the roads may form a script that aggression is appropriate when driving.

"The contagion notion is diffusion," said Novaco. "Part of the spreading is that it makes salient various scripts for aggressive behavior on the roadways."

But road "rage" may be a misnomer. Anger—an emotion—can be a trigger for aggression, defined as an act intended to harm, but need not be present for the behavior to occur.

This is likely to be the case in general: Changes in emotion may impact behavior but behavioral contagion can occur without emotional contagion.

Yet the very basic underlying process between emotional and behavioral contagion may be the same. Our facial muscles twitch, and we infer that we are happy. We see someone looking ill, we feel our internal bodily sensations—perhaps our heart is beating rapidly or we're breathing shallowly because we're anxious about the situation—and we interpret these signs that we are about to pass out because we also took in the gas fumes.

Communicable Dis-ease

There are a number of personality and situational factors that both strengthen and weaken the likelihood that contagion will occur.

Although we are wired to respond to other people, there is also a tremendous amount of variability in individuals' ability to transmit their emotions to others. More outgoing and expressive individuals tend to be better transmitters, or more successful at having you feel what they feel, according to Hatfield.

Think about the person in the office who is hard to feel happy around when he or she is upset. That person may not criticize or denigrate you, but you might start feeling miserable nonetheless. Chances are this individual communicates feelings very

strongly, perhaps by scowling or sighing deeply. By noticing that person's mood, consciously or not, one may be more likely adopt it.

This expressiveness can be taught, said Cacioppo. And, we can still be affected even if we know that people are intentionally trying to influence us, as in the case of cheerleaders at a pep rally.

On the other side, more easily infected people tend to be more observant of others, and may be of lower status in the situation.

"You have to actually pay attention to the person to be able to clue in to what's going on," said Barsade.

There are also conditions under which contagion is more likely to spread.

Disinhibitory situational factors, such as anonymity and ease of escape, can increase the likelihood of a behavior's occurrence—especially those that are typically considered inappropriate, like aggression, which people typically try to minimize—according to Novaco.

Despite the pervasive nature of contagion, we often don't attribute changes in mood or behavior to the people around us. Barsade explicitly asks her participants after experiments what factors they think might have influenced their performance. Hardly anyone mentions the moods of other people.

Awareness may be important, however.

"The person who's aware can start to control it, modulate it," said Sy. "Some people are able."

If parents have a bad day at work, they may be able to consciously tell themselves they shouldn't let the interaction with the boss affect how they treat their children.

"If they're not aware of that and they go home and they don't know it's the boss that caused it, they might shift that blame to their kids," said Sy. "When it's conscious, you have a better chance of controlling how it's going to impact you."

However, we are surprisingly bad at controlling emotions, according to Hatfield; and even when we can modulate our moods we tend to be able to do so only in spurts.

Hatfield cites the example of being with family during the holidays. You can remain pleasant with your family and resist feeling irritable for a couple of hours, but after that you'll probably be yearning for the hotel where you can take a nap.

However, if one continues to remain in that stressful situation, "people start getting tired, and then start mimicking other people's behavior. It's a surprisingly short time."

Rooted in biology but supported by social and situational factors, contagion—whether of nausea or of happiness—is a powerful process and an almost unavoidable fact of being human.

On the other hand, if people want to avoid being infected, what's an easy way to try and foil the attempt?

"Be oblivious," said Hatfield. "Fifteen-year-old boys are great at it."

SHIRLEY WANG is a freelance writer in New Haven, Connecticut.

From *APS Observer*, Vol. 19, no. 2, February 2006. Copyright © 2006 by American Psychological Society. Reprinted by permission via the Copyright Clearance Center.

Competent Jerks, Lovable Fools, and the Formation of Social Networks

New research shows that when people need help getting a job done, they'll choose a congenial colleague over a more capable one. That has big implications for every organization—and not all of them are negative

Tiziana Casciaro and Miguel Sousa Lobo

One of management's greatest challenges arises from a natural tension inherent in every organization. People are brought together because they have the variety of skills that, in concert, are needed to carry out a complex activity. But this variety inevitably leads to fragmentation of the organization into silos of specialized knowledge and activity.

It's an understatement to say that resolving this tension is crucial to success in today's knowledge-based and collaborative business environment. How do you ensure that relevant information gets transferred between two parts of an organization that have different cultures? How do you encourage people from units competing for scarce corporate resources to work together? How do you see to it that the value of a cross-functional team is more, not less, than the sum of its parts?

The answers to such questions lie not in an examination of organization charts but largely in an understanding of informal social networks and how they emerge. Certainly, organizations are designed to ensure that people interact in ways necessary to get their jobs done. But all kinds of work-related encounters and relationships exist that only partly reflect these purposefully designed structures. Even in the context of formal structures like cross-functional teams, informal relationships play a major role.

In this article, we offer somewhat surprising insights into how informal networks take shape in companies—that is, how people choose those they work with. We then discuss some of the benefits and drawbacks of this phenomenon and offer ways for managers to mitigate its negative effects and leverage the positive ones.

How We Choose Work Partners

When given the choice of whom to work with, people will pick one person over another for any number of reasons: the prestige of being associated with a star performer, for example, or the hope that spending time with a strategically placed superior will further their careers. But in most cases, people choose their work partners according to two criteria. One is competence at the job (Does Joe know what he's doing?). The other is likability (Is Joe enjoyable to work with?). Obviously, both things matter. Less obvious is how much they matter—and exactly how they matter.

To gain some insight into these questions, we studied four organizations selected to reflect a wide range of attributes—for-profit and nonprofit, large and small, North American and European. We asked people to indicate how often they had work-related interactions with every other person in the organization. We then asked them to rate all the other people in the company in terms of how much they personally liked each one and how well each did his or her job. (For a more-detailed description of the studies, see the sidebar "Who Is Good? Who Is Liked?")

These two criteria—competence and likability—combine to produce four archetypes: the competent jerk, who knows a lot but is unpleasant to deal with; the lovable fool, who doesn't know much but is a delight to have around; the lovable star, who's both smart and likable; and the incompetent jerk, who ... well, that's self-explanatory. These archetypes are caricatures, of course: Organizations usually—well, much of the time—weed out both the hopelessly incompetent and the socially clueless. Still, people in an organization can be roughly classified using a simple matrix. (Indeed, with relative ease you can probably populate the four boxes depicted in the exhibit "Whom Would You Choose?" with the names of people in your own company.)

Our research showed (not surprisingly) that, no matter what kind of organization we studied, everybody wanted to work with the lovable star, and nobody wanted to work with the incompetent jerk. Things got a lot more interesting, though, when people faced the choice between competent jerks and lovable fools.

Ask managers about this choice—and we've asked many of them, both as part of our research and in executive education programs we teach—and you'll often hear them say that when it comes to getting a job done, of course competence trumps likability. "I can defuse my antipathy toward the jerk if he's competent, but I can't train someone who's incompetent," says the CIO at a large engineering company. Or, in the words of a knowledge management executive in the IT department of a professional services firm: "I really care about the skills and expertise you bring to the table. If you're a nice person on top of that, that's simply a bonus."

But despite what such people might say about their preferences, the reverse turned out to be true in practice in the organizations we analyzed. Personal feelings played a more important role in forming work relationships—not friendships at work but job-oriented relationships—than is commonly acknowledged. They were even more important than evaluations of competence. In fact, feelings worked as a gating factor: We found that if someone is strongly disliked, it's almost irrelevant whether or not she is competent; people won't want to work with her anyway. By contrast, if someone is liked, his colleagues will seek out every little bit of competence he has to offer. And this tendency didn't exist only in extreme cases; it was true across the board. Generally speaking, a little extra likability goes a longer way than a little extra competence in making someone desirable to work with.

Of course, competence is more important than likability in some people's choice of work partners. But why do so many others claim that to be the case? "Choosing the lovable fool over the competent jerk looks unprofessional," suggests a marketing manager at a personal products company. "So people don't like to admit it—maybe not even to themselves."

Yet is such a choice unprofessional? Is it a mistake to steer clear of the competent jerk when we have a job to do? Sometimes, yes. We may forgo the opportunity to tap a competent jerk's knowledge and skills because we don't want to deal with his patronizing, brusque, or otherwise unpleasant attitude—which is arguably a modest price to pay for the valuable assistance he can provide. We may even shun the jerk simply to deny him the satisfaction of lording his knowledge over us.

But there are justifiable reasons to avoid the jerk. Sometimes it can be difficult to pry the needed information from him simply because he is a jerk. And knowledge often requires explanation to be useful—you might, for instance, want to brainstorm with someone or ask follow-up questions—and this kind of interaction may be difficult with a competent jerk. Furthermore, in order to learn, you often have to reveal your vulnerabilities,

which also may be difficult with the competent jerk—especially if you are afraid of how this might affect your reputation in his eyes or in the eyes of others to whom he may reveal your limitations. By contrast, the lovable fool may be more likely to freely share whatever (albeit modest) information or skills he has and, without any intention of gaining an advantage, help others put them to use.

The Likability Bias: Pros and Cons

Some people are liked pretty much universally. In other cases, likability is relative: One person's friend may be another one's jerk. This is because our positive feelings can result from people's inherent attributes or from the situations we find ourselves in with them. This distinction is important to keep in mind as we try to manage this tendency of people to favor likability over competence in their choice of work partners.

Social psychologists have long known that we like people who are similar to us; people we are familiar with; people who have reciprocal positive feelings about us; and people who are inherently attractive, either in their appearance or their personality—that is, they are considerate, cheerful, generous, and so on. Each of these sources of personal likability can contribute, for better or worse, to the formation of an informal network.

For Better. That we like people who are similar to us—for example, in their background, their beliefs, their interests, their personal style—is one of the most solidly documented findings in the social sciences. After all, these people make us feel good because they reaffirm the validity of our own characteristics and attitudes. But there's a business, as well as a psychological, benefit when similar people choose to work together: Their similar values, ways of thinking, and communication styles help projects flow smoothly and quickly.

Benefits also result when we work with people who aren't necessarily similar, but are familiar, to us. When you launch into a task with those you already know, you don't waste a lot of time figuring out what to expect from them or explaining what you mean every time you say something. In addition, because you are usually relatively comfortable with individuals you know, you're likely to be more accepting of their differences.

We also like to work with people who seem to like us. This can produce a virtuous circle in which everyone is more open to new ideas, more willing to help, and more trusting than would typically be the case. A similarly positive environment can be created if you work with someone who has an attractive personality—someone who is empathetic, for example, or generous. You know that you'll have liberal access to her intellectual resources, however abundant or modest they may be, and are likely to reciprocate by freely sharing your own knowledge.

And a person who is physically attractive? Well, in such a case, the job you do together can be, in some indefinable way, simply a bit more enjoyable than usual.

For Worse. One of the greatest drawbacks of choosing to work with similar people is the limited range of perspectives that a homogeneous group often brings to bear on a problem. A diverse collection of colleagues—whatever the tensions and misunderstandings that arise because of their differences—provides an array of perspectives that can lead to truly innovative approaches to accomplishing a task.

Even groups composed not of similar souls but merely of people who are very familiar with one another miss the chance to integrate the fresh perspective that new players bring to a project. Working with the same old colleagues can also dampen debate: People may hesitate to challenge or reject a bad idea put forward by someone they know and like.

There is also an obvious downside when we gravitate toward people because they like us or because they are pleasant to work with. These individuals, however terrific they may be, aren't necessarily the ones most suited to tackling the task at hand. The required expertise or knowledge may lie elsewhere, in someone who in fact doesn't like us that much or isn't attractive.

One other danger of people working primarily with those they like: They may simply have a good time and get nothing done. An experienced venture capitalist recalls the case of a very capable manager who hired individuals based on his personal affinity with them. "His team had a great time going out for a beer, but the quality of their work was seriously compromised," says the dismayed investor. "If you keep hiring only people you like, you can kill a company."

The objective, therefore, is to leverage the power of liking while avoiding the negative consequences of people's "affect-based choice"—to use the psychological term—of work partners. Keep in mind that we're not talking here about formal work relationships: You work with your boss and your direct counterparts in other divisions whether you like them or not. We're talking only about people's choices of informal, though work-related, interactions. Even so, that doesn't preclude executives from doing some things that will positively affect those interactions and the often task-crucial informal networks that grow out of them.

We offer three basic approaches. First, where possible, manufacture liking in critical relationships. Second, carefully position universally likable people so they can bridge organizational divides. Third, to put it bluntly, work on the jerks. The first tactic acknowledges that whether you like someone or not may depend on the situation. The second and third tactics acknowledge that being a jerk or being likable can be an intrinsic characteristic of a person, almost regardless of the situation.

Manufacture Liking

Given the central role that our feelings about people play in our work relationships, is there anything a manager can do to foster positive feelings toward one another? The answer, perhaps surprisingly, is yes.

Promote familiarity. In a well-known psychological experiment, a person shown a photograph of himself and a re-versed image of the same picture consistently preferred the reversed photograph—simply because it was the image he was used to seeing in the mirror! And just as people like the images they're used to seeing, so they tend to like other people they're used to seeing around—they, too, are known and predictable. Familiarity is, in turn, one of the reasons why physical proximity strongly affects the degree to which people like each other: Research has shown that regular exposure to someone generally increases the comfort and pleasure of interaction.

The power of familiarity to generate positive interpersonal feelings argues for some careful thinking about the design of office space. This could involve anything from mixing up people's work spaces ("I generally don't care for people in Finance, but I've actually grown to like Sarah since she moved into the next office") to creating areas in an office that foster informal, watercooler-style chats.

You can also design processes that give people an opportunity simply to become acquainted and thus make them more comfortable with each other. The "peer assist," a knowledge management process in which team members aim to capture the expertise of other colleagues before starting a project, generally involves some initial interaction—say, a cocktail party—the evening before work begins and any work-specific goals are addressed. This allows people to get to know one another a bit, independently from the work at hand, while relationships are still emotionally neutral and haven't yet been subjected to any task-related interference, such as the potentially competing interests of the assisting and assisted parties. Less formally, all-office get-togethers on Friday afternoons can be more than culture- and morale-building exercises. They offer an opportunity for people from different functions and units to become familiar with one another, thus making it easier for them to share knowledge in the future.

Redefine similarity. Similarities can be created where they might not naturally arise. It's no secret, for example, that marketers and researchers tend to be wary of one another. Their personalities, as well as their departmental allegiances, are generally very different. But if you create a product management team that includes both marketers and researchers, there is a chance their similar identities as "Product X people" may begin to feel stronger than their dissimilar identities as "marketing people" and "R&D people." Superimposition of the shared identity, by overriding natural differences, may lead to increased cross-functional cooperation, both formal and informal.

Foster bonding. Often, however, cooperation fails to emerge despite a redefinition of similarities. Where there exists powerful forces of distrust or animosity, either because of strong dissimilarities (for instance, loyalty to different premerger companies) or because of a troubled history (years of competition between functional areas over budget allocations, for example), you won't be able to get people to like each other simply by inviting them to some TGIF gatherings or by sticking them on a cross-functional team. Promoting positive feelings in those circumstances requires stronger methods.

One involves putting people through an intense cooperative experience. In a famous experiment conducted more than 40 years ago by social psychologist Muzafer Sherif, groups of 11- and 12-year-old boys were brought together in a camp setting. Initially, they were randomly assigned to two groups. These were kept separate to foster ties within each group, and competitive activities were designed to produce animosity between the two groups. Then, to see if exposure to one another in a fun environment could reduce the hostility that had been generated, the competitive activities were suspended, and the boys got together for such benign activities as watching movies. In fact, though, hostility increased, with fights erupting at every turn. Sherif figured that something else was needed: a situation that would force the boys to cooperate with one another. So he created several. For instance, a truck taking the two groups on a camping trip broke down, and all of the boys had to push it up a steep hill to get it going again. Over time, episodes like this decreased hostility and, by the end of the camp experience, the number of boys who said that they had a best friend in the other group quadrupled.

The Outward Bound-style off-site experiences used by many companies are based on this venerable psychological principle. Such tactics can be problematic, however, because novelty and authenticity are critical to their success. The moment they become trite or feel manufactured, they lose their effectiveness. The challenge for managers, therefore, is to constantly find new ways to take advantage of this old concept.

Leverage the Likable

What should managers do to make effective use of people—fools or otherwise—who are likable almost regardless of the situation? Perhaps the best way to capitalize on their personal qualities is to have them play the role of "affective hubs"—people who, because they are liked by a disproportionate number of people, can bridge gaps between diverse groups that might not otherwise interact.

We don't necessarily like such people because they are similar or familiar to us. More likely, we are drawn to their attractive personality traits, sophisticated social skills, and old-fashioned "chemistry"—a chemistry that may arise from our sense that these people genuinely like us. Such individuals aren't necessarily the best performers (although they can be—that's the lovable star). More commonly, because of the time they devote to interacting with people, they may actually lag slightly behind their peers in terms of measurable performance. But their ability to establish positive working relationships between groups that would otherwise tend to be disconnected can be crucial to an organization's success. Managers can do several things to get the most out of such people.

Identify them. Attentive managers know if they have someone who could play—or is already playing—the role of an affective hub. But most managers aren't closely enough attuned to the emotional dimension of work to recognize such an indi-

vidual. Take the case of an employee in one company's IT department. She was the person who dealt with breakdowns in the technical infrastructure of the company. Although less technically proficient than many of her colleagues, she acted, in the words of one, "as a coral reef barrier when the user community in the company had problems. Because she was liked by everyone, she could deflate users' frustration and anger, insulating us geeks from complaints and allowing us to solve the problem." After she was laid off in a cost-cutting move, her job was divided among more technically competent people. The result? "It was a disaster," according to her former colleague.

Granted, it's often difficult for a manager several steps up in the firm to identify and assess the value of such a person. One aid is the increasingly common 360-degree evaluation, which typically includes questions about how pleasant someone is to deal with. A more systematic approach is to perform a social network analysis with surveys whose questions are specifically designed to collect information on relationships between workers and on the structure of the network formed by those relationships.

Protect them. Even when affective hubs are identified and their value to the company is acknowledged, such soft contributions may be deemed less important than more quantifiable ones. When told about the concept of affective hubs, members of a management team at a large technology company exclaimed almost in unison: "Damn, we just fired him!" They went on to describe someone who was beloved within and outside the organization, a person other people would turn to when they wanted to make contact with someone in another part of the business or at an alliance partner. "It's not just that he knew everybody," according to one member of the team. "It's that everybody really liked him, and they were happy to do him a favor." Even though people were aware of his critical informal role, it wasn't enough to save him from being one of the first to go in a round of downsizing.

Position them strategically. Clearly, you don't want to waste the talents of an affective hub by letting the person languish in a job that is only loosely connected with other functions. Such individuals should be put in a position to link people from different parts of the organization who might otherwise resist—or never think of—collaborating with one another. Affective hubs also are useful in positions central to the diffusion of new ideas. Think, for example, of a program designed to communicate new practices or principles throughout an organization. How do you select participants? Do you chose managers? Star performers? Or do you chose the people who, because others will listen to them, are going to be good evangelists for the new ideas?

Work on the Jerk

Competent jerks represent a missed opportunity for the organization because so much of their expertise goes untapped.

Whom Would You Choose?

To test our theory of work relationships, we conducted a series of social network surveys at four organizations: an entrepreneurial technology company in Silicon Valley, a unit of a multinational IT corporation, a U.S. university, and the Spanish country office of a global luxury goods corporation. We also surveyed a large group of MBA students at a U.S. business school. In all, we collected data about more than 10,000 work relationships.

We conducted multiple studies for two reasons. First, we wanted to see if the findings would remain consistent across different industries, types of organizations, and national cultures. Second, we wanted to see if the findings would remain consistent if we used different measures of likability, competence, and work-related interaction. For example, the definition of work interaction in the survey questions ranged from the very general ("We interact at work"—in which any kind of work-related interaction counted, whether formal or informal, but not other unrelated socializing) to the more specific ("When I have a question or issue about my job, I go to this person for advice or help" or "When I need to engage in creative problem solving regarding my job, I go to that person to help me think out of the box and consider different aspects of the problem innovatively"). Although our results clearly were limited to the five groups we studied, the consistency of the findings on both counts was striking.

Our analysis of the responses took into account biases often present when someone is asked to rate other people. We corrected, for instance, for the fact that some people are generally very generous with their ratings and others are very stingy. We took into account the fact that people working in the same department or in the same part of the building would naturally interact more frequently, regardless of liking or competence. And we adjusted for the fact that evaluations of competence and likability tend to go together: If I like you, I'm more likely to rate you as competent, and, conversely, if we've worked together in the past, I'll tend to like you better. We were able to disentangle this overlap in our analysis, as well. For details of our statistical approach, see our working paper at www.people.hbs.edu/tcasciaro/AffectInstrumentalTies.pdf.

Dealing with jerks is so unpleasant that colleagues simply can't be bothered with them. What can you do with such people?

Reassess their contribution. The individual performance of the competent jerk is great. But how does he contribute to the performance of the organization as a whole? Does he help the people who work with him or actually hinder them? Take the case of an investment bank that hired an extraordinary rainmaker in a difficult and highly profitable market the bank wanted to enter.[1] Unfortunately, the qualities that made the new hire a phenomenal producer in this rough-and-tumble market also alienated lots of his colleagues. Over time, it became clear that the newcomer's manner was violating the culture of respect and polite behavior that helped define the company. What, then, to do about it?

Reward good behavior; punish bad behavior. If the contributions of the competent jerk are significant, it's probably worth trying to turn him into a tolerated, even if not actively liked, star performer. Changing the behavior of adults is never a straightforward proposition, of course, but some things can be done. Jerks who can be charming when they wish—but choose to do so only when convenient—may respond to incentives. The rainmaker was one of those. He could be very charming to potential clients but was not to his coworkers. So when it came time for him to be considered for a managing director position, the bank denied him the promotion.

Socialize and coach. Although the rainmaker could have quit, taking his revenue-generating skills with him, he did not. His boss adopted an aggressive coaching stance, scolding for bad behavior immediately after the fact, rather than waiting for a year-end performance review. The boss was effective in explaining in detail how the behavior was self-defeating—information that a self-interested and ambitious individual is likely to take to heart. After coaching from his boss, the rainmaker's behavior improved, and he was promoted the following year. (Sadly, there are people who are disliked because they are socially incompetent and probably never will be truly charming. For them, interpersonal-skills training, rather than incentive-based coaching, may be preferable.)

Reposition. If likable people can improve an organization when they operate in highly interdependent roles, competent jerks will probably do best when they work independently. There is often a place for people who don't need to be liked so long as they get their jobs done—even if you must sacrifice widespread access to their expertise.

■

Obviously, simply being liked doesn't mean a person is valuable to an organization. We all know the fellow that people adore whose performance is continually disappointing—to the point that his colleagues end up disliking him because he repeatedly lets them down. We all know the woman who builds relationship after relationship that ultimately go nowhere, at least as far as the organization is concerned.

Still, it's easy to be mistakenly dazzled by a high performer, even if his expertise is never tapped or shared because people don't want to work with him. And too many managers fail to appreciate the benefits that a likable person can offer an organization, particularly if those benefits come at the expense of some measure of performance. Building an environment in which people like one another—whether by creating situations that make liking people easy, by fostering those likable people who can play the role of an affective hub, or by improving the behavior of competent jerks—can help all employees work more hap-

COLLEGE LIBRARY

pily and productively and encourage the formation of strong and smoothly functioning social networks.

Reference

"Rob Parson at Morgan Stanley (A), (B), (C) (Abridged), (D)," HBS case nos. 9-498-054, 9-498-055, 9-498-057, and 9-498-058.

TIZIANA CASCIARO (tcasciaro@hbs.edu) is an assistant professor of organizational behavior at Harvard Business School in Boston. **MIGUEL SOUSA LOBO** (mlobo@duke.edu) is an assistant professor of decision sciences at Duke University's Fuqua School of Business in Durham, North Carolina.

Reprinted by permission of *Harvard Business Review,* Vol. 83, Issue 6, June 2005, pp. 92-99. Copyright © 2005 by the Harvard Business School Publishing Corporation, all rights reserved.

Isn't She Lovely?

If you think that physical appeal is strictly a matter of personal taste and cultural bias, think again. Who you find attractive, say psychobiologists, is largely dictated by evolutionary needs and hardwired into your brain

BRAD LEMLEY

She's cute, no question. Symmetrical features, flawless skin, looks to be 22 years old—entering any meat-market bar, a woman lucky enough to have this face would turn enough heads to stir a breeze. But when Victor Johnston points and clicks, the face on his computer screen morphs into what a mesmerized physicist might call a discontinuous state of superheated, crystallized beauty. "You can see it. It's just so extraordinary," says Johnston, a professor of biopsychology at New Mexico State University who sounds a little in love with his creation.

The transformation from pretty woman to knee-weakening babe is all the more amazing because the changes wrought by Johnston's software are, objectively speaking, quite subtle. He created the original face by digitally averaging 16 randomly selected female Caucasian faces. The morphing program then exaggerated the ways in which female faces differ from male faces, creating, in human-beauty-science parlance, a "hyperfemale." The eyes grew a bit larger, the nose narrowed slightly, the lips plumped, and the jaw contracted. These are shifts of just a few millimeters, but experiments in this country and Scotland are suggesting that both males and females find "feminized" versions of averaged faces more beautiful.

Johnston hatched this little movie as part of his ongoing study into why human beings find some people attractive and others homely. He may not have any rock-solid answers yet, but he is far from alone in attempting to apply scientific inquiry to so ambiguous a subject. Around the world, researchers are marching into territory formerly staked out by poets, painters, fashion mavens, and casting directors, aiming to uncover the underpinnings of human attractiveness.

The research results so far are surprising—and humbling. Numerous studies indicate that human beauty may not be simply in the eye of the beholder or an arbitrary cultural artifact. It may be an ancient, hardwired, universal, and potent behavior-driver, on a par with hunger or pain, wrought through eons of evolution that rewarded reproductive winners and killed off losers. If beauty is not truth, it may be health and fertility: Halle Berry's flawless skin may rivet moviegoers because, at some deep level, it persuades us that she is parasite-free and conse-

quently good mating material. Acquired, individual preferences factor in, but research increasingly indicates that their influence is much smaller than many of us would care to know. While romantic writers blather about the transcendence of beauty, Elizabethan poet Edmund Spenser more than 400 years ago pegged the emerging scientific thesis: "Beauty is the bait which with delight allures man to enlarge his kind."

Implications of human-beauty research range from the practical—providing cosmetic surgeons with pretty-people templates—to the political and philosophical. Landmark studies show that attractive males and females not only garner more attention from the opposite sex, they also get more affection from their mothers, more money at work, more votes from the electorate, more leniency from judges, and are generally regarded as more kind, competent, healthy, confident, and intelligent than their big-nosed, weak-chinned counterparts. (Beauty is considered such a valuable trait by some that one entrepreneur recently put up a Web site offering to auction off the unfertilized ova of models.)

Human attractiveness research is a relatively young and certainly contentious field—the allure of hyperfemales, for example, is still hotly debated—but those on its front lines agree on one point: We won't conquer "looks-ism" until we understand its source. As psychologist Nancy Etcoff, author of the 1999 book *Survival of the Prettiest*, puts it: "The idea that beauty is unimportant or a cultural construct is the real beauty myth. We have to understand beauty, or we will always be enslaved by it."

The modern era of beauty studies got a big push 20 years ago with an awkward question in a small, airless room at Louisiana State University in Baton Rouge. Psychology graduate student Judith Langlois was defending her doctoral dissertation—a study of how preschool children form and keep friendships—when a professor asked whether she had factored the kids' facial attractiveness into her conclusions. "I thought the question was way off the mark," she recalls. "It might matter for college students, but little kids?"

After stammering out a noncommittal answer—and passing the examination—she resolved to dig deeper, aiming to determine the age at which human beings could perceive physical attractiveness.

Langlois, who had joined the faculty at the University of Texas at Austin, devised a series of experiments. In one, she had adults rate photos of human faces on a spectrum from attractive to unattractive. Then she projected pairs of high- and low-rated faces in front of 6-month-old infants. "The result was straightforward and unambiguous," she declares. "The babies looked longer at the attractive faces, regardless of the gender, race, or age of the face." Studies with babies as young as 2 months old yielded similar results. "At 2 months, these babies hadn't been reading *Vogue* magazine," Langlois observes dryly.

Her search for the source of babies' precocious beauty-detection led her all the way back to nineteenth-century research conducted by Sir Francis Galton, an English dilettante scientist and cousin of Charles Darwin. In the late 1870s, Galton created crude, blurry composite faces by melding mug-shot photographs of various social subgroups, aiming to prove that each group had an archetypal face. While that hypothesis fizzled—the average criminal looked rather like the average vegetarian—Galton was shocked to discover that these averaged faces were better looking than nearly all of the individuals they comprised. Langlois replicated Galton's study, using software to form digitally averaged faces that were later judged by 300 people to be more attractive than most of the faces used to create them.

Human beings may be born "cognitive averagers," theorizes Langlois. "Even very young infants have seen thousands of faces and may have already constructed an average from them that they use for comparison."

Racial preferences bolster the idea, say some scientists. History shows that almost universally when one race first comes into contact with another, they mutually regard each other as homely, if not freakish. Etcoff relates that a delegation of Japanese samurai visiting the United States in 1860 observed that Western women had "dogs' eyes," which they found "disheartening." Early Western visitors to Japan thought the natives' epicanthic folds made the eyes appear sleepy and small. In each case, Etcoff surmises, the unfamiliar race most likely veered from the internal, averaged ideal.

But why would cognitive averaging have evolved? Evolutionary biology holds that in any given population, extreme characteristics tend to fall away in favor of average ones. Birds with unusually long or short wings die more often in storms. Human babies who are born larger or smaller than average are less likely to survive. The ability to form an average-mate template would have conveyed a singular survival advantage.

Inclination toward the average is called koinophilia, from the Greek words *koinos*, meaning "usual," and *philos*, meaning "love." To Langlois, humans are clearly koinophiles. The remaining question is whether our good-mate template is acquired or innate. To help solve the mystery, Langlois's doctoral student Lisa Kalakanis has presented babies who are just 15 minutes old with paired images of attractive and homely faces. "We're just starting to evaluate that data," says Langlois.

But koinophilia isn't the only—or even supreme—criterion for beauty that evolution has promoted, other scientists argue. An innate yearning for symmetry is a major boon, contend biologists Anders Moller and Randy Thornhill, as asymmetry can signal malnutrition, disease, or bad genes. The two have found that asymmetrical animals, ranging from barn swallows to lions, have fewer offspring and shorter lives. Evolution would also logically instill an age preference. Human female fertility peaks in the early 20s, and so do assessments of female attractiveness. Between 1953 and 1990, the average age of *Playboy* centerfold models—who are presumably selected solely for sexual appeal—was 21.3 years. Similarly, Johnston has found that the beauty of a Japanese female face is judged to be at its peak when its perceived age is 22.4 years. Because men are fertile throughout most of their adult lives, their attractiveness ratings—while dropping as they age past their late 20s—remain relatively higher as their perceived age increases. As Johnston puts it, "Our feelings of beauty are exceptionally well tuned to the age of maximum fertility."

Still, a species can stagnate without some novelty. When competition for mates is intense, some extreme traits might help to rivet a roving eye. "A male peacock is saying, 'Look at me, I have this big tail. I couldn't grow a tail this big if I had parasites,'" says Johnston. "Even if the trait is detrimental to survival, the benefit in additional offspring brought about by attracting females can more than compensate for the decrease in longevity." The concept seems applicable to humans, too, because it helps to resolve a nagging flaw in average-face studies. In many of them, "there were always a few individual faces in the population that were deemed even prettier than the average," says Etcoff. "If average were always best, how could that be?"

Psychologist David Perrett of the University of St. Andrews in Scotland aimed to find out by creating two averaged faces—one from a group of women rated attractive and another from men so judged. He then compared those faces with averaged faces constructed from a larger, random set of images. The composites of the beautiful people were rated more appealing than those made from the larger, random population. More surprising, when Perrett exaggerated the ways in which the prettiest female composite differed from the average female composite, the resulting face was judged to be even more attractive.

"It turned out that the way an attractive female face differs from an average one is related to femininity," says Perrett. "For example, female eyebrows are more arched than males'. Exaggerating that difference from the average increases femininity," and, in tandem, the attractiveness rating. In the traffic-stopping female face created for this experiment, 200 facial reference points all changed in the direction of hyperfemininity: larger eyes, a smaller nose, plumper lips, a narrower jaw, and a smaller chin.

"All faces go through a metamorphosis at puberty," observes Johnston. "In males, testosterone lengthens the jaw. In females, estrogen makes the hips, breasts, and lips swell." So large lips, breasts, and hips combined with a small jaw "are all telling you that I have an abundant supply of estrogen, so I am a fertile female." Like the peacock, whose huge tail is a mating advantage but a practical hindrance, "a small jaw may not, in fact, be as efficient for eating," Johnston says. But it seems attractive because it emphasizes *la différence;* whatever survival disadvantage comes along with a small jaw is more than made up for by the chance to produce more babies, so the trait succeeds.

Along with his morphing program, Johnston approached the hyperfemale hypothesis through another route. Starting with 16 computer-generated random female Caucasian faces, he had visitors to his Web site rate the attractiveness of each face on a scale of one to nine. A second generation of faces was then computed by selecting, crossing, and mutating the first generation in proportion to beauty ratings. After 10,000 people from around the world took part in this merciless business, the empirically derived fairest-of-them-all was born. Facial measurements confirm that she is decidedly hyperfemale. While we might say she is beautiful, Johnston more accurately notes that the face displays "maximum fertility cues."

Johnston's findings have set off a ruckus among beauty scientists. In a paper titled "Attractive Faces Really Are Only Average," Langlois and three other researchers blast the notion that a deviation from the average—what they term "facial extremes"—explains attractiveness better than averageness does. The findings of Perrett and his team, she says, are "artifacts of their methodology," because they used a "forced-choice" scenario that prevented subjects from judging faces as equally attractive. "We did the same kind of test, but gave people a rating scale of one to five," says Langlois. "When you do it that way, there is no significant difference—people would tell us that, basically, the two faces looked like twins." Langlois argues that if extremes create beauty, "then people with micro-jaws or hydrocephalic eyes would be seen as the most beautiful, when, in fact, eyes that are too big for a head make that head unattractive."

As the world becomes more egalitarian, beauty becomes more inclusive.

But for Etcoff, circumstantial evidence for the allure of some degree of hyperfemininity is substantial. "Female makeup is all about exaggerating the feminine. Eye makeup makes the brow thinner, which makes it look farther from the eye," which, she says, is a classic difference between male and female faces. From high hair (which skews facial proportions in a feminine direction, moving up the center of gravity) to collagen in lips to silicone in breasts, women instinctively exaggerate secondary female sex characteristics to increase their allure. "Langlois is simply wrong," declares Johnston. In one of his studies, published last year in *Psychophysiology*, both male and female subjects rated feminized pictures as more attractive. Further, male subjects attached to electrical-brain-activity monitors showed a greater response in the P3 component, a measure of emotional intensity. "That is, although both sexes know what is attractive, only the males exhibit an emotional response to the feminized picture," Johnston says.

And what about male attractiveness? It stands to reason that if men salivate for hyperfemales, women should pursue hypermales—that is, men whose features exaggerate the ways in which male faces differ from female ones. Even when adjusted for differing overall body size, the average male face has a more pronounced brow ridge, more sunken eyes, and bushier brows that are set closer to the eyes. The nose and mouth are wider, the lower jaw is wider and longer. Ramp up these features beyond the norm, and you've got a hunk, right?

There's no question that a dose of this classic "maleness" does contribute to what is now called handsome. Actor Brad Pitt, widely regarded as a modern paradigm of male attractiveness, is a wide-jaw guy. Biologically speaking, he subconsciously persuades a female that he could chew more nutrients out of a leafy stalk than the average potential father of her children—a handy trait, in hunter-gatherer days anyway, to pass on to progeny.

But a woman's agenda in seeking a mate is considerably more complex than simply whelping strong-jawed kids. While both men and women desire healthy, fertile mates, a man can—and, to some extent, is biologically driven to—procreate with as many women as possible. Conversely, a woman "thinks about the long haul," notes Etcoff. "Much of mate choice is about finding a helpmate to bring up the baby." In several studies, women presented with the hypermale face (the "Neanderthal type" as Etcoff puts it) judged its owner to be uncaring, aggressive, and unlikely to be a good father.

Female preferences in male faces oscillate in tandem with the menstrual cycle, suggests a study conducted by Perrett and Japanese researchers and published last June in *Nature*. When a woman is ovulating, she tends to prefer men with more masculine features; at less fertile times in her monthly cycle, she favors male faces with a softer, more feminine look. But amid the hoopla that this widely publicized finding generated, a critical fact was often overlooked. Even the "more masculine" face preferred by the ovulating women was 8 percent feminized from the male average (the less masculine face was 15 to 20 percent feminized). According to Perrett's study, even an averagely masculine face is too male for comfort.

To further complicate the male-appeal picture, research indicates that, across the board in mating species, an ugly guy can make up ground with status and/or wealth. Etcoff notes that female scorpion flies won't even look at a male unless his gift— a tasty bit of insect protein—is at least 16 square millimeters wide. The human situation isn't all that different. Anthropologist John Marshall Townsend showed photos of beautiful and homely people to men and women, and described the people in the photos as being in training for either low-, medium-, or high-paying positions—waiter, teacher, or doctor. "Not surprisingly, women preferred the best-looking man with the most money," Etcoff writes, "but below him, average-looking or even unattractive doctors received the same ratings as very attractive teachers. This was not true when men evaluated women. Unattractive women were not preferred, no matter what their status."

It's all a bit bleak. Talk to enough psychobiologists, and you get the impression that we are all rats—reflexively, unconsciously coupling according to obscure but immutable circuitry. But beauty researchers agree that, along with natural selection and sexual selection, learned behaviors are at least part of the attractiveness radar. In other words, there is room for individuality—perhaps even a smattering of mystery—in this business of attraction between humans.

"Human beauty really has three components," says Johnston. "In order of importance, there's natural selection, which leads to the average face and a limited age range. Then there's sexual selection," which leads men, at least, to be attracted to exaggerated feminine traits like the small lower jaw and the fuller lips. "Finally, there's learning. It's a fine-tuning mechanism that allows you to become even more adapted to your environment and culture. It's why one person can say 'She's beautiful' and another can say, 'She's not quite right for me.'"

The learned component of beauty detection is perhaps most evident in the give-and-take between races. While, at first meeting, different racial groups typically see each other as unattractive, when one race commands economic or political power, members of other races tend to emulate its characteristics: Witness widespread hair straightening by American blacks earlier in this century. Today, black gains in social equity are mirrored by a growing appreciation for the beauty of such characteristically black features as relatively broader noses and tightly curled hair. "Race is a cultural overlay on beauty and it's shifting," says Etcoff.

She adds that human appearance is about more than attracting sex partners. "There was a cartoon in the *New Yorker*. A mother and daughter are in a checkout line. The girl is saying to the cashier, 'Oh, no, I *do* look like my mother, with her *first* nose!' As we make ourselves more beautiful, we take away things like family resemblance, and we may realize that's a mistake. Facial uniqueness can be a wonderful emotional tag. Human beings are always looking for kinship as well as beauty."

Midway between goats and gods, human beings can find some accommodation between the notion that beauty is all and that it is nothing. "Perhaps it's best to enjoy the temporary thrill, to enjoy being a mammal for a few moments, and then do a reality check and move on," writes Etcoff. "Our brains cannot help it, but we can."

From *Discover*, February 2000, pp. 43-49. Copyright © 2000 by Brad Lemley. Reprinted by permission of the author.

If It's Easy Access That Really Makes You Click, Log On Here

Stupid Cupid! Karen Gold searches for the e-spot

KAREN GOLD

From: Gold, Karen

To: Ben-Ze'ev, Aaron—psychologist, philosopher and author of *Love Online: Emotions on the Internet*

Subject: Does cybersex count as cheating on your partner, or is it just an adolescent game sustained by chocolate pixels?

KG: If we were doing this interview face to face, you'd know if I was a 50-year-old man pretending to be a 22-year-old lesbian. We're not, and so you don't. Does that make it impossible for either of us to believe anything the other is saying?

AB: One paradoxical feature of online romantic relationships is that they encourage deception and sincerity. The anonymity of cyberspace and the voluntary nature of online self-presentation allow people to present themselves inaccurately. In one survey, 48 per cent of users said they changed their age "occasionally" and 23 per cent did so "often".

Furthermore, 38 per cent changed their race online, and 5 percent admitted to changing their sex occasionally.

But online relationships also encourage many people to present a more accurate picture of their true self. People can express themselves more freely because they are more anonymous and hence less vulnerable. Many people present themselves honestly online. This is especially true if the relationship grows.

KG: Are the emotions people feel in online relationships the same as the ones they experience face to face? Is the experience of cybersex comparable to real sex?

AB: The emotions are similar, but the role of imagination online is greater. Many people testify that their online sexual experience has been the most intense and wild sex they have ever had. One 32-year-old woman, married for the second time, claims: "The sexual release from cybering has been a great experience and the arousal factor is just magnificent."

Emotions in online relationships incorporate more intellectual elements.

The weight of conversation is far greater in online relationships than in offline relationships.

A woman who has participated in cybersex writes: "The best sex, obviously, is with someone literate enough to 'paint a picture' describing activities or thoughts. I suppose that in face-to-face activities, someone stupid could still be extraordinarily sexy. But stupid doesn't work online, at least not for me."

KG: What kind of person seeks love online? What kind of person finds it?

AB: All kinds. Online relationships increase your chances of finding a more suitable and exciting partner because it's easier to identify willing people and cheaper and less risky to conduct the relationship. The computer's ability to sort people by characteristics is much greater than in offline circumstances, so it's easier to find people with attributes you like.

For example, an obese woman who feels insecure approaching new people face to face because of her weight may interact online with people who share her interests. When she reveals that she is overweight, some people may not want to continue the correspondence. But others may find her physical size irrelevant or her other characteristics very attractive.

For such people, who have to break a lot of eggs to make an omelette, cyberspace provides many eggs. Millions of people eagerly wait for you on the net every moment of the day.

KG: You say cyber relationships last a few months on average. Is there a pattern to them?

AB: There are many types of online relationships. It's hard to find a pattern, but I distinguish three major types:
- relationships intended to find an offline sexual or romantic partner

- cyberflirting and cybersex
- profound online-only romantic relationships.

KG: Do women have an advantage in online relationships? They're generally better communicators than men, and you say in your book that they feel less inhibited—raunchy even—online than in person. They're not being judged on how they look, though that might be an advantage for some men, too. What difference does all this make?

AB: Online relationships are advantageous for all people whose communicative and intellectual abilities are better than their looks.

Because external appearance generally has more weight in men's judgement of women than in women's judgement of men, it does benefit women. It lets people get to know each other without the heavy burden of the attractiveness stereotype.

Thus, someone writes about his online girlfriend: "She is not even my type when it comes to physical attraction, but she is now the most beautiful girl I have ever met and will ever meet." The reduced concern about external appearance allows women to enjoy sex more and to be much freer in this respect. As one woman said: "It was great not having to worry about being unattractive."

KG: The way you describe online affairs—more soul-searching, more intense, more fleeting, easy to switch off, easy to replace—makes them sound…well… rather adolescent. Aren't the people engaging in them just avoiding grown-up relationships?

AB: Online interactions might be considered a kind of virtual laboratory in which people can explore each other and experiment. In this sense, they are similar to the games that children play that allow them to develop, in a relatively safe and benign way, social skills for adult life. Indeed, cyberspace has been characterised as an amazing sex toy.

There's nothing wrong with playing the way children do as long as we know the boundaries between the game and reality. In cyberspace, such boundaries are often blurred.

KG: Isn't it dangerous when they are? Fantasy can be addictive. If people confuse fantasy with reality—if they talk about being more profoundly satisfied by virtual sex and virtual relationships than by real sex and real relationships—aren't

they losing touch with reality? And where does this leave their real-life partners and spouses?

AB: You're absolutely right. There is such danger. The great seductiveness of cyberspace and the ease of becoming involved in online affairs bring risks. People are easily carried away.

Moreover, cyberspace doesn't merely satisfy needs, it creates new needs that often cannot be met. Thus, the apparent ease of finding true and everlasting love in cyberspace creates the need to have such "perfect" love. Of course, that is far from simple to achieve. Online affairs are like a new toy with which the human race has not yet learnt how to play. People may confuse the toy with reality and ruin their life.

Cybering is similar, in some senses, to taking drugs. Both provide easy access to pleasure that is often based on virtual realities. Whereas drugs artificially stimulate pleasure centres in the brain, online conversations artificially stimulate pleasure centres in the mind. The price can be high for our overall performance and for those close to us in our offline lives.

KG: How widespread do you think cyber relationships will become? Have you ever had one? Will all this be contractualised some day: in marriage perhaps we'll promise to forsake all others, online as well as off?

AB: I know many people who have had online relationships. I haven't. The internet has changed the romantic domain, and this process will accelerate.

It will modify social forms such as marriage and cohabitation, and romantic practices relating to courtship, casual sex, committed romantic relationships and romantic exclusivity.

I think we can expect more relaxation of social and moral norms concerning romantic exclusivity. It will be difficult to avoid the vast amount of tempting alternatives entirely. The notion of "betrayal" will become less common. But I think the values placed on stability and stronger commitment will increase as well.

By the way, are you a 50-year-old man or an attractive 42-year-old woman, as it seems from your questions?

AARON BEN-ZE'EV is a psychologist, philosopher and rector of the University of Haifa. *Love Online: Emotions on the Internet* is published by Cambridge University Press on February 14, £18.95.

From *The Times Higher Education Supplement*, February 13, 2004. Copyright © 2004 by Times Supplements Ltd. Reprinted by permission of Karen Gold and The Times Higher Education Supplement.

Brokeback Mountain:
A Gay and a Universal Love Story

ILENE SERLIN

A young, gay client left my office, and I reflected on her urgent questions. She was intent on explaining to me the difference between enjoying being submissive in sex and enjoying the dominance or cruelty of her partner. One of her main issues, she said, is that she cannot have an orgasm or feel passion with this partner, who is stable and loves her greatly, but only with someone who is emotionally cruel or unavailable. My client was turning 30 years old and wanted to settle down. She had been with the same partner for three years and was desperate at her inability to feel passion. Although I appreciate the importance of these subtle distinctions of sexual identity, equality, and love, I am also aware of the many gaps in my own understanding and of the stereotypes that I, as a heterosexual psychotherapist, hold.

Looking at *Brokeback Mountain* as a lesson in sexual identity and relationship issues is only one of the ways it would be useful for psychologists to discuss this film with clients and one another. We should be as informed as possible about the nuances of all kinds of love and be aware of our own biases and perspectives. But are the concerns in this film only about gay love? I believe that the issues raised by this film are compelling and universal themes of passion, authenticity, loneliness, and partnership. These are the very human questions that show up in all great dramas: Can any romantic love that is fueled by challenges, secrecy, and idyllic settings live in the real world? Does domestic routine always kill passion? Is romantic love inevitably tragic?

Setting

Brokeback Mountain is an exquisite story about two cowboys who fall in love. It is based on a short story written by Wyoming resident E. Annie Proulx, who won the Pulitzer prize for *The Shipping News*. First published in *The New Yorker* in 1997, it also appeared in the book *Close Range: Wyoming Stories*. The screenplay was adapted by Larry McMurtry and Diana Ossana, and the film was brilliantly directed by Ang Lee, director of *Crouching Tiger, Hidden Dragon* and *Sense and Sensibility*. The score was created by Gustavo Santaolla (*Motorcycle Diaries*) and contains excerpts from Merle Haggard, Willie Nelson, and Rufus Wainwright. Poetic visual images of the Western landscape iconography were created by Rodrigo Prieto. The film was produced by James Shamus, is rated R, and runs for 134 min.

The story is about two young men in 1963 who are hired to work for a rancher in Signal, Wyoming. The inarticulate and solitary Ennis Del Mar, played by Heath Ledger, and Jack Twist (Jake Gyllenhaal) both come from families of emotional cruelty, and one stormy night they find refuge in their tent and each others' arms. Although Ennis immediately says, "You know I ain't queer," and Jack says, "Me neither," their passion continues to smolder. After the summer, Ennis returns home to marry his childhood sweetheart (Michelle Williams, Ledger's real-life partner), and Jack goes to Texas and marries a rich boss's daughter (Anne Hathaway). Over the next 20 years, they continue to meet periodically for "fishing trips" on their idyllic mountain, while their respective marriages deteriorate. Scenes of silent male camaraderie taking place in wide open spaces are juxtaposed against images of the banality of domestic family life.

Brokeback Mountain: Why Is It Relevant?

I went to see the film on the evening after I met with my client, and the 10:00 p.m. showing was sold out in San Francisco. Although *Brokeback Mountain* has sold out houses in liberal New York and Los Angeles, it is not just a gay or liberal film. It won seven Golden Globe nominations and was screened at the Venice International Film Festival, and more advance tickets for *Brokeback Mountain* were sold in a metroplex in Plano, Texas, than for the blockbuster film *King Kong*. Other movies with gay characters this year, such as Capote and Rent, had urban or campy settings, but *Brokeback Mountain* takes place in America's heartland. It is impossible to dismiss the film as a plot designed by latte-sipping liberals or Chelsea faux cowboys. Set in the same year as Martin Luther King, Jr.'s, march on Washington and the publication of Betty Friedan's book *The Feminine Mystique*, the film shows the heartening progress we have made on civil rights since 1963. Even though the film was released around the time that the president "cynically flogged a legally superfluous (and unpassable) constitutional amendment banning same-sex marriage for the sole purpose of whipping up the basest hostilities of his electoral base" (Rich, 2005, p. 13), polls are nevertheless showing that a large majority of Americans support equal rights for gay couples if the relationship is not called *marriage*.

Brokeback Mountain: Psychological Issues

The film's postmodern layering of perspectives and issues about identity, alienation, and the need for connection (Gergen, 1991) is revealed by a look at the fascinating array of review titles. Some examples include "Masculinity and Its Discontents in Marlboro Country" (Dargis, 2005), "Two Gay Cowboys Hit a Home Run" (Rich, 2005), "Cowboys, Just Like in the Movies" (Trebay, 2005), and "Love Story With One Difference" (2005). Robert Roten (2005), from the Laramie Movie Scope, called it a "modern story about 'star-crossed lovers,'" a modern "Romeo and Jack." Rob Nelson called it "Midnight Cowboys, Lonesome Doves," and Roger Ebert said it was "as observant as work by Bergman" (*Brokeback Mountain*, n.d.).

Reviewers and writers have quite different ideas about what the film is about. Proulx, the author of the short story on which the film is based, has said that it is "about two confused young men 'beguiled by the cowboy myth'" (Dargis, 2005, p. 13). The irony is that the protagonists are not actually cowboys but technically shepherds. Dargis noted that *Brokeback Mountain* is a film about identity ("On Brokeback, the two men are neither straight nor gay, much less queer; they are lovers, which probably accounts for the category confusion that has greeted the film"; p. 13), and Rich (2005) made the same point tongue in cheek, calling it "a heavily promoted American movie depicting two men having sex" (p. 13). Epidemiologists attempting to categorize sexually transmitted diseases have the same problem with mixed identities, having no categories for men who have sex with other men but do not identify as gay. Being gay in American poses special questions and challenges about identity formation (Cass, 1979; Coleman, 1982; Isay, 1996).

Brokeback Mountain is also a film about the challenging societal factors that impinge on gay relationships. The film has been called a "landmark in the troubled history of America's relationship to homosexuality" (Rich, 2005, p. 13); Proulx's story "Brokeback Mountain" was written six years before Stonewall became a new frontier for gay rights, and gay student Matthew Shepard was murdered near Laramie, Wyoming, on October 6, 1998, the year after the story was published. Shepherd was pistol whipped by two men he met at a bar, tied to a split rail fence with his own shoelaces, and left to die in the cold. Consensual sex between two men was still a crime in some American states until 2002, when the Supreme Court reversed the sodomy laws; therefore, critic Trebay (2005) called the film a documentary that shows the violence so often part of gay men's experience. Other reviewers have pointed out that the problem in the film is not caused by the wife and family of the men but by their bullying bosses and shaming fathers—the patriarchy itself.

Noteworthy for clinicians are also the terrible alienation, depression, and loneliness that come with being gay in America (Herek, 1989). The name of one of the two protagonists, Ennis, brilliantly played by Ledger, means *island*, and we see him as unable to fully connect with either Jack, his wife, or his children. Jack, the other protagonist, played seductively by Gyllenhaal, is also lonely in his cold family—his wealthy and insensitive wife and in-laws. Both men live a secretive double life, and neither is able to commit authentically to either life. One rancher from Wyoming who was interviewed in a review (Trebay, 2005, p. 1) spoke of his great loneliness and said that he had considered suicide.

Another theme of *Brokeback Mountain* is purely a visual element—the power of nonverbal communication. From the grunting and wrestling between the two men and their use of silence, pauses, and body language, we feel their bond (Birdwhistell, 1970). They use understatement to make their points, as when Jack summarizes the whole story of the relationship as, "That ol' Brokeback got us good." The camera work echoes the poetic use of imagery, lingering on distant mountaintops and clear streams. The imagery even gets campy, as when the smoldering looks and shots of men's butts in tight jeans have the audience snickering. In psychotherapy, the nonverbal level is often minimized by our verbal, goal-directed, male therapeutic model. Because nonverbal and visual imagery are so directly connected to dreams and the unconscious, it would be helpful for therapists to be aware of this aspect of the therapeutic process.

Another layer of the film is archetypal. The image of the Western frontier is mythic in the American imagination, and the film shows the power of the imagination over reality. For example, the era of the cowboy actually existed for a relatively short time in American history—from the end of the large-scale cattle drives after the Civil War to the advent of the use of rail to move cattle. By the time movies were created, this era was over. The myth of wide open spaces lives on in the collective unconscious and symbolizes freedom to be oneself, away from the stifling conformity of domesticity and technology. Part of this myth shows the conflict between nature and culture in the human psyche. Other Western films that show this conflict and also have sexual overtones include John Wayne and Monty Cliff in *Red River*, Gary Cooper and Lloyd Bridges in *High Noon*, and Rock Hudson and James Dean in *Giant*. Outsiders have always been drawn to this freedom, as shown in the John Wayne genre. Even artists who perpetuated the myth, such as Aaron Copland, who wrote *Billy the Kid* and *Rodeo*, were outsiders; Copland was a Jewish boy from Brooklyn who was a Communist sympathizer and more comfortable in Paris than the West (J. Weisgall, personal communication, December 26, 2005). Agnes de Mille, the choreographer of *Oklahoma*, was the ugly duckling and outsider of the famous Hollywood de Mille family, and *Oklahoma* was one of the first American musicals that captured the hearts and minds of the American public. In the political arena, Ronald Reagan and Arnold Schwartzenegger (Serlin, 2003) posed before pictures of Teddy Roosevelt, evoking the myth of the rugged individualistic cowboy. However, the myth of freedom is an ideal and not real; for example, cowboy Rock

Hudson spent his life living in the closet. The myth of the wild West shows the tension between the real and the ideal.

As Carl Jung (1958), Rollo May (1975, 1991), and others have shown, the influence of mythic images is as significant as the reality of human thoughts, feelings, and behavior. Mythic images can be used in psychotherapy as a template to see one's own personal mythology (Feinstein & Krippner, 1988) and also images of male partnership (Beebe, 1993). In the case of my psychotherapy client, for example, her mythology was partly about her need for freedom, commitment and flight, and doomed love. Myths capture the paradoxical complexity of human nature, whereas much modern psychology emphasizes a one-dimensional approach to diagnosis or treatment. For example, the trend toward manualized methods that help clients replace negative thoughts with positive ones, or those that emphasize happiness while leaving out tragedy, miss the drama of human life. Instead of fixing symptoms, a mythic approach to psychology aims to help people deal with the real complexity between individuation and adjustment to reality, freedom and fate, and multiple selves and identities. From a mythic perspective, as Shakespeare wrote in *As You Like It*, "all the world's a stage," and we play many roles.

Finally, a mythic perspective allows us to see that, like great art, life comes in genres. Is *Brokeback Mountain* a tragedy? Both heroes leave the community and go off to the island or paradise to find themselves—a theme often found in Shakespeare. Yet can they individuate, or are societal factors such as homophobia and intolerance too strong? Greek tragedies portray the tension between freedom and fate. Is *Brokeback Mountain* in the genre of forbidden love?

Because everything else in the cowboys' life changed, but their love lasted all their life, I see this film as showing the enduring power of love. The director set out to sympathetically portray the challenges of two men in love and the human need to live an authentic life. To this end, he succeeds magnificently. The acting by Ledger may win him an Academy Award nomination, and the score and cinematography support the action

seamlessly. In short, *Brokeback Mountain* introduces many complex psychological issues that would be valuable for psychologists to see and understand.

References

Beebe, J. (1993). Towards an image of male partnership. In R. Hopcke (Ed.), Same-sex love and the path to wholeness. Boston: Shambhala.

Birdwhistell, R. (1970). Kinesis and context: Essays in body motion communication. Philadelphia: University of Pennsylvania Press.

Brokeback mountain (2005). (n.d.). Retrieved January 30, 2005, from www.rottentomatoes.com.

Cass, V. C. (1979). Homosexual identity formation: A theoretical model. Journal of Homosexuality, 4(3), 219–235.

Coleman, E. (1982). Developmental stages of the coming out process. Journal of Homosexuality, 7(2), 31–43.

Dargis, M. (2005, December 18). Masculinity and its discontents in Marlboro country. New York Times, p. 13.

Feinstein, D., & Krippner, S. (1988). Personal mythology. Los Angeles: Tarcher.

Gergen, K. (1991). The saturated self. New York: Basic Books.

Herek, G. M. (1989). Hate crimes against lesbians and gay men: Issues for research and policy. American Psychologist, 44, 948–955.

Isay, R. (1996). Becoming gay: A journey to self-acceptance. New York: Pantheon Books.

Jung, C. G. (1958). Psyche and symbol (V. de Laszlo, Ed.). New York: Doubleday.

"Love Story with one difference." (2005, December 23). Palm Beach Post.

May, R. (1975). The courage to create. New York: Bantam Books.

May, R. (1991). The cry for myth. New York: Norton.

Rich, F. (2005, December 18). Two gay cowboys hit a home run. New York Times, p. 13.

Roten, R. (2005, October 9). Brokeback Mountain: A song of doomed love for cowboys. Laramie Movie Scope.

Serlin, I. (2003, October 10). Image vs. reality: Daddy will take care of you. San Francisco Chronicle.

Trebay, G. (2005, December 18). Cowboys, just like in the movies. New York Times, Section 9, pp. 1, 6.

From *PsycCritiques*, March 15, 2006, Vol. 51 (11). Copyright © 2006 by American Psychological Association. Reprinted by permission. http://psycinfo.apa.org

UNIT 7
Social Biases

Unit Selections

Key Points to Consider

- What are stigma, prejudice, stereotyping, and discrimination? Can you give examples of each? Can any of these ever have positive effects?

- What are the effects of stigma on self-esteem? Is self-esteem an exclusively desirable attribute? When does stigma not create negative effects?

- What is racial categorization? Are such categories appropriate? How are they used (or misused)?

- How do you feel about the illegal immigrant issue? Does it have far-reaching effects, i.e. beyond our border states? Are some people angrier about this issue than others? Why?

- How do teachers' expectations affect students? How do biased teachers' appraisals of minority children affect those children? Do biased teachers have an effect on other children? Are there classroom techniques to overcome the effects of bigoted teachers or students?

- What is discrimination? Is it legal? How is it practiced if it is illegal? How does the average American feel about prejudice and discrimination?

Student Web Site
www.mhcls.com/online

Internet References
Further information regarding these Web sites may be found in this book's preface or online.

NAACP Online: National Association for the Advancement of Colored People
http://www.naacp.org
National Civil Rights Museum
http://www.civilrightsmuseum.org
United States Holocaust Memorial Museum
http://www.ushmm.org/
Yahoo—Social Psychology
http://www.yahoo.com/Social_Science/Psychology/disciplines/social_psychology/

A young boy named Daniel sat quietly, very quietly at the dinner table. Danny was typically chatty and eager to share the day's events with his mother and father. This particular evening, however, Danny was neither talkative nor happy. His parents soon noted the change in his demeanor and asked him what was wrong. Danny kept telling them that everything was fine, but his parents persisted. The change in Danny was too noticeable to ignore. After dinner, Danny's mother went to his room and found him crying. She comforted her child and prodded him to share with her what the events of the day.

Danny told the following story. In the morning, he got on the school bus, rode to school, and eagerly finished the school day. In the afternoon, he readied himself for the ride home. The bus ride was uneventful until he stepped off the bus. In a nearby car, a man called and motioned to him to approach. At first the man seemed friendly and told Danny that in the car were some toys specially made for boys Danny's age. Although Danny had been warned by his parents not to talk to strangers, Danny finally acquiesced to the man's seemingly well-meaning entreaties. When Danny got in the man's car, the car sped off to a remote location where the man sexually molested Danny.

The man warned Danny not to tell anyone or he would kill Danny's dog. Danny was terrified. The man drove Danny back to the neighborhood, dropped him off, and sped off. When Danny's parents came home, at first they did not notice how dejected he was. After he revealed the story about the man to his mother, his parents phoned the police who quickly came to their home. The boy was so shattered by what had happened to him and so worried about what to tell the police that he became mute. Danny's mother and father retold the story as best they could.

While Danny and his parents were being interviewed by the police, Danny's father revealed something quite incredible. His father stated to the officers that the man who had molested Danny was an African-American. Danny never told his father this, because *it was not true*. This piece of information led the investigating detectives in the wrong direction. When the man was eventually apprehended, he was White. The story is true, but the names and a few details have been changed.

You should be asking yourself, "Why would Danny's parents say the assailant was Black?" Was it an innocent or intentional mistake? Or did they just assume that when bad things happen to Whites, African-Americans must be responsible. You should also ask yourself if minority groups perceive Whites as the root cause of their troubles.

The interrelated issues of *prejudice*, *discrimination* and *stereotyping* are the topics of the present unit. To relate these terms to the story about Danny, you should know that his parents were very bigoted and simply assumed that someone outside of their own group *must* have committed the crime. Understand that social biases can be both positive (favorable) and negative (harmful). It is the harmful ones, such as the racial prejudice held by Danny's parents, that most concern social psychologists.

Now, let us define the above terms as they relate to social biases. *Prejudice* can be defined as an attitude toward another person or group that is based solely on group membership. An example would be that a middle-aged woman lives near your campus and believes that all college students are wild and drunk. She has little to no respect or liking for them. If you are a college student you *must* be wild and drunk in her opinion, no matter how sober and studious you really are.

Discrimination is a companion to prejudice in that it is the behavioral manifestation of prejudice. In other words, *discrimination* is an action taken against (or occasionally in favor of) a certain individual because of his or her group membership. Continuing the example of the middle-aged woman: suppose she has an apartment to rent, and several interested individuals visit to preview the home and discuss the monthly rental and lease. The woman briskly cuts short any college student's appointment. She absolutely refuses to rent to any of them much less be courteous. When a middle-aged, recently widowed woman inspects the space, the landlord immediately suggests that she is the perfect tenant and leases it to her.

Not all bigots act on their biases. The presence of prejudice does not mean that discrimination always occurs. One significant reason is that federal and state laws now prohibit discrimination against certain protected groups. Recognize, though, that attitudes and beliefs are more difficult to legislate than actions. Some people retain their stereotypes and prejudices but do not actively discriminate against others. In fact, social psychological research has documented that both prejudice and discrimination still exist but have become more subtle and covert than in the past—at least in the United States.

The third term related to social bias is stereotypes. *Stereotypes* are widespread generalizations about certain groups of people that have little if any basis in fact. The middle-aged landlord's stereotype of college students as drunk and wild may have been based solely on her experience one night when a handful of students poured onto her street from a nearby bar and caused boisterous commotions that kept her awake—and angry. Be-cause this event stood out in her mind, she stereotyped all college students the same way: rowdy, disorderly, and inebriated.

Unit 7 contains five articles on prejudice, discrimination, and stereotypes. Jennifer Crocker and Brenda Major, two of the leading social psychologists on stigma and biases, describe their intensive research program. The two scientists explain research on how stigma is related to self-esteem. Interestingly, some of their studies have shown that stigma is not always detrimental. Instead, Crocker and Major have found that stigmatized people often use their own groups for social comparison rather than compare themselves to the majority.

The second article, entitled "Leaving Race Behind," by Amitai Etzioni reviews the use of racial categories by the government and others. He concludes that such categories are contrived and artificial and therefore useless. Etzioni claims that we all need education about diversity and about accepting one another for who we are and not for what category we fit in.

"Lowered Expectations" is an article about the school performance of minority children. All too often, teachers stereotype minority students and therefore expect poorer performance from them compared to White students. Such expectations often do result in worse performance by minority children, fulfilling the teacher's expectations. Author Zak Stambor addresses techniques teachers can utilize to reduce the ill effects of such expectations.

"Change of Heart," by Adam Goodheart, addresses discrimination which can result from stereotyping. Despite public policy, discrimination in the U.S. still occurs in housing, employment, and education. The author shares with us the results of two recent public opinion surveys that show discrimination is decreasing over time.

The Self-Protective Properties of Stigma: Evolution of a Modern Classic

JENNIFER CROCKER
Department of Psychology
University of Michigan

BRENDA MAJOR
Department of Psychology
University of California at Santa Barbara

We thank Trish Devine for nominating our work as a modern classic and Ralph Erber and Lenny Martin for giving us this opportunity to reflect on how these ideas originated and evolved over time and how others have used them. Our original idea about the self-protective functions of social stigma germinated for a long time, and there are people who directly and indirectly shaped our ideas, some of whom probably have no idea how they influenced us.

The origins of this work, at least in the mind of one of us (Jennifer Crocker) can be traced to a 1982 invitation to attend a summer institute on Stigma and Interpersonal Relations at the Center for Advanced Study in the Behavioral Sciences at Stanford University. Crocker applied to the summer institute because a secretary put the flyer in her mailbox, and it sounded interesting. She had been studying cognitive processes in stereotyping so thought her work was possibly relevant to stigma, although frankly she wasn't sure.

The summer institute was directed by Dale Miller and Bob Scott; included an interdisciplinary group of psychologists, sociologists, education researchers, anthropologists, and historians; and was a truly exciting intellectual experience. Each morning the stigma scholars met as a group to discuss readings that someone in the group had identified as important or interesting. Among those readings was Porter and Washington's *Annual Review of Sociology* chapter on Black identity and self-esteem, which argued that contrary to popular wisdom and a lot of psychological theorizing, Blacks do not always suffer from low self-esteem (Porter & Washington, 1979). At the time, it was a puzzling finding to Crocker, but not particularly relevant to her work on subtyping and stereotype change, and she didn't think further about it.

Over the next few years at Northwestern University, Crocker's research evolved to include more emotional processes, and she began to study the relations among self-esteem, threats to the self, and prejudice. Established wisdom suggested that people who are low in self-esteem are more prejudiced, but her research indicated that when threatened, high self-esteem people are more likely to derogate out-groups or think their group is superior to out-groups (Crocker & Luhtanen, 1990; Crocker, Thompson, McGraw, & Ingerman, 1987).

In 1985, Crocker left Northwestern (their choice, not hers) and joined the faculty at the State University of New York at Buffalo. Her second semester there, she gave a lecture on stereotyping and prejudice in her Introduction to Social Psychology course. After the class, an African American student approached her, observing that she sometimes wondered whether people were prejudiced against her. For example, she said, she drove a new red car, and recently a White man in a pickup truck almost hit her. She wondered if it could have happened because he was prejudiced against her. Although Crocker couldn't give her an answer, the conversation connected in Crocker's mind with the Porter and Washington (1979) article on race and self-esteem. She thought that the uncertainty, or attributional ambiguity that this student had experienced about whether she was the target of prejudice might account for high self-esteem in African Americans.

As Crocker thought about this, she realized that her colleague, Brenda Major, had a research paradigm that might be really useful for studying this phenomenon of attributional ambiguity. Major was interested in why highly attractive women did not have higher self-esteem than those who were less attractive and had done a study showing that attractive women were less likely to think they had written a good essay when the man who praised their essay could see them, because the blinds were up on a one-way mirror, than when the man couldn't see them because the blinds were down (Major, Carrington, & Carnevale, 1984). When the blinds were up, the women suspected he had ulterior motives for praising their essay, and they were less likely to believe they had written a really good essay. Less attractive women did not show this effect.

Crocker scurried to Major's office to talk about this idea and the connection with her previous research. Major was intrigued by

Crocker's idea about attributional ambiguity as an explanation for the lack of self-esteem differences between members of stigmatized and nonstigmatized groups. Major also saw connections and implications that had escaped Crocker and broadened the scope of the idea. Attributional ambiguity, she suggested, might not be the only reason that Blacks do not show the low self-esteem predicted by many theories. She suggested that the tendency to make in-group social comparisons and the tendency to devalue certain domains that one's group doesn't tend to succeed in might also protect self-esteem. Major had been studying the phenomenon of "paradoxical contentment" among working women, who are underpaid relative to men yet just as satisfied with their pay. Her research showed that women's tendency to compare their pay with that of other women, instead of comparing it with that of men, could help to explain this paradoxical contentment—women often didn't realize that they were discriminated against, because they didn't know that men made more than them (Major, 1987). Another explanation that had been offered for this effect was that women simply don't care about money as much as men do. Major argued that this might be so because women held a dim view of their prospects of making money. That is, women devalued money as a self-protective device, because they knew that as women they were unlikely to earn a lot. Major had also just finished writing an article with Kay Deaux exploring how targets' self-beliefs and goals interact with perceivers' stereotypical expectations to influence gender-linked behavior (Deaux & Major, 1987). The connection between Major's ideas and research interests and those of Crocker was clear was compelling, and a collaboration was born.

We decided to write a grant proposal to fund some research. Our graduate students (including Bruce Blaine, Wayne Bylsma, Cathy Cozzarelli, Riia Luhtanen, Oscar Romero, Monica Schneider, and Maria Testa) worked with us on designing some studies, and we submitted the proposal. In the meantime, we thought the ideas themselves were compelling enough that we should write them up. Over the next few months, we began conducting studies and wrote a draft of "The Self-Protective Properties of Stigma" (Crocker & Major, 1989).

We knew from the outset that our ideas could be misinterpreted. We were careful not to say that stigmatized people are motivated to perceive prejudice against them. Rather, we said that when those who are stigmatized explain negative outcomes as being due to discrimination rather than as being due to "internal, stable, and global causes" (Crocker & Major, 1989, p. 613) it can have the consequence of protecting self-esteem. And we were worried that people would interpret our article as claiming that stigma, or prejudice, has no harmful consequences, which we were not claiming.

From the beginning, we also realized that stigma was not always self-protective. Our article (Crocker & Major, 1989) included a section on moderating factors, including the time since the acquisition, concealability, internalization of negative attitudes, responsibility for the condition, and centrality of the stigma in the self-concept. And we also recognized and outlined in our article the potential costs of attributional ambiguity, in-group social comparisons, and devaluation for motivation.

Initial Tests of Our Ideas and Where They Led Us

Our initial attempts to test our ideas in the laboratory met with some frustration. We needed to manipulate positive and negative outcomes in ways that were realistic enough to potentially affect self-esteem, to examine whether attributions to stigma, in-group comparisons, or devaluation could protect self-esteem. Creating believable and ethical manipulations that would have an impact became a challenge. Also, we found that the introduction to psychology pool of research participants included few African American students who could participate in our research, so it would take many semesters to recruit enough participants to fill out the design of a study. That was the original impetus for conducting the studies on women who feel overweight. We also naively assumed that we could use a trait measure of self-esteem as a dependent variable in our studies. Although we sometimes were able to find effects on measures of trait self-esteem, in other studies the effects were only significant for depressed affect. Eventually, we realized we needed to measure state self-esteem. We created a state version of the Rosenberg (1965) self-esteem scale and devised an early implicit measure of state self-esteem for this purpose (Bylsma, Tomaka, Luhtanen, Crocker, & Major, 1992).

Our early attempts to study attributional ambiguity underscored the importance of considering the perceived legitimacy of stigmatization from the target's perspective. Although women and African Americans showed some self-protective consequences of attributing negative evaluations to prejudice (Crocker, Voelkl, Testa, & Major, 1991), overweight women who thought they were rejected because of their weight showed drops in self-esteem (Crocker, Cornwell, & Major, 1993). Early on, we began thinking about the idea that some stigmatized people, especially those who feel responsible for their condition, might feel less deserving of positive outcomes and more deserving of negative outcomes. Hence, they might not attribute negative outcomes to prejudice and, even if they do, they might not be protected by such attributions (Crocker & Major, 1994; Major, 1994). These ideas led to another grant proposal and related research (e.g., Major, Gramzow, et al., 2002; Quinn & Crocker, 1999).

Our early studies also taught us that the self-protective strategies we proposed were more complicated than we initially presumed. For example, one of our first devaluing experiments examined whether men and women would personally devalue a trait if they learned that the other gender group scored higher on it than their own gender group. Men devalued the trait, as we had predicted, but women tended not to (Schmader & Major, 1999). In another study we found that African American college students valued school just as much as did European American students, even though the former recognized that their ethnic group did not do as well in school as the latter group. African American students were more likely than European American students, however, to say that their self-esteem did not depend on their performance in school. These studies led us to recognize the difference between devaluing a domain and disengaging one's self-esteem from that domain (Schmader, Major, & Gramzow, 2001).

Our initial studies also led to the insight that attributionally ambiguous positive outcomes can have negative effects on self-esteem and affect. African American students who were favorably evaluated by a European American peer showed a drop in self-esteem (relative to their initial levels) if the evaluator knew their race. This did not occur if the evaluator did not know their race (Crocker et al., 1991). Our attempts to understand this surprising finding led us to consider the conditions under which those who are stigmatized might distrust positive feedback or believe that it does not reflect their true level of deserving (Major & Crocker, 1993). This finding also led to another grant proposal and to explorations of the affective implications of ostensibly positive acts, such as being the beneficiary of assumptive help (Schneider, Major, Luhtanen, & Crocker, 1996), pity (Blaine, Crocker, & Major, 1995), or preferential selection procedures (Major, Feinstein, & Crocker, 1994).

What Others Have Done With Our Ideas

One of the first people to find our work useful was Claude Steele. Steele was just beginning his work on stigma and the underperformance of African American students—work on the phenomenon that has since been called stereotype threat (Steele, 1992; Steele, 1997). His idea that African American students may disidentify with school as a way of maintaining self-esteem shared our perspective on self-esteem protection and devaluation processes among members of stigmatized groups.

Our work led other scholars to reexamine differences in personal self-esteem between members of stigmatized and nonstigmatized groups. Meta-analyses revealed that although African Americans do have higher self-esteem than European Americans (Gray-Little & Hafdahl, 2000; Twenge & Crocker, 2002), other stigmatized groups, such as the overweight (Miller & Downey, 1999), and other ethnic groups, such as Asian Americans, Hispanic Americans, and Native Americans (Twenge & Crocker, 2002), on average have lower self-esteem than those who are not stigmatized. Other researchers found that people with concealable stigmas had lower self-esteem than those who were not stigmatized, whereas those with nonconcealable stigmas did not (Frable, Platt, & Hoey, 1998). These findings raise interesting and still unresolved questions about why some stigmatized groups have high self-esteem and others do not.

Other researchers, assuming that we had claimed that those who are stigmatized are motivated to perceive prejudice against them, tested whether members of stigmatized groups minimize or maximize their likelihood of being a target of prejudice. In a widely cited study, Ruggiero and Taylor (Ruggiero & Taylor, 1995) reported that those who are stigmatized do not attribute their negative outcomes to discrimination unless discrimination is virtually certain in the situation. This finding cast doubt on the hypothesis that those who are stigmatized might attribute attributionally ambiguous negative outcomes to discrimination. Subsequent work by other researchers, however, failed to replicate this finding (e.g., Inman, in press; Kaiser & Miller, 2001a), and other studies purportedly showing it were later retracted (Ruggiero & Marx, 2001). Other researchers explored how attributions to discrimination are affected by individual-differences factors, such as race-rejection sensitivity (Mendoza-Denton, Downey, Purdie, Davis, & Pietrzak, 2002) and stigma consciousness (Pinel, 1999), and situational factors, such as the attitudes of the evaluator and the clarity of prejudice cues (Operario & Fiske, 2001).

Our hypothesis that attributing outcomes to prejudice can protect the self-esteem of those who are stigmatized proved most generative, as well as most controversial. Nyla Branscombe and her colleagues, for example, argued that because group membership is an aspect of self, attributions to prejudice against the group implicate the self and hence are damaging to personal self-esteem. They showed that chronically perceiving oneself or one's group as a victim of pervasive prejudice is negatively correlated with self-esteem and well-being among members of stigmatized groups such as African Americans (Branscombe, Schmitt, & Harvey, 1999). These findings contradicted our speculation that "People who believe that they personally are frequent victims of discrimination … may have high self-esteem" (Crocker & Major, 1989, p. 621). Other researchers, however, found that once the positive correlation between individuals' perceptions that they are targets of racial discrimination and their chronic sensitivity to rejection in interpersonal relationships is controlled, the negative correlation between perceptions of racial discrimination and personal self-esteem is no longer significant (Mendoza-Denton et al., 2002). In retrospect, it is perhaps not surprising that a chronic perception that one has been a victim of discrimination is negatively related to self-esteem, given that this perception is likely to reflect not only attributional processes but also the frequency and severity of discrimination to which an individual has been exposed, as well as personal dispositions to perceive rejection. The implications of perceived prejudice for psychological well-being continue to be a topic of considerable interest to researchers. We urge researchers to be more precise in their use of terms and measurement of constructs, as well as to resist inferring causation from correlation.

Researchers also followed up on our ideas by exploring the conditions under which attributions to discrimination are and are not psychologically beneficial. For example, although attributing negative outcomes to discrimination results in less depressed affect than does attributing them to an internal, stable, global cause such as a lack of ability (Major, Kaiser, & Mc Coy, 2003), it does not result in less negative affect compared with attributing negative outcomes to a purely external cause, such as another person's being a jerk (Schmidt & Branscombe, 2002). Researchers also demonstrated that attributing negative outcomes to discrimination could be socially costly. African American targets who blame a negative outcome on discrimination are disliked and seen as troublemakers by European American students, regardless of the probability that discrimination was actually the cause of their outcome (Kaiser & Miller, 2001b).

Researchers have also explored alternative ways in which those who are stigmatized may cope with prejudice and discrimination. Drawing on social identity theory (Tajfel & Turner, 1979), Branscombe and her colleagues hypothesized that those who are stigmatized may cope with perceived discrimination by identifying more strongly with their in-group. This increased group identification, in turn, is hypothesized to lead to higher personal and collective self-esteem (e.g., Branscombe et al., 1999).

What We Have Done With Our Ideas

In the years since the publication of our article (Crocker & Major, 1989), Crocker's work has wandered far afield from the original questions that drove us. A serendipitous finding in another line of research led her to think of the issue of stigma and self-esteem in a different way. Specifically, in a study of collective, or group-based, self-esteem (Crocker, Luhtanen, Blaine, & Broadnax, 1994), she found that for White and Asian students, private and public collective self-esteem were highly correlated, whereas for African American students, they were uncorrelated. In other words, how White students view their social groups is strongly linked to how they think others view their groups, whereas for Black students, their view of their groups was disconnected from how they think others view them. This suggested to Crocker that Blacks and Whites might have different sources of self-esteem, with Whites' self-esteem being more based in others' regard and approval (following Cooley, 1902/1956, and Mead's, 1934, suggestions), whereas Blacks' self-esteem was more disconnected from others' approval. Subsequent research has supported this view (Crocker & Blanton, 1999). This line of thinking took Crocker in an entirely new direction, in which the focus of her work became contingencies of self-worth (Crocker & Wolfe, 2001). Although the impetus for this work was her interest in stigma and self-esteem, in her current work this is a side interest. Things have a way of cycling back, however, and Crocker's current interest in the costs of pursuing self-esteem has implications for the experience of prejudice and stigma that may bring her back to this topic.

Major continues to study responses to stigmatization, from a perspective that integrates justice theories with self-esteem theories. She argues that among those who are stigmatized, motives to protect personal and social identity often conflict with motives to justify existing status arrangements (Major & Schmader, 2001). Her current work examines how beliefs about the legitimacy of group status differences affect the use of self-protective strategies among members of disadvantaged and advantaged groups. She finds that members of lower status groups who believe their lower group status is legitimate are unlikely to devalue an attribute or domain in which higher status groups excel. However, if they are led to question the legitimacy of status differences, they do show the devaluing pattern we had predicted (Schmader, Major, Eccleston, & McCoy, 2001). Status legitimacy beliefs also affect the likelihood of attributing negative outcomes to discrimination. The more members of lower status groups (e.g., Hispanic Americans, women) endorse ideologies that legitimize their lower status (such as the belief in individual mobility), the less likely they are to attribute rejection by a member of a higher status group to discrimination. Just the opposite relationship is observed when members of higher status groups (European Americans, men) are rejected by a member of a lower status group (Major, Gramzow, et al., 2002). These findings are reminiscent of her earlier research on "paradoxical contentment" among members of disadvantaged groups and illustrate that things really do have a way of cycling back! Major also continues to study the nature and antecedents, as well as psychological and behavioral consequences, of believing that one is a target of discrimination. Indeed, the contradictory findings and controversies that plague research in this area impelled her recently to undertake a review and revision of our original attributional ambiguity perspective (Major, McCoy, & Quinton, 2002).

We continue to be fascinated by the question of how people cope with threatened or devalued identities and, in particular, how it is that some people manage to maintain a sense of self-respect and dignity in the face of people, circumstances, and institutions that devalue them. We are honored that our collaboration has inspired the work of others, and we are delighted that after so many years of concentrating on the "perpetrators" of prejudice, our field has begun to give more attention to the psychological predicaments experienced by the targets of prejudice.

Note

Jennifer Crocker, Department of Psychology, University of Michigan, Ann Arbor, MI 48109-1109. E-mail: jcroccker@umich.edu

References

Blaine, B., Crocker, J., & Major, B. (1995). The unintended negative consequences of sympathy for the stigmatized. *Journal of Applied Social Psychology, 25,* 889–905.

Branscombe, N. R., Schmitt, M. T., & Harvey, R. D. (1999). Perceiving pervasive discrimination among African Americans: Implications for group identification and well-being. *Journal of Personality and Social Psychology, 77,* 135–149.

Bylsma, W. H., Tomaka, J., Luhtanen, R., Crocker, J., & Major, B. (1992). Response latency as an index of temporary self-evaluation. *Personality and Social Psychology Bulletin, 18,* 60–67.

Cooley, C. H. (1956). *Human nature and the social order.* New York: Schocken. (Original work published 1902)

Crocker, J., & Blanton, H. (1999). Social inequality and self-esteem: The moderating effects of social comparison, legitimacy, and contingencies of self-esteem. In T. R. Tyler, R. Kramer, & O. John (Eds.), *The social self* (pp. 171–191). Mahwah, NJ: Lawrence Erlbaum Associates, Inc.

Crocker, J., Cornwell, B., & Major, B. M. (1993). The stigma of overweight: Affective consequences of attributional ambiguity. *Journal of Personality and Social Psychology, 64,* 60–70.

Crocker, J., & Luhtanen, R. K. (1990). Collective self-esteem and ingroup bias. *Journal of Personality and Social Psychology, 58,* 60–67.

Crocker, J., Luhtanen, R., Blaine, B., & Broadnax, S. (1994). Collective self-esteem and psychological well-being among White, Black, and Asian college students. *Personality and Social Psychology Bulletin, 20,* 502–513.

Crocker, J., & Major, B. (1989). Social stigma and self-esteem: The self-protective properties of stigma. *Psychological Review, 96,* 608–630.

Crocker, J., & Major, B. (1994). Reactions to stigma: The moderating role of justifications. In M. P. Zanna & J. M. Olson (Eds.), *The psychology of prejudice: The Ontario symposium* (Vol. 7, pp. 289–314). Hillsdale, NJ: Lawrence Erlbaum Associates, Inc.

Crocker, J., Thompson, L., McGraw, K., & Ingerman, C. (1987). Downward comparison, prejudice, and evaluation of others: Effects of self-esteem and threat. *Journal of Personality and Social Psychology, 52,* 907–916.

Crocker, J., Voelkl, K., Testa, M., & Major, B. M. (1991). Social stigma: Affective consequences of attributional ambiguity. *Journal of Personality and Social Psychology, 60,* 218–228.

Crocker, J., & Wolfe, C. T. (2001). Contingencies of self-worth. *Psychological Review, 108,* 593–623.

Deaux, K., & Major, B. (1987). Putting gender into context: An integrative model of gender-related behavior. *Psychological Review, 94,* 369–389.

Frable, D. E. S., Platt, L., & Hoey, S. (1998). Concealable stigmas and positive self-perceptions: Feeling better around similar others. *Journal of Personality and Social Psychology, 74,* 909–922.

Gray-Little, B., & Hafdahl, A. R. (2000). Factors influencing racial comparisons of self-esteem: A quantitative review. *Psychological Bulletin, 126,* 26–54.

Inman, M. L. (in press). Do you see what I see?: Similarities and differences in victims' and observers' perceptions of discrimination. *Social Cognition.*

Kaiser, C. R., & Miller, C. T. (2001a). Reacting to impending discrimination: Compensation for prejudice and attributions to discrimination. *Personality and Social Psychology Bulletin, 27,* 1357–1367.

Kaiser, C. R., & Miller, C. T. (2001b). Stop complaining! The social costs of making attributions to discrimination. *Personality and Social Psychology Bulletin, 27,* 254–263.

Major, B. (1987). Gender, justice, and the psychology of entitlement. In P. Shaver & C. Hendrick (Eds.), *Review of personality and social psychology* (Vol. 7, pp. 124–148). Beverly Hills, CA: Sage.

Major, B. (1994). From social inequality to personal entitlement: The role of social comparisons, legitimacy appraisals, and group membership. In M. P. Zanna (Ed.), *Advances in experimental and social psychology* (Vol. 26, pp. 293–355). San Diego: Academic.

Major, B., Carrington, P. I., & Carnevale, P. (1984). Physical attractiveness and self-esteem: Attributions of praise from an other-sex evaluator. *Personality and Social Psychology Bulletin, 10,* 43–50.

Major, B., & Crocker, J. (1993). Social stigma: The affective consequences of attributional ambiguity. In D. Mackie & D.L. Hamilton (Eds.), *Affect, cognition and stereotyping: Interactive processes in group perception* (pp. 345–370). San Diego, CA: Academic.

Major, B., Feinstein, J., & Crocker, J. (1994). Attributional ambiguity of affirmative action. *Basic and Applied Social Psychology, 15,* 113–141.

Major, B., Gramzow, R., McCoy, S., Levin, S., Schmader, T., & Sidanius, J. (2002).

Attributions to discrimination: The role of group status and legitimizing ideology. *Journal of Personality and Social Psychology, 82,* 269–282.

Major, B., Kaiser, C. R., & McCoy, S. K. (2003). It's not my fault: When and why attributions to prejudice protect self-esteem. *Personality and Social Psychology Bulletin, 29,* 772–781.

Major, B., McCoy, S. K., & Quinton, W. (2002). Antecedents and consequences of attributions to discrimination: Theoretical and empirical advances. In M. P. Zanna (Ed.), *Advances in Experimental Social Psychology* (Vol. 34, pp. 251–349). San Diego: Academic.

Major, B., & Schmader, T. (2001). Legitimacy and the construal of social disadvantage. In J. Jost & B. Major (Eds.), *The psychology of legitimacy: Emerging perspectives on ideology, power, and intergroup relations* (pp. 176–204). New York: Cambridge University Press.

Mead, G. H. (1934). *Mind, self, and society.* Chicago: University of Chicago Press.

Mendoza-Denton, R., Downey, G., Purdie, V. J., Davis, A., & Pietrzak, J. (2002). Sensitivity to race-based rejection: Implications for African-American students' college experience. *Journal of Personality and Social Psychology, 83,* 896–918.

Miller, C. T., & Downey, K. T. (1999). A meta-analysis of heavyweight and self-esteem. *Personality and Social Psychology Review, 3,* 68–84.

Operario, D., & Fiske, S. T. (2001). Ethnic identity moderates perceptions of prejudice: Judgments of personal versus group discrimination and subtle versus blatant bias. *Personality and Social Psychology Bulletin, 27,* 550–561.

Pinel, E. C. (1999). Stigma consciousness: The psychological legacy of social stereotypes. *Journal of Personality and Social Psychology, 76,* 114–128.

Porter, J. R., & Washington, R. E. (1979). Black identity and self-esteem: A few studies of Black self-concept, 1968–1978. *Annual Review of Sociology, 5,* 53–74.

Quinn, D. M., & Crocker, J. (1999). When ideology hurts: Effects of feeling fat and the Protestant ethic on the psychological well-being of women. *Journal of Personality and Social Psychology, 77,* 402–414.

Rosenberg, M. (1965). *Society and the adolescent self-image.* Princeton, NJ: Princeton University Press.

Ruggiero, K. M., & Marx, D. M. (2001). Retraction. "Less pain and more to gain: Why high-status group members blame their failure on discrimination." *Journal of Personality and Social Psychology, 81,* 178.

Ruggiero, K. M., & Taylor, D. M. (1995). Coping with discrimination: How disadvantaged group members perceive the discrimination that confronts them. *Journal of Personality and Social Psychology, 68,* 826–838.

Schmader, T., & Major, B. (1999). The impact of ingroup vs. outgroup performance on personal values. *Journal of Experimental Social Psychology, 35,* 47–67.

Schmader, T., Major, B., Eccleston, C., & McCoy, S. (2001). Devaluing domains in response to threatening intergroup comparisons: Perceiving legitimacy and the status-value asymmetry. *Journal of Personality and Social Psychology, 80,* 736–753.

Schmader, T., Major, B., & Gramzow, R. (2001). Coping with ethnic stereotypes in the academic domain: Perceived injustice and psychological disengagement. *Journal of Social Issues, 57,* 93–112.

Schmidt, M. T., & Branscombe, N. R. (2002). The internal and external causal loci of attributions to prejudice. *Personality and Social Psychology Bulletin, 28,* 620–628.

Schneider, M. E., Major, B., Luhtanen, R., & Crocker, J. (1996). When help hurts: Social stigma and the costs of assumptive help. *Personality and Social Psychology Bulletin, 22,* 201–209.

Steele, C. M. (1992, April). Race and the schooling of Black Americans. *Atlantic, 269,* 68–78.

Steele, C. M. (1997). A threat in the air: How stereotypes shape intellectual identity and performance. *American Psychologist, 52,* 613–629.

Tajfel, H., & Turner, J. C. (1979). An integrative theory of intergroup conflict. In S. Worchel & W. Austin (Eds.), *Psychology of intergoup relations* (Vol. 2, pp. 7–24). Chicago: Nelson-Hall.

Twenge, J., & Crocker, J. (2002). Race, ethnicity, and self-esteem: Meta-analyses comparing Whites, Blacks, Hispanics, Asians, and Native Americans, including a commentary on Gray-Little and Hafdahl (2000). *Psychological Bulletin, 128,* 371–408.

From *Psychological Inquiry,* Vol. 14, No. 3/4, 2003, pp. 232-237. Copyright © 2003 by Lawrence Erlbaum Associates, Inc. Reprinted by permission.

Leaving Race Behind: Our Growing Hispanic Population Creates a Golden Opportunity

AMITAI ETZIONI

Some years ago the United States government asked me what my race was. I was reluctant to respond because my 50 years of practicing sociology—and some powerful personal experiences—have underscored for me what we all know to one degree or another, that racial divisions bedevil America, just as they do many other societies across the world. Not wanting to encourage these divisions, I refused to check off one of the specific racial options on the U.S. Census form and instead marked a box labeled "Other." I later found out that the federal government did not accept such an attempt to de-emphasize race, by me or by some 6.75 million other Americans who tried it. Instead the government assigned me to a racial category, one it chose for me. Learning this made me conjure up what I admit is a far-fetched association. I was in this place once before. When I was a Jewish child in Nazi Germany in the early 1930s, many Jews who saw themselves as good Germans wanted to "pass" as Aryans. But the Nazi regime would have none of it. Never mind, they told these Jews, we determine who is Jewish and who is not. A similar practice prevailed in the Old South, where if you had one drop of African blood you were a Negro, disregarding all other facts and considerations, including how you saw yourself.

You might suppose that in the years since my little Census-form protest the growing enlightenment about race in our society would have been accompanied by a loosening of racial categories by our government. But in recent years the United States government has acted in a deliberate way to make it even more difficult for individuals to move beyond racial boxes and for American society as a whole to move beyond race.

Why the government perpetuates racialization and what might be done to diminish the role of race in our lives are topics that have become especially timely as Hispanics begin to take a more important role demographically, having displaced African-Americans as the largest American minority. How Hispanics view themselves and how they are viewed by others are among the most important factors affecting whether or not we can end race as a major social divide in America.

Treating people differently according to their race is as un-American as a hereditary aristocracy, and as American as slavery. The American ethos was formed by people who left the social stratification of the Old World to live in a freer, more fluid society. They sought to be defined by what they accomplished, not by what they were born with. As Arthur M. Schlesinger Jr. puts it in his book The Disuniting of America, one of the great virtues of America is that it defines individuals by where they are going rather than by where they have been. Achievement matters, not origin. The national ideal says that all Americans should be able to compete as equals, whatever their background.

American society has been divided along racial lines since its earliest days. Racial characterizations have trumped the achievement ideal; people born into a non-white race, whatever their accomplishments, have been unable to change their racial status. Worse, race has often been their most defining characteristic, affecting most, if not all, aspects of their being.

As a result, we have been caught, at least since the onset of the civil rights movement, in an ambivalence. On the one hand, we continue to dream of the day when all Americans will be treated equally, whatever their race; we rail against—and sometimes punish—those who discriminate according to race in hiring, housing, and social life. At the same time, we have ensconced in law many claims based on race: requirements that a given proportion of public subsidies, loans, job training, educational assistance, and admission slots at choice colleges be set aside for people of color. Many Americans, including African-Americans, are uneasy about what some people consider reverse discrimination. Courts have limited its scope; politicians have made hay by opposing it; and some of its beneficiaries feel that their successes are hollow because they are unsure whether their gains reflect hard-won achievements or special favors. There must be a better way to deal with past and current injustice. And the rapid changes in American demographics call for a reexamination of the place of race in America.

Enter the Hispanic

We have grown accustomed to thinking about America in black and white, and might well have continued to do so for decades to come except that Hispanics complicate this simplistic scheme: they do not fit into the old racial categories. Some Hispanics appear to many Americans to be black (for example, quite a few Cuban-Americans), others as white (especially immigrants from Argentina and Chile), and the appearance of still others is hard for many people to pigeonhole. Anyone seeing the lineup of baseball players honored as Major League Baseball's "Latino Legends Team" would find that the players vary from those who are as fair-skinned as Roger Clemens to those who are as dark-skinned as Jackie Robinson. More important by far, survey after survey shows that most Hispanics object to being classified as either black or white. A national survey conducted in 2002 indicated that 76 percent of Hispanics say the standard racial categories used by the U.S. Census do not address their preferences. The last thing most of those surveyed desire is to be treated as yet another race—as "brown" Americans.

Hispanics would have forced the question of how we define one another even if they were just another group of immigrants among the many that have made America what it is. But Hispanics are not just one more group of immigrants. Not only have Hispanic numbers surpassed those of black Americans, who until 2003 made up America's largest minority group, Hispanics have been reliably projected to grow much faster than African-Americans or any other American group. Thus, according to the Census, in 1990 blacks constituted 12 percent of the population and Hispanics 9 percent. By 2000, Hispanics caught up with blacks, amounting to 12.5 percent of the population compared to 12.3 percent for blacks. By 2050, Hispanics are projected to be 24.3 percent of the American population, compared to 14.7 percent for blacks. In many cities, from Miami to Los Angeles, in which African-Americans have been the largest minority group, Hispanics' numbers are increasingly felt. While once Hispanics were concentrated in the areas bordering Mexico, their numbers are now growing in places like Denver, St. Paul, and even New England.

Immigration fuels the growth of Hispanics relative to the growth of African-Americans because Latin American immigration, legal and illegal, continues at an explosive pace, while immigration from Africa is minuscule. Hispanics also have more children than African-Americans. During the most recent year for which data is available, 2003-2004, one of every two people added to America's population was Hispanic. And while black Americans have long been politically mobilized and active, Hispanics are just beginning to make their weight felt in American politics.

The rapid growth in the number, visibility, and power of Hispanics will largely determine the future of race in America, a point highlighted by Clara E. Rodriguez in her book Changing Race: Latinos, the Census, and the History of Ethnicity in the U.S. If Hispanics are to be viewed as brown or black (and some on the left aspire to color them), and above all if Hispanics develop the sense of disenfranchisement and alienation that many African-Americans have acquired (often for very good reasons), then America's immutable racial categories will only deepen.

If, on the other hand, most Hispanics continue to see themselves as members of one or more ethnic groups, then race in America might be pushed to the margins. Racial categories have historically set us apart; ethnic categories are part of the mosaic that makes up America. It has been much easier for an individual to assimilate from an ethnic perspective than from a racial one. Race is considered a biological attribute, a part of your being that cannot be dropped or modified. Ethnic origin, in contrast, is where you came from. All Americans have one hyphen or another attached to their ethnic status: we're Polish-, or German-, or Anglo-, or Italian-Americans. Adding Cuban-Americans or Mexican-Americans to this collage would create more comfortable categories of a comparable sort.

The Race Trap

Many people take it for granted that genes determine race, just as genes determine gender. And we also tend to believe that racial categories are easy to discern (though we all know of exceptions).

One way to show how contrived racial divisions actually are is to recall that practically all of the DNA in all human beings is the same. Our differences are truly skin deep. Moreover, the notion that most of us are of one race or another has little basis in science. The Human Genome Project informs us not only that 99.9 percent of genetic material is shared by all humans, but also that variation in the remaining 0.1 percent is greater within racial groups than across them. That is, not only are 99.9 percent of the genes of a black person the same as those of a white person, but the genes of a particular black person may be more similar to the genes of a white person than they are to another black person.

This point was driven home to college students in a sociology class at Penn State in April 2005. Following their professor's suggestion, the students took DNA tests that had surprising results. A student who identified himself as "a proud black man" found that only 52 percent of his ancestry traced back to Africa, while the other 48 percent was European. Another student who said she takes flak from black friends for having a white boyfriend found that her ancestry was 58 percent European and only 42 percent African. These two students are not alone: an estimated one-third of the African-American population has European ancestry.

Which people make up a distinct race and which are considered dark-skinned constantly changes as social prejudices change. Jewish-, Slavic-, Irish-, and Polish-Americans were considered distinct races in the mid-19th and early 20th centuries— and dark races at that, as chronicled in great detail in Matthew Frye Jacobson's book Whiteness of a Different Color: European Immigrants and the Alchemy of Race and in a well-documented book by Noel Ignatiev, How the Irish Became White. Ignatiev found that in the 1850s, Irish people were considered non-white in America and were frequently referred to as "niggers turned inside out." (Blacks were sometimes called "smoked Irish.")

The capriciousness of racial classifications is further highlighted by the way the U.S. Census, the most authoritative and widely used source of social classifications, divides Americans into races. When I ask my students how many races they think there are in America, they typically count four: white, black, Asian, and Native American. The Census says there are 15 racial categories: white, African-American, American Indian/Alaska Native, Asian Indian, Chinese, Filipino, Japanese, Korean, Vietnamese, "other Asian," Native Hawaiian, Guamanian/Chamorro, Samoan, and "other Pacific Islander," and as of 2000 one more for those who feel they are of some other race. (Hispanic is not on this list because the Census treats Hispanic as an ethnicity and asks about it on a separate question, but immediately following that question, the Census asks, "So what is your race, anyhow?")

The arbitrary nature of these classifications is demonstrated by the Census Bureau itself, which can change the race of millions of Americans by the stroke of a pen. The Census changed the race of Indian- and Pakistani-Americans from white in 1970 to Asian in 1980. In 1930 the Census made Mexicans into a different race but then withdrew this category. Similarly, Hindu made a brief appearance as a race in the 1930 and 1940 Censuses but was subsequently withdrawn.

Anthropologists have found that some tribes do not see colors the way many of us do; for instance, they do not "see" a difference between brown and yellow. Members of these tribes are not colorblind, but some differences found in nature (in the color spectrum) simply don't register with them, just as young American children are unaware of racial differences until someone introduces them to these distinctions. We draw a line between white and black, but people's skin colors have many shades. It is our social prejudices that lead us to make sharp racial categories.

I am not one of those postmodernists who, influenced by Nietzsche and Foucault, claim that there are no epistemological truths, that all facts are a matter of social construction. I disagree with Nietzsche's description of truth as "a mobile army of metaphors, metonyms, and anthropomorphisms—in short a sum of human relations, which have been enhanced, transposed, and embellished poetically and rhetorically and which after long use seem firm, canonical, and obligatory to a people." However, there is no doubt that social construction plays a significant role in the way we "see" racial differences, although our views may in turn be affected by other factors that are less subject to construction, for example, historical differences.

Most important is the significance we attribute to race and the interpretations we impose on it. When we are told only that a person is, say, Asian-American, we often jump to a whole list of conclusions regarding that person's looks, intelligence, work ethic, character; we make the same sort of jumps for Native Americans, blacks, and other races. Many things follow from these knee-jerk characterizations: whether we will fear or like this person, whether we will wish to have him or her as a neighbor or as a spouse for one of our children—all on the basis of race. In short, we load on to race a great deal of social importance that is not a reflection of the "objective" biological differences that exist. To paraphrase the UNESCO Constitution, racial divisions are made in the minds of men and women, and that is where they will have to be ended.

Defining the Hispanic

If racial categories have long been settled, the social characterization of the Hispanic is up for grabs. We still don't know whether Hispanics will be defined as a brown race and align themselves with those in the United States who are or who see themselves as marginalized or victimized—or if they will be viewed as a conglomerate of ethnic groups, of Mexican-Americans, Cuban-Americans, Dominican-Americans, and so forth, who will fit snugly into the social mosaic.

The term Hispanic was first used in the Census in 1980. Before that, Mexican-Americans and Cuban-Americans were classified as white (except when a Census interviewer identified an individual as the member of a different racial group). Until 1980, Hispanics were part of the great American panorama of ethnic groups. Then the Census combined these groups into a distinct category unlike any other. It was as if the federal government were to one day lump together Spanish-, Italian-, and Greek-Americans into a group called "Southern European" and begin issuing statistics on how their income, educational achievements, number of offspring, and so on compare to those of Northern Europeans.

And as we've seen, those who define themselves as Hispanic are asked to declare a race. In the 1980 Census, the options included, aside from the usual menu of races, that ambiguous category "Other." There were 6.75 million Americans, including me, who chose this option in 1980. Most revealing: 40 percent of Hispanics chose this option. (Note that they—and I—chose this category despite the nature of the word Other, which suggests the idea of "not being one of us." Had the category been accorded a less loaded label, say "wish not to be identified with any one group," it seems likely that many millions more would have chosen this box.)

To have millions of Americans choose to identify themselves as "Other" created a political backlash because Census statistics are used both to allocate public funds to benefit minority groups and to assess their political strength. Some African-American groups, especially, feared that if African-Americans chose "Other" instead of marking the "African-American" box, they would lose public allotments and political heft.

But never underestimate our government. The Census Bureau has used a statistical procedure to assign racial categories to those millions of us who sought to butt out of this divisive classification scheme. Federal regulations outlined by the Office of Management and Budget, a White House agency, ruled that the Census must "impute" a specific race to those who do not choose one. For several key public policy purposes, a good deal of social and economic data must be aggregated into five racial groups: white, black, Asian, American Indian or Alaska Native, and native Hawaiian or other Pacific Islander. How does the government pick a race for a person who checked the "Other" box? They turn to the answers for other Census questions: for example, income, neighborhood, education level, or last name. The resulting profiles of the U.S. population (referred to as the "age-race modified profile") are then used by government agencies in allotting public funds and for other official and public purposes.

But the Census isn't alone in oversimplifying the data. Increasingly, other entities, including the media, have treated Hispanics as a race rather than an ethnic group. This occurs implicitly when those who generate social data—such as government agencies or social scientists—break down the data into four categories: white, black, Asian, and Hispanic, which is comparable to listing apples, oranges, bananas, and yams. In their profile of jail inmates, the Bureau of Justice statistics lists inmates' origins as "white, black, Hispanic, American Indian/Alaska Native, Asian/Pacific Islander, and more than one race." The New York Times ran a front-page story last September in which it compared the first names used by whites, blacks, Asians, and Hispanics. Replace the word Hispanics with the name of another ethnic group, say Jews, and the unwitting racial implication of this classification will stand out.

Still other studies include Hispanics when they explicitly refer to racial groups. For example, a 2001 paper by Sean Reardon and John T. Yun examines what they call "racial balkanization among suburban schools," where there is increased segregation among black, Hispanic, and Asian students. A 2005 Seattle Times story uses racial terminology when it reports "Latinos have the fewest numbers among racial groups in master's-of-business programs nationwide, with about 5,000 enrolling annually." Similarly, The San Diego Union Tribune states: "A brawl between Latino and black students resulted in a lockdown of the school and revealed tensions between the two largest racial groups on campus."

A handful of others go a step further and refer to Hispanics as a brown race. For example, following the recent Los Angeles mayoral election, The Houston Chronicle informed us that "Villaraigosa's broad-based support has analysts wondering whether it is evidence of an emerging black-brown coalition." And, National Public Radio reported: "There is no black and brown alliance at a South Central Los Angeles high school."

One way or another, all of these references push us in the wrong direction—toward racializing Hispanics and deepening social divisions. America would be best served if we moved in the opposite direction.

A New Taxonomy

Thus far, workers at the U.S. Census Bureau, following the White House's instructions, seem determined to prevent any de-emphasis of race. They are testing iterations of the wording for the relevant questions in the 2010 Census—but all of these possibilities continue to require people to identify themselves by race. Moreover, Census bureaucrats will continue to impute race to those who refuse to do so themselves, ignoring the ever-growing number of people, especially Hispanics, who do not fit into this scheme.

Imagine if instead the federal government classified people by their country (or countries) of origin. For some governmental purposes, it might suffice to use large categories, such as Africa (which would exclude other so-called black groups, such as Haitians and West Indians that are now included in references to "black" Americans), Asia, Europe, Central America, and South America (the last two categories would not, of course, in-

clude Spain). For other purposes, a more detailed breakdown might work better—using regions such as the Middle East and Southeast Asia, for example—and if still more detail was desired, specific countries could be used, as we do for identifying ethnic groups (Irish, Polish, Cuban, Mexican, Japanese, Ethiopian, and so on). Kenneth Prewitt, a former director of the U.S. Census Bureau, has suggested the use of ethnic categories. As we have seen, ethnic origins carry some implications for who we are, but these implications decline in importance over time. Above all, they do not define us in some immutable way, as racial categories do. A category called something like "wish not to be identified with any particular group" should be included for those who do not want to be characterized even by ethnicity or for others who view themselves as having a varied and combined heritage.

The classification of Americans who are second-generation, and beyond, highlights the importance of the no-particular-group category. Although a fourth-generation Italian-American might still wish to be identified as Italian, he might not, particularly if he has grandparents or parents who are, say, Greek, Korean, and Native American. Forcing such a person to classify himself as a member of one ethnic group conceals the significance of the most important American development in social matters: out-marriage. Out-marriage rates for all groups other than African-Americans are so high that most of us will soon be tied to Americans of a large variety of backgrounds by the closest possible social tie, the familial one. Approximately 30 percent of third-generation Hispanics and 40 percent of third-generation Asians marry people of a different racial or ethnic origin. Altogether, the proportion of marriages among people of different racial or ethnic origins has increased by 72 percent since 1970. The trend suggests more of this in the future. Even if your spouse is of the same background, chances are high that the spouse of a sibling or cousin will represent a different part of the American collage. At holidays and other family events, from birthdays to funerals, we will increasingly be in close connection with "Others." Before too long most Americans will be "Tiger Woods" Americans, whose parental heritage is black, Native American, Chinese, Caucasian, and Thai. Now is the time for our social categories to reflect this trend—and its capacity for building a sense of one community—rather than conceal it.

Where Do We Go from Here?

Changing the way we divide up society will not magically resolve our differences or abolish racial prejudices. Nor does a movement toward a colorblind nation mean that we should stop working for a more just America. A combination of three major approaches that deal with economic and legal change could allow us to greatly downgrade the importance of race as a social criterion and still advance social justice. These approaches include reparations, class-based social programs, and fighting discrimination on an individual basis.

To make amends for the grave injustice that has been done to African-Americans by slavery and racial prejudice, as well as to bring to a close claims based on past injustices—and the sense of victimhood and entitlement that often accompanies these claims—major reparations are called for. One possible plan might allot a trillion dollars in education, training, and housing vouchers to African-Americans over a period of 20 years. (The same sort of plan might be devised for Native Americans.)

Such reparations cannot make full compensation for the sins of slavery, of course. But nothing can. Even so, if Jews could accept restitution from Germany and move on (Germany and Israel now have normal international relations, and the Jewish community in Germany is rapidly growing), could not a similar reconciliation between black and white Americans follow reparations? A precedent in our own history is the payment of reparations to Japanese-Americans because of their internment in World War II. In 1988, the U.S. government issued a formal apology in the Civil Liberties Act and awarded $20,000 to each living person who had been interned. About 80,000 claims were awarded, totaling $1.6 billion.

Part of the deal should be that once reparations are made for the sins against African-Americans in the past, black people could no longer claim special entitlements or privileges on the basis of their race. Reparations thus would end affirmative action and minority set-asides as we have known them.

At the same time, Americans who are disadvantaged for any reason not of their own doing—the handicapped; those who grew up in parts of the country, such as Appalachia, in which the economy has long been lagging; those whose jobs were sent overseas who are too old to be retrained—would be given extra aid in applying for college admissions and scholarships, housing allowances, small-business loans, and other social benefits. The basis for such aid would be socio-economic status, not race. The child of a black billionaire would no longer be entitled to special consideration in college admissions, for instance, but the child of a poor white worker who lost his job to outsourcing and could not find new employment would be.

Social scientists differ in their estimates of the extent to which differences in opportunity and upward mobility between blacks and whites are due to racial prejudice and the extent to which they are due to economic class differences. But most scholars who have studied the matter agree that economic factors are stronger than racial ones, possibly accounting for as much as 80 percent of the differences we observe. A vivid example: In recent years, Wake County in North Carolina made sure that its public school classes were composed of students of different economic backgrounds, disregarding racial and ethnic differences. The results of this economic integration overshadowed previous attempts to improve achievement via racial integration. While a decade ago, only 40 percent of blacks in grades three through eight scored at grade level, in the spring of 2005, 80 percent did so.

Class differences affect not only educational achievement, health, and job selection, but also how people are regarded or stereotyped. Fifty years ago, a study conducted at Howard University showed that although adjectives used to describe whites and blacks were quite different, that variance was greatly reduced when class was held constant. People described upperclass whites and upper-class blacks in a remarkably similar fashion, as intelligent and ambitious. People also described lower-class whites and lower-class blacks in a similar way, as dirty and ignorant. The author concluded that "stereotypes vary more as a function of class than of race."

If race-based discrimination were a thing of the past, and black Americans were no longer subjected to it, then my argument that reparations can lead to closure would be easier to sustain. Strong evidence shows, however, that discrimination remains very much with us. A 1990 Urban Institute study found that when two people of different races applied for the same job, one in eight times the white was offered the job and an equally qualified African-American was not. Another Urban Institute study, released in 1999, found that racial minorities received less time and information from loan officers and were quoted higher interest rates than whites in most of the cities where tests were conducted.

The victims of current racial discrimination should be fully entitled to remedies in court and through such federal agencies as the Equal Employment Opportunity Commission. These cases should be dealt with on an individual basis or in a class-action suit where evidence exists to support one. Those who sense discrimination should be required to prove it. It shouldn't be assumed that because a given workplace has more people of race x than race y, discrimination must exist.

A Vision of the Future

In the end, it comes down to what Americans envision for our future together: either an open society, in which everyone is equally respected (an elusive goal but perhaps closer at hand than we realize), or an even more racialized nation, in which "people of color" are arrayed in perpetual conflict with white people. The first possibility is a vision of America as a community in which people work out their differences and make up for past injustices in a peaceful and fair manner; the other is one in which charges of prejudice and discrimination are mixed with real injustices, and in which a frustrated sense of victimhood and entitlement on the one hand is met with guilt and rejection on the other.

A good part of what is at stake is all too real: the distribution of assets, income, and power, which reparations, class-based reforms, and the courts should be able to sort out. But don't overlook the importance of symbols, attitudes, and feelings, which can't be changed legislatively. One place to start is with a debate over the official ways in which we classify ourselves and the ways we gather social data, because these classifications and data are used as a mirror in which we see ourselves reflected.

Let us begin with a fairly modest request of the powers that be: Give us a chance. Don't make me define my children and myself in racial terms; don't "impute" a race to me or to any of the millions of Americans who feel as I do. Allow us to describe ourselves simply as Americans. I bet my 50 years as a sociologist that we will all be better for it.

AMITAI ETZIONI is University Professor at George Washington University and the author of The Monochrome Society.

From *American Scholar*, Vol. 75, issue 2, Spring 2006, pp. 20-31. Copyright © 2006 by Amitai Etzioni. Reprinted by permission of the journal and Amitai Etzioni.

Lowered Expectations

At the Southwestern Psychological Association Annual Convention, Joshua Aronson suggested ways to counteract the harmful affects of stereotypes about minorities' intellectual abilities.

ZAK STAMBOR

As a third-grader in Austin, Texas, in 1969, psychologist Joshua Aronson, PhD, looked like many grade-schoolers; a long, thick, coffee-colored muddle of hair drooped down his forehead and over his ears and neck. And despite—or perhaps because of—the mop top, his teacher, Mrs. Williams, loved him. He was one of her favorite and best performing students.

The following year his family moved to California. His hair was the same but his teacher was not. Mr. Tomlin, his new teacher, had a short, spiky crew cut and disliked "long hairs"—even when those long hairs were 9 years old. He thought they were dirty and dumb, and he humiliated Aronson on the first day of class. From that point on, until he reached college, Aronson struggled in school and, in turn, his school placed him in remedial classes.

"A really good teacher can change your life, and a bad one can too," said Aronson, a New York University psychology and education professor, at the Southwestern Psychological Association (SWPA) Annual Convention, held in Austin in April.

Based on his own experience and the research that it helped spark, Aronson suggested that in most situations human intelligence reflects a social transaction: When one person in the social interaction holds a negative stereotype of the other person, like Mr. Tomlin's notion of long hairs' intelligence, it can cause the stereotyped person to mirror the other's expectation.

Aronson further suggested that if teachers focused on counteracting negative stereotypes of certain groups' academic abilities, like those of blacks, Hispanics and women, they could help to dramatically improve those groups' performance. "Even if we can't get better teachers, we can improve the system," he said. "We should be stressing belongingness, engagement and challenges."

Fragile Intelligence

Aronson urged psychologists to pay attention to their psychological fathers. His own work builds on research that emerged in the 1960s when psychologists like his father and fellow conference speaker Elliot Aronson, PhD, investigated social influence, and Claude Steele, PhD, first proposed the underpinnings for the concept of stereotype threat—the fear that one will be reduced to the negative stereotype of one's group. "You don't want to confirm a negative stereotype, or even a positive stereotype, because it ... pegs you," Aronson said.

For instance, when Aronson was working with a realtor to buy a house in Austin, she asked him, "Why are you Jews so good with money?" The realtor explained that nearly every Jewish person she had ever worked with had wanted to live in the most exclusive areas. Aronson explained to her about the dangers of such stereotypes, and she apologized. But later when they went to lunch he was caught in a Catch-22. If he offered to buy the realtor's lunch it would confirm her stereotype, and if he didn't he would confirm another stereotype about Jewish people—that they are cheap.

And for many blacks in America, he's found that the threat posed by the subject of intelligence can be extremely damaging.

In a 1995 study in the *Journal of Personality and Social Psychology* (Vol. 69, No. 5, pages 797–811), Steele worked with Aronson to examine whether reducing stereotype threat could bolster threatened group members' academic performance. The researchers had black and white students take a difficult standardized verbal test. Half the students were told that the test measured their intellectual ability; the other half were told it was unrelated to ability. They found that the black students who were told that the test measured their intellectual ability did significantly worse on the test than the black students in the other group—even after Aronson adjusted the scores to eliminate any differences in the students' academic abilities. The finding points to the stereotype threat to their intelligence, brought on by attaching the intelligence label to the test.

In subsequent studies, Aronson has found that teachers can trigger stereotype threat by having students identify their race, which can apparently hamper black students' performance, or gender, which can interfere with women's performance on math tests. The findings help explain the black-white and male-female achievement gaps in National Center for Educational Statistics reports for more than 40 years, he said.

Reducing Threat

Reflecting on the inability of his former teacher, Mr. Tomlin, to shake the notion that long-haired children are dumb, Aronson pointed to cognitive dissonance theory, developed by Leon Festinger, PhD—his father Elliot's graduate school mentor at Stanford University from 1957 to 1959. The theory suggests that people are powerfully motivated to maintain consistent beliefs—like long-haired children are dumb—even when that belief is irrational or even maladaptive.

To address the problem, Aronson suggested that schools incorporate programs like the "jigsaw classroom"—a concept conceived by Elliot Aronson to help integrate minority students into predominately white Austin schools in 1971. In the program, a teacher assigns students to racially and academically mixed groups. Each member of the group learns one piece of academic material and teaches it to the others in their group. Elliot Aronson found that the project appears to boost students' reliance on each other, fondness of each other and of school, and their self-esteem.

Moreover, the program doesn't have to be interracial to work, since discord and bullying occurs in all schools, he added. "I invented jigsaw to get kids to work together and not compete," said Elliot Aronson during a discussion with SWPA President Paul R. Nail, PhD, following his son's address. "It makes them interdependent and breaks barriers to help them work as colleagues, not enemies."

The key to jigsaw and other such programs is that they challenge and push students and teachers' expectations, said Joshua Aronson.

"We need for teachers and the system to understand that intelligence is malleable—and it needs nurturing," he said.

From *Monitor on Psychology,* Vol. 37 (6), June 2006, pp. 26-27. Copyright © 2006 by American Psychological Association. Reprinted by permission. No further distribution without permission from the American Psychological Association.

Change of Heart

A landmark survey reveals that most Americans are open to sharing their life, work, and even love with people of a different color. So why do tensions remain?

ADAM GOODHEART

The rural Maryland county where I live, barely an hour from the Washington, D.C., Beltway, is a place whose soul is not just divided but fractured. There are still small towns here that feel like the Old South, where whites talk about "colored people" and blacks in their late 40s remember such things as farming with mules and horses and attending segregated schools. But there are newer communities, too: sprawling tracts of identical suburban houses whose middle-class residents—black as well as white—think little about the past and care even less. In their midst, a small but growing Hispanic population has started to thrive, drawn by the economic opportunities that change has brought.

Many parts of our country today look something like this. When President Lyndon Johnson's Kerner Commission famously prophesied in 1968 a future of "two societies, one black, one white," it was wrong. What we have now is a multiplicity of Americas, often sharing the same neighborhood, but rarely the same mindset.

The good news is that in the 50 years since the Supreme Court ruled in favor of school desegregation in the case of *Brown* v. *Board of Education,* there have been some dramatic changes in Americans' attitudes toward race and equality. Today, most Americans—55 percent—think that the state of race relations is either very or somewhat good, according to a landmark telephone survey of 2,002 people conducted last November and December by the Gallup Organization for AARP and the Leadership Conference on Civil Rights (LCCR). Yet disheartening divisions between the races persist. Such is the complicated picture painted by "Civil Rights and Race Relations," the largest and most comprehensive race-relations survey of blacks, Hispanics, and whites that Gallup has ever undertaken.

The most astonishing progress has been made in two areas that hit closest to home for most Americans: interracial relationships and the neighborhoods we live in. Consider that 70 percent of whites now say they approve of marriage between whites and blacks, up from just 4 percent in a 1958 Gallup poll. Such open-mindedness extends across racial lines: 80 percent

of blacks and 77 percent of Hispanics also said they generally approve of interracial marriage. Perhaps even more remarkable, a large majority of white respondents—66 percent—say they would not object if their own child or grandchild chose a black spouse. Blacks (86 percent) and Hispanics (79 percent) were equally accepting about a child or grandchild's marrying someone of another race.

When it comes to choosing neighbors, an inclusive spirit again prevails: majorities of blacks, whites, and Hispanics all say they would rather live in racially mixed neighborhoods than surround themselves with only members of their own group. "It's hard now to imagine the level of fear and anxiety that Americans felt about these issues just a few decades ago," says Taylor Branch, who won a Pulitzer Prize in 1989 for his history of the Civil Rights Movement, *Parting the Waters: America in the King Years, 1954-1963*. "The idea [among whites] that you might have a black colleague or customer or neighbor has now become relatively commonplace except in a few scattered pockets." Similarly, slight majorities of whites and Hispanics and a little less than half of blacks think that minorities should try to blend in with the rest of American culture rather than maintain their own separate identities.

The data did show a significant generation gap: young Americans (ages 18-29) of all races were more likely than older respondents (65-plus) to favor the retention of distinctive cultures. But this is not necessarily a step backward. "Younger people are more likely to have been exposed in school to the idea that multiculturalism is a positive thing, that it's not necessarily bad when certain groups desire to be among their own kind," suggests the eminent Harvard sociologist William Julius Wilson. "This is a phenomenon of just the last couple of decades."

When it comes to future expectations, however, in certain respects the picture is as bleak as ever. Sixty-three percent of Americans think that race relations will always be a problem for our country—a view that varies little whether the respondents are white, black, or Hispanic. That's up sharply from the 42 percent who felt similarly in a study done in 1963, when most Americans were seeing television images of African Americans

128

Survey Insights

Our respondents told us that they…

1. Would not object to a child or grandchild's marrying someone of another race.

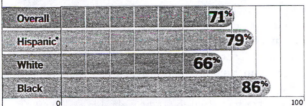

Overall	71%
Hispanic*	79%
White	66%
Black	86%

* Black Hispanics were asked about marrying whites;
white Hispanics were asked about marrying blacks.

2. Prefer to live in a neighborhood that is mostly mixed.

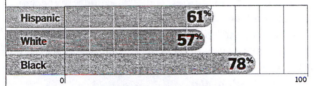

Hispanic	61%
White	57%
Black	78%

3. Believe race relations will always be a problem in the U.S.

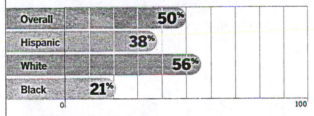

Overall	63%
Hispanic	60%
White	62%
Black	72%

4. Think all or most of the goals of Dr. Martin Luther King Jr. and the Civil Rights Movement have been achieved.

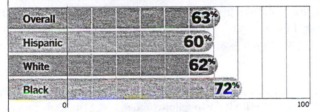

Overall	50%
Hispanic	38%
White	56%
Black	21%

5. Have been denied a rental or an opportunity to buy a home.

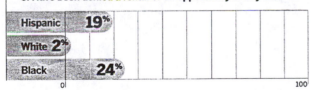

Hispanic	19%
White	2%
Black	24%

*Civil Rights and Race Relations," a study commissioned by AARP and the LCCR and conducted by the Gallup Organization, is based on telephone interviews with 2,002 people 18 years of age or older from households in the continental United States. All polling was conducted between November 11 and December 14, 2003. The respondents included 915 whites and oversamples of 446 blacks and 551 Hispanics. In addition, 90 who belonged to other groups or gave no racial or ethnic affiliation were interviewed. The results were weighted to reflect the actual representation of each group in the U.S. population. ("Whites" refers to non-Hispanic whites; "black" refers to non-Hispanic blacks; and the "Hispanic" category includes all Hispanics, whether they identified as black or as white or did not specify a racial category.) The margin of error at the 95 percent confidence level for that total national sample is +/-5.1 percentage points. +/-6.7 percentage points for whites, +/-8.5 percentage points for blacks, and +/-6.2 percentage points for Hispanics.

withstanding police dogs and fire hoses but believed the Civil Rights Movement would eventually prevail. (Indeed, respondents over 65, who remember the 1960s well, were the ones most likely to remain optimistic, while those under 30—of all races—were the least hopeful.)

"There was a sense then that eventually truth and justice would win out," recalls Julian Bond, who as a founder of the Student Nonviolent Coordinating Committee (SNCC) led some of the earliest sit-ins and is now chairman of the National Association for the Advancement of Colored People (NAACP). "Maybe people are looking back and realizing we haven't come as far as we'd hoped."

A large majority of Americans of all ages and races does agree that the 20th-century crusade for civil rights was a watershed in our nation's history. In addition, most people of all backgrounds also believe that the movement has benefited not just blacks and other minorities but all Americans. This is a remarkable degree of unanimity for an issue that violently divided so many families and communities just a generation or two ago.

"The Civil Rights Movement has had enormous collateral effects for everyone from gays to members of religious minorities, and especially for women," Branch says. "These effects have been felt in every university, every corporation, and even, I'd venture to say, almost every American household, down to the level of who does the dishes and changes the diapers."

But when it comes to gauging the ultimate success or failure of the struggle, members of different races diverge sharply. While 56 percent of whites say they believe that "all or most" of the goals of Dr. Martin Luther King Jr. and the 1960s Civil Rights Movement have been achieved, only 21 percent of blacks agree with them. A similar margin divides whites' and blacks' opinions on how much of a role the movement will continue to have: 66 percent of blacks think it will be "extremely important" to the United States in the future, compared with only 23 percent of whites. "Many whites have a misconception of the Civil Rights Movement as something with a few limited goals that have already been achieved," Branch suggests.

Similarly, the AARP-LCCR survey found vast gulfs between different groups' perceptions of how minorities are treated today. Seventy-six percent of white respondents think that blacks are treated "very fairly" or "somewhat fairly," but only 38 percent of blacks agree with them; nearly one-third, in fact, say that members of their race are treated "very unfairly." (Hispanics fall in the middle: they are more or less evenly divided about the treatment of their own group as well as that of blacks.) And while 61 percent of whites believe that blacks have achieved equality in the realm of job opportunities, just 12 percent of African Americans concur.

How is it that we can all share the same land, the same history, and yet reach such different conclusions? The disparities start to make sense when you look at the most fundamental measure of each group's current happiness: economic prosperity.

Blacks are more than twice as likely as whites to say that their personal finances are in "poor shape"; they are also more than twice as likely to say they worry constantly about whether their family's income will be enough to pay the bills. Hispanics appear to be feeling similar or even greater degrees of financial stress. And indeed, their concerns are legitimate: nationally, the median household income is $35,500 among blacks, $40,000 among Hispanics, and $55,318 among whites, according to the most recent figures available from the U.S. Census Bureau.

"Were we to have solved all the problems that we tried to take on, there would be relative parity today," Bond says. "The fact that there is still an enormous wealth gap between blacks and whites is evidence of the continuing legacy of segregation and even of slavery."

What explains these persistent economic disparities? Continued prejudice, plain and simple. Half a century after *Brown*, a minuscule 8 percent of African Americans could claim that they had ever in their lives been denied admittance to a school on account of race. Yet other forms of discrimination persist. A third reported that they had been passed over for a job because they are black, a third said they had been blocked from promotion, and a quarter said they had been denied an opportunity to rent or buy housing. Only slightly fewer Hispanics said they had experienced similar forms of prejudice.

Even more than such dramatic instances of racism, it is the less obvious, day-to-day examples of prejudice that are a continuing, grinding burden on minorities in America. Nearly half of all blacks reported having experienced at least one form of discrimination in the last 30 days, in settings ranging from stores (26 percent) to restaurants and theaters (18 percent) to public transportation (10 percent). The figures for Hispanics were at nearly the same level. Perhaps most troubling of all, a surprising 22 percent of blacks and 24 percent of Hispanics said they had, in the past month, been the victims of prejudice in an interaction with the police.

For the record, a significant number of white Americans maintain that they, too, are sometimes penalized on the basis of race: 21 percent report that they have been the victims of reverse discrimination, especially in the workplace. And many seem unaware or even dismissive of continuing prejudice against other groups: nearly half insist that society treats them no better than blacks. But the majority of whites—52 percent—say they support affirmative action for blacks, as do 81 percent of blacks and 66 percent of Hispanics. So while an uncomfortably large number of Americans remain in denial about persistent discrimination against minorities, an even larger percentage, it seems, want to do the right thing.

Like the American countryside, the AARP-LCCR survey results are a landscape of layers: old outlooks and new perceptions, 20th-century memories and 21st-century expectations. One of the most unexpected results came when the polltakers asked participants to consider the prediction that by 2050 the majority of Americans will be nonwhite. Only about 13 percent of each group said this would be a bad thing; most Americans said it simply won't matter.

So, as their country changes, perhaps Americans—more than they are often given credit for—are ready to change along with it. Indeed, the revolution that *Brown* started will likely continue through the next 50 years and beyond. "We did much," Bond says, "but there's much left to do."

ADAM GOODHEART is a fellow of the C. V. Starr Center for the Study of the American Experience at Washington College in Chestertown, Maryland.

From *AARP The Magazine*, May/June 2004. Copyright © 2004 by Adam Goodheart. Reprinted by permission of the Wylie Agency, Inc.

Thin Ice: "Stereotype Threat" and Black College Students

When capable black college students fail to perform as well as their white counterparts, the explanation often has less to do with preparation or ability than with the threat of stereotypes about their capacity to succeed. Educators at Stanford who tested this hypothesis report their findings and propose solutions.

CLAUDE M. STEELE

The buildings had hardly changed in the thirty years since I'd been there. "There" was a small liberal-arts school quite near the college that I attended. In my student days I had visited it many times to see friends. This time I was there to give a speech about how racial and gender stereotypes, floating and abstract though they might seem, can affect concrete things like grades, test scores, and academic identity. My talk was received warmly, and the next morning I met with a small group of African-American students. I have done this on many campuses. But this time, perhaps cued by the familiarity of the place, I had an experience of déjà vu. The students expressed a litany of complaints that could have come straight from the mouths of the black friends I had visited there thirty years earlier: the curriculum was too white, they heard too little black music, they were ignored in class, and too often they felt slighted by faculty members and other students. Despite the school's recruitment efforts, they were a small minority. The core of their social life was their own group. To relieve the dysphoria, they went home a lot on weekends.

I found myself giving them the same advice my father gave me when I was in college: lighten up on the politics, get the best education you can, and move on. But then I surprised myself by saying, "To do this you have to learn from people who part of yourself tells you are difficult to trust."

Over the past four decades African-American college students have been more in the spotlight than any other American students. This is because they aren't just college students; they are a cutting edge in America's effort to integrate itself in the thirty-five years since the passage of the Civil Rights Act. These students have borne much of the burden for our national experiment in racial integration. And to a significant degree the success of the experiment will be determined by their success.

Nonetheless, throughout the 1990s the national college-dropout rate for African-Americans has been 20 to 25 percent higher than that for whites. Among those who finish college, the grade-point average of black students is two thirds of a grade below that of whites.

The finger-pointing debate over the underperformance of black undergraduates has missed one big culprit—"stereotype threat." This is the threat of being viewed through the lens of a negative stereotype, or the fear of doing something that would inadvertantly confirm that stereotype.

A recent study by William Bowen and Derek Bok, reported in their book *The Shape of the River*, brings some happy news: despite this underachievement in college, black students who attend the most selective schools in the country go on to do just as well in postgraduate programs and professional attainment as other students from those schools. This is a telling fact in support of affirmative action, since only these schools use affirmative action in admissions. Still, the underperformance of black undergraduates is an unsettling problem, one that may alter or hamper career development, especially among blacks not attending the most selective schools.

Attempts to explain the problem can sound like a debate about whether America is a good society, at least by the standard of racial fairness, and maybe even about whether racial integration is possible. It is an uncomfortably finger-pointing debate. Does the problem stem from something about black students themselves, such as poor motivation, a distracting peer culture, lack of family values, or—the unsettling suggestion of *The Bell Curve*—genes? Or does it stem from the conditions of blacks' lives: social and economic deprivation, a society that views blacks through the lens of diminishing stereotypes and low expectations, too much coddling, or too much neglect?

In recent years this debate has acquired a finer focus: the fate of middle-class black students. Americans have come to view the disadvantages associated with being black as disadvantages primarily of social and economic resources and opportunity. This assumption is often taken to imply that if you are black and come from a socioeconomically middle-class home, you no longer suffer a significant disadvantage of race. "Why should the son of a black physician be given an advantage in college admission over the son of a white delivery-truck driver?" This is a standard question in the controversy over affirmative action. And the assumption behind it is that surely in today's society the disadvantages of race are overcome when lower socioeconomic status is overcome.

But virtually all aspects of underperformance—lower standardized-test scores, lower college grades, lower graduation rates—persist among students from the African-American middle class. This situation forces on us an uncomfortable recognition: that beyond class, something racial is depressing the academic performance of these students.

Some time ago I and two colleagues, Joshua Aronson and Steven Spencer, tried to see the world from the standpoint of these students, concerning ourselves less with features of theirs that might explain their troubles than with features of the world they see. A story I was told recently depicts some of these. The storyteller was worried about his friend, a normally energetic black student who had broken up with his longtime girlfriend and had since learned that she, a Hispanic, was now dating a white student. This hit him hard. Not long after hearing about his girlfriend, he sat through an hour's discussion of *The Bell Curve* in his psychology class, during which the possible genetic inferiority of his race was openly considered. Then he overheard students at lunch arguing that affirmative action allowed in too many underqualified blacks. By his own account, this young man had experienced very little of what he thought of as racial discrimination on campus. Still, these were features of his world. Could they have a bearing on his academic life?

My colleagues and I have called such features "stereotype threat"—the threat of being viewed through the lens of a negative stereotype, or the fear of doing something that would inadvertently confirm that stereotype. Everyone experiences stereotype threat. We are all members of some group about which negative stereotypes exist, from white males and Methodists to women and the elderly. And in a situation where one of those stereotypes applies—a man talking to women about pay equity, for example, or an aging faculty member trying to remember a number sequence in the middle of a lecture—we know that we may be judged by it.

Like the young man in the story, we can feel mistrustful and apprehensive in such situations. For him, as for African-American students generally, negative stereotypes apply in many situations, even personal ones. Why was that old roommate unfriendly to him? Did that young white woman who has been so nice to him in class not return his phone call because she's afraid he'll ask her for a date? Is it because of his race or something else about him? He cannot know the answers, but neither can his rational self fully dismiss the questions. Together they raise a deeper question: Will his race be a boundary to his experience, to his emotions, to his relationships?

With time he may be weary of the extra vigilance these situations require and of what the psychologists Jennifer Crocker and Brenda Major have called the "attributional ambiguity" of being on the receiving end of negative stereotypes. To reduce this stress he may learn to care less about the situations and activities that bring it about—to realign his self-regard so that it no longer depends on how he does in the situation. We have called this psychic adjustment "disidentification." Pain is lessened by ceasing to identify with the part of life in which the pain occurs. This withdrawal of psychic investment may be supported by other members of the stereotype-threatened group—even to the point of its becoming a group norm. But not caring can mean not being motivated. And this can have real costs. When stereotype threat affects school life, disidentification is a high price to pay for psychic comfort. Still, it is a price that groups contending with powerful negative stereotypes about their abilities—women in advanced math, African-Americans in all academic areas—may too often pay.

Measuring Stereotype Threat

Can stereotype threat be shown to affect academic performance? And if so, who would be most affected—stronger or weaker students? Which has a greater influence on academic success among black college students—the degree of threat or the level of preparation with which they enter college? Can the college experience be redesigned to lessen the threat? And if so, would that redesign help these students to succeed academically?

As we confronted these questions in the course of our research, we came in for some surprises. We began with what we took to be the hardest question: Could something as abstract as stereotype threat really affect something as irrepressible as intelligence? Ours is an individualistic culture; forward movement is seen to come from within. Against this cultural faith one needs evidence to argue that something as "sociological" as stereotype threat can repress something as "individualistic" as intelligence.

To acquire such evidence, Joshua Aronson and I (following a procedure developed with Steven Spencer) designed an experiment to test whether the stereotype threat that black students might experience when taking a difficult standardized test could depress their performance on the test to a statistically reliable degree. In this experiment we asked black and white Stanford students into our laboratory and gave them, one at a time, a thirty-minute verbal test made up of items from the advanced Graduate Record Examination in literature. Most of these students were sophomores, which meant that the test was particularly hard for them—precisely the feature, we reasoned, that would make this simple testing situation different for our black participants than for our white participants.

In matters of race we often assume that when a situation is objectively the same for different groups, it is *experienced* in the same way by each group. This assumption might seem especially reasonable in the case of "standardized" cognitive tests. But for black students, difficulty with the test makes the negative stereotype relevant as an interpretation of their performance, and of them. They know that they are especially likely to be seen as having limited ability. Groups not stereotyped in this way don't experience this extra intimidation. And it is a serious intimidation, implying as it does that they may not belong in walks of life where the tested abilities are important—walks of life in which they are heavily invested. Like many pressures, it may not be experienced in a fully conscious way, but it may impair their best thinking.

This is exactly what Aronson and I found. When the difficult verbal test was presented as a test of ability, black students performed dramatically less well than white students, even though we had statistically matched the two groups in ability level. Something other than ability was involved; we believed it was stereotype threat.

But maybe the black students performed less well than the white students because they were less motivated, or because their skills were somehow less applicable to the advanced material of this test. We needed some way to determine if it was indeed stereotype threat that depressed the black students' scores. We reasoned that if stereotype threat had impaired their performance on the test, then reducing this threat would allow their performance to improve. We presented the same test as a laboratory task that was used to study how certain problems are generally solved. We stressed that the task did not measure a person's level of intellectual ability. A simple instruction, yes, but it profoundly changed the meaning of the situation. In one stroke "spotlight anxiety," as the psychologist William Cross once called it, was turned off—and the black students' performance on the test rose to match that of equally qualified whites.

Aronson and I decided that what we needed next was direct evidence of the subjective state we call stereotype threat. To seek this, we looked into whether simply sitting down to take a difficult test of ability was enough to make black students mindful of their race and stereotypes about it. This may seem unlikely. White students I have taught over the years have sometimes said that they have hardly any sense of even having a race. But blacks have many experiences with the majority "other group" that make their race salient to them.

We again brought black and white students in to take a difficult verbal test. But just before the test began, we gave them a long list of words, each of which had two letters missing. They were told to complete the words on this list as fast as they could. We knew from a preliminary survey that twelve of the eighty words we had selected could be completed in such a way as to relate to the stereotype about blacks' intellectual ability. The fragment "—ce," for example, could become "race." If simply taking a difficult test of ability was enough to make black students mindful of stereotypes about their race, these students should complete more fragments with stereotype-related words. That is just what happened. When black students were told that the test would measure ability, they completed the fragments

with significantly more stereotype-related words than when they were told that it was not a measure of ability. Whites made few stereotype-related completions in either case.

What kind of worry is signaled by this race consciousness? To find out, we used another probe. We asked participants on the brink of the difficult test to tell us their preferences in sports and music. Some of these, such as basketball, jazz, and hip-hop, are associated with African-American imagery, whereas others, such as tennis, swimming, and classical music, are not. Something striking emerged: when black students expected to take a test of ability, they spurned things African-American, reporting less interest in, for instance, basketball, jazz, and hip-hop than whites did. When the test was presented as unrelated to ability, black students strongly preferred things African-American. They eschewed these things only when preferring them would encourage a stereotypic view of themselves. It was the spotlight that they were trying to avoid.

Stereotype Threat Versus Self-fulfilling Prophecy

Another question arises: Do the effects of stereotype threat come entirely from the fear of being stereotyped, or do they come from something internal to black students—self-doubt, for example?

Beginning with George Herbert Mead's idea of the "looking-glass self," social psychology has assumed that one's self-image derives in large part from how one is viewed by others—family, school, and the broader society. When those views are negative, people may internalize them, resulting in lower self-esteem—or self-hatred, as it has been called. This theory was first applied to the experience of Jews, by Sigmund Freud and Bruno Bettelheim, but it was also soon applied to the experience of African-Americans, by Gordon Allport, Frantz Fanon, Kenneth Clark, and others. According to the theory, black students internalize negative stereotypes as performance anxiety and low expectations for achievement, which they then fulfill. The "self-fulfilling prophecy" has become a commonplace about these students. Stereotype threat, however, is something different, something external: the situational threat of being negatively stereotyped. Which of these two processes, then, caused the results of our experiments?

Joshua Aronson, Michael Lustina, Kelli Keough, Joseph Brown, Catherine Good, and I devised a way to find out. Suppose we told white male students who were strong in math that a difficult math test they were about to take was one on which Asians generally did better than whites. White males should not have a sense of group inferiority about math, since no societal stereotype alleges such an inferiority. Yet this comment would put them under a form of stereotype threat: any faltering on the test could cause them to be seen negatively from the standpoint of the positive stereotype about Asians and math ability. If stereotype threat alone—in the absence of any internalized self-doubt—was capable of disrupting test performance, then white males taking the test after this comment should perform less well than white males taking the test without hearing the comment. That is just what happened. Stereotype threat impaired intellectual functioning in a group unlikely to have any sense of group inferiority.

In science, as in the rest of life, few things are definitive. But these results are pretty good evidence that stereotype threat's impairment of standardized-test performance does not depend on cueing a pre-existing anxiety. Steven Spencer, Diane Quinn, and I have shown how stereotype threat depresses the performance of accomplished female math students on a difficult math test, and how that performance improves dramatically when the threat is lifted. Jean-Claude Croizet, working in France with a stereotype that links poor verbal skills with lower-class status, found analogous results: lower-class college students performed less well than upper-class college students under the threat of a stereotype-based judgment, but performed as well when the threat was removed.

Is everyone equally threatened and disrupted by a stereotype? One might expect, for example, that it would affect the weakest students most. But in all our research the most achievement-oriented students, who were also the most skilled, motivated, and confident, were the most impaired by stereotype threat. This fact had been under our noses all along—in our data and even in our theory. A person has to care about a domain in order to be disturbed by the prospect of being stereotyped in it. That is the whole idea of disidentification—protecting against stereotype threat by ceasing to care about the domain in which the stereotype applies. Our earlier experiments had selected black students who identified with verbal skills and women who identified with math. But when we tested participants who identified less with these domains, what had been under our noses hit us in the face. None of them showed any effect of stereotype threat whatsoever.

These weakly identified students did not perform well on the test: once they discovered its difficulty, they stopped trying very hard and got a low score. But their performance did not differ depending on whether they felt they were at risk of being judged stereotypically.

Why Strong Students Are Stereotype-threatened

This finding, I believe, tells us two important things. The first is that the poorer college performance of black students may have another source in addition to the one—lack of good preparation and, perhaps, of identification with school achievement—that is commonly understood. This additional source—the threat of being negatively stereotyped in the environment—has not been well understood. The distinction has important policy implications: different kinds of students may require different pedagogies of improvement.

The second thing is poignant: what exposes students to the pressure of stereotype threat is not weaker academic identity and skills but stronger academic identity and skills. They may have long seen themselves as good students—better than most. But led into the domain by their strengths, they pay an extra tax on their investment—vigilant worry that their future

will be compromised by society's perception and treatment of their group.

This tax has a long tradition in the black community. The Jackie Robinson story is a central narrative of black life, literature, and journalism. *Ebony* magazine has run a page for fifty years featuring people who have broken down one or another racial barrier. Surely the academic vanguard among black college students today knows this tradition—and knows, therefore, that the thing to do, as my father told me, is to buckle down, pay whatever tax is required, and disprove the damn stereotype.

That, however, seems to be precisely what these students are trying to do. In some of our experiments we administered the test of ability by computer, so that we could see how long participants spent looking at different parts of the test questions. Black students taking the test under stereotype threat seemed to be trying too hard rather than not hard enough. They reread the questions, reread the multiple choices, rechecked their answers, more than when they were not under stereotype threat. The threat made them inefficient on a test that, like most standardized tests, is set up so that thinking long often means thinking wrong, especially on difficult items like the ones we used.

Philip Uri Treisman, an innovator in math workshops for minority students who is based at the University of Texas, saw something similar in his black calculus students at the University of California at Berkeley: they worked long hours alone but they worked inefficiently—for example, checking and rechecking their calculations against the correct answers at the back of the book, rather than focusing on the concepts involved. Of course, trying extra hard helps with some school tasks. But under stereotype threat this effort may be misdirected. Achievement at the frontier of one's skills may be furthered more by a relaxed, open concentration than by a strong desire to disprove a stereotype by not making mistakes.

Sadly, the effort that accompanies stereotype threat exacts an additional price. Led by James Blascovich, of the University of California at Santa Barbara, we found that the blood pressure of black students performing a difficult cognitive task under stereotype threat was elevated compared with that of black students not under stereotype threat or white students in either situation.

In the old song about the "steel-drivin' man," John Henry races the new steam-driven drill to see who can dig a hole faster. When the race is over, John Henry has prevailed by digging the deeper hole—only to drop dead. The social psychologist Sherman James uses the term "John Henryism" to describe a psychological syndrome that he found to be associated with hypertension in several samples of North Carolina blacks: holding too rigidly to the faith that discrimination and disadvantage can be overcome with hard work and persistence. Certainly this is the right attitude. But taken to extremes, it can backfire. A deterioration of performance under stereotype threat by the skilled, confident black students in our experiments may be rooted in John Henryism.

This last point can be disheartening. Our research, however, offers an interesting suggestion about what can be done to overcome stereotype threat and its detrimental effects. The success of black students may depend less on expectations and motivation—things that are thought to drive academic performance—than on trust that stereotypes about their group will not have a limiting effect in their school world.

How To Reduce Stereotype Threat

Putting this idea to the test, Joseph Brown and I asked, How can the usual detrimental effect of stereotype threat on the standardized-test performance of these students be reduced? By strengthening students' expectations and confidence, or by strengthening their trust that they are not at risk of being judged on the basis of stereotypes? In the ensuing experiment we strengthened or weakened participants' confidence in their verbal skills, by arranging for them to have either an impressive success or an impressive failure on a test of verbal skills, just before they took the same difficult verbal test we had used in our earlier research. When the second test was presented as a test of ability, the boosting or weakening of confidence in their verbal skills had no effect on performance: black participants performed less well than equally skilled white participants. What does this say about the commonsense idea that black students' academic problems are rooted in lack of self-confidence?

What did raise the level of black students' performance to that of equally qualified whites was reducing stereotype threat—in this case by explicitly presenting the test as racially fair. When this was done, blacks performed at the same high level as whites even if their self-confidence had been weakened by a prior failure.

These results suggest something that I think has not been made clear elsewhere: when strong black students sit down to take a difficult standardized test, the extra apprehension they feel in comparison with whites is less about their own ability than it is about having to perform on a test and in a situation that may be primed to treat them stereotypically. We discovered the extent of this apprehension when we tried to develop procedures that would make our black participants see the test as "race-fair." It wasn't easy. African-Americans have endured so much bad press about test scores for so long that, in our experience, they are instinctively wary about the tests' fairness. We were able to convince them that our test was race-fair only when we implied that the research generating the test had been done by blacks. When they felt trust, they performed well regardless of whether we had weakened their self-confidence beforehand. And when they didn't feel trust, no amount of bolstering of self-confidence helped.

Policies for helping black students rest in significant part on assumptions about their psychology. As noted, they are typically assumed to lack confidence, which spawns a policy of confidence-building. This may be useful for students at the academic rearguard of the group. But the psychology of the academic vanguard appears different—underperformance appears to be rooted less in self-doubt than in social mistrust.

Education policy relevant to non-Asian minorities might fruitfully shift its focus toward fostering racial trust in the schooling situation—at least among students who come to school with good skills and high expectations. But how should this be done? Without particulars this conclusion can fade into banality, suggesting, as Alan Ryan has wryly put it in *Liberal Anxieties and Liberal Education*, that these students "will hardly be able to work at all unless everyone else exercises the utmost sensitivity to [their] anxieties." Sensitivity is nice, but it is an awful lot to expect, and even then, would it instill trust?

That is exactly what Geoffrey Cohen, Lee Ross, and I wondered as we took up the question of how a teacher or a mentor could give critical feedback across the "racial divide" and have that feedback be trusted. We reasoned that an answer to this question might yield insights about how to instill trust more broadly in the schooling environment. Cohen's hunch was that niceness alone wouldn't be enough. But the first question had to be whether there was in fact a racial divide between teachers and students, especially in the elite college environment in which we worked.

We set up a simple experiment. Cohen asked black and white Stanford students one at a time to write essays about their favorite teachers, for possible publication in a journal on teaching. They were asked to return several days later for feedback on their essays. Before each student left the first writing session, Cohen put a Polaroid snapshot of the student on top of his or her essay. His ostensible purpose was to publish the picture if the essay was published. His real purpose was to let the essay writers know that the evaluator of their writing would be aware of their race. When they returned days later, they were given constructive but critical feedback. We looked at whether different ways of giving this feedback engendered different degrees of trust in it.

We found that neither straight feedback nor feedback preceded by the "niceness" of a cushioning statement ("There were many good things about your essay") was trusted by black students. They saw these criticisms as probably biased, and they were less motivated than white students to improve their essays. White students took the criticism at face value—even as an indication of interest in them. Black students, however, faced a different meaning: the "ambiguating" possibility that the criticism was motivated by negative stereotypes about their group as much as by the work itself. Herein lies the power of race to make one's world insecure—quite apart from whatever actual discrimination one may experience.

But this experiment also revealed a way to be critical across the racial divide: tell the students that you are using high standards (this signals that the criticism reflects standards rather than race), and that your reading of their essays leads you to believe that they can meet those standards (this signals that you do not view them stereotypically). This shouldn't be faked. High standards, at least in a relative sense, should be an inherent part of teaching, and critical feedback should be given in the belief that the recipient can reach those standards. These things go without saying for many students. But they have to be made explicit for students under stereotype threat. The good news of this study is that when they *are* made explicit, the students trust and respond to criticism. Black students who got this kind of feedback saw it as unbiased and were motivated to take their essays home and work on them even though this was not a class for credit. They were more motivated than any other group of students in the study—as if this combination of high standards and assurance was like water on parched land, a much needed but seldom received balm.

Reassessing The Test-score Gap

There is, of course, another explanation for why black college students haven't fared well on predominantly white campuses: they aren't prepared for the competition. This has become an assumption of those who oppose affirmative action in college admissions. Racial preference, the argument goes, brings black students onto campuses where they simply aren't prepared to compete.

The fact most often cited in support of the underpreparation explanation is the lower SAT scores of black students, which sometimes average 200 points below those of other students on the same campus. The test-score gap has become shorthand for black students' achievement problems. But the gap must be assessed cautiously.

First, black students have better skills than the gap suggests. Most of the gap exists because the proportion of blacks with very high SAT scores is smaller than the corresponding proportions of whites and Asians. Thus when each group's scores are averaged, the black average will be lower than the white and Asian averages. This would be true even if the same admissions cut-off score were used for each group—even if, for example, affirmative action were eliminated entirely. Why a smaller proportion of blacks have very high scores is, of course, a complex question with multiple answers, involving, among other things, the effects of race on educational access and experience as well as the processes dwelt on in this article. The point, though, is that blacks' test-score deficits are taken as a sign of underpreparation, whereas in fact virtually all black students on a given campus have tested skills within the same range as the tested skills of other students on the campus.

In any case, the skills and preparation measured by these tests also turn out not to be good determinants of college success. As the makers of the SAT themselves tell us, although this test is among the best of its kind, it measures only about 18 percent of the skills that influence first-year grades, and even less of what influences subsequent grades, graduation rates, and professional success.

Indulge a basketball analogy that my colleagues Jay Rosner and Lee Ross and I have developed. Suppose that you were obliged to select a basketball team on the basis of how many of ten free throws a player makes. You'd regret having to select players on the basis of a single criterion. You'd know that free-throw shooting involves only a few of the skills that go into basketball—and, worse, you'd know that you'd never pick a Shaquille O'Neal.

You'd also wonder how to interpret a player's score. If he made ten out of ten or zero out of ten, you'd be fairly confident about making a judgment. But what about the kid who makes five, six, or seven? Middling scores like these could be influenced by many things other than underlying potential for free-throw shooting or basketball playing. How much practice was involved? Was the kid having a good or a bad day? Roughly the same is true, I suggest, for standardized-test scores. Are they inflated by middle-class advantages such as prep courses, private schools, and tours of European cathedrals? Are they deflated by race-linked experiences such as social segregation and being consistently assigned to the lower tracks in school?

In sum, black college students are not as underprepared in academic skills as their group score deficit is taken to suggest. The deficit can appear large, but it is not likely to be the sole cause of the troubles they have once they get on campus.

Showing the insufficiency of one cause, of course, does not prove the sufficiency of another. My colleagues and I believed that our laboratory experiments had brought to light an overlooked cause of poor college performance among non-Asian minorities: the threat to social trust brought about by the stereotypes of the larger society. But to know the real-life importance of this threat would require testing *in situ*, in the buzz of everyday life.

To this end Steven Spencer, Richard Nisbett, Kent Harber, Mary Hummel, and I undertook a program aimed at incoming first-year students at the University of Michigan. Like virtually all other institutions of higher learning, Michigan had evidence of black students' underachievement. Our mission was clear: to see if we could improve their achievement by focusing on their transition into college life.

We also wanted to see how little we could get away with—that is, to develop a program that would succeed broadly without special efforts. The program (which started in 1991 and is ongoing) created a racially integrated "living and learning" community in a 250-student wing of a large dormitory. It focused students on academic work (through weekly "challenge" workshops), provided an outlet for discussing the personal side of college life (through weekly rap sessions), and affirmed the students' abilities (through, for example, reminding them that their admission was a vote of confidence). The program lasted just one semester, although most students remained in the dormitory wing for the rest of their first year.

Still, it worked: it gave black students a significant academic jump start. Those in the program (about 15 percent of the entering class) got better first-year grades than black students outside the program, even after controlling for differences between these groups in the skills with which they entered college. Equally important, the program greatly reduced underperformance: black students in the program got first-year grades almost as high as those of white students in the general Michigan population who entered with comparable test scores. This result signaled the achievement of an academic climate nearly as favorable to black students as to white students. And it was achieved through a concert of simple things that enabled black students to feel racially secure.

One tactic that worked surprisingly well was the weekly rap sessions—black and white students talking to one another in an informal dormitory setting, over pizza, about the personal side of their new lives in college. Participation in these sessions reduced students' feelings of stereotype threat and improved grades. Why? Perhaps when members of one racial group hear members of another racial group express the same concerns they have, the concerns seem less racial. Students may also learn that racial and gender stereotypes are either less at play than they might have feared or don't reflect the worst-feared prejudicial intent. Talking at a personal level across group lines can thus build trust in the larger campus community. The racial segregation besetting most college campuses can block this experience, allowing mistrust to build where cross-group communication would discourage it.

Our research bears a practical message: although stereotypes held by the larger society may be hard to change, it is possible to create educational niches in which negative stereotypes are not felt to apply— and which permit a sense of trust that would otherwise be difficult to sustain.

Our research bears a practical message: even though the stereotypes held by the larger society may be difficult to change, it is possible to create niches in which negative stereotypes are not felt to apply. In specific classrooms, within specific programs, even in the climate of entire schools, it is possible to weaken a group's sense of being threatened by negative stereotypes, to allow its members a trust that would otherwise be difficult to sustain. Thus when schools try to decide how important black-white test-score gaps are in determining the fate of black students on their campuses, they should keep something in mind: for the greatest portion of black students—those with strong academic identities—the degree of racial trust they feel in their campus life, rather than a few ticks on a standardized test, may be the key to their success.

CLAUDE M. STEELE is the Lucie Stern Professor in the Social Sciences at Stanford University. His articles have appeared in *The New York Times* and *The American Prospect*.

From *The Atlantic Monthly* by Claude M. Steele, pp. 44-47, 50-54. Copyright © 1999 by Claude M. Steele. Reprinted by permission.

UNIT 8
Violence and Aggression

Unit Selections

Key Points to Consider

- What effect does culture have in the demonstration of aggression and violence?

- What differences exist in the aggressive behaviors exhibited by men versus women? Why do you think these gender differences exist?

- Think about the last time that you were threatened by aggressive behavior; what factors do you believe led to the situation?

- Every day the network news reports engulf us in statistics relative to violence; how does this affect you and those that you know?

Student Web Site

www.mhcls.com/online

Internet References

Further information regarding these Web sites may be found in this book's preface or online.

MINCAVA: Minnesota Center Against Violence and Abuse
  http://www.mincava.umn.edu

National Consortium on Violence Research
  http://www.nicic.org/Library/020733

Jacob was a quiet baby, but he was adorable with his full cheeks, blonde hair, and blue eyes. Jake was his parent's first child, and his mother lavished him with attention and affection. She was so proud of him when a shopper at the grocery store would stop her to take a closer look. At other times, his mother would sit in the park and watch all the toddlers playing. As she compared Jake to the other children, she thought he was the cutest and smartest of all.

Everything changed for Jake when he entered kindergarten. Not only was Jake smaller than the other children, he was younger and a bit slower. The teacher noticed this immediately and began giving Jake the extra attention he seemed to need. Although he was only five, the added help embarrassed him. The other children noticed, too. A few of them wondered out loud why Jake never seemed to get his projects finished on time or done well.

By the time Jake entered first grade, he had fallen hopelessly behind. Other children knew the alphabet and colors; Jake did not. In response to his needs, Jake's first grade teacher placed him in the "Sparrows" reading group. Other children were assigned to the "Robins" or the "Swallows" groups. Jake's classmates soon realized that the Sparrows were the slowest reading group of all. They read easier books and progressed less quickly than did the other two groups.

Some of the children taunted and bullied the Sparrows on the playground or refused to allow them to participate in projects. Jake was on the receiving end of the most hurtful behavior by his classmates. After occasionally admonishing her students, the teacher felt helpless to change the other children's negativity toward Jake.

When Jake started falling behind in school, his father became harsh and critical, especially when Jake was held back and repeated first grade. His mother tried to stand up to her husband on Jake's behalf but did not succeed so eventually withdrew from the dispute. The recurring criticism by his father made young Jake retreat to his room and cry. He did so as softly as possible so his father would not call him "a baby."

When Jake entered second grade, he was a different child. He was angry, sullen, and brooding. Jake seemed to smolder when the other children came near him, and he rejected any nurturing efforts on the part of his teacher and mother. Late one afternoon, when his mother was at the store, Jake once again brought home a failing report card. Not only were his grades low, his teacher had noted in several places Jake's lack of effort and lack of cooperation with the other children. Jake's father was furious and called him "stupid." Jake went upstairs, climbed to the top of his father's closet, pulled out the shotgun, and killed his father with a single blast. He then pumped ten more bullets into the lifeless body. Then Jake ran away.

Sadly, the above story is true. Why do children tease other children? How do humans become so angry that they kill one another? The issue of aggression is the primary subject of Unit 8. Four articles introduce you to the causes, consequences of, and solutions to violence and aggression in society.

The first article details research on media violence. Televisions, movies, video games, and other forms of media introduce violence every day to American homes. Nancy Signorielli, writing about prime-time violence, provides an excellent summary of the effects of media violence. She concludes that the amount of violence has not decreased much, but the type of brutality and its outcomes have changed—for the worse.

The second article is "How Psychology Can Help Explain the Iraqi Prisoner Abuse." After reviewing the types of abuse, the article summarizes the results of and likens the abuse to Zimbardo's now famous mock prison research. In the research, the behavior of guards became so atrocious that the investigation was terminated early.

Bullying by and of school children is another important form of abuse and is discussed in this unit. Why bullying occurs and how to intervene when it happens are the topics of "Bullying: It Isn't What it Used to Be."

Social psychologists are very concerned about the causes and consequences of violence and aggression. Their work would be incomplete if they did not also offer methods for managing these behaviors. Manning and Robertson, in "Influencing, Negotiating, and Conflict Handling," review research that demonstrates not only is negotiation effective, it goes *beyond* simple conflict management.

A Bi-Cultural Perspective on World Views

ILHAM AL-SARRAF

Rooted in its Islamic history, Iraqi culture and education stress absolutes, generally calling for a monolithic society believing in the one God: "Allah". However, there are fundamental differences between Shiaa and Sunni interpretations of Islam, based on politics involving the followers of the Prophet Mohammed 1400 years ago. The Shiaa considered themselves the followers of the teaching of the prophet and his descendents "or his household lineage—who were the 12 Imams". The Shiaa had to go underground due to persecution by the Sunni rulers of that time. The Sunnis had four schools of thoughts, from four scholars who interpreted and taught the Quran according to their knowledge.

There were several differences between the two groups, involving interpretations of the Quran. Two models of interpretation were either literal or philosophical. Some Sunnis took certain texts literally; for example "God has eyes over his worshipers". No questions were allowed.

The Shiaa philosophically interpreted the Quran in an esoteric manner, instead of God literally has eyes, they stated metaphorically, that "God is overseeing his worshipers". Another difference involved the issue of human destiny: Is life predetermined or do we have choices? Shiaa believed that human beings have "choices in life", as the authors of our lives. We make choices and face the consequences (but, Allah ultimately judges and his will prevails).

In this worldview, Allah gives believers choices, but cautions them about going astray. The Sunni worldview believes that humans are "predetermined" by the will of Allah from birth and that "one's destiny is written on one's forehead the day you are born". Kismet!

The Shiaa believe in "Ijtihad/Jihad" juristic reasoning as a struggle to incorporate the reason more in their faith in a proactive manner, finding the truth first in the Quran (in the Hadith or "the sayings of Muhammad"), then, in case of conflict, with the guidance of an Islamic scholar (called "Almarga-Ayattallah Imam" or the source of knowledge). The Sunnis rely only on the literal Quran and the Hadith for guidance.

The teachings of Islam are reinforced with fear and prohibitions ("Haram"); one dares not to question instructions given by the family, school or society. Most of the Iraqi schools' teachings were from the Sunni ideology. The oppressed Shiaa feared to have their own schools, confining their teachings to their homes and places of worship.

Both groups believe the purpose of humans is to be the guardians of Earth, where they are tested on their endurance and acceptance. Joy and happiness belong to the devil. (It is better to walk behind those who make you cry, than those who make you laugh.) They are taught the rewards of the hereafter are the real existence; the Earth life is nothing but a casing to the true kernel. Heaven is promised to those who follow Islam and its teaching with full obedience.

Both believe in total and categorical obedience to the faith, no questions allowed although today the young generation is asking questions before total submission. Believers submit to the will of Allah; the Arabic word "Inshaa-Allah" is never far from one's lips. To be called a "nonbeliever" is the worse condemnation a person has to endure in society; it is worse than God's condemnation! Social pressure, creating very rigid norms, controls the population. This structure provides safety and security in a plural-collective enmeshment. (An Arabic proverb states "In a plural way of living, suffering becomes a celebration".) Thus, there is uniformity in practice that few would dare to violate.

Transcending the differences between Shiaa and Sunni, a uniformity and obedience to concepts are created by the popular culture. These cultural norms surpass religious guidance. The tribal traditions and customs were reinforced by selected Quranic verses that cannot be questioned. You can imagine how this contrasts with the U.S., where one feels free to listen to others views, where the world is not universally presented as black or white, right or wrong.

This foundational world view with its faith has organized and structured Iraqi society for decades, giving a sense of safety to believers although it provided for few, if any, personal choices. However, the last forty years of oppression and struggle to survive has forced Iraqis through many transitions that have reshaped their lives, beliefs, values, faith, and consciousness, at both emotional and cognitive levels. Circumstances beyond their control, or so it seems to them, has caused deep transformations. Let me illustrate some of them.

From 1968, submission to a ruthless dictator who ruled with iron fist and intimidation caused the people of Iraq to completely lose their sense of trust in anyone, often even their own children. A splitting of the personality went beyond private and public personas. Different sub-personalities were created to deal with family members, close friends, co-workers, neighbors, and authority figures. Everyone needed to be constantly vigilant. The inability to exercise any freedom—to feel, to think, to talk, to express any discontent—leads people to suppress their human rights and adhere to blind obedience. Iraqis perceived they had No choice.

From 1991, submission to severe sanctions denied them essential materials for everyday living. It degraded, humiliated, and marginalized them below sub-human. They began to plead, beg, and bargain with their dictator, the Superpower, and the United Nations about their suffering, but the three pointed at each other and turned a deaf ear to the Iraqi pleas. Eventually reality sets in: No one in the world cares. Learned helplessness, depression, and apathy eventually lead to dissociation and, in many cases, undiagnosed psychosis. Control of their own destiny is out of their reach again.

During the period from 1994–1996, the only option seemed to be submission to the will of Allah ("He will not give us more than what we can handle"). The attitude became one of "this must be our destiny". "This dreadful living must be a punishment from up above for how bad we have been. Even Allah forsakes us". The continuous bombings from the air were defiantly perceived as Allah's wrath. The abyss was so deep during the middle 1990's that all one saw was the walking dead, on automatic and literally "predetermined by higher power". They waited for external help; from within came only self-blame and anger at their failure to overcome the atrocities and injustice.

From 1997 to 2000, the youth began to express their frustrations by personalizing religion. A private religion was something that no one could take away from them. Their worship moved from an external power to recognition of some autonomy, exercised from within. Trepidation and fear of retaliation by the dictator or the West were kept at bay. Creativity in their behaviors, with traditions and norms no longer keeping them from expressing their discontent against social stratification, prohibitions, and the rigid interpretations of the Quran, began shaping a new consciousness. What used to be "shameful, humiliating and dishonoring behaviors " no longer held. A sense of internal control of their destiny begot an attitude of a triumph over victimization!

By 2000, this sense of an underground freedom began to roll back boundaries. The ability to bring in income, the ability to earn and to participate in society restored their shattered dignity and pride. There was a revival of life, living for the day, being carefree, enjoying hedonism, and being deaf to the world around them. They began to overcome their misery. With joy in their statements came a feeling that "I am the one responsible, I

have nothing to lose". With this attitude, they challenged the "we-collective cultural practices".

But by 2004, the war, terrorism, and internal conflicts had reversed the progression; regression arrived with plummeting speed. At first, the news of being liberated/invaded hit hard the newly freed Iraqi population. Fear, joy, and terror ran an ambivalent range of emotions when the coalition marched into Baghdad. Ridding the population of Saddam was a dream come true, but what followed was the nightmare they all feared.

Self-determination was again taken away, replaced by the occupation of the Superpower. Their behaviors had to regress to old familiar patterns of a power outside of themselves. Material promises failed to materialize. A government to represent their needs became torn by violence, foreign terrorists, internal terrorists, invasion by a foreign power, open borders, no laws, no army or police, and no legislative body with the power to execute or implement. With a temporary central government Iraqis saw themselves as powerless again.

Able only to stand by and observe others determining their future, only ignited anger kept at bay for a long time. Releasing the pent-up rage resulted in the attitude "we have nothing to lose". Having tasted the freedom of self-motivation and being co-creators of their destiny only for a short period of time makes civil war the inevitable outcome, providing evidence for the Darwinian theory "Survival of the Fittest".

The current breakdown of cultural and societal systems causes nothing but chaos in cognitive and emotional levels of the Iraqi consciousness. People trampled upon, then unsuccessfully attempting to be proactive and to participate in creating their own destiny led to a psychotic breakdown.

Historically, unable to tolerate differences among themselves, the Shiaa, the Sunni, the Kurds, the Childanian, and many minorities who for a long time were muffled and intolerant of one another's differences must today expand their world views to incorporate differences and a higher level of consciousness if the society is to survive.

ILHAM HEATHER AL-SARRAF, Ph.D., MFT, received her doctorate at California Graduate Institute, Master of Art in Educational Psychology at University-Northridge. Dr. Al-Sarraf is employed at Kaiser Permanente in addition to her thriving private practice in the Los Angeles area.

Editors' Note: We requested the writer to take the perspective of an objective observer and provide examples of how world views in Iraq can differ from the dominant world views in the United States. We further asked for illustrations of how those worldviews might have changed over time.

Updated version of an article from *The AHP Perspective* Magazine, October/November 2005. Copyright © 2005 by the Association for Humanist Psychology. Reprinted by permission of the author, Ilham Heather Al-Sarraf, and the Association for Humanistic Psychology. www.ahpweb.org

Anger on the Road

A psychologist presented research at the Rocky Mountain Psychological Association conference on the characteristics of angry drivers and what can be done to make the roads safer.

MELISSA DITTMANN

Someone cuts you off while you're driving on the highway or steals the parking space you've been patiently waiting for. Is your first instinct to (a) take a deep breath and move on; (b) honk and then move on; or (c) repeatedly honk, yell out and pound your fists against your steering wheel, wondering how the other person even got a driver's license in the first place?

Those high-anger drivers who have the latter response are a source of alarm for counseling psychologist Jerry Deffenbacher, PhD, who notes that even typically calm, reasonable people can sometimes turn into warriors behind the wheel; when provoked, they yell obscenities, wildly gesture, honk and swerve in and out of traffic, and may endanger their lives and others.

Deffenbacher—a psychology professor at Colorado State University—highlighted his research on the personality, aggressiveness and risk-taking characteristics of high-anger drivers during an invited address at the Rocky Mountain Psychological Association conference, in Phoenix. In his research, high-anger drivers—who identify themselves as such—are assessed on their driving tendencies through questionnaires, driving diaries, computer driving simulations and imagery exercises. From these studies, Deffenbacher has created relaxation and imagery interventions to help counter road rage and make the nation's roads safer.

"The good news is that we can do something about [road rage]," Deffenbacher said. "We can reduce it and modify it somewhat to make people feel better on the road."

Characteristics of Angry Drivers

The need is evident: The AAA Foundation for Traffic Safety found that between 1990 and 1996 road rage contributed to 218 deaths and 12,610 injuries. The study analyzed 10,037 police reports and newspaper stories about traffic accidents that led to violence. What's more, AAA found that road rage incidents increased nearly 7 percent each year within that six-year period. Some experts blame the increase on longer commutes, which have led to more people on the roads.

To find out what's instigating more road rage, Deffenbacher compares aggressiveness, risk-taking and personality traits of high-anger drivers with those of low-anger drivers—those who focus their attention on safe driving, rethink anger-provoking situations in less negative ways and use calming or distracting behaviors, such as turning on the radio.

His studies revealed that high-anger drivers:

- **Engage in hostile, aggressive thinking.** High-anger drivers report more judgmental and disbelieving thoughts about other drivers than low-anger drivers do. For example, they're more likely to insult other drivers or state disbelief about the way others drive. They also have more vengeful and retaliatory thoughts about other drivers, sometimes plotting ways to physically harm them.

- **Take more risks on the road.** High-anger drivers in his studies report more risky behavior in the prior three months than low-anger drivers do. They more often speed—usually 10 to 20 miles per hour over the speed limit—rapidly switch lanes, tailgate and enter an intersection when a light turns red.

- **Get angry faster and behave more aggressively.** High-anger drivers most commonly reported the following aggressive behaviors: swearing or name-calling, driving while angry, yelling at the driver or honking in anger. They were angry slightly more than two times a day and averaged just over two aggressive behaviors per day, whereas low-anger drivers were angry slightly less than once per day and averaged less than one aggressive behavior per day. This pattern held for low- and high-anger drivers who drove equally as often and an equivalent number of miles.

- **Have more accidents.** In driving simulations, high-anger drivers have twice as many car accidents—either from a collision with another vehicle or off-road crash. They also report more near-accidents and receive more speeding tickets. However, the two groups are equal in the number of accidents they have that involve major injuries;

Deffenbacher speculated that's because these types of crashes are a rare occurrence anyway.

- **Experience more trait anger, anxiety and impulsiveness.** High-anger drivers are more likely to get in a car angry, which may stem from work or home stress. They generally tend to express anger in more outward and less controlled ways as well as react impulsively.

That said, high-anger drivers are not angry all the time when they drive, Deffenbacher noted. For example, when they drive on unimpeded country roads—as they did in one of his study's computer-program simulations—high- and low-anger drivers report similar levels of low anger.

"Anger is not a chronic experience for high-anger drivers, but something prompted by different triggers or events on the road," Deffenbacher said. "It's about encountering provocations—events on the road that are frustrating and provoking in some way—and then what they bring to the wheel [that determines] how angry they will get."

Making the Roads Safer

Encouragingly, a combination of cognitive and relaxation interventions have shown promise for reducing road rage among high-anger drivers, Deffenbacher said. He has done several studies geared to enhance safe driving behaviors by testing relaxation interventions and cognitive restructuring, or reframing of negative events.

For example, in his studies, college student participants who reported high-anger driving and wanted to seek counseling for it were assigned to attend eight therapy sessions in-

volving either relaxation or cognitive relaxation therapy. In the relaxation-only condition, the researchers taught students deep breathing and other basic relaxation techniques. In the cognitive-relaxation therapy condition, they taught students similar relaxation methods but added cognitive change strategies as well. Both groups practiced skills to better control their anger while visualizing anger-provoking driving situations, such as someone cutting them off in traffic, and then practiced these skills when they were actually driving.

His studies have shown that both interventions are equally effective in curbing road rage. But, he noted, they don't take away a person's anger completely—rather they reduce the frequency and intensity of it.

Taken together, "The studies suggest that relaxation, cognitive-relaxation and cognitive-behavioral interventions can lower anger behind the wheel, aggressive anger expression and aggression, and lower general anger as well," Deffenbacher said.

Further Reading

Deffenbacher, J.L., Deffenbacher, D.M., Lynch, R.S., & Richards, T.L. (2003). Anger, aggression and risky behavior: A comparison of high and low anger drivers. *Behaviour Research and Therapy,* 41(6), 701–718.

Deffenbacher, J.L., Filetti, L.B., Richards, T.L., Lynch, R.S., & Oetting, E.R. (2003). Characteristics of two groups of angry drivers. *Journal of Counseling Psychology,* 50(2), 123–132.

Deffenbacher, J.L., & McKay, M. *Overcoming situational anger and general anger: A protocol for the treatment of anger based on relaxation, cognitive restructuring and coping skills training.* Oakland, CA: New Harbinger.

From *Monitor on Psychology*, Vol. 36 (6), June 2005, pp. 26-28. Copyright © 2005 by American Psychological Association. Reprinted by permission. No further distribution without permission from the American Psychological Association.

Bullying: It Isn't What It Used To Be

JANICE SELEKMAN
JUDITH A. VESSEY

Many adults can remember a time during their childhood when either they felt like they were being bullied or they were bullies themselves. Others can remember the discomfort they felt knowing that classmates were being bullied, but doing nothing about it. While some will argue that bullying is just a rite of passage for children, most will now disagree based on the increase in violent behavior in today's society and the increased morbidity and mortality that result. This article will explore the current state of bullying behavior among today's youth and the role nurses play.

Defining Bullying

Before bullying can be addressed, it must be defined. Usually schools are the organizing force to address bullying, and it should be the responsibility of the "players" within the school environment to decide what they consider to be bullying behaviors. These "players" must include students, faculty (including the school nurse), administrators, and parents. Optional participants may be mental health care providers, social workers, and law enforcement.

The National Association of School Nurses (NASN) (2003) has defined bullying as "dynamic and repetitive persistent patterns of verbal and/or non-verbal behaviors directed by one or more children on another child that are *intended to deliberately inflict physical, verbal, or emotional abuse* in the presence of a real or perceived power differential." Compare the above definition to one from the United Kingdom. "Bullying is long-standing violence, physical or psychological, conducted by an individual or group and directed *against an individual who is not able to defend himself* in the actual situation, with a *conscious desire to hurt,* threaten or frighten that individual or put him under stress" (Thompson, Arora & Sharp, 2002, p. 4).

The concepts in italics are important, in that they appear in most definitions of bullying in some form. They include: (a) aggressive behavior or intentional "harm doing" by one person or a group; (b) the behaviors are carried out repeatedly and over time; and (c) bullying is targeted towards someone less powerful (Nansel et al., 2001; Oleweus, 1997). No matter which way bullying behaviors are analyzed, the bottom line is that "bullying is violence."

The definitions should assist the "players" in identifying what is not bullying. Examples would include (a) students who just don't like each other; (b) playful teasing between friends; and (c) a physical fight between two students of equal stature and strength who are angry at each other. (Anger does not imply bullying.) It is important to differentiate bullying behaviors that occur only once from bullying, which is more chronic. Care should be taken to not label every child who displays the former as a bully.

The Bullying Spectrum of Behaviors

Teasing refers to "verbal and/or nonverbal behaviors among peers that are generally humorous and playful, but may be annoying to the recipient on another level" (Vessey, Swanson, & Hagedorn, 1995). It is often a healthy way for children to send useful messages or show interest in another student. When it is funny to both parties, it can help build interpersonal relationships. How a child responds to the teasing depends on his or her past relationship with the instigator. Children's interpretation of the teasing affects their response. If a child cannot see the humor in the comment or action, or if the victim feels intimidated by either a real or perceived power differential, even if it is unintended, then it may no longer be interpreted as teasing. Consequently, the impact of teasing is based on how the victim of the "tease" interprets what is said or done. Good-natured teasing can deteriorate into ridicule and mean-spirited taunts, or be interpreted that way, if the recipient feels threatened (Vessey, Carlson, & David, 2003). With playful teasing on one end of the spectrum, the continuum continues to bullying and then on to more severe violence.

Manifestations of Bullying

Familiar forms of bullying include physical or psychosocial/verbal acts, all of which have a psychological impact. Common physical acts of bullying include:

- actions causing physical injury (hitting, punching, kicking, tripping)
- taking money, lunch, or homework
- taking or damaging belongings of others
- engaging in extortion
- embarrassing by snapping the bra, lifting the skirt, pulling down pants

Psychosocial/verbal manifestations may be subtler. They include:

- using insults, name calling, or threats
- humiliating in front of peers; spreading rumors about the person or his/her family
- shunning or excluding
- slamming books
- gesturing
- setting one person against another ("You can join but you have to drop them as your friends.")

There is also the act of coercing others to steal from or bully a victim. This is referred to as "bully by proxy" and occurs when one bully tells another person what to do to a victim (Thompson et al., 2002).

The newest form of bullying is "online bullying." It can be extremely vicious. Those who use this medium often feel that they cannot be held accountable. Social inhibitions of face-to-face confrontation are eased allowing the bully to write things that they would never say to someone's face … and then to send it out for all to see. While the home was once a safe haven from bullying behaviors, online bullying can occur 24 hours a day and be shared with many more people. School officials often do little in these situations since they argue that the behaviors occurred off of school grounds; however, the messages are often passed around in school.

Regardless of the form, it must be recognized that all bullying is aggression, although not all aggression is bullying, and aggression is a form of violence.

Where Does Bullying Occur?

Bullying occurs anywhere there is an absence of adults. Kids learn to engage in these behaviors "under the radar" of adult supervision; the most common locations for bullying to occur include to and from school, on the bus, in the cafeteria, in the halls, at the lockers, in the gym locker room, and on the playground.

Who Are the Children Involved?

It is estimated that 3 out of 10 students are either bullies or victims of bullies. Thirteen percent are bullies; 11% are victims; and 6% are both (Fox, Elliott, Kerlikowske, Newman, & Christeson, 2003). For children in grades 6 through 10, this translates into 3.7 million children who bully other children each year and 3.2 million who are victims (Fox et al., 2003). Bullying occurs equally by children of both genders. Boys are more likely to be physical while girls resort to more "social toxicity."

Bullying occurs throughout the school-age years, starting in elementary school. "The prevalence of nasty teasing/bullying has two peaks: in early elementary school (ages 7-8) and again in middle school (ages 11-14)" (NASN, 2003, p. 1). While bullying behaviors can certainly be seen in toddlers and preschoolers, they can only be considered bullying when the child reaches "a certain level of awareness and understanding" (Thompson et al., 2002, p. 18) of an intent to hurt. The child has to be aware that what they are doing is called bullying and that it is not an accept-

able way to behave because of its consequences for the victim and others in the group. Early signs that a child is developing this awareness are seen in the child who forcefully takes possessions from another child or hurts another; shows pleasure at the child's reaction; and appears unconcerned when disciplined for the action.

Bullying decreases during the high school years, but it still occurs, often with very negative outcomes. The same behaviors seen in young people can also be seen in adults; however, in adulthood it is called harassment. Whatever it is called and whenever it occurs, its consequences can be devastating.

What Influences Bullying Behaviors

There is no difference in bullying behaviors based on geography or locale (e.g., urban, suburban, or rural settings), race/ethnicity, or socio-economic status. Bullies often come from homes where aggressive methods are used to manage difficult situations (Thompson et al., 2002). Certainly parental attitudes regarding bullying behaviors as well as parental disciplinary measures can send messages to children and teens about what behaviors are appropriate and which ones will get a response by the parent. Other influences include role models and violence on television and in the movies, as well as those portrayed in videogames. When bullies see that parents and teachers will not interfere in the bullying process, this is a message that the behaviors can continue.

Why Does Bullying Occur?

The need for perceived power and control results in a feeling of dominance and an achieved status, even if only in the eyes of the bully and those who watch and often fear him or her. Bullying is perceived as a demonstration of being "tough." Yet, for all of its violence, bullying is a social activity. Rarely is it just done on a one-to-one basis. While the victim may be alone, the bully often has a "fan club" around to share the "success."

Who Is the Victim?

Victims are often identified as being "different" from their peers (Bernstein & Watson, 1997). This may be in their height, stature, choice of clothes, mannerisms, beliefs, lack of coordination, disabilities, craniofacial abnormalities (i.e., big ears, braces, or glasses), or sexual orientation. These are frequently the children and adolescents who are described as "weird" by their peers, such as the computer geeks. They may be the ones who are highly disliked by their classmates or those who are neither liked nor disliked. This latter group often holds no status in the peer group; it is as if they do not exist.

Victims may already be anxious and insecure and have a lowered self-esteem and poorer social skills. They appear to be more annoyed by and less tolerant of teasing by their classmates (Vessey, 1999).

What About the Bystanders?

It was noted above that the bully rarely acts alone. Frequently there are "watchers" or bystanders who watch the process occur. As observers, they act as collaborators; they fuel the bully to show off to the peers and receive a vicarious thrill from watching, even though they do nothing. Some refer to them as "bully-assistants" or reinforcers; they are certainly accessories to the crime.

Watchers are reluctant to intervene because they believe that the bully will come after them if they do, or they may be concerned that they would not be successful if they tried. Other reasons for lack of intervention on the part of "watchers" is "It's none of my business;" "I thought someone else was reporting it;" or they may actually believe that the victim deserves the abuse. Those who do stand up for the victim underestimate how important their contribution is.

The Sequelae of Being a Bully

"Bullying is an early warning that bullies may be headed toward more serious antisocial behavior" (Fox et al., 2003, p. 1). Bullies were found to be seven times more likely to carry a weapon to school than non-bullies. In addition, nearly 60% of boys who were classified as bullies in grades 6 through 9 were convicted of at least one crime by the age of 24; 40% of them had three or more convictions by age 24 (Fox et al.). Children who are bullies also are more likely to engage in criminal activities after reaching adulthood—everything from simple assault to rape and murder. Because bullying is violence, there are legal consequences of being involved in violent acts that may involve the police.

The Sequelae of Being a Victim

Those who are bullied often suffer the psychological complications that result (Hawker & Boulton, 2000). These may include sleep disturbances (e.g., nightmares); psychosomatic complaints; irritability; increased frequency of illness and disease related to chronic stress; and regression to younger behaviors, such as enuresis, comfort habits, and nail biting. Within the school environment, the victim may have impaired concentration, decreased academic performance, truancy from school (to prevent bullying from occurring), or absence from special school activities or certain classes. They may fear rejection, being excluded or ignored, feeling betrayed, or being ridiculed in class with the spread of nasty rumors.

They may feel lonely and isolated from their friends and classmates. Peers can provide a sense of acceptance and belonging; close friendships can result in intimacy, loyalty, and emotional support. The victim may feel they are without any of this support. They have lowered self-esteem, increased anxiety, and increased depression. They may actually suffer from post traumatic stress disorder (PTSD) (Thompson et al., 2002). Young people who are bullied are five times more likely to be depressed than those who were not (Fox et al, 2003). This may result in suicidal thoughts. Bullied boys are four times more likely

to be suicidal, whereas bullied girls are eight times more likely to be suicidal (Fox et al.).

Seventy-five percent of the school shootings over the past decade have been related to bullying and feeling persecuted, threatened, attacked, or injured prior to the incident (Fox et al., 2003).

What Interventions Do NOT Work?

The worst thing anyone can do is to do nothing or assume that bullying behaviors are harmless. Equally harmful is instructing youths to fight back. Responsible adults cannot discount or minimize these behaviors or reports of them. Comments such as "Just ignore them," "Stand up and fight," "Kids will be kids," "Kids sure can be cruel," "It's just a small minority of kids," or "This will prepare you for the real world" are neither helpful nor supportive to the victim and allow bullying to continue. Equally damaging are comments such as, "You must have done something to bring it on yourself" or "You deserved it."

Certain school approaches are also ineffective. These include the misinterpretation of bullying behavior as anger and using anger management strategies as a way of coping. When two children do not like each other, it may be helpful to use lines such as, "If you can't say anything nice, don't say it at all" or "Stay away from each other." It might also be helpful to assist in displacing anger by punching a pillow or punching bag. However, these are inappropriate strategies for bullying.

Also inappropriate are peer mediation approaches—unless there is significant adult input and support. There is too much stress on the victim to be in these situations. Zero tolerance policies with no other programs in place are also not effective, as they do not address the behaviors and give direction as to how to change them. Lastly, disciplining the bully without providing adequate safeguards for the victim often place the victim at greater risk.

Helpful Interventions

The best intervention is communication. Parents should be encouraged to talk to their children to discuss the child's view of bullying, what causes people to bully each other, how it feels to be bullied or to bully others, and the effects bullying behaviors have on students who are victims and the bystanders. Parents also can offer suggestions as to how to handle bullies or role play responses.

Schools can incorporate discussions of bullying behaviors in classes that discuss history and laws. Examples from history and politics, including information on prejudice can help student explore what society would be like if bullying behavior was acceptable. Schools can have group discussions about how to stop bullying and the moral dilemmas faced when encountering bullying behavior (Thompson et al., 2002).

All school personnel as well as parents need to promote trust—trust that the adult will be there for them and protect them and trust that they will do something about the problem. Adults need to be aware that bullying occurs. Children do not want their parents and teachers to over-react or take control, which may be one of the reasons that they do not share details of the problem with adults.

All environments that respond to children need to be intolerant of bullying behaviors. Adults need to be positive role models in managing relationships. They can emphasize sharing, helping, and caring. They can demonstrate and mandate of others that they respect others and others' property. Even the Golden Rule can be used—Do unto others as you would have others do unto you.

Schools should adopt "codes of behavior" for all members of the school community. For classroom exercises that require teams or partners, teachers should assign students to groups to prevent someone from always being the last to be chosen. Care must be taken to assure that the bully and victim are not paired together. Students need to learn conflict resolution, both through formal lessons and informally at the time of untoward incidents. Whenever possible, the victim should be surrounded by supportive students. Lastly, strategies need to be developed that encourage students to tell a staff member or the school nurse when bullying is occurring; the same principles can be used as when the students find weapons.

The victim can be empowered to keep logs or diaries of what happened, where it happened, who was present, what was said or done, and how they felt. This assists the student to stay calmer and make mental notes about what is happening. The victims can be assisted with assertiveness training as well as rehearsal skills; scripts can be used to help the victim know how to respond. If they are open to it, give them ideas of how to decrease their vulnerability, whether it is how to dress or how they carry themselves. Involve them with peers and promote attachment to others.

It is especially important to promote positive self-esteem and enhance resiliency. One school nurse reported that a fifth grade girl who was being bullied would often come to the school nurse's office for respite. The school nurse applauded her for her smile and told her that every day she wanted the girl to stop in the office and smile so that she, the nurse, could start her day smiling back.

When dealing with the bully, it is important to have a clear direct honest message to avoid interactions. Make a basic simple statement of what you do or do not want to happen. Establish ground rules so that the bully and victim can coexist, although they never have to become friends.

Teach all children, especially the "watchers," that everyone has the responsibility to help and that no one has the right to hurt others. Children need to understand their role in promoting or preventing these behaviors. They may also need to be empowered to band together and protect their classmates. They can be the buffers or the defenders of the student being bullied and can distract the bully so that the victim can escape or can surround the victim to offer protection and support. Thompson et al. (2002) calls them the "befrienders."

The watchers should not provide an audience for the bully. it is hard to bully without the support from peers, and their absence will reduce his power base. Students should also sign an agreement regarding the ethical use of the Internet and make

HRSA's Stop Bullying Now Campaign

Because of the extent of bullying among today's youths, the United States Department of Health and Human Services, the Health Resources Administration, and the Maternal Child Health Bureau have recently launched the largest bullying prevention effort and media campaign ever. Specifically geared to reach middle school youths between the ages of 9-13 years of age, a variety of materials are available for youths, parents, and other interested adults. Materials include:

- Public Service Announcements for print, radio, and TV that target youths or adults
- An interactive Web site for middle-school children
- "Webisodes": animated stories about bullying and appropriate responses to it
- Tip Sheets for Adults

All materials are free for your use and are available through: www.StopBullyingNow.hrsa.gov

sure that they define bullying to include actions that are either on or off school grounds, in writing or in person.

Bullying first must be tackled at the group level and involve the whole school community, since it is a collective responsibility. Curricula that emphasize conflict resolution and empathy training may be of help. Policies also must be in place with consequences for bullying clearly articulated and be consistently applied in response to specific bullying incidents. "School staff retain the ultimate responsibility for ensuring the welfare of pupils" (Thompson et al., 2002, p. 128).

Conclusion

Bullying is abuse and abuse is not tolerated. It is present in every school in America. Some children say that it is a bigger problem than drugs and alcohol. Every child has a right to be protected from oppression. The goal for children is to promote success in school, social ties, and productive lives. They need to be taught that everyone has the responsibility to help and that no one has the right to hurt others.

References

Bernstein, J.Y., & Watson, M.W. (1997). Children who are targets of bullying: A victim pattern. *Journal of Interpersonal Violence, 124*, 483–498.

Fox, J., Elliott, D., Kerlikowske, R., Newman, S., & Christeson, W. (2003). *Bullying prevention is crime prevention.* Washington, DC: Fight Crime: Invest in Kids.

Hawker, S.J., & Boulton, M.J. (2000). Twenty years research on peer victimization and psychosocial maladjustment: A meta-analytic review of cross sectional studies. *Journal of Child Psychology and Psychiatry, 41,* 441–455.

Nansel, R., Overpeck, M., Pilla, R., Ruan, W., Simons-Morton, B., & Scheidt, P. (2001). Bully behaviors among U.S. youth: Prevalence and association with psychosocial adjustment. *Journal of the American Medical Association, 285*(16), 2094–2100.

National Association of School Nurses (NASN). (2003). *Peer bullying. Issue brief: School health nursing services role in health care.* Retrieved September 7, 2003, from www.nasn.org/ briefs/ bullying.htm.

Oleweus, D. (1997). Bully/victim problems in school: Facts and intervention. *European Journal of Psychology of Education, 12,* 495–510.

Thompson, D., Arora, T., & Sharp, S. (2002). *Bullying: Effective strategies for long term improvement,* London: Routledge/ Falmer.

Vessey, J. (March, 1999). Bully-proof your child. *The Johns Hopkins Health Insider, 2*(4), 8.

Vessey, J.A., Carlson, K., & David, J. (2003). Helping children who are being teased or bullied. *Nursing Spectrum, 7,* 14–16.

Vessey, J.A., Swanson, M.N., & Hagedorn, M.I. (1995). Teasing: Who says names will never hurt you? *Pediatric Nursing, 21,* 297–300.

JANICE SELEKMAN, DNSc, RN, is Professor, Department of Nursing, University of Delaware, Newark, DE.

JUDITH A. VESSEY, PhD, MBA, PNP, FAAN, is the Lelia Holden Carroll Professor, Boston College, William F. Connell School of Nursing, Chestnut Hill, MA.

From *Pediatric Nursing,* May/June 2004, pp. 246-249. Copyright © 2004 by Pediatric Nursing. Reprinted by permission.

Influencing, Negotiating Skills and Conflict-Handling: Some Additional Research and Reflections

This paper examines the connection between influencing, negotiation and conflict-handling. Using newly gathered data, it develops earlier articles on the relationships between negotiation and influencing by linking them to the associated area of conflict-handling. The new data confirm the authors' view that negotiation is best seen as an aspect of influencing and that, although both are associated with conflict-handling, they go beyond this. The new findings reinforce concerns about the role of negotiation and suggest some situations in which negotiation may be appropriate and some where it may not be suitable. As earlier, these findings have implications for the way training in these areas is carried out and how managers can make effective use of influencing, negotiation and conflict-handling.

TONY MANNING AND BOB ROBERTSON

Introduction

This paper looks at some of the ways in which approaches to both influencing and negotiation are related to conflict-handling. In particular, it develops the findings of an earlier pair of articles (Manning and Robertson, 2003) on the connection between influencing and negotiation. These were based on the analysis of data collected by the authors, in their capacity as training and development practitioners, and concluded that it is beneficial to see negotiation as one type of influencing. One implication of this, for both training and managerial effectiveness, was the danger of assuming that negotiating skills are appropriate to all influencing situations. This raised further questions about the key ways in which influence situations vary and the skills that are appropriate, and inappropriate, to the different situations.

These issues can be further explored by looking at the relationship between conflict-handling and influencing, which in line with the above, can be taken to include negotiation. Conflict-handling, influencing and negotiating are inter-linked concepts. It is, therefore, informative to investigate the inter-relationships through further empirical research as this may throw further light on the approaches to different types of influencing situations.

Additional data have been collected by one of the authors, Tony Manning, on the use by individuals of various conflict-handling modes, along with their influencing strategies and styles, and negotiating skills. The data are based on the responses to three established psychometric instruments: the Thomas-Kilmann conflict mode instrument (Thomas and Kilmann, 1974); the influencing strategies and styles profile (ISSP) developed by Tony Manning (Manning and Robertson, 2003);

the negotiating skills questionnaire (NSQ) prepared by Manning and Robertson (2003). The Thomas-Kilmann model is outlined in Figure 1. The latter two instruments were described in the previous articles and are summarised below.

The ISSP

The six influencing strategies are as follows.

1. *Reason* – using reason, information and logic to justify a request,
2. *Assertion* – making a direct request for what we want,
3. *Exchange* – working together for the best overall result – offering an exchange of benefits,
4. *Courting favour* – bringing oneself into favour with the other person,
5. *Coercion* – threatening to use, or actually using, some kind of sanction,
6. *Partnership* – getting the support of others at all levels.

The three dimensions of influence are as follows.

1. *Strategist-opportunist. Strategists* tend to use reason, assertion and partnership to influence others, but avoid courting favour and exchange. They are likely to be clear about what they want to achieve, to have thought about why they want it and to have identified who they need to influence to get it. *Opportunists* tend to use courting favour and exchange to influence others, but avoid reason, assertion and partnership. They are likely to be less clear about who they need to influence, about what and why and respond more opportunistically in the face-to-face situation.

Figure 1 The Thomas-Kilmann model of conflict-handling

This model is concerned with an individual's behaviour in conflict situations, using the definition of conflict noted above Thomas and Kilmann identify two dimensions to describe a person's behaviour in a conflict situation:

- *Assertiveness* – the extent to which the individual attempts to satisfy his or her own concerns
- *Cooperativeness* – the extent to which the individual attempts to satisfy the other person's concerns.

These two dimensions are used to define five specific methods of dealing with conflicts or conflict-handling modes:

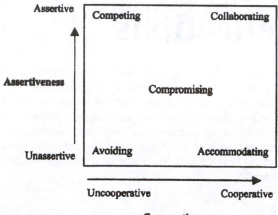

The five conflict-handling modes described by Thomas and Kilmann are outlined briefly below:-

1. *Competing* – assertive and uncooperative: pursues own concerns at the other person's expense; power-oriented: uses whatever power seems appropriate to win one's own position.

2. *Collaborating* – assertive and co-operative: attempts to work with the other person to find some solution which fully satisfies both parties; involves identifying the underlying concerns of both parties.

3. *Compromising* – intermediate in both assertiveness and cooperatives: seeks to find a mutually acceptable solution which partially satisfies both sides without fully meeting all concerns to everyone's satisfaction.

4. *Avoiding* – unassertive and uncooperative: the individual pursues neither their own goal nor the other person's goals; involves not addressing the issue.

5. *Accommodating* – unassertive and cooperative: neglects their own concerns to satisfy the concerns of the other person

2. *Collaborator-battler.* Collaborators tend to use partnership, reason, exchange and courting favour to influence others but not coercion and assertion. They engage collaboratively in a rational partnership with others for the overall good. Battlers tend to use coercion and assertion but not partnership, reason, exchange and courting favour. They concentrate on getting across exactly what they want to achieve and the sanctions they are prepared to use if they do not achieve it.

3. *Bystander-shotgun.* In addition to the two independent dimensions of influence described above, statistical analysis shows there is a third factor that is independent of the other two dimensions and relates to the overall level or frequency of influence attempts strategies. Using terms derived from Kipnis and Schmidt (1998), although in a slightly different way, we refer to this dimension as the "Bystander versus Shotgun" scale. Bystanders engage in relatively few influence attempts, using little of any influence strategies. This may be associated with a low need to influence others at work and/or limited power to influence. However, it may also involve the more judicious use of influence strategies

4. *Shotguns* engage in a relatively large number of influence attempts, using a lot of all strategies. This may be associated with a high need to engage in influence attempts and/or the possession of significant and varied sources of power. However, it may also be associated with the non-judicious use of influence strategies.

NSQ

This measure allows respondents to compare their negotiating skills against a model of good negotiating practice. The following are the main *stages in the process* of negotiation.

1. *Preparation* – establishing the issues, getting quality information, preparing the case and preparing for the encounter.
2. *The opening phase* – creating a positive climate, stating your case and finding out their case.
3. *Getting movement to reach agreement* – challenging their case, responding to challenges on your case, making concessions, trading or linking and moving to reach agreement.
4. *Closure* – summarising and recording agreements, establishing monitoring and review procedures and building for the future.

Within these four stages, there are a number of issues which run through the whole process of negotiation. They are as follows.

1. *Clarity of focus.* Defining the issues, having a clear and simple case, using different types of information from a variety of sources, taking time before making decisions, agreeing the outcome, monitoring and reviewing.
2. *Flexibility of strategy.* Finding out about the other party and what they want, taking a long term perspective, planning around issues rather than in a strict sequence and using concessions, adjournments and whatever is necessary to reach an agreement.
3. *Win-win-values.* Having respect for the other party and what they want, considering a wide range of options and outcomes, ensuring both parties clearly present their case, and cooperating openly to achieve mutually acceptable outcomes.
4. *Win-win-interactive skills.* Showing personal warmth, seeking information and clarification throughout, summarising and testing understanding of what is said, and being open and non-defensive. This paper begins by examining the relationship between conflict-handling, influencing and negotiation. This sets the scene for a more detailed examination of the links between conflict-handling and influencing and conflict-handling and negotiation. This reinforces the view that negotiation is only one method of influencing and, once again, highlights the dangers of assuming that negotiating skills are appropriate to all influence situations. It also illustrates that negotiation may not be appropriate in all conflict situations. It may be appropriate in certain circumstances, but there are also situations in which it is likely to be inappropriate.

Conflict-Handling, Influencing and Negotiation

Conflict-handling is defined by Thomas and Kilmann (1974) as situations in which the concerns of two people appear to be incompatible. This suggests a clear link with influencing and negotiation as both can be seen as possible means by which any conflict could be resolved. By definition, influencing involves trying to get another person to do what they might otherwise not do. As such, it can contribute to reducing the apparent incompatibility between those involved in a conflict. Negotiation is one form of influencing and is about trying to achieve win-win. It is a process of compromise, involving parties with different sets of objectives and values, based on their different vested interests. It is, by its vary nature, a process intended to decrease the incompatibility between the parties involved.

The above refers to a situation where conflict can be said to be overt in that both parties recognise that their concerns are not compatible. This seems to be the situation envisaged by Thomas and Kilmann (1974). Conflict in their model is overt at least to the extent that both parties accept that, at a particular moment, their concerns seem to be incompatible.

However, the use of influencing and negotiation is not confined to this state of affairs. Both can be used where the parties believe their concerns to be consistent with each other. Each of the two sides in a negotiation, for example, may believe that the other wishes to reach an agreement and that the purpose of the negotiation is to settle the terms of the agreement. In these circumstances, however, influencing and negotiation have the potential to cause conflict. Any attempt to persuade someone to do something, which they might not otherwise do, for instance, must carry the risk that it will expose concerns "which appear to be incompatible".

It is clear that the concepts of conflict-handling, influencing and negotiating are inter-linked. However, this only tells us a certain amount about how they are inter-related and further empirical research is needed to investigate the relationships further. The following discussion attempts to do this.

Influencing and Conflict-Handling

The framework for looking at influencing strategies and styles is described by Manning and Robertson (2003). It identifies six influencing strategies and two dimensions of style, each with two polar extremes, although in this paper we also include an additional dimension of influencing style also with two polar extremes. Figure 1 provides some further information on this instrument.

Thirty-three individuals, all participants on training courses concerned with influencing skills, completed both the Thomas-Kilmann conflict mode instrument and the ISSP. It was, therefore, possible to establish the relationships between these two sets of variables. Appendix 1 shows the correlation matrix for conflict-handling modes and influencing strategies and styles.

Some tentative conclusions can be drawn from this about the relationship between conflict-handling and influencing. With respect to the six *influencing strategies,* it appears to confirm the view that different strategies relate to different circumstances. Coercion, for example, is strongly associated with competition as an approach to handling conflict; and exchange is related to collaboration.

It also suggests that the various approaches to conflict-handling can be treated as aspects of influencing. Reason, for example, unlike all other influencing strategies, is not related to any particular conflict-handling mode which implies that influencing strategies go beyond handling conflict. Some strategies like partnership and courting favour are associated with avoidance of conflict and thus, cover situations where incompatible concerns may not surface. They approach this situation differently, however. Partnership is about friendly cooperation and collaboration while courting favour may be linked to grasping an opportunity to "get into someone's good books".

Similar points can be made in terms of the *influencing styles.* For example, collaborators tend to use a lot of collaboration but not competition, whereas battlers do the opposite and tend to use a competition most but lack collaboration. This confirms that different people prefer to act in different ways and, in line with the argument that different strategies are appropriate in different circumstances, can help to explain why, in some cases, influencing attempts can result in successful conflict-handling, but may not succeed in others, where a different approach would be appropriate.

It also appears that shotguns tend to use avoidance and, to a lesser extent, a lack of compromise, while bystanders tend not to use avoidance, but show some willingness to compromise. This suggests that more attempts at influence do not mean more facing up to and dealing with conflicts but less, along with less willingness to compromise on such issues. This adds further support to the view that it is the strategy of influencing which is chosen that is likely to be important in any situation. Again, influencing may be the broader category as it covers both overt conflict and situations where conflict may not necessarily follow an attempt at influencing.

Negotiating and Conflict-Handling

Thirty-one individuals, all participants on training courses concerned with negotiating skills, completed both the Thomas-Kilmann conflict mode instrument and the NSQ. Once again, it was, therefore, possible to establish the relationships between these two sets of variables. Appendix 2 shows the correlation matrix for conflict-handling modes and stages and issues in negotiating.

The results provide some support for the behaviours associated with a win-win approach to negotiation. One example is that the conflict-handling mode of collaboration is related to the preparation and opening phases of the negotiation: it is here when the most significant attempts to find a solution acceptable to both parties are likely to be made. Further, this mode is directly linked to the key issue of a win-win approach. The conflict-handling mode of avoidance is negatively related to all four stages of negotiation, which is consistent with the notion that skilled negotiators do attempt to address explicitly the issues in a negotiation. This idea is reinforced by the fact that low avoidance is also associated with a flexibility of approach to negotiation.

The general pattern of relationships between an individual's approach to negotiating and his or her approach to conflict-handling, therefore, is very clear: skilled negotiators tend to use low avoidance and high collaboration modes of conflict-handling. To a lesser extent, skilled negotiators also show a preparedness to use accommodation and compromise, whilst avoiding competition.

Overall, therefore, only some of the modes of conflict-handling (collaborating, compromising and accommodation) appear to be consistent with negotiation. Further, Appendix 1 suggests a link between the influencing strategy of assertion and the conflict-handling mode of avoidance. Once again, there seems to be a support for the notion that negotiation can be seen as a subset of influencing.

Thomas and Kilmann (1974) make it clear that there is no "one best" approach to handling conflict and that all approaches might be effective in particular circumstances. They also provide some guidance on the appropriate use of each of the five modes. In the light of the finding that skilled negotiators tend to use certain conflict-handling modes but not others, it may be useful to look at the three conflict-handling modes which are used successfully in negotiation and consider both when they may be appropriate. Effectively, this develops the guidance provided by Thomas and Kilmann.

Negotiation is fundamentally a collaborative, win-win approach to conflict resolution. Collaboration is likely to be particularly useful:

- to find integrative solutions without compromising either sets of concerns;
- when your objective is to learn and find out the other party's views;
- to merge insights from people with different perspectives on a problem;
- to gain commitment by incorporating the other's concerns into a consensual decision; and
- to work through hard feelings which have interfered with interpersonal relationships.

Negotiation may involve accommodating as an element of conflict-handling. Accommodating is likely to be useful:

- when you realise you are wrong;
- to avoid further damage in a situation which is not going well;
- when the issues are more important to the other party than to you;
- as a goodwill gesture, to build-up credit points for later issues which are important to you; and when preserving harmony and avoiding disruption are important.

Negotiation may also involve compromising as an element conflict-handling. Compromise is likely to be useful:

- when your goals are only moderately important;
- when there is an equal balance of power and strong commitment to mutually exclusive goals; and
- as a temporary settlement, expedient solution or back up mode.

The other two modes of conflict-handling, avoiding and competing are not used by skilled negotiators. However, if negotiation is seen as one possible approach among several options to any situation, both may be appropriate in certain circumstances. Avoiding is likely to be useful:

- when the issue is trivial or symptomatic of another more basic issue;
- when you perceive no possibility of satisfying your concerns, perhaps because of an adverse balance of power;
- when the potential damage of confronting an issue outweighs its resolution;

Appendix 1.

Table AI Correlation matrix for conflict-handling modes and influencing strategies and styles (N = 33)

	Competition	Collaboration	TKCM Compromise	Avoidance	Accommodation
ISSP strategies					
Reason	−0.06	−0.04	0.08	0.06	−0.06
Assertion	−0.06	−0.05	−0.11	0.19	0.00
Exchange	−0.10	0.28	−0.21	0.11	−0.02
Courting favour	0.04	−0.12	−0.17	0.16	0.03
Coercion	0.31	−0.22	−0.07	−0.03	−0.15
Partnership	−0.25	0.11	−0.09	0.30	−0.04
ISSP style dimensions					
Total (bystander-shotgun)	−0.05	−0.01	−0.15	0.22	−0.07
AF1 (strategist-opportunist)	0.10	0.07	−0.20	−0.01	0.05
AF2 (collaborator-battler)	0.37	−0.24	−0.12	0.05	−0.11

Appendix 2.

Table AII Correlation matrix for conflict-handling modes and negotiating stages and issues (N = 31)

NSQ	Competition	Collaboration	TKCM Compromise	Avoidance	Accommodation
Stages in the process					
Preparation	−0.26	0.22	−0.04	−0.11	0.26
Opening phase	0.05	0.36	0.01	−0.41	−0.01
Movement	−0.02	0.12	−0.09	−0.12	0.09
Closure	−0.08	−0.02	0.08	−0.01	0.05
Key issues throughout the process					
Clarity of focus	−0.04	0.29	−0.11	−0.21	0.10
Flexibility of approach	−0.04	0.12	0.17	−0.32	0.06
Win-win values and approach	−0.09	0.17	0.14	−0.25	0.06
Win-win interpersonal skills	0.02	0.04	−0.14	−0.04	0.11
Negotiating skills – total score	−0.10	0.25	−0.04	−0.23	0.14

- to let people cool down, reduce tensions, regain perspective and composure; and when gathering more information is more important than making an immediate decision.

Competition is likely to be useful:

- when quick, decisive action is vital, e.g. emergencies;
- when issues are important and where unpopular courses of action need implementing;
- when issues are vital to organisation welfare, when you know you are right; and
- to protect yourself against people who take advantage of non-competitive behaviour.

Conclusion

The conclusions drawn from the analysis of the research data presented above reinforce the conclusion arrived at in our previous pair of articles, that it is important for those providing training and development activities to recognise that negotiating is not a paradigm for all influence situations. Negotiating is an appropriate method of influencing and conflict-handling in certain conditions and situations, although other methods of in-fluencing and conflict-handling are likely to be more appropriate in contrasting conditions and situations. Training and development activities should reflect the legitimacy of a variety of approaches to interpersonal influence and conflict-handling, and give due consideration to an equal diversity of situations and the particular skills appropriate to each other. Negotiation has a place, is fine in its place but is best kept in its place.

References

Kipnis, D. and Schmidt, S.M. (1988), "Upward-influence styles: relationships with performance evaluations, salary and stress", *Administrative Science* Quarterly. Vol. 33, pp. 528–42.

Manning, T. and Robertson, B. (2003), Influencing and negotiating skills: some research and reflections—Part I: influencing strategies and styles. Part II: influencing styles and negotiating skills, *Industrial and Commercial Training*, Vol. 35 Nos 1/2, pp. 60–6, pp. 11–15.

Thomas, K. (1976), "Conflict and conflict management", in Dunnette, M.D. (Ed.), *Handbook of Industrial and Organisational Psychology*. Wiley, New York, NY.

Thomas, K.W. and Kilmann, R.H. (1974), *Thomas-Kilmann Conflict Mode Instrument,* Xicom.

From *Industrial and Commercial Training,* Vol. 36, No. 3, 2004, pp. 104-109. Copyright © 2004 by Emerald Group Publishing Ltd. Reprinted by permission.

UNIT 9

Altruism, Helping and Cooperation

Unit Selections

Key Points to Consider

- What characteristics do individuals who demonstrate prosocial behavior share in common?

- What situational factors affect prosocial behavior?

- Why is there a tendency for a group of bystanders to be less likely than an individual to provide assistance to a person in trouble?

- What role does culture play in prosocial behavior?

- Do you think that some helping behavior is motivated by anticipated gain (as in the egoistic model)? Why?

Student Web Site

www.mhcls.com/online

Internet References

Further information regarding these Web sites may be found in this book's preface or online.

Americans With Disabilities Act Document Center
http://www.jan.wvu.edu/links/adalinks.htm

Give Five
http://www.independentsector.org/give5/givefive.html

University of Maryland Diversity Database
http://www.inform.umd.edu/EdRes/Topic/Diversity/

A young woman believed in regular exercise and in relaxing after work. While her coworkers gathered at a local pub to discuss the latest gossip at work, she would go home, grab a bottle of water, and her MP3 player and go for a brisk walk. She generally followed the same itinerary, but on this particular day, she decided to cross a large park because one of the roads on her usual route was under construction. She wanted to avoid the noise, the dust, and snarled traffic.

Because she had earphones on, she did not here the man sprinting up behind her. The next thing she knew, she was hurled to the ground. Her headphones had fallen off but she still clutched the water bottle. As the man began to tear at her clothes, she pummeled him with the bottle, but she had drunk too much water for the bottle to be effective. When the bottle didn't stop him, she started screaming, "Help me; help me, please."

Would anyone come? Would this man get what he wanted? Would he leave her dead or alive? As she screamed for the second time, her assailant tried to cover her mouth with his hand. The grip of his other hand momentarily released so that she could push him off. She got up and started to run. He just as quickly pursued her. As she ran, she screamed again until he caught her and threw her to the ground. As she fell, she remembered what she had learned in a women's self-defense course—to yell loudly "I don't know you; get away."

This time the struggling pair was seen by several people in the park. A young man walking a dog nearby heard her desperate screams and ran to her. The young man pulled the attacker off the woman. The rescuer's big dog snarled and barked and bit at the stranger, who finally ran off. The young man asked if the victim was all right, called 911 on his cell phone, and grabbed his dog. Together they awaited the arrival of the medics and the police.

Is this story usual or unusual, not so much in regard to the woman's assault, but with respect to the fact that someone actually responded to cries for help. Every day someone somewhere needs help in our society, but just how helpful are people? Who are the helpers and rescuers? Which victims will they help? Why do some people not respond to the pleas of others? Under what circumstances will people help rather than just watch?

The topics of this unit are helping, altruism, and cooperation—positive social behaviors. "Helping" and "cooperation" are readily understood terms by the average American. But what is altruism? Most social psychologists define *altruism* as helping another *at a cost to the helper*. The cost might be lost time, threats to personal safety, money donated, or anything else that the helper offers up.

The first article of this unit, "The Compassionate Instinct," explores twenty-first century viewpoints relative to altruism and prosocial behavior. Are such good works obsolete in our fast-paced society? Dacher Keltner explores if there is a biological basis for helping and how today's society may be influenced by evolution. The question of whether we are hard-wired to help one another is posed.

Our second article discusses the role of self-satisfaction in giving. Do we show compassion just to improve how we view ourselves? "Gift Giving's Hidden Strings" adds insight about motives to help others and how twenty-first century society may affect altruism.

The last article in this unit explores another concept—social justice. *Social justice* essentially means a person's perception that the outcomes or rewards of his or her effort are fair and just. Most people have an acute sense of fairness when they interact with others, although what they perceive as fair for themselves may not be what they interpret as fair for others. Skitka and Crosby analyze past research on fairness and cooperation, as well as point out future research in new directions.

The Compassionate Instinct

Think humans are born selfish? Think again.

Dacher Keltner reveals the compassionate side to human nature.

DACHER KELTNER

Humans are selfish. It's so easy to say. The same goes for so many assertions that follow. Greed is good. Altruism is an illusion. Cooperation is for suckers. Competition is natural, war inevitable. The bad in human nature is stronger than the good.

These kinds of claims reflect age-old assumptions about emotion. For millennia, we have regarded the emotions as the fount of irrationality, baseness, and sin. The idea of the seven deadly sins takes our destructive passions for granted. Plato compared the human soul to a chariot: the intellect is the driver and the emotions are the horses. Life is a continual struggle to keep the emotions under control.

Even compassion, the concern we feel for another being's welfare, has been treated with downright derision. Kant saw it as a weak and misguided sentiment: "Such benevolence is called soft-heartedness and should not occur at all among human beings," he said of compassion. Many question whether true compassion exists at all—or whether it is inherently motivated by self-interest.

Recent studies of compassion argue persuasively for a different take on human nature, one that rejects the preeminence of self-interest. These studies support a view of the emotions as rational, functional, and adaptive—a view which has its origins in Darwin's *Expression of Emotion in Man and Animals*. Compassion and benevolence, this research suggests, are an evolved part of human nature, rooted in our brain and biology, and ready to be cultivated for the greater good.

The Biological Basis of Compassion

First consider the recent study of the biological basis of compassion. If such a basis exists, we should be wired up, so to speak, to respond to others in need. Recent evidence supports this point convincingly. University of Wisconsin psychologist Jack Nitschke found in an experiment that when mothers looked at pictures of their babies, they not only reported feeling more compassionate love than when they saw other babies; they also demonstrated unique activity in a region of their brains associated with the positive emotions. Nitschke's finding suggests that this region of the brain is attuned to the first objects of our compassion—our offspring.

But this compassionate instinct isn't limited to parents' brains. In a different set of studies, Joshua Greene and Jonathan Cohen of Princeton University found that when subjects contemplated harm being done to others, a similar network of regions in their brains lit up. Our children and victims of violence—two very different subjects, yet united by the similar neurological reactions they provoke. This consistency strongly suggests that compassion isn't simply a fickle or irrational emotion, but rather an innate human response embedded into the folds of our brains.

In other research by Emory University neuroscientists James Rilling and Gregory Berns, participants were given the chance to help someone else while their brain activity was recorded. Helping others triggered activity in the caudate nucleus and anterior cingulate, portions of the brain that turn on when people receive rewards or experience pleasure. This is a rather remarkable finding: helping others brings the same pleasure we get from the gratification of personal desire.

The brain, then, seems wired up to respond to others' suffering—indeed, it makes us feel good when we can alleviate that suffering. But do other parts of the body also suggest a biological basis for compassion?

Helping others triggers the same brain activity as the gratification of personal desire.

It seems so. Take the loose association of glands, organs, and cardiovascular and respiratory systems known as the autonomic nervous system (ANS). The ANS plays a primary role in regulating our blood flow and breathing patterns for different kinds of actions. For example, when we feel threatened, our heart and breathing rates usually increase, preparing us either to confront or flee from the threat—the so-called "fight or flight" response. What is the ANS profile of compassion? As it turns out, when young children and adults feel compassion for others, this emotion is reflected in very real physiological changes: Their heart rate goes down from baseline levels, which prepares them not to fight or flee, but to approach and sooth.

Then there's oxytocin, a hormone that floats through the bloodstream. Research performed on the small, stocky rodents known as prairie voles indicates that oxytocin promotes long-term bonds and commitments, as well as the kind of nurturing behavior—like care for offspring—that lies at the heart of compassion. It may account for that overwhelming feeling of warmth and connection we feel toward our offspring or loved ones. Indeed, breastfeeding and massages elevate oxytocin levels in the blood (as does eating chocolate). In some recent studies I've conducted, we have found that when people perform behaviors associated with compassionate love—warm smiles, friendly hand gestures, affirmative forward leans—their bodies produce more oxytocin. This suggests compassion may be self-perpetuating: Being compassionate causes a chemical reaction in the body that motivates us to be even more compassionate.

Signs of Compassion

According to evolutionary theory, if compassion is truly vital to human survival, it would manifest itself through nonverbal signals. Such signals would serve many adaptive functions. Most importantly, a distinct signal of compassion would soothe others in distress, allow people to identify the good-natured individuals with whom they'd want long-term relationships, and help forge bonds between strangers and friends.

Research by Nancy Eisenberg, perhaps the world's expert on the development of compassion in children, has found that there is a particular facial expression of compassion, characterized by oblique eyebrows and a concerned gaze. When someone shows this expression, they are then more likely to help others. My work has examined another nonverbal cue: touch.

Previous research has already documented the important functions of touch. Primates such as great apes spend hours a day grooming each other, even when there are no lice in their physical environment. They use grooming to resolve conflicts, to reward each other's generosity, and to form alliances. Human skin has special receptors that transform patterns of tactile stimulation—a mother's caress or a friend's pat on the back—into indelible sensations as lasting as childhood smells. Certain touches can trigger the release of oxytocin, bringing feelings of warmth and pleasure. The handling of neglected rat pups can reverse the effects of their previous social isolation, going as far as enhancing their immune systems.

My work set out to document, for the first time, whether compassion can be communicated via touch. Such a finding would have several important implications. It would show that we can communicate this positive emotion with nonverbal displays, whereas previous research has mostly documented the nonverbal expression of negative emotions such as anger and fear. This finding would also shed light on the social functions of compassion—how people might rely on touch to soothe, reward, and bond in daily life.

In my experiment, I put two strangers in a room where they were separated by a barrier. They could not see one another, but they could reach each other through a hole. One person touched the other on the forearm several times, each time trying to convey one of 12 emotions, including love, gratitude, and compassion. After each touch, the person touched had to describe the emotion they thought the toucher was communicating.

Imagine yourself in this experiment. How do you suppose you might do? Remarkably, people in these experiments reliably identified compassion, as well as love and the other ten emotions, from the touches to their forearm. This strongly suggests that compassion is an evolved part of human nature—something we're universally capable of expressing and understanding.

Compassion as a Source of Altruism

Feeling compassion is one thing; acting on it is another. We still must confront a vital question: Does compassion promote altruistic behavior? In an important line of research, Daniel Batson has made the persuasive case that it does. According to Batson, when we encounter people in need or distress, we often imagine what their experience is like. This is a great developmental milestone—to take the perspective of another. It is not only one of the most human of capacities; it is one of the most important aspects of our ability to make moral judgments and fulfill the social contract. When we take the other's perspective, we feel an empathic state of concern and are motivated to address that person's needs and enhance that person's welfare, sometimes even at our own expense.

In a compelling series of studies, Batson exposed participants to another's suffering. He then had some participants imagine that person's pain, but he allowed those participants to act in a self-serving fashion—for example, by leaving the experiment.

Within this series, one study had participants watch another person receive shocks when he failed a memory task. Then they were asked to take shocks on behalf of the participant, who, they were told, had experienced a shock trauma as a child. Those participants who had reported that they felt compassion for the other individual volunteered to take several shocks for that person, even when they were free to leave the experiment.

In another experiment, Batson and colleagues examined whether people feeling compassion would help someone in distress, even when their acts were completely anonymous. In this study female participants exchanged written notes with another person, who quickly expressed feeling lonely and an interest in spending time with the participant. Those participants feeling compassion volunteered to spend significant time with the other person, even when no one else would know about their act of kindness.

Taken together, our strands of evidence suggest the following. Compassion is deeply rooted in human nature: it has a biological basis in the brain and body. Humans can communicate compassion through facial gesture and touch, and these displays of compassion can serve vital social functions, strongly suggesting an evolutionary basis of compassion. And when experienced, compassion overwhelms selfish concerns and motivates altruistic behavior.

Cultivating Compassion

We can thus see the great human propensity for compassion and the effects compassion can have on behavior. But can we actually cultivate compassion, or is it all determined by our genes?

Compassion is deeply rooted in our brains, our bodies, and in the most basic ways we communicate.

Recent neuroscience studies suggest that positive emotions are less heritable—that is, less determined by our DNA—than the negative emotions. Other studies indicate that the brain structures involved in positive emotions like compassion are more "plastic"—subject to changes brought about by environmental input. So we might think about compassion as a biologically based skill or virtue, but not one that we either have or don't have. Instead, it's a trait that we can develop in an appropriate context. What might that context look like? For children, we are learning some answers.

Some researchers have observed a group of children as they grew up, looking for family dynamics that might make the children more empathetic, compassionate, or likely to help others. This research points to several key factors.

First, children securely attached to their parents, compared to insecurely attached children, tend to be sympathetic to their peers as early as age three and a half, according to the research of Everett Waters, Judith Wippman, and Alan Sroufe. In contrast, researchers Mary Main and Carol George found that abusive parents who resort to physical violence have less empathetic children.

Developmental psychologists have also been interested in comparing two specific parenting styles. Parents who rely on *induction* engage their children in reasoning when they have done harm, prompting their child to think about the consequences of their actions and how these actions have harmed others. Parents who rely on *power assertion* simply declare what is right and

wrong, and resort more often to physical punishment or strong emotional responses of anger. Nancy Eisengerg, Richard Fabes, and Martin Hoffman have found that parents who use induction and reasoning raise children who are better adjusted and more likely to help their peers. This style of parenting seems to nurture the basic tools of compassion: an appreciation of others' suffering and a desire to remedy that suffering.

Parents can also teach compassion by example. A landmark study of altruism by Pearl and Samuel Oliner found that children who have compassionate parents tend to be more altruistic. In the Oliners' study of Germans who helped rescue Jews during the Nazi Holocaust, one of the strongest predictors of this inspiring behavior was the individual's memory of growing up in a family that prioritized compassion and altruism.

Concluding Thoughts

Human communities are only as healthy as our conceptions of human nature. It has long been assumed that selfishness, greed, and competitiveness lie at the core of human behavior, the products of our evolution. It takes little imagination to see how these assumptions have guided most realms of human affairs, from policy making to media portrayals of social life.

But clearly, recent scientific findings forcefully challenge this view of human nature. We see that compassion is deeply rooted in our brains, our bodies, and in the most basic ways we communicate. What's more, a sense of compassion fosters compassionate behavior and helps shape the lessons we teach our children.

Of course, simply realizing this is not enough; we must also make room for our compassionate impulses to flourish. What follows are three essays that can help us do just that. They examine three institutions—marriage, education, and health care—and describe how and why we should infuse each of them with more compassion. Their proposals are as concrete as they are insightful. These essays provide ample evidence to show what we can gain from more compassionate marriages, schools, and hospitals. They do more than make us reconsider the purpose of three important social institutions. They offer a blueprint for a more compassionate world.

DACHER KELTNER, Ph.D., a co-editor of *Greater Good*, is a professor of psychology at the University of California, Berkeley, and a co-director of the UC-Berkeley Center for the Development of Peace and Well-Being.

From *Greater Good*, Vol. I, Issue 1, Spring 2004, pp. 6-9. Copyright © 2004 by Greater Good. Reprinted by permission. For more information, please visit www.greatergoodmag.org.

Gift Giving's Hidden Strings

Good deeds do help a Scrooge—even when the motives are mixed.

G. JEFFREY MACDONALD

Materialism run amok—or the sweet spirit of giving? Every year the holidays tend to raise the same questions about gifts. Does the traditional year's end exchange of presents and charitable offerings bring out the best in humanity—or simply hide other forms of self-interest?

In recent years, Americans have become a more giving people, according to data from the Center on Philanthropy at Indiana University. Charitable donations more than doubled from $119 billion in 1994 to $241 billion in 2002. But the main reason for the increase, says Eugene Tempel, executive director of the center, is a selfish one: new tax benefits for donors.

Givers of all things from cards to parties, from a treat for a colleague to a check for charity, expect some measure of reward in return for doing good deeds, according to behavioral experts and spiritual leaders alike. And yet, some add, even selfish giving can be a force for good—especially because motives tend to represent at least a bit of both the good and the bad.

"There's a lot of evidence to say Ebenezer Scrooge is healthier and happier as a result of his generosity," says Stephen Post, a bioethics professor at Case Western Reserve University and executive director of the Institute for Research on Unlimited Love. "There's a different kind of self that is benefiting in Scrooge's case, a deeper self. Most motivations [for giving] are mixed, but the deeper self still benefits when the giving is prudential, but not crass."

"People give because it makes them feel good. That's a very selfish motivator for giving," says Dr. Tempel. "When you give, you feel good about yourself."

But that's not all bad, says Julie Salamon, author of the new book "Rambam's Ladder: A Meditation on Generosity and Why It Is Necessary to Give." Like most psychologists and ethicists, she holds no illusions about the possibility of pure altruism. What matters more is to climb from the lowest type of giving (begrudging) to the highest types—anonymous gifts to strangers and gifts that enable others to attain self-sufficiency.

There are, however, some dismaying signs of the state of charitable giving in the United States. For all of America's heightened giving, more and more gifts to institutions come with restrictions, Tempel says, which suggests a diminished level of trust and a mounting desire to control how donations are used.

For example, United Methodists next year will debate a proposal to enable member churches to specify how their gifts to the denomination are used. According to the Rev. Scott Campbell, pastor of Harvard-Epworth United Methodist Church in Cambridge, Mass., the proposal tells a larger story of individual control eclipsing the communal decisionmaking processes of yesteryear.

Donors increasingly "want to be assured that their own particular agenda is being served by anything they support," Mr. Campbell says. "This is something fairly new with regard to how widespread the practice has become."

And if politics were not sufficient to corrupt giving motives, what anthropologists term "the reciprocity principle" just might be. Give a gift and the recipient, no matter the culture or the era, feels obliged to respond in kind. This type of giving is meant to induce guilt, shame, and indebtedness, and therefore ranks high in the hierarchy of types of giving.

"To receive an unexpected gift is more a bane than a blessing," says Prof. Martin Bolt, a social psychologist at Calvin College in Grand Rapids, Mich. "The experts at this are the Hare Krishnas, who give away flowers and then ask for donations. Are you going to take the flower and not give a donation? What kind of a Scrooge are you?"

Yet upon a sea of mixed motives and corrupting temptations in the giving season, behavioral experts say they see reasons for hope. Personal gain in a crass sense is hardly the sole reason for giving, according to new research on empathy. Professor Bolt says the findings show people can transcend their own primary self-interest when they see what another person sees and feel what another feels. They think, "I want to relieve their suffering," and act on that basis.

Of course, even the most compassionate gift is apt to be given with hopes of feeling what's known as the "helper's high." But that type of personal gain raises few concerns.

"I don't think we should look into every corner of our hearts for unselfish motivations," Professor Post says. "No one acts from absolute selflessness or absolute selfishness."

Even without motives that are entirely pure, Post suggests, giving can have a powerfully positive impact both on those who give and those who receive.

"The major motivation and wise goal of gift giving should be elevation of the human spirit, to develop [in the receiver and giver alike] profound virtues of gratitude, generosity, and kindness," says Post.

"This is what puts gift giving more on the side of the angels."

From *The Christian Science Monitor*, December 24, 2003. Copyright © 2003 by Christian Science Monitor. Reprinted by permission via the Copyright Clearance Center.

Trends in the Social Psychological Study of Justice

Justice is one of the most basic and potentially important social psychological areas of inquiry. The assumption that others will be fair is what makes social cooperation possible. This article provides a brief review of trends, both historical and current, in the social psychological study of justice and provides an introduction for a special issue of Personality and Social Psychology Review devoted to social psychological theorizing and research on the role that justice plays in human affairs. This overview highlights some exciting new directions injustice theorizing and research, including new uses of identity's ties to justice reasoning, increased attention to negative justice and moral emotion, as well as a greater emphasis on integrative and contingent, rather than competing, social psychological models of justice.

LINDA J. SKITKA
Department of Psychology
University of Illinois at Chicago

FAYE J. CROSBY
Department of Psychology
University of California, Santa Cruz

Justice research has a rich history in social psychology. Social psychologists cannot determine what is just or unjust, but we can document how people think and feel about justice issues. We can study people's behavior, and chart how matters of fairness are associated with various thoughts, feelings, and actions on the part of individual and groups.

In the four decades that social psychologists have been conducting research on social justice, a number of changes have occurred. During the 1960s and 1970s, the primary guiding metaphor of justice research was that of *homo economics*. Equity theorists assumed that people's concern with justice was primarily rooted in a desire to maximize their long- or short-term self-interests. Social interactions were conceptualized as forms of exchange and the focus was on distributions. Early challenges to the hegemony of equity theory—including Melvin Lerner's (1971) path-breaking work on the justice motive and Morton Deutsch's (1975) insistence that proportionality was only one of several basics for determining justice—exposed some of the limitations of equity theory but still conceived of justice in terms of allocations. The same implicit focus on allocations may be said of Susan Opotow's (e.g. 1994, 1996) important work on the "scope of justice," work that described how fair-minded people can be cruel to those outside their moral community.

It was during the late 1970s and the 1980s that a concern with procedural justice replaced the exclusive focus on distributive justice. As Thibaut and Walker (1975), Deutsch (1979), and Leventhal (1980; Leventhal, Karoza, & Fry, 1980) were among the first to note, people care not only about the content of decisions, they also care about how the decisions are made. A number of studies showed that people will remain attached to their groups and satisfied with the authority figures if they think the authorities have followed fair procedures, even if the authorities have rendered a decision that adversely affects them (see Tyler & Smith, 1998, for a review).

Considerable justice research during the 1970s, 1980s, and 1990s primarily sought to gauge the relative importance of distributive and procedural justice concerns for people in a variety of settings. Meanwhile, other research looked instead at the reasons why procedural justice matters. Under the strong leadership of Tom Tyler and Alan Lind (e.g., Lind & Tyler, 1988; Tyler, 1989; Tyler & Lind, 1992), many researchers documented that procedures communicate important information about social worth and value to involved parties. People need to feel they are valued and respected members of the group, and they need to take pride in their group membership. A number of studies have found that people feel that even unfavorable outcomes are fair so long as they are treated with courtesy and respect.

Now, in the new millennium, more shifts in justice theorizing and research appear to be underway. Several researchers have become cognizant of the contingent nature of procedural justice. As happened earlier with equity theory, procedural justice studies have increasingly come to recognize that procedural fairness matters in some situations and for some subjects and not in or for others. Meanwhile, other researchers are seeking to enumerate the properties of procedural justice. Still other researchers are moving beyond what might be called *positive justice* to examine the reactions of people to situations in which a harm has been done or an injustice has been committed. How people react cognitively, emotionally, and behaviorally to unfairness is currently a topic of intense research activity.

The goal of this special issue of *Personality and Social Psychology Review* is to present samples of some of the current theorizing in the social psychology of justice. The issue includes some newcomers to the field, like Julie Exline and her colleagues, some established scholars, like Carolyn Hafer and Linda Skitka, and some of the pioneers, like Melvin Lerner, Faye Crosby, Tom Tyler, and John Darley. In a sense, then, our issue contains the current conceptualizations of three generations of scholars.

When do people care about social justice? The article by Linda Skitka (this issue) attempts to answer this and other basic questions. Specifically, she proposes an Accessible Identity Model (AIM) that predicts that people will be more likely to think about justice when identity concerns are particularly salient The AIM also posits that people's definitions of what is fair or unfair depends on which aspect of identity—the material, social, or personal or moral—dominates their working self-concept. Different justice norms, values, and expectations are predicted to be linked in memory to different aspects of identity, and therefore will be more cognitively accessible in contexts that prime different identity-relevant goals or values.

Like Skitka, Susan Clayton and Susan Opotow (this issue) similarly focus on the links between justice and identity concerns. Clayton and Optotow argue that "who" is included in one's scope of justice will shape people's justice reasoning in important ways. Whereas Skitka focuses on different levels of individual identity (how people see themselves as individuals with material, social, and personal standing), Clayton and Optotow focus instead on differences that arise from conceiving of oneself as an individual or as a representative of a broader group (e.g., as a rancher or environmentalist). Their article explores the contours of justice reasoning when one's individual interests might be at odds with one's sense of self as part of a larger group. Just as it is important to consider differences in individual perspective, Clayton and Optotow review evidence that to understand how people reason about fairness, it is important to know whether people are taking the perspective of themselves as individuals or of as more morally inclusive groups (e.g., women, all of humanity, or all living things).

Carolyn Hafer and Jim Olson (this issue) review research on the scope of justice, or the boundaries people seem to draw between those who are covered by considerations of justice and those who are not As a construct, the "scope of justice" has been invoked to help account for a host of phenomena such as mass internment, genocide, and slavery. Experimental evidence has seemed to corroborate models about the scope of justice. Hafer and Olson point to a number of possible alternative explanations, however, for these experimental findings and articulate other interpretations of the historical evidence than the ones originally articulated by Opotow (e.g., 1994, 1996). Hafer and

Olson note that people outside the scope of justice sometimes receive positive outcomes, and people within the scope of justice sometimes are harmed—and moreover, are harmed in the name of justice. In short, conceptions of justice also involve punishment, vengeance, and harm, regardless of where the lines of the scope of justice are drawn. Hafer and Olson present an agenda for future research that can help to tease apart when harm is done because the harmed ones lie outside the harmdoer's moral community and when harm is done because, on the contrary, the harmed ones lie within it.

What about when harm has already been done? John Darley and Thane Pittman's article (this issue) presents a review of the retributive justice literature, an area of inquiry that is gaining increasing momentum in the justice literature. Their review of the literature leads to an integrated model of retributive justice. Specifically, their model proposes that the attribution people make for why a perpetrator inflicted harm will lead to different levels of moral outrage. Accidental, negligent, and intentional harm will lead to respectively higher levels of moral outrage. People's level of moral outrage in response to harm is used as a psychological barometer that predicts what is needed for justice to be done. Darley and Pittman's model predicts that low levels of moral outrage lead to low perceived need for punishment, whereas moderate levels of moral outrage lead people to demand compensatory reactions to make the victim "whole," or to return him or her to a preharm state. High levels of moral outrage lead people to feel that justice requires not only compensation, but also retribution, such as payment of punitive in addition to compensatory damages.

Retribution is not the only possible reaction to harm. Research on forgiveness represents another emerging area of psychological inquiry that has been gaining momentum in recent years. Julie Exline, Everett Worthington, Jr., Peter Hill, and Michael McCullough (this issue) review recent trends in law, management, philosophy, theology, and psychology that point to forgiveness as being increasingly discussed as a viable alternative to retribution. Although the very young field of forgiveness studies can be a minefield that can conflate "ought" with "is," and prescription with description, these authors provide an objective review of the research to date on the precursors and consequences of forgiveness, and outline five questions important for future research, including the following: (a) the development of a clear and consistent definition of forgiveness; (b) exploration of whether forgiveness encourages or deters future offenses; (c) whether people believe there are some offenses that cannot, or perhaps should not, be forgiven; (d) exploration of the motivational underpinnings of the desire to forgive; and (e) exploring whether variables that affect perceptions of justice or injustice similarly relate to people's desire to forgive.

The article by Tom Tyler and Steven Blader (this issue) looks at justice issues less from the point of view of the actor and more from the point of view of those who are, as it were "acted upon." Tyler and Blader review the current literature on procedural justice and integrate the insights of that now vast literature into a revised model of procedural fairness, the Group Engagement Model This version of the model, like its predecessors, focuses on the role of fair treatment in validating people's social identities.

Whether people's social identities are validated or invalidated by fair or unfair procedures, in turn, plays an important role in people's subsequent thoughts, feelings, and behavior. Tyler and Blader's article extends previous work on procedural justice by differentiating between the consequences of procedural treatment for voluntary and involuntary cooperation with authorities. It also proposes that people's reactions to material outcomes do not directly affect variables like cooperation, but rather influence social identity that, in turn, affects cooperation.

Much of the vitality of social justice research derives from the pan-disciplinary nature of the research. Since the days of J. Stacy Adams (1965), justice researchers have combined organizational with social psychology. For example, scholars like Alan Lind and Tom Tyler (e.g., Lind & Tyler, 1988). Gerald Greenberg (e.g., Greenberg, 1993: Greenberg & Wiethoff, 2001), and Rob Folger and Russell Cropanzano (e.g., Folger & Cropanzano, 1998). have stepped outside the ivory tower and gathered data from legal settings, businesses, and other organizational contexts to test various hypotheses about the psychology of justice. In the tradition of pan-disciplinary research on justice. Faye Crosby and Jamie Franco (this issue) seek to develop insights into social justice theorizing by looking closely at the field of public policy. Rather than working deductively from theory to generate predictions for research, furthermore. Crosby and Franco work inductively from a controversial social problem to arrive at important new insights that can guide subsequent justice theorizing and research. Specifically, Crosby and Franco note that for all the attention lavished on issues of procedural justice, little thought has been given to what may be the most basic question of all: How can those who have been privileged by a system accommodate to changes in system roles, given that neither they nor anyone else is operating in the Rawlsian "veil of ignorance" when the rules are changed?

Like Crosby and Franco (this issue), Dave Schroeder, Julie Steel, Andria Woodell, and Alicia Bembenek (this issue) provide a novel perspective on justice theorizing and research by bridging different areas of substantive inquiry. Specifically, Schroeder et al. see the conflict between individual and group outcomes that lies at the heart of social dilemmas as prime examples of the contexts where questions of justice and fairness are especially likely to emerge. Their review of the social dilemma literature provides important insight into the conditions when people will be more likely to be concerned about distributive, procedural, retributive, and restorative justice. Their review illustrates the benefits of studying justice in contexts that allow relationships to emerge and that include opportunities for the social and interactive aspects of justice decision making to unfold, rather than relying exclusively on single-shot encounters or decisions to inform justice theorizing and research.

Finally, the capstone article of this special issue is one by Melvin Lerner, who provides a historical review and critique of the justice literature from his unique position as one of the field's senior statesmen. His article outlines some cautionary messages for justice researchers. Specifically, he argues that justice theorists need to take a more nuanced look at whether experimental manipulations or measures arouse or tap a set of justice-based cognitions, or instead, simply elicit impression-managed adherence to normative conventions.

Visible Shifts in Justice Theorizing and Research

Taken together, the articles included in this special issue illustrate some developments in the social psychological study of justice. One clear trend is the concern with identity. Another is the attention to what might be called *negative justice*—that is, what happens after wrongs have occurred. A third is increased attention given to contingent models, that is, to models that specify the boundary conditions when different considerations are likely to be especially important in people's conceptions of justice. A fourth development that is discernable is the return to emotion. For a while, all of social psychology appeared to concentrate on cold cognitions; today, feelings about justice (and about the self and others in justice-related situations) are understood as representing important components of the social psychology of justice. For example, the articles by Darley and Pittman and Exline et al. clearly reveal the important role of moral emotions in how people think about justice. Gaining a better understanding of moral emotion more generally as well as how it relates to the social psychology of justice, is an exciting new frontier for justice researchers to explore.

The articles in this issue also reveal important intersections between justice theorizing and other areas of social psychological inquiry, and illustrate how greater cross-boundary research can facilitate work in justice, as well as other areas of social psychology. For example, research and theorizing that focuses on contemporary social problems, like affirmative action, are especially important in revealing new insights into both the psychological foundations of people's objections to affirmative action, and because it can reveal important and previously neglected gaps in theory, such as rule change as a procedural justice issue. Relating social dilemma research and theories to justice provides another excellent example of how bridging different areas of inquiry can do much to inform each one.

Our ultimate goal in putting together this issue was to fan the flames of interest in social psychological justice theory and research, and to showcase the many new developments that are emerging in the social psychological study of questions relating to justice and fairness. We hope for a two-fold outcome. First, we hope that the research agendas of social psychologists currently doing research injustice will benefit from incorporating some of the innovations in justice theorizing that this issue presents into their current thinking and work. Second, we hope that social psychologists working in other areas will have an increased recognition of the importance of justice as an area of social psychological inquiry. To a considerable degree, negotiating how the benefits and burdens of social cooperation are to be allocated across persons—the fundamental focus of justice theory and research—is one of the most central of all social psychological questions. We therefore hope that this special issue facilitates a broader recognition of the importance of justice as a social psychological construct worthy of both additional study and inclusion as a chapter in social psychology textbooks.

References

Adams. S. I. (1965). Inequity in social exchange. In L. Berkowiltz (Ed.), *Advances in experimental social psychology, Vol 2* (pp. 267–299). New York: Academic.

Clayton, S., & Opotow, S. (2003). Justice and identity: Changing perspectives on what is fair. *Personality and Social Psychology Review 7,* 298–310.

Crosby. F. J., & Franco. J. L (2003). Connections between the ivory tower and the multicolored world: Linking abstract theories of social justice to the rough and tumble of affirmative action. *Personality and Social Psychology Review, 7,* 362–373.

Darley, J. M., & Pittman, T. S. (2003). The psychology of compensatory and retributive justice. *Personality and Social Psychology Review, 7,* 324–336.

Deutsch, M. (1975). Equity, equality, and need: What determines which value win be used as the basis of distributive justice? *Journal of Social Issues, 31*(4), 137–149.

Deutsch, M. (1979). Education and distributive justice: Some reflections on grading systems. *American Psychologist, 34,* 391–401.

Exline, J. J., Worthington. E. L., Jr., Hill, P., & McCullough. M. E. (2003). Forgiveness and justice: A research agenda for social and personality psychology. *Personality and Social Psychology Review, 7,* 337–348.

Folger, R., & Cropanzano, R. (1998). *Organizational justice and human resource management.* Thousand Oaks, CA: Sage

Greenberg, J. (1993). Justice and organizational citizenship: A commentary on the state of the science. *Employee Responsibilities and Rights Journal, 6,* 249–256.

Greenberg, J., & Wietholf, C. (2001). Organizational justice as proaction and reaction: Implications for research and application. In R. Cropanzano (Ed.) *Justice in the workplace: From theory to practice, Vol. 2* (pp. 271–302). Mahwah, NJ: Lawrence Erlbaum Associates, Inc.

Hafer, C. L., & Olson, J. M. (2003). An analysis of empirical research on the scope of justice. *Personality and Social Psychology Review, 7,* 311–323.

Lerner. M. J. (1971). Justified self-interest and responsibility for suffering: A replication and extension. *Journal of Human Relations, 19,* 550–559.

Lerner, M. J. (2003). The justice motive: Where social psychologists found it, how they lost it, and why they may not find it again. *Personality and Social Psychology Review, 7,* 388–399.

Leventhal, G. S. (1980). What should be done with equity theory? In K. J. Gergen. M. S. Greenberg, & R. H. Willis (Eds.). *Social exchange: Advances in theory and research* (pp. 27–55). New York: Plenum.

Leventhal, G. S., Karuza, J., & Fry, W. R. (1980). Beyond fairness: A theory of allocation preferences. In G. Mikula (Ed.) *Justice and social interaction* (pp. 167–218). New York: Springer-Verlag.

Lind, E. A., & Tyler, T. R. (1988). *The social psychology of procedural justice.* New York Plenum.

Opotow, S. (1994). Predicting protection: Scope of justice and the natural world. *Journal of Social Issues, 50,* 49–63.

Opotow, S. (1996). Is justice finite? The case of environmental inclusion. In L. Montada & M. Lerner (Eds.), *Social justice in human relations: Current societal concerns about justice. Vol. 3* (pp. 213–230). New York Plenum.

Schroeder, D. A., Steel. J. E., Woodell, A. J., & Bembenek, A. F. (2003). Justice within social dilemmas, *Personality and Social Psychology Review, 7,* 374–387.

Skitka, L. J. (2003). Of different minds: An accessible identity model of justice reasoning. *Personality and Social Psychology Review, 7,* 286–297.

Thibaut, J., & Walker. L. (1975). *Procedural justice: A psychological analysis.* Hillside. NJ: Lawrence Erlbaum Associates, Inc.

Tyler, T. R. (1989). The psychology of procedural justice: A test of the group-value model. *Journal of Personality and Social Psychology, 57,* 830–838.

Tyler, T. R., & Blader, S. L. (2003). The Group Engagement Model: Procedural justice, social identity, and cooperative behavior. *Personality and Social Psychology Review, 7,* 349–361.

Tyler, T. R., & Lind, E. A. (1992). A relational model of authority in groups. In M. Zanna (Ed.), *Advances in experimental social psychology, Vol. 4* (pp. 595–629). Boston: McGraw-Hill.

Tyler, T., & Smith. H. J. (1998). Social justice and social movements. In D. T. Gilbert & S. T. Fiske (Eds.), *The handbook of social psychology, Vol. 2* (4th ed., pp. 595–629). New York McGraw-Hill.

From *Personality and Social Psychology Review,* Vol. 7, No. 4, November 1, 2003, pp. 282-285. Copyright © 2003 by Lawrence Erlbaum Associates, Inc. Reprinted by permission.

UNIT 10
Group Processes

Unit Selections

Key Points to Consider

- What are the various styles of leadership? Are leaders more important than group members? Can leaders change their leader style? How does a change in leader style change the group or the organization? Or does it?

- How do most followers or group members interact with their leaders? When do followers become toxic? How can a leader tell when his or her followers are causing dysfunction in the group?

- What does classic social psychological research demonstrate about human group behavior? Does group behavior always result in some negative outcome? What are some of the negative effects of the group or the leader on the individual? What are some of the positive effects?

- What is groupthink? What are its causes and symptoms? How can it be avoided? Do you know any historic instances where groupthink has caused a catastrophe?

- How is a stadium full of sports fans different from other groups? How is typical fan behavior different from fanatical fan behavior? What causes a fan to be fanatical?

Student Web Site
www.mhcls.com/online

Internet References
Further information regarding these Web sites may be found in this book's preface or online.

Center for the Study of Group Processes
http://www.uiowa.edu/~grpproc/
Collaborative Organizations
http://www.workteams.unt.edu

In American schools, all too often cliques form, children are ostracized, and fights break out. Popularity, fitting in, and recognition by other students, teachers, and coaches dominate the thinking of many junior and senior high school pupils.

An experienced eighth grade teacher became concerned with the exclusion of her only Asian student from groups in her classroom. Despite her best efforts at teaching about diversity and cultural sensitivity, her other students just did not put any of the information into practice. She spoke to other teachers and the principle about her Asian student's situation. The teacher reported that Ho was chosen last for student teams, was not invited to play with the other boys at recess, was teased by some of his classmates for his accent, and was generally ignored by the girls, although some had begun flirting with other boys. No one to whom the teacher spoke had any helpful advice; in fact, each listener complained that the same conditions prevailed in other classrooms.

One night at dinner, the distressed and frustrated teacher grumbled to her family that the situation was absolutely exasperating. The teacher's daughter who was studying social psychology at the nearby community college sympathized and then shared information about noted psychologist Elliott Aronson's jigsaw classroom technique.

In a jigsaw classroom, master groups learn pieces of material about a particular topic. A likely topic might be Passover. One master group would learn about the general teachings of Judaism. Another master group would learn about specific reasons Passover is celebrated. A third group might learn how Passover is celebrated by contemporary Jews and so on.

The master groups next break into jigsaw groups, comprised of one member from each master group such that every aspect

learned by the master groups about Passover is represented. In the jigsaw groups, if a member does not contribute or has trouble expressing him- or herself, it is incumbent on the remaining members to improve that member's performance or all will fail. The jigsaw classroom scientifically has been confirmed to enhance children's cooperation, increase interactions with less popular children, and improve classroom climate.

How happy the teacher was to hear about this method! She questioned why so few teachers knew or practiced this teaching approach. She could not wait to learn more and implement the jigsaw technique in her classroom.

Groups not only play a special role in students' lives, they are a significant part of all of our lives. Groups surround us at work, places of worship, on the streets, and even in our homes. While families are our primary groups, there certainly are other groups—formal and informal, large and small—that impact us.

In this final unit of the anthology, we will contemplate group dynamics. Because there are at least two major components of most groups—leaders and followers—we will consider both. In the first subsection of this unit, the emphasis is on leadership. In the first article, David Rooke and William Torbert suggest that there are seven different types of leaders and that leaders can transform themselves from one type to another. When leaders evolve in such a fashion, their organizations can also transform or so claim the authors.

The second selection on leadership discusses how followers affect leaders. Lynn Offerman presents information and advice to leaders about how their followers might try to influence the leader. Sycophants, for example, use flattery or agreement with the leader to attract approval from the leader. Offerman suggests that such followers are toxic to group performance.

The second part of this unit pertains to group dynamics, especially the members of a group. Three additional articles round out the collection of essays. In "To Err Is Human," noted science writer Bruce Bower explains that the study of group dynamics is crucial to better group performance. He reviews classic and contemporary research on such important dynamics as obedience to authority, bystander apathy, and conformity—all processes induced by virtue of being a member of a group and most of which have negative outcomes.

Other phenomena can make groups ineffectual, too. Groupthink, a well-established phenomenon in the social psychology literature, also results in poor and sometimes disastrous decision making. During *groupthink*, group members become self-righteous, exclude outside opinions, and make no alternate strategies if their plan fails. Groupthink is the theme of the penultimate selection by Vicki Kemper. Kemper reveals that groupthink may well have triggered the decision to invade Iraq and instigated the miscalculations about the aftermath of the invasion.

Finally, a recent article on sports fans addresses collective group behavior. A collective is a large, loosely knit group that morphs several times during its existence. Collectives are thought to take on a life and personality of their own and may be responsible for yet further negative behaviors of groups. A large group of people at a nightclub is one such example; many of them may die when a fire starts because of the rapidly changing group dynamics and lack of good leadership. Sports fans represent another collective group. We all know sports fans that are fanatical. Social psychologists are studying what makes fanatical fans different from other sports fans.

Seven Transformations of Leadership

Leaders are made, not born, and how they develop is critical for organizational change.

David Rooke and William R. Torbert

Most developmental psychologists agree that what differentiates leaders is not so much their philosophy of leadership, their personality, or their style of management. Rather, it's their internal "action logic"—how they interpret their surroundings and react when their power or safety is challenged. Relatively few leaders, however, try to understand their own action logic, and fewer still have explored the possibility of changing it.

They should, because we've found that leaders who do undertake a voyage of personal understanding and development can transform not only their own capabilities but also those of their companies. In our close collaboration with psychologist Susanne Cook-Greuter—and our 25 years of extensive survey-based consulting at companies such as Deutsche Bank, Harvard Pilgrim Health Care, Hewlett-Packard, NSA, Trillium Asset Management, Aviva, and Volvo—we've worked with thousands of executives as they've tried to develop their leadership skills. The good news is that leaders who make an effort to understand their own action logic can improve their ability to lead. But to do that, it's important first to understand what kind of leader you already are.

The Seven Action Logics

Our research is based on a sentence-completion survey tool called the Leadership Development Profile. Using this tool, participants are asked to complete 36 sentences that begin with phrases such as "A good leader ... ," to which responses vary widely;

"... cracks the whip."

"... realizes that it's important to achieve good performance from subordinates."

"... juggles competing forces and takes responsibility for her decisions."

By asking participants to complete sentences of this type, it's possible for highly trained evaluators to paint a picture of bow participants interpret their own actions and the world around them; these "pictures" show which one of seven developmental action logics—Opportunist, Diplomat, Expert, Achiever, Individualist, Strategist, or Alchemist—currently functions as a leader's dominant way of thinking. Leaders can move through

these categories as their abilities grow, so taking the Leadership Development Profile again several years later can reveal whether a leader's action logic has evolved.

Over the past 25 years, we and other researchers have administered the sentence-completion survey to thousands of managers and professionals, most between the ages of 25 and 55, at hundreds of American and European companies (as well as nonprofits and governmental agencies) in diverse industries. What we found is that the levels of corporate and individual performance vary according to action logic. Notably, we found that the three types of leaders associated with below-average corporate performance (Opportunists, Diplomats, and Experts) accounted for 55% of our sample. They were significantly less effective at implementing organizational strategies than the 30% of the sample who measured as Achievers. Moreover, only the final 15% of managers in the sample (Individualists, Strategists, and Alchemists) showed the consistent capacity to innovate and to successfully transform their organizations. To understand how leaders fall into such distinct categories and corporate performance, let's look in more detail at each leadership style in turn, starting with the least productive (and least complex).

The Opportunist

Our most comforting finding was that only 5% of the leaders in our sample were characterized by mistrust, egocentrism, and manipulativeness. We call these leaders Opportunists, a title that reflects their tendency to focus on personal wins and see the world and other people as opportunities to be exploited. Their approach to the outside world is largely determined by their perception of control—in other words, how they will react to an event depends primarily on whether or not they think they can direct the outcome. They treat other people as objects or as competitors who are also out for themselves.

Opportunists tend to regard their bad behavior as legitimate in the cut and thrust of an eye-for-an-eye world. They reject feedback, externalize blame, and retaliate harshly. One can see this action logic in the early work of Larry Ellison (now CEO of Oracle). Ellison describes his managerial style at the start of his career as "management by ridicule." "You've got to be good at intellectual intimidation and rhetorical bullying," he once told Matthew Symonds of the *Economist*. "I'd excuse my behavior by telling myself I was just having 'an open and honest debate.' The fact is, I just didn't know any better."

Few Opportunists remain managers for long, unless they transform to more effective action logics (as Ellison has done). Their constant firefighting, their style of self-aggrandizement, and their frequent rule breaking is the antithesis of the kind of leader people want to work with for the long term. If you have worked for an Opportunist, you will almost certainly remember it as a difficult time. By the same token, corporate environments that breed opportunism seldom endure, although Opportunists often survive longer than they should because they provide an exciting environment in which younger executives, especially, can take risks. As one ex-Enron senior staffer said, "Before the fall, those were such exciting years. We felt we could do anything, pull off everything, write our own rules. The pace was wild, and we all just rode it." Of course, Enron's shareholders and pensioners would reasonably feel that they were paying too heavily for that staffer's adventure.

The Diplomat

The Diplomat makes sense of the world around him in a more benign way than the Opportunist does, but this action logic can also have extremely negative repercussions if the leader is a senior manager. Loyally serving the group, the Diplomat seeks to please higher-status colleagues while avoiding conflict. This action logic is focused on gaining control of one's own behavior—more than on gaining control of external events or other people. According to the Diplomat's action logic, a leader gains more enduring acceptance and influence by cooperating with group norms and by performing his daily roles well.

In a support role or a team context, this type of executive has much to offer. Diplomats provide social glue to their colleagues and ensure that attention is paid to the needs of others, which is probably why the great majority of Diplomats work at the most junior rungs of management, in jobs such as frontline supervisor, customer service representative, or nurse practitioner. Indeed, research into 497 managers in different industries showed that 80% of all Diplomats were at junior levels. By contrast, 80% of all Strategists were at senior levels, suggesting that managers who grow into more effective action logics—like that of the Strategist—have a greater chance of being promoted.

Diplomats are much more problematic in top leadership roles because they try to ignore conflict. They tend to be overly polite and friendly and find it virtually impossible to give challenging feedback to others. Initiating change, with its inevitable conflicts, represents a grave threat to the Diplomat, and he will avoid it if at all possible, even to the point of self-destruction.

Consider one Diplomat who became the interim CEO of an organization when his predecessor died suddenly from an aneurysm. When the board split on the selection of a permanent successor, it asked the Diplomat to carry on. Our Diplomat relished his role as a ceremonial figurehead and was a sought-after speaker at public events. Unfortunately, he found the more conflictual requirements of the job less to his liking. He failed, for instance, to replace a number of senior managers who had serious ongoing performance issues and were resisting the change program his predecessor had initiated. Because the changes were controversial, the Diplomat avoided meetings, even planning business trips for the times when the senior team would meet. The team members were so frustrated by the Diplomat's attitude that they eventually resigned en masse. He "resolved" this crisis by thanking the team publicly for its contribution and appointing new team members. Eventually, in the face of mounting losses arising from this poor management, the board decided to demote the Diplomat to his former role as vice president.

The Expert

The largest category of leader is that of Experts, who account for 38% of all professionals in our sample. In contrast to Opportunists, who focus on trying to control the world around them, and Diplomats, who concentrate on controlling their own behavior. Experts try to exercise control by perfecting their knowledge, both in their professional and personal lives. Exercising watertight thinking is extremely important to Experts. Not surprisingly, many accountants, investment analysts, marketing researchers, software engineers, and consultants operate from the Expert action logic. Secure in their expertise, they present hard data and logic in their efforts to gain consensus and buy-in for their proposals.

Experts are great individual contributors because of their pursuit of continuous improvement, efficiency, and perfection. But as managers, they can be problematic because they are so completely sure they are right. When subordinates talk about a my-way-or-the-highway type of boss, they are probably talking about someone operating from an Expert action logic. Experts tend to view collaboration as a waste of time ("Not all meetings are a waste of time—some are canceled!"), and they will frequently treat the opinion of people less expert than themselves with contempt. Emotional intelligence is neither desired nor appreciated. As Sun Microsystems' CEO Scott McNealy put it: "I don't do feelings; I'll leave that to Barry Manilow."

It comes as no surprise, then, that after unsuccessfully pleading with him to scale back in the face of growing losses during the dot-com debacle of 2001 and 2002, nearly a dozen members of McNealy's senior management team left.

The Achiever

For those who hope someday to work for a manager who both challenges and supports them and creates a positive team and interdepartmental atmosphere, the good news is that a large proportion, 30%, of the managers in our research measured as Achievers. While these leaders create a positive work environment and focus their efforts on deliverables, the downside is that their style often inhibits thinking outside the box.

Achievers have a more complex and integrated understanding of the world than do managers who display the three previous action logics we've described. They're open to feedback and realize that many of the ambiguities and conflicts of everyday life are due to differences in interpretation and ways of re-

Seven Ways of Leading

Different leaders exhibit different kinds of action logic—ways in which they interpret their surroundings and react when their power or safety is challenged. In our research of thousands of leaders, we observed seven types of action logics. The least effective for organizational leadership are the Opportunist and Diplomat; the most effective, the Strategist and Alchemist. Knowing your own action logic can be the first step toward developing a more effective leadership style. If you recognize yourself as an Individualist, for example, you can work, through both format and informal measures, to develop the strengths and characteristics of a Strategist.

Action Logic	Characteristics	Strengths	% of research sample profiling at this action logic
Opportunist	*Wins any way possible.* Self-oriented; manipulative; "might makes right."	Good in emergencies and in sales opportunities.	5%
Diplomat	*Avoids overt conflict.* Wants to belong; obeys group norms; rarely rocks the boat.	Good as supportive glue within an office; helps bring people together.	12%
Expert	*Rules by logic and expertise.* Seeks rational efficiency.	Good as an individual contributor.	38%
Achiever	*Meets strategic goals.* Effectively achieves goals through teams; juggles managerial duties and market demands.	Well suited to managerial roles; action and goal oriented.	30%
Individualist	*Interweaves competing personal and company action logics.* Creates unique structures to resolve gaps between strategy and performance.	Effective in venture and consulting roles.	10%
Strategist	*Generates organizational and personal transformations.* Exercises the power of mutual inquiry, vigilance, and vulnerability for both the short and long term.	Effective as a transformational leader.	4%
Alchemist	*Generates social transformations.* Integrates material, spiritual, and societal transformation.	Good at leading society-wide transformations.	1%

lating. They know that creatively transforming or resolving clashes requires sensitivity to relationships and the ability to influence others in positive ways. Achievers can also reliably lead a team to implement new strategies over a one- to three-year period, balancing immediate and long-term objectives. One study of ophthalmologists in private practice showed that those who scored as Achievers had lower staff turnover, delegated more responsibility, and had practices that earned at least twice the gross annual revenues of those run by Experts.

Achievers often find themselves clashing with Experts. The Expert subordinate, in particular, finds the Achiever leader hard to take because he cannot deny the reality of the Achiever's success even though he feels superior. Consider Hewlett-Packard, where the research engineers tend to score as Experts and the lab managers as higher-level Achievers. At one project meeting, a lab manager—a decided Achiever—slammed her coffee cup on the table and exclaimed, "I *know* we can get 18 features into this, but the customers want delivery some time this century, and the main eight features will do." "Philistine!" snorted one engineer, an Expert. But this kind of conflict isn't always destructive. In fact, it provides much of the fuel that has ignited—and sustained—the competitiveness of many of the country's most successful corporations.

The Individualist

The Individualist action logic recognizes that neither it nor any of the other action logics are "natural"; all are constructions of one self and the world. This seemingly abstract idea enables the 10% of Individualist leaders to contribute unique practical value to their organizations; they put personalities and ways of relating into perspective and communicate well with people who have other action logics.

What sets Individualists apart from Achievers is their awareness of a possible conflict between their principles and their actions, or between the organization's values and its implementation of those values. This conflict becomes the source of tension, creativity, and a growing desire for further development.

Individualists also tend to ignore rules they regard as irrelevant, which often makes them a source of irritation to both colleagues and bosses. "So, what do you think?" one of our clients asked us as he was debating whether personal to let go of one of his star performers, a woman who had been measured as an individualist. Sharon (not her real name) had been asked to set up an offshore shared service function in the Czech Republic in order to provide IT support to two separate and internally competitive divisions operating there. She formed a highly cohesive team within budget and so far ahead of schedule that she quipped that she was "delivering services before Group Business Risk had delivered its report saying it can't be done."

> **Initiating change, with its inevitable conflicts, represents a grave threat to the Diplomat, and he will avoid it if at all possible, even to the point of self-destruction.**

The trouble was that Sharon had a reputation within the wider organization as a wild card. Although she showed great political savvy when it came to her individual projects, she put many people's noses out of joint in the larger organization because of her unique, unconventional ways of operating. Eventually, the CEO was called in (not for the first time) to resolve a problem created by her failure to acknowledge key organizational processes and people who weren't on her team.

Many of the dynamics created by different action logics are illustrated by this story and its outcome. The CEO, whose own action logic was that of an Achiever, did not see how he could challenge Sharon to develop and move beyond creating such problems. Although ambivalent about her, he decided to retain her because she was delivering and because the organization had recently lost several capable, if unconventional, managers.

So Sharon stayed, but only for a while. Eventually, she left the company to set up an off shoring consultancy. When we examine in the second half of this article how to help executives transform their leadership action logics, we'll return to this story to see how both Sharon and the CEO might have succeeded in transforming theirs.

The Strategist

Strategists account for just 4% of leaders. What sets them apart from Individualists is their focus on organizational constraints and perceptions, which they treat as discussable and transformable. Whereas the Individualist masters communication with colleagues who have different action logics, the Strategist masters the second-order organizational impact of actions and agreements. The Strategist is also adept at creating shared visions across different action logics—visions that encourage both and organizational transformations. According to the Strategist's action logic, organizational and social change is an iterative developmental process that requires awareness and close leadership attention.

Strategists deal with conflict more comfortably than do those with other action logics, and they're better at handling people's instinctive resistance to change. As a result, Strategists are highly effective change agents. We found confirmation of this in our re-

cent study often CEOs in six different industries. All of their organizations had the stated objective of transforming themselves and had engaged consultants to help with the process. Each CEO filled out a Leadership Development Profile, which showed that five of them were Strategists and the other five fell into other action logics. The Strategists succeeded in generating one or more organizational transformations over a four-year period; their companies' profitability, market share, and reputation all improved. By contrast, only two of the other five CEOs succeeded in transforming their organizations—despite help from consultants, who themselves profiled as Strategists.

Strategists are fascinated with three distinct levels of social interplay: personal relationships, organizational relations, and national and international developments. Consider Joan Bavaria, a CEO who, back in 1985, measured as a Strategist. Bavaria created one of the first socially responsible investment funds, a new subdivision of the investments industry, which by the end of 2001 managed more than $3 trillion in funds. In 1982, Bavaria founded Trillium Asset Management, a worker-owned company, which she still heads. She also co-wrote the CERES Environmental Principles, which dozens of major companies have signed. In the late 1990s, CERES, working with the United Nations, created the Global Reporting Initiative, which supports financial, social, and environmental transparency and accountability worldwide.

Here we see the Strategist action logic at work. Bavaria saw a unique moment in which to make ethical investing a viable business, then established Trillium to execute her plan. Strategists typically have socially conscious business ideas that are carried out in a highly collaborative manner. They seek to weave together idealist visions with pragmatic, timely initiatives and principled actions. Bavaria worked beyond the boundaries of her own organization to influence the socially responsible investment industry as a whole and later made the development of social and environmental accountability standards an international endeavor by involving the United Nations. Many Achievers will use their influence to successfully promote their own companies. The Strategist works to create ethical principles and practices beyond the interests of herself or her organization.

The Alchemist

The final leadership action logic for which we have data and experience is the Alchemist. Our studies of the few leaders we have identified as Alchemists suggest that what sets them apart from Strategists is their ability to renew or even reinvent themselves and their organizations in historically significant ways. Whereas the Strategist will move from one engagement to another, the Alchemist has an extraordinary capacity to deal simultaneously with many situations at multiple levels. The Alchemist can talk with both kings and commoners. He can deal with immediate priorities yet never lose sight of long-term goals.

Alchemists constitute 1% of our sample, which indicates how rare it is to find them in business or anywhere else. Through an extensive search process, we found six Alchemists who were willing to participate in an up-close study of their daily actions.

Though this is obviously a very small number that cannot statistically justify generalization, it's worth noting that all six Alchemists shared certain characteristics. On a daily basis, all were engaged in multiple organizations and found time to deal with issues raised by each. However, they were not in a constant rush—nor did they devote hours on end to a single activity. Alchemists are typically charismatic and extremely aware individuals who live by high moral standards. They focus intensely on the truth. Perhaps most important, they're able to catch unique moments in the history of their organizations, creating symbols and metaphors that speak to people's hearts and minds. In one conservative financial services company in the UK, a recently appointed CEO turned up for work in a tracksuit instead of his usual pinstripes but said nothing about it to anyone. People wondered whether this was a new dress code. Weeks later, the CEO spoke publicly about his attire and the need to be unconventional and to move with greater agility and speed.

A more celebrated example of an Alchemist is Nelson Mandela. Although we never formally profiled Mandela, he exemplifies the Alchemist action logic. In 1995. Mandela symbolized the unity of a new South Africa when he attended the Rugby World Cup game in which the Springboks, the South African national team, were playing. Rugby had been the bastion of white supremacy, but Mandela attended the game. He walked on to the pitch wearing the Springboks' jersey so hated by black South Africans, at the same time giving the clenched fist salute of the ANC, thereby appealing, almost impossibly, both to black and white South Africans. As Tokyo Sexwale, ANC activist and premier of South Africa's Gauteng province, said of him: "Only Mandela could wear an enemy jersey. Only Mandela would go down there and be associated with the Springboks … All the years in the underground, in the trenches, denial, self-denial, away from home, prison, it was worth it. That's all we wanted to see."

Evolving as a Leader

The most remarkable—and encouraging—finding from our research is that leaders can transform from one action logic to another. We have, in fact, documented a number of leaders who have succeeded in transforming themselves from Experts into Achievers, from Achievers into Individualists, and from Individualists into Strategists.

Take the case of Jenny, one of our clients, who initially measured as an Expert. She became disillusioned with her role in her company's PR department and resigned in order to, as she said, "sort out what I really want to do." Six months later, she joined a different company in a similar role, and two years after that we profiled her again and she still measured as an Expert. Her decision to resign from the first company, take a "sabbatical," and then join the second company had made no difference to her action logic. At that point, Jenny chose to join a group of peer leaders committed to examining their current leadership patterns and to experimenting with new ways of acting. This group favored the Strategist perspective (and the founder of the group was profiled as an Alchemist), which in the end helped Jenny's development. She learned that her habit of consistently

taking a critical position, which she considered "usefully objective," isolated her and generated distrust. As a result of the peer group's feedback, she started a series of small and private experiments, such as asking questions rather than criticizing. She realized that instead of seeing the faults in others, she had to be clear about what *she* could contribute and, in doing so, started the move from an Expert to an Achiever. Spiritually, Jenny learned that she needed an ongoing community of inquiry at the center of her life and found a spiritual home for continuing reflection in Quaker meetings, which later supported (and indeed signaled) her transition from an Achiever to an Individualist.

Two years later, Jenny left the second job to start her own company, at which point she began profiling as a Strategist. This was a highly unusual movement of three action logics in such a short time. We have had only two other instances in which a leader has transformed twice in less than four years.

As Jenny's case illustrates, there are a number of personal changes that can support leadership transformation, Jenny experienced loss of faith in the system and feelings of boredom, irritability, burnout, depression, and even anger. She began to ask herself existential questions. But another indication of a leader's readiness to transform is an increasing attraction to the qualities she begins to intuit in people with more effective action logics, jenny, as we saw, was drawn to and benefited hugely from her Strategist peer group as well as from a mentor who exhibited the Alchemist action logic. This search for new perspectives often manifests itself in personal transformations: The ready-to-transform leader starts developing new relationships. She may also explore new forms of spiritual practice or new forms of centering and self-expression, such as playing a musical instrument or doing tai chi.

External events can also trigger and support transformation. A promotion, for example, may give a leader the opportunity to expand his or her range of capabilities. Earlier, we cited the frustration of Expert research engineers at Hewlett-Packard with the product and delivery attitude of Achiever lab managers. Within a year of one engineer's promotion to lab manager, a role that required coordination of others and cooperation across departments, the former Expert was profiling as an Achiever. Although he initially took some heat ("Sellout!") from his former buddies, his new Achiever awareness meant that he was more focused on customers' needs and clearer about delivery schedules. For the first time, he understood the dance between engineers trying to perfect the technology and managers trying to deliver on budget and on schedule.

Changes to a manager's work practices and environment can also facilitate transformation. At one company we studied, leaders changed from Achievers to Individualists partly because of simple organizational and process changes. At the company's senior manager meetings, for example, executives other than the CEO had the chance to lead the meetings; these opportunities, which were supported by new spirit of openness, feedback, and frank debate, fostered professional growth among many of the company's leaders.

Planned and structured development interventions are another means of supporting leadership transformation. We worked with a leading oil and gas exploration company on developing the already high-level capabilities of a pool of future senior managers; the managers were profiled and then interviewed by two consultants who explored each manager's action logic and how it constrained and enabled him or her to perform current and recent roles. Challenges were discussed as well as a view of the individual's potential and a possible developmental plan. After the exercise, several managers, whose Individualist and Strategist capabilities had not been fully understood by the company, were appreciated and engaged differently in their roles. What's more, the organization's own definition of leadership talent was refrained to include the capabilities of the Individualist and Strategist action logics. This in turn demanded that the company radically revisit its competency framework to Incorporate such expectations as "sees issues from multiple perspectives" and "creates deep change without formal power."

Now that we've looked generally at some of the changes and interventions that can support leadership development, let's turn to some specifics about how the most common transformations are apt to take place.

From Expert to Achiever

This transformation is the most commonly observed and practiced among businesspeople and by those in management and executive education. For the past generation or more, the training departments of large companies have been supporting the development of managers from Experts into Achievers by running programs with titles like "Management by Objectives," "Effective Delegation," and "Managing People for Results" These programs typically emphasize getting results through flexible strategies rather than through one right method used in one right way.

Observant leaders and executive coaches can also formulate well-structured exercises and questions related to everyday work to help Experts become aware of the different assumptions they and others may be making. These efforts can help Experts practice new conversational strategies such as, "You may be right, but I'd like to understand what leads you to believe that." In addition, those wishing to push Experts to the next level should consider rewarding Achiever competencies like timely delivery of results, the ability to manage for performance, and the ability to implement strategic priorities.

> **What sets Alchemists apart from Strategists is their ability to renew or even reinvent themselves and their organizations in historically significant ways.**

Within business education, MBA programs are apt to encourage the development of the more pragmatic Achievers by frustrating the perfectionist Experts. The heavy workloads, use of multidisciplinary and ambiguous case studies, and teamwork requirements all promote the development of Achievers. By contrast, MSc programs, in particular disciplines such as finance or marketing research, tend to reinforce the Expert perspective.

Still, the transition from Expert to Achiever remains one of the most painful bottlenecks in most organizations. We've all heard the eternal lament of engineers, lawyers, and other professionals whose Expert success has saddled them with managerial duties, only to estrange them from the work they love. Their challenge becomes working as highly effective Achievers who can continue to use their in-depth expertise to succeed as leaders and managers.

From Achiever to Individualist

Although organizations and business schools have been relatively successful in developing leaders to the Achiever action logic, they have, with few exceptions, a dismal record in recognizing, supporting, and *actively* developing leaders to the Individualist and Strategist action logics, let alone to the Alchemist logic. This is not surprising. In many organizations, the Achiever, with his drive and focus on the endgame, is seen as the finish line for development: "This is a competitive industry—we need to keep a sharp focus on the bottom line."

The development of leaders beyond the Achiever action logic requires a very different tack from that necessary to bring about the Expert-to-Achiever transformation. Interventions must encourage self-awareness on the part of the evolving leader as well as a greater awareness of other worldviews. In both business and personal relationships, speaking and listening must come to be experienced not as necessary, taken-for-granted ways of communicating predetermined ideas but as intrinsically forward-thinking, creative actions. Achievers use inquiry to determine whether they (and the teams and organization to which they belong) are accomplishing their goals and how they might accomplish them more effectively. The developing Individualist, however, begins to inquire about and reflect on the goals themselves—with the aim of improving future goals. Annual development plans that set new goals, are generated through probing and trusting conversation, are actively supported through executive coaching, and are carefully reviewed at the end of the cycle can be critical enablers at this point. Yet few boards and CEOs appreciate how valuable this time investment can be, and it is all too easily sacrificed in the face of short term objectives, which can seem more pressing to leaders whose action logics are less developed.

Let's go back to the case of Sharon, the Individualist we described earlier whose Achiever CEO wasn't able to manage her. How might a coach or consultant have helped the CEO feel less threatened by Sharon and more capable of supporting her development while also being more open to his own needs and potential? One way would have been to try role-playing, asking the CEO to play Sharon while the coach or consultant enacts the CEO role. The role-playing might have gone as follows:

"Sharon, I want to talk with you about your future here at our company. Your completion of the Czech project under budget and ahead of time is one more sign that you have the initiative, creativity, and determination to make the senior team here. At the same time, I've had to pick up a number of pieces after you that I shouldn't have had to. I'd like to brainstorm together about how you can approach future projects in a way that eliminates this hassle and gets key players on your side. Then, we can chat several times over the next year as you begin to apply whatever new principles we come up with. Does this seem like a good use of our time, or do you have a different perspective on the issue?"

Note that the consultant in the CEO's role offers clear praise, a clear description of a limitation, a proposed path forward, and an inquiry that empowers the CEO (playing Sharon) to reframe the dilemma if he wishes. Thus, instead of giving the CEO one-way advice about what he should do, the coach enacts a dialogic scenario with him, illustrating a new kind of practice and letting the CEO judge whether the enacted relationship is a positive one. The point is not so much to teach the CEO a new conversational repertoire but to make him more comfortable with how the Individualist sees and makes sense of the world around her and what feedback may motivate her to commit to further learning. Such specific experiments with new ways of listening and talking can gradually dissolve the fears associated with transformational learning.

To Strategist and Beyond

Leaders who are moving toward the Strategist and Alchemist action logics are no longer primarily seeking personal skills that will make them more effective within existing organizational systems. They will already have mastered many of those skills. Rather, they are exploring the disciplines and commitments entailed in creating projects, teams, networks, strategic alliances, and whole organizations on the basis of collaborative inquiry. It is this ongoing practice of reframing inquiry that makes them and their corporations so successful.

The path toward the Strategist and Alchemist action logics is qualitatively different from other leadership development processes. For a start, emergent Strategists and Alchemists are no longer seeking mentors to help them sharpen existing skills and to guide them toward influential networks (although they may seek spiritual and ethical guidance from mentors). Instead, they are seeking to engage in mutual mentoring with peers who are already part of their networks (such as board members, top managers, or leaders within a scientific discipline). The objective of this senior-peer mentoring is not, in conventional terms, to increase the chances of success but to create a sustainable community of people who can challenge the emergent leader's assumptions and practices and those of his company, industry, or other area of activity.

We witnessed just this kind of peer-to-peer development when one senior client became concerned that he, his company, and the industry as a whole were operating at the Achiever level. This concern, of course, was itself a sign of his readiness to transform beyond that logic. This executive—the CEO of a dental hygiene company—and his company were among the most successful of the parent company's subsidiaries. However, realizing that he and those around him had been keeping their heads down, he chose to initiate a research project—on introducing affordable dental hygiene in developing countries—that was decidedly out of the box for him and for the corporation.

The CEO's timing was right for such an initiative, and he used the opportunity to engage in collaborative inquiry with colleagues across the country. Eventually, he proposed an educational and charitable venture, which the parent company funded. The executive was promoted to a new vice presidency for international ventures within the parent company—a role he exercised with an increased sense of collaboration and a greater feeling of social responsibility for his company in emerging markets.

Formal education and development processes can also guide individuals toward a Strategist action logic. Programs in which participants act as leaders and challenge their conventional assumptions about leading and organizing are very effective. Such programs will be either long term (one or two years) or repeated, intense experiences that nurture the moment-to-moment awareness of participants, always providing the shock of dissonance that stimulates them to reexamine their worldviews. Path-breaking programs of this type can be found at a few universities and consultancies around the globe. Bath University in the UK, for instance, sponsors a two-year master's degree in responsibility and business practice in which students work together during six one-week get-togethers. These programs involve small-learning teams, autobiographical writing, psychodrama, deep experiences in nature, and a yearlong business project that involves action and reflection. Interestingly, many people who attend these programs report that these experiences have had the transformative power of a life-altering event, such as a career or existential crisis or a new marriage.

Leadership Teams and Leadership Cultures Within Organizations

So far, our discussion has focused on the leadership styles of individuals. But we have found that our categories of leadership styles can be used to describe teams and organizations as well. Here we will talk briefly about the action logics of teams.

Over the long term, the most effective teams are those with a Strategist culture, in which the group sees business challenges as opportunities for growth and learning on the part of both individuals and the organization. A leadership team at one of the companies we worked with decided to invite managers from across departments to participate in time-to-market new product teams. Seen as a risky distraction, few managers volunteered, except for some Individualists and budding Strategists. However, senior management provided sufficient support and feedback to ensure the teams' early success. Soon, the first participants were promoted and leading their own cross-departmental teams. The Achievers in the organization, seeing that others were being promoted, started volunteering for these teams. Gradually, more people within the organization were experiencing shared leadership, mutual testing of one another's assumptions and practices, and individual challenges that contributed to their development as leaders.

Sadly, few companies use teams in this way. Most senior manager teams operate at the Achiever action logic—they prefer unambiguous targets and deadlines, and working with clear strategies, tactics, and plans, often against tight deadlines. They thrive in a climate of adversity ("When the going gets tough, the tough get going") and derive great pleasure from pulling together and delivering. Typically, the team's leaders and several other members will be Achievers, with several Experts and perhaps one or two Individualists or Strategists (who typically feel ignored). Such Achiever teams are often impatient at slowing down to reflect, are apt to dismiss questions about goals and assumptions as "endless philosophizing," and typically respond with hostile humor to creative exercises, calling them "off-the-wall" diversions. These behaviors will ultimately limit an Achiever team's success.

The situation is worse at large, mature companies where senior management teams operate as Experts. Here, vice presidents see themselves as chiefs and their "teams" as an information-reporting formality. Team life is bereft of shared problem-solving, decision-making, or strategy formulating efforts. Senior teams limited by the Diplomat action logic are even less functional. They are characterized by strong status differences, undiscussable norms, and ritual "court" ceremonies that are carefully stage-managed.

Individualist teams, which are more likely to be found in creative, consulting, and nonprofit organizations, are relatively rare and very different from Achiever, Expert, and Diplomat teams. In contrast to Achiever teams, they may be strongly reflective; in fact, excessive time may be spent reviewing goals, assumptions, and work practices. Because individual concerns and input are very important to these teams, rapid decision making may be difficult.

But like individual people, teams can change their style. For instance, we've seen Strategist CEOs help Individualist senior teams balance action and inquiry and so transform into Strategist teams. Another example is an Achiever senior team in a financial services company we worked with that was emerging from two years of harsh cost cutting during a market downturn. To adapt to a changing and growing financial services market, the company needed to become significantly more visionary and innovative and learn how to engage its workforce. To lead this transforma-

tion, the team had to start with itself. We worked with it to help team members understand the constraints of the Achiever orientation, which required a number of interventions over time. We began by working to improve the way the team discussed issues and by coaching individual members, including the CEO. As the team evolved, it became apparent that its composition needed to change: Two senior executives, who had initially seemed ideally suited to the group because of their achievements, had to be replaced when it became clear that they were unwilling to engage and experiment with the new approach.

During this reorientation, which lasted slightly more than two years, the team became an Individualist group with emergent Strategist capabilities. The CEO, who had profiled at Achiever/Individualist, now profiled as a Strategist, and most other team members showed one developmental move forward. The impact of this was also felt in the team's and organization's ethos: Once functionally divided, the team learned to accept and integrate the diverse opinions of its members. Employee surveys reported increased engagement across the company. Outsiders began seeing the company as ahead of the curve, which meant the organization was better able to attract top talent. In the third year, bottom- and top-line results were well ahead of industry competitors.

The leader's voyage of development is not an easy one. Some people change little in their lifetimes; some change substantially. Despite the undeniably crucial role of genetics, human nature is not fixed. Those who are willing to work at developing themselves and becoming more self-aware can almost certainly evolve over time into truly transformational leaders. Few may become Alchemists, but many will have the desire and potential to become Individualists and Strategists. Corporations that help their executives and leadership teams examine their action logics can reap rich rewards.

DAVID ROOKE (david@harthill.co.uk) is a partner at Harthill Consulting in Hewelsfield, England. **WILLIAM R. TORBERT** (torbert@bc.edu) is a professor at Boston College's Carroll School of Management in Massachusetts. They are coauthors of *Action Inquiry: The Secret of Timely and Transforming Leadership* (Berrett-Koehler, 2004).

Reprinted by permission of *Harvard Business Review,* April 2005, pp. 67-76. Copyright © 2005 by the Harvard Business School Publishing Corporation, all rights reserved.

When Followers Become Toxic

Few leaders realize how susceptible they are to their followers' influence. A good set of values, some trusted friends, and a little paranoia can prevent them from being led astray.

LYNN R. OFFERMANN

Douglas MacArthur once said, "A general is just as good or just as bad as the troops under his command make him." Almost as he made that remark, his country's president was proving the point. For in late 1961, John F. Kennedy, bowing to pressure from his advisers, agreed to the escalation of American intervention in Vietnam. Among the advisers pressuring him was the senior author of a report recommending military intervention. And that adviser's trusted friend—an American general—was chosen by the president to lead the new U. S. command in Saigon. Given his loyalties, the general wanted to make sure things looked good on the surface, so he stifled evidence from the field about potential setbacks and obstacles in Vietnam, making it tough for the president to discern the truth.

That, according to author and journalist David Halberstam, was how President Kennedy and his advisers led the United States into Vietnam. The story starkly illustrates just how easily, and with the best of intentions, loyal and able followers can get their leaders into trouble. If an accomplished politician like Kennedy could be misled in this way, it's no surprise that today's business leaders often fall into the same trap. No matter who we are, we are all influenced by those around us. Some of us are leaders, but we are *all* followers. Indeed, Ken Lay, the disgraced ex-chairman of Enron, may not be entirely wrong in blaming unscrupulous subordinates and advisers for his company's demise. As an executive coach to senior leaders in a variety of industries for more than 20 years, I've seen firsthand just how easily followers can derail executive careers.

How does it happen? In the following pages, I draw both on my experience as a consultant and executive coach and on decades of research in organizational psychology to describe when and why leaders become vulnerable to being led astray by their followers. In some cases, as the Kennedy story illustrates, effective leaders can end up making poor decisions because able and well-meaning followers are united and persuasive about a course of action. This is a particular problem for leaders who attract and empower strong followers; these leaders need to become more skeptical and set boundaries. At other times,

leaders get into trouble because they are surrounded by followers who fool them with flattery and isolate them from uncomfortable realities. Charismatic leaders, who are most susceptible to this problem, need to make an extra effort to unearth disagreement and to find followers who are not afraid to pose hard questions. Charismatic or not, all leaders run the risk of delegating to unscrupulous followers. There's probably little they can do to completely guard against a determined corporate Iago, but leaders who communicate and live a positive set of values will find themselves better protected.

When the Majority Rules

Although many leaders pride themselves on their willingness to take unpopular stands, research has consistently demonstrated that most people—including leaders—prefer conformity to controversy. And the pressure to conform rises with the degree of agreement among those around you. Even if widespread agreement doesn't actually exist, the very appearance of it can be hard to resist.

One of the most striking pieces of evidence for this was a series of experiments conducted in the 1950s by psychologist Solomon Asch. Asch showed participants a vertical line and then asked them to judge which of three other lines was most similar in length to the test line. Participants who made judgments on their own chose the correct answer 99% of the time. Yet when other participants answered as part of a group in which fake respondents had been coached to pick a particular incorrect line, almost three-quarters of the unknowing participants made at least one wrong choice and one-third of them conformed to the group choice half the time.

It's worth noting that the participants conformed without any pressure from the fake respondents. Indeed, the fake respondents were strangers whom the participants were unlikely to see ever again. In workplace situations where continued interactions are expected and where there may be concern about possible loss of face, one would reasonably expect conformity to be even more marked. What's more, most business decisions are urgent, complex, and ambiguous, which encourages people to depend on the views of others. We should hardly be surprised, therefore, to find that the ethical and capable individuals who served on the boards of companies like WorldCom and Enron turned "into credulous, compliant apparatchiks more focused on maintaining collegiality than maximizing long-term profitability," as the *Washington Post* put it.

What happens is that leaders faced with a united opposition can start to question their own judgment. And they should question themselves—the reason that unanimity is such a powerful influencing force is simply that the majority often is right. In general, research shows that using social proof—what others think or do—to determine our behavior leads us to make fewer mistakes than opposing the majority view does. But as even the smartest leaders have had to learn the hard way, the majority can be spectacularly wrong.

People tend to be what psychologists call "cognitive misers," preferring the shortcuts of automatic thinking over considered examination.

One reason that even well-informed experts so often follow the crowd is that people by nature tend to be what psychologists call "cognitive misers," preferring the shortcuts of automatic thinking over considered examination. These shortcuts can help us to process information more quickly but can also lead to monumental errors. For instance, product designers may assume that if they like a product, everyone will. Yet the flop of Dell's Olympic line of desktop and workstation computers taught managers there that products must appeal to more than the company's own technically savvy workforce. As Michael Dell put it, "We had gone ahead and created a product that was, for all intents and purposes, technology for technology's sake rather than technology for the customer's sake."

Cognitive miserliness can be reinforced by culture. In the United States, for instance, Americans have long tolerated—even encouraged—people who form and express quick opinions. It is not a reflective society. Americans like to brainstorm and move on. That shortcut mentality can be particularly dangerous if the opinions are presented publicly, because people will then advance their views tenaciously.

In such public forums, it falls to the leader to push followers to examine their opinions more closely. Alfred P. Sloan, the former chairman of GM, understood this very well. He once said at the close of an executive meeting: "Gentlemen, I take it we are all in complete agreement on the decision here. I propose we postpone further discussion until our next meeting to give ourselves time to develop disagreement and perhaps gain some understanding of what the decision is all about."

Another factor contributing to the power of the majority is that leaders worry about undermining their employees' commitment. This is a reasonable concern. Leaders do need to be care-

ful about spending their political capital, and overruling employees one too many times can demotivate them. Indeed, there are times when going along with the majority to win commitment is more important than making the "right" decision. (For more on when it's wise to go along with the majority, see the box "Joining the Opposition") But other times, leaders need to listen instead to the single, shy voice in the background, or even to their own internal doubts. As Rosalynn Carter once said," A leader takes people where they want to go. A great leader takes people where they don't necessarily want to go but ought to be." In going against the tide, the leader will sometimes boost rather than undermine his or her credibility.

Fooled by Flattery

Being swept along by their followers isn't the only form of influence that leaders need to be wary of. Sometimes, follower influence takes the subtler and gentler form of ingratiation. Most people learn very early in life that a good way to get people to like you is to show that you like them. Flattery, favors, and frequent compliments all tend to win people over. Leaders, naturally, like those who like them and are more apt to let those they are fond of influence them.

For their part, followers think that being on the boss's good side gives them some measure of job security. To an extent, they're probably right; even a recent *Forbes* guide to surviving office parties recommends: "Try to ingratiate yourself. In this market, people are hired and kept at their companies for their personal skills." Indeed, a recent study indicated that successful ingratiators gained a 5% edge over other employees in performance evaluations. This kind of margin by itself won't get someone ahead, but in a competitive market, it might well tip the scale toward one of two people up for a promotion.

Everyone loves a sincere compliment, but those who already think highly of themselves are most susceptible to flattery's charms. In particular, leaders predisposed toward narcissism may find their narcissistic tendencies pushed to unhealthy levels when they are given heavy doses of follower ingratiation. Gratuitous ingratiation can create a subtle shift in a leader's attitude toward power. Instead of viewing power as something to be used in the service of the organization, clients, and stakeholders, the leader treats it as a tool to further personal interests, sometimes at the expense of others in and outside the organization. This happens as a leader starts to truly believe his press and comes to feel more entitled to privileges than others. People often cite Jack Welch's retirement deal as an example of executive entitlement gone haywire. The resulting furor drew public scorn for a longstanding corporate icon.

But one of the most serious problems for leaders who invite flattery is that they insulate themselves from the bad news they need to know. In her memoir, Nancy Reagan relates how then—Vice President George Bush approached her with concerns about Chief of Staff Donald Regan. Mrs. Reagan said she wished he'd tell her husband, but Bush replied that it was not his role to do so. "That's exactly your role," she snapped. Yet followers who have witnessed the killing of previous messengers of unwelcome news will be unlikely to volunteer for the role.

Joining the Opposition

The leader who automatically rejects his followers' opinions can be as unwise as one who unthinkingly goes along with them. In fact, there are times when it is advisable to go along with followers who are plainly wrong.

A senior executive in the health care field recently faced a united front of followers in an acquired facility. The followers wanted the executive to retain a popular manager despite an outside consultant's report that strongly recommended the manager's dismissal. Staff members felt that the manager had been wrongly blamed for the unit's problems and that the unit had been mishandled, underfunded, and generally "done in" by previous management.

Although the senior executive was under pressure from her COO to dismiss the manager, she chose to keep and support him—and watch carefully. By choosing this course, the executive won the support and confidence of hundreds of employees who saw procedural justice in her willingness to give the manager a chance. With the full support of her staff, the executive then went on to lead a turnaround of the facility in short order, exceeding the COO's expectations. Indeed, the executive built so much credibility through her actions that she was eventually able to dismiss the manager, with the staff understanding that he had had a fair chance but had failed.

The executive recognized not only the unanimity of employees but also the importance of winning their buy in and commitment. She chose, intentionally, to defer to the staff's wishes in order to demonstrate her fairness and openness. After all, the employees could have been correct in their assessment. Even though that didn't turn out to be the case, the leader's considered decision to go along with her reports likely resulted in a better outcome than if she had summarily rejected their opinions.

Samuel Goldwyn's words resonate strongly: "I want you to tell me exactly what's wrong with me and with MGM even if it means losing your job." As more staff ingratiate or hold back criticism, the perception of staff unanimity, often at the expense of the organization's health, increases as well.

The rare individual who won't join an ingratiating inner circle of followers is typically seen as a bad apple by both the leader and her peers. Even when this perception problem is acknowledged, it is tough to fix. Despite widespread publicity after the 1986 space shuttle *Challenger* disaster about the dangers of failing to attend to negative news, NASA is once again facing charges of having downplayed possible liftoff problems just before the *Columbia* disaster. In both cases, engineers allegedly did not inform senior NASA executives of safety concerns; they either withheld information or presented it in ways that diminished its importance or feasibility. Obviously, this tendency to withhold information is not limited to government agencies. Bill Ford, the new CEO of Ford Motor Company, believes that isolation at the top has been a big problem at Ford—a problem he has spent considerable time trying to rectify by a variety of means, including forcing debate and discussion among executives and having informal, impromptu discussions with employees at all levels.

In dealing with ingratiation, leaders need to begin by reflecting on how they respond to both flattery and criticism. In considering a follower's advice or opinion, ask yourself if you would respond differently if a staff member you disliked made the same comment, and why. Are followers really free to voice their honest assessments, or are they jumped on whenever they deviate from your opinions? Bill Ford makes a point of thanking people whom he has overruled because he wants them to know that their honesty is appreciated. One simple test of whether you're getting the feedback you need is to count how many employees challenge you at your next staff meeting. As Steven Kerr, chief learning officer of Goldman Sachs, says: "If you're not taking flak, you're not over the target."

Organizational mechanisms can also help. Greater exposure to external feedback from clients, well-run 360-degree feedback programs, and executive coaching may be more likely to reveal the full truth. It's hard to lead from a pedestal; open channels of communication can keep a leader far better grounded.

For honest feedback, some CEOs rely on longtime associates or family members, people who may even take pleasure at times in letting some of the air out of the executive's balloon. (Your teenage children might particularly enjoy this, though they might not have as much insight into your business). Bill Gates, for instance, has said that he talks to his wife, Melinda, every night about work-related issues. In particular, he credits her with helping him handle the transition period when he turned over the Microsoft CEO title to his old friend Steve Ballmer. Ballmer, too, has been one of Gates's closest advisers. Gates says of this peer relationship with Ballmer: "It's important to have someone whom you totally trust, who is totally committed, who shares your vision, and yet who has a little bit different set of skills and who also acts as something of a check on you." And Gates's well-known friendship with fellow billionaire and bridge buddy Warren Buffer serves as a sounding board for both men. Disney's Michael Eisner had a similar relationship with Frank Wells, until Wells's death in 1994, with Wells enjoying the role of devil's advocate, challenging Eisner to ensure that the best decisions got made.

It's worth remembering the words of cartoonist Hank Ketchum: "Flattery is like chewing gum. Enjoy it, but don't swallow it."

Six Ways to Counter Wayward Influences

There's no guaranteed means of ensuring that you won't be misled by your followers. But adhering to these principles may help.

1. **Keep vision and values front and center.** It's much easier to get sidetracked when you're unclear about what the main track is.

2. **Make sure people disagree.** Remember that most of us form opinions too quickly and give them up too slowly.

3. **Cultivate truth tellers.** Make sure there are people in your world you can trust to tell you what you need to hear, no matter how unpopular or unpalatable it is.

4. **Do as you would have done to you.** Followers look to what you do rather than what you say. Set a good ethical climate for your team to be sure your followers have clear boundaries for their actions.

5. **Honor your intuition.** If you think you're being manipulated, you're probably right.

6. **Delegate, don't desert.** It's important to share control and empower your staff, but remember who's ultimately responsible for the outcome. As they say in politics, "Trust, but verify."

In his book *You're Too Kind*, journalist Richard Stengel gives an account of flattery through the ages, noting that "the history of how ministers have used flattery to control leaders did not begin with Henry Kissinger's relentless and unctuous toadying to Richard Nixon. … Cardinal Richelieu was a famous user of flattery … and he was a famous sucker for it himself." Stengel argues that corporate VPs who suck up to their bosses are no different than the less powerful chimpanzees who subordinate themselves to more powerful ones in the animal world. Though it may feel great at the time, stroking a leader's ego too much, and protecting him or her from needed information, can have negative consequences for both the leader and the organization. It's worth remembering the words of cartoonist Hank Ketchum: "Flattery is like chewing gum. Enjoy it, but don't swallow it."

Powers Behind the Throne

Caught between the Scylla of follower unanimity and the Charybdis of flattery, leaders might be tempted to keep their followers at a distance. But in today's world, this is simply not an option. CEOs of major firms cannot know everything about their own organizations. In coaching senior executives, I often hear them lamenting that they don't have full knowledge of what's happening in their companies. They report sleepless nights because they've been forced to make decisions based on incomplete information. They must rely on others for full, accurate, and unbiased input as well as for many operational decisions.

From the follower's point of view, this presents wonderful opportunities. He can learn and practice new skills as the leader relies on him more and more, and he may be presented with new opportunities for advancement and reward. At the same time, however, it opens the door for the occasional follower who uses his newfound power to serve his own interests more than the company's.

So how can leaders guard against that problem? They can begin by keeping ethical values and corporate vision front and center when delegating and monitoring work. Only then can they be certain that followers have a clear framework and

boundaries for their actions. As Baxter CEO Harry Kraemer says, the key to ensuring that followers do the right thing is "open communication of values … over and over and over again."

Leaders can also protect themselves and their companies by setting good examples. Followers—especially ingratiators—tend to model themselves after their leaders. Thus, straightforward leaders are less likely to be manipulated than manipulative leaders are. And a leader who is seen to condone or encourage unethical behavior will almost certainly get unethical behavior in his ranks. Take the case of former WorldCom CEO Bernie Ebbers, who allegedly ridiculed attempts to institute a corporate code of conduct as a waste of time even as he pressed his followers to deliver double-digit growth. He shouldn't have been surprised to find that junior WorldCom executives cooked the books or at least turned a blind eye when others did.

Although competency is generally a good basis on which to grant followers greater influence, leaders need to avoid letting followers influence them based on competency alone. As W. Michael Blumenthal, former chairman and CEO of Unisys, once said, "When did I make my greatest hiring mistakes? When I put intelligence and energy ahead of morality." The danger here is that astute but unscrupulous followers can find ways of pushing their leaders in unethical directions and may even use the leader's stated values against him. Suggestions like "I know you like saving money, so you'll love the idea of…," followed by a shady proposal, force leaders into the position of having to choose between eating their words and accepting the proposal.

At the end of the day, leaders have to rely on their instincts about people. Fortunately, there is good news in this respect. Research by psychologist Robert Zajonc suggests that we process information both affectively and cognitively and that we experience our feeling toward something a split second before we intellectualize it. If leaders are attentive, therefore, they may be able to tune in to a fleeting feeling that something is not quite right or that they are being manipulated before they rationalize and accept what they would be better off rejecting. For example, one tactic favored by manipulative followers is to create a false sense of urgency to rush the leader into an uninformed decision. Recognizing that you're being pushed too fast and reserving judgment for a time may save you from an action you may regret.

One simple test of whether you're getting the feedback you need is to count how many employees challenge you at your next staff meeting.

It's not only the people you delegate to that you have to watch, it's also *what* you delegate. Clearly, leaders can never delegate their own responsibilities without peril. Smart leaders understand that even well-intentioned followers have their own ambitions and may try to usurp tasks that properly belong to their leaders. Harry Stonecipher, former president and COO of Boeing, likes to point to the great polar explorer Ernest Shackleton as an example of a leader who knew what responsibilities he could and couldn't afford to delegate. Stranded on an ice pack and crossing 800 miles of stormy seas in an open boat, Shackleton knew the deadly consequences of dissension and therefore focused his attention on preserving his team's unity. He was happy to delegate many essential tasks to subordinates, even putting one man in charge of 22 others at a camp while he sailed off with the remainder of the crew to get assistance. But the one task he reserved for himself was the management of malcontents, whom he kept close by at all times. Amazingly, the entire crew survived the more than 15-month ordeal in fairly good health, and eight members even joined Shackleton on a subsequent expedition.

■

By understanding how followers are capable of influencing them, top executives can improve their leadership skills. They can choose to lead by steadfastly refusing to fall prey to manipulative forces and try to guide the way toward more open and appropriate communications.

Followers, for their part, can better understand their power to inappropriately influence leaders. Once they recognize the danger they pose to their leaders—and ultimately to themselves ingratiators may come to realize that isolating leaders from reality can be as costly to themselves as to the company's shareholders. Realizing the value of dissent may force followers to take more care in forming and promoting their opinions.

Understanding that some tasks are best left to a leader may help followers to know where to stop and leaders to know what not to give away. In the final analysis, honest followers have just as great an investment in unmasking manipulative colleagues as their leaders do.

LYNN R. OFFERMANN is a professor of organizational sciences and psychology at George Washington University in Washington, DC, and the director of the university's doctoral program in industrial and organizational psychology.

Reprinted by permission of *Harvard Business Review*, 82 (1) January 2004. Copyright © 2004 by the Harvard Business School Publishing Corporation, all rights reserved.

To Err Is Human

Influential research on our social shortcomings attracts a scathing critique

BRUCE BOWER

I t's a story of fear, loathing, and crazed college boys trapped in perhaps the most notorious social psychology study of all time. In the 1971 Stanford Prison Experiment, psychologist Philip G. Zimbardo randomly assigned male college students to roles as either inmates or guards in a simulated prison. Within days, the young guards were stripping prisoners naked and denying them food. The mock prisoners were showing signs of withdrawal and depression. In light of the escalating guard brutality and apparent psychological damage to the prisoners, Zimbardo halted the study after 6 days instead of the planned 2 weeks.

Zimbardo and his colleagues concluded that anyone given a guard's uniform and power over prisoners succumbs to that situation's siren call to abuse underlings. In fact, this year, in a May 6 Boston Globe editorial, Zimbardo asserted that U.S. soldiers granted unrestricted power at Iraq's Abu Ghraib prison inevitably ended up mistreating detainees—just as the college boys did in the famous experiment.

Rot, says psychologist S. Alexander Haslam of the University of Exeter in England. No broad conclusions about the perils of belonging to a powerful group can be drawn from the Stanford study, in his view. Abuses by the college-age guards stemmed from explicit instructions and subtle cues given by the experimenters, Haslam asserts.

However one interprets the Stanford Prison Experiment, it falls squarely in the mainstream of social psychology. Over the past 50 years, researchers have described how flaws in study participants' behaviors and thinking create all sorts of mishaps in social situations.

This accounting of our monumental aptitude for ineptitude and cruelty has appealed both to social scientists and to the public; these experiments are among the most celebrated products of social science.

They're also profoundly misleading, say Joachim I. Krueger of Brown University in Providence, R.I., and David C. Funder of the University of California, Riverside. Mainstream social psychology emphasizes our errors at the expense of our accomplishments, the two psychologists contend. Also, because the work uses artificial settings, it doesn't explain how social behaviors and judgments work in natural situations, they believe.

In an upcoming *Behavioral and Brain Sciences*, Krueger and Funder compare much of current social psychology to vision research more than a century ago. At that time, visual illusions were considered reflections of arbitrary flaws in the visual system.

In 1896, a French psychologist proposed that visual illusions arise from processes that enable us to see well in natural contexts. For instance, during their years of visual experience, people come to achieve accurate depth perception by perceiving a line with outward-pointing tails as farther away than a line with inward-pointing tails. The result is the illusion that a line is longer when adorned with outward-facing tails than with inward-facing ones.

Subsequently, vision scientists unraveling illusions focused on elements of visual skill rather than on apparent shortcomings in the visual system. Krueger and Funder propose what they say is a similar shift—in which psychologists will consider how different behaviors and thought patterns might have practical advantages, even if they sometimes lead to errors.

Many social psychologists continue to search for what they regard as inherent flaws in people's behaviors and attitudes. In several responses published with Krueger and Funder's critique, these researchers describe their work as a necessary first step toward identifying ways to improve our social lives by learning to avoid errors in behavior and thought.

Krueger prefers an alternative approach. "A more balanced social psychology would seek to understand how people master difficult behavioral and cognitive challenges and why they sometimes lapse," he says.

Today, investigators interested in how evolution, culture, and the brain shape mental life are already on this track, Krueger says, as they probe the accuracy and practical impact of various social behaviors and beliefs.

Group Peril Social psychology's pioneers, with few exceptions, believed that individuals lose their moral compass in groups and turn into "irrational, suggestible, and emotional brutes," Krueger and Funder argue. Laboratory studies in the 1950s and 1960s laid the groundwork for the Stanford Prison Experiment by probing volunteers' conformity in the face of social pressure, chilling obedience to cruel authority figures, and unwillingness to aid needy strangers.

Yet the underlying complexity of such findings has often been ignored, Krueger and Funder say. In 1956, for instance, Solomon Asch placed individual volunteers in groups where everyone else had been instructed to claim that drawings of short lines were longer than drawings of long lines. Most of the time, volunteers acceded to the crowd's bizarre judgments.

Asch also studied conditions where volunteers simultaneously tended to resist conformity's pull. For example, when two volunteers entered a group, they often supported each other in a minority opinion. However, the story of individuals' submission to strange group beliefs received far more public attention than the other findings did.

Stanley Milgram upped the ante in 1974 by studying obedience to a malevolent authority figure. In his notorious work, an experimenter relentlessly ordered participants to deliver what they thought were ever-stronger electrical shocks to an unseen person whose moans and screams could be heard. As many as 65 percent of participants administered what they must have thought were highly painful, and perhaps even lethal, voltages (*SN: 6/20/98, p. 394*).

In further experiments, Milgram found that in certain conditions, obedience to the instruction to shock someone dropped sharply. These included situations in which two authorities gave contradicting orders or the experimenter gave instructions to shock himself. Yet these variations were overlooked, and Milgram's work achieved fame as a dramatic exposé of our obediently brutal natures.

A third set of studies demonstrated a seemingly uncaring side to human nature. This work grew out of the infamous 1964 murder of a New York City woman. Dozens of apartment dwellers did nothing as they heard the woman's screams and watched her being stabbed to death.

Bibb Latané of Florida Atlantic University in Boca Raton and John Darley of Princeton University set up simulated emergency situations in the late 1960s and demonstrated that the proportion of people attempting to aid a person in need declined as the number of bystanders increased. The presence of others depresses a person's sense of obligation to intervene in an emergency, as each bystander waits for someone else to act first, the researchers concluded. The nature of certain social situations encourages people to act in unseemly ways, Darley says.

Krueger and Funder don't draw that conclusion from these studies and others like them. They counter that there may be underlying factors, such as concerns for personal safety derived from real-life experiences, that make that behavior more sensible than it seems.

Our responses to real-life situations remain poorly understood, they contend. In their view, researchers have yet to probe thoroughly how behaviors emerge from the interplay between individuals' personalities and the situations in which they find themselves.

Guards Gone Wild The Stanford Prison Experiment offers a dramatic example of how scientists who agree with Krueger and Funder's critique can revise and draw new lessons from a classic social psychology investigation.

After noting the scarcity of research inspired by Zimbardo's report, Exeter's Haslam organized his own exploration of group power in December 2001. Because the 1971 Stanford experiment later attracted charges of ethical transgressions, an independent, five-person ethics committee monitored the new study.

Haslam built an institutional environment with three cells for 10 prisoners and quarters for five guards inside a London film studio, where cameras recorded all interactions. In May 2002, the British Broadcasting Corporation, which funded the project, aired four 1-hour documentaries on the "BBC Prison Study." Academic papers on the study are currently in preparation.

Haslam's interests differed significantly from those of Zimbardo. He wanted to draw conclusions about groups with hierarchies and, after setting up some ground rules, he removed himself from what went on.

Before the study got under way, guards were asked to come up with their own set of prison rules and punishments for violators. Haslam had stipulated that on the study's third day guards could promote any prisoners to guard status who showed "guardlike qualities" and that the prisoners would know about that provision.

In contrast, Zimbardo in the earlier experiment told guards that it was necessary to exert total control over prisoners' lives and to make them feel scared and powerless.

From the start, the guards in Haslam's experiment found it difficult to trust one another and work together. Moreover, unlike the guards in the earlier experiment, they were generally reluctant to impose their authority on prisoners.

On the third day, one prisoner received a promotion to guard. The remaining prisoners then began to identify strongly as a group and to challenge the legitimacy of the guards' rules and punishments.

A new prisoner entered the study on day 5 and began to question the guards' power and certain aspects of the study, such as what they regarded as excessive heating of the prison. From then on, in a rapidly shifting chain of events, prisoners broke out of their cells, and guards joined prisoners in what they called a commune.

However, two guards and two prisoners fomented a counterrevolution to set up strict authoritarian rule. Instead of opposing that group, the members of the commune became demoralized and depressed. As the situation deteriorated, Haslam's team stopped the experiment after 8 days, 2 days before its scheduled conclusion.

The BBC Prison Study indicates that tyranny doesn't arise simply from one group having power over another, Haslam says. Group members must share a definition of their social roles to identify with each other and promote group solidarity. In his study, volunteers assigned to be prison guards had trouble wielding power because they failed to develop common assumptions about their roles as guards.

"It is the breakdown of groups and resulting sense of powerlessness that creates the conditions under which tyranny can triumph," Haslam holds.

The Hot Hand Gets an Assist
An Irrational Belief Scores in Basketball

Professional basketball players and coaches rarely pay much attention to psychology experiments. Yet they scoffed in 1985 after psychologist Thomas Gilovich of Cornell University and two colleagues published a report that claimed to debunk the popular belief that hoopsters who hit several shots in a row have a "hot hand" and are likely to score on their next shot, as well.

Over an entire season, individual members of the Philadelphia 76ers exhibited constant probabilities of making and flubbing their shots, regardless of whether the immediately preceding shots had been hits or misses, Gilovich's team found. So, strings of successful shots don't reflect a shooter's hot hand.

Although belief in the hot hand is irrational, there may still be good reason to heed an illusory hot hand in a basketball game, says psychologist Bruce D. Burns of Michigan State University in East Lansing. Teams that preferentially distribute the ball to players on shooting streaks score more points than teams that don't, Burns asserted in the February *Cognitive Psychology*.

Gilovich's National Basketball Association (NBA) data show that scoring streaks occur more often among the best overall shooters, Burns notes. When players regard a string of scores by a teammate as a cue to set him up for more shots, they are favoring the strongest player.

Using a model of hot-hand behavior and computer simulations of basketball games based on the NBA data, Burns estimated that a professional team that follows the hot-hand rule scores one extra basket every seven or eight games. That's a small advantage, but enough to make a difference over a season.

Hot-hand beliefs probably boost team scoring to a greater extent in pick-up basketball games, where players know much less about their teammates' shooting abilities than NBA pros do, Burns says.—B.B.

Imperfect Minds During the past several decades, social psychology has moved from reveling in people's bad behavior to documenting faults in social thinking, according to Krueger and Funder. This shift reflects the influence of investigations, launched 30 years ago, by psychologists studying decision-making. That work showed that people don't use strict standards of rationality to decide what to buy or to make other personal choices.

Investigators have uncovered dozens of types of errors in social judgment. However, methodological problems and logical inconsistencies mar much of the evidence for these alleged mental flaws, Krueger and Funder assert.

For instance, volunteers who scored poorly on tests of logical thinking, grammatical writing, and getting jokes tended to believe that they had outscored most of their peers on those tests, according to a 1999 report by Cornell's Justin Kruger and David Dunning. In contrast, high scorers on these tests slightly underestimated how well they had done compared with others.

Kruger and Dunning concluded that people who are incompetent in a task can't recognize their own ineptitude, whereas expertise in a task leads people to assume that because they perform well, most of their peers must do the same.

Kruger, however, says, "This study exemplifies the rush to the conclusion that most people's social-reasoning abilities are deeply flawed."

Krueger and Funder hold that the results are undermined by a statistical effect known as regression to the mean. If participants take two tests, each person's score on the second test tends to revert toward the average score of all test takers. Thus, a person who had scored high on the first test is more likely to score lower on a second test. Similarly, low scorers from the first test will tend to come in higher on a second test than on the first. So, the Kruger and Dunning finding doesn't necessarily indicate that low scorers lack insight into the quality of their performance, Krueger adds.

In a published response, Dunning doesn't counter the statistical challenge but says that his results have been confirmed by further studies. He contends that, in general, social psychologists "would do well to point out people's imperfections so that they can improve upon them."

Krueger and Funder follow another scientific path. Instead of assuming that behavior and thinking are inherently flawed, they see errors as arising out of adaptive ways of interacting with the world.

"It is the breakdown of groups and resulting sense of powerlessness that creates the conditions under which tyranny can triumph."
—S. Alexander Haslam, University of Exeter

Krueger studies whether individuals see themselves in an unduly positive light and, if they do, whether such self-inflation contains benefits as well as costs.

Funder observes exchanges between pairs of volunteers to study how each individual assesses the other's personality. He determines which of the cues emitted by one person are detected by the other person and how they lead to an opinion about the first volunteer's personality.

While encouraging psychologists to look at positive aspects of social interactions, neither researcher harbors any illusions that what the two call the "reign of errors" in social psychology is about to end. They'd rather not add another mental mistake to the list.

From *Science News*, August 14, 2004, pp. 106-108. Copyright © 2004 by Science Service Inc. Reprinted by permission via the Copyright Clearance Center.

Senate Intelligence Report

Groupthink Viewed as Culprit in Move to War

VICKI KEMPER

Washington—The 1961 Bay of Pigs invasion. The escalation of the Vietnam War. The go-ahead for launching the space shuttle Challenger.

Groupthink, an insular style of policy-making, has been identified as a chief culprit in all. And Friday, the Senate Intelligence Committee added to those the process leading to the 2003 decision to attack Saddam Hussein.

Irving Janis, a Yale psychologist, coined the term in 1972 to describe a decision-making process in which officials are so wedded to the same assumptions and beliefs that they ignore, discount or even ridicule information to the contrary. When members of a cohesive, homogeneous group value unanimity and agreement on one course of action more than a realistic appraisal of alternatives, they are engaging in groupthink.

Experts said Friday that groupthink was not entirely responsible for the acceptance of faulty intelligence information on Iraq, but that the Bush administration was, by design, particularly susceptible to that dangerous style of decision-making.

"Groupthink is more likely to arise when there is a strong premium on loyalty and when there is not a lot of intellectual range or diversity within a decision-making body," said Stephen M. Walt, academic dean of Harvard University's Kennedy School of Government.

All organizations and presidential administrations face the same risk, Walt said. He added that the report specifically indicted the intelligence community, but that others, including Democratic lawmakers and the media, also failed to challenge basic assumptions about Iraq's weapons capability.

"When a president makes a decision about something, there is a tendency to get on the train rather than throwing yourself in front of it," Walt said. "Whatever Bush's flaws may be, indecision is not one of them."

Business schools and political scientists are among those who warn would-be policy-makers and managers of the dangers of groupthink. CRM Learning, a company specializing in developing products for leadership and management development, has been selling its popular Groupthink video program since the 1970s.

The commonly cited "symptoms" of groupthink are a fundamental overconfidence that gives members an illusion of invulnerability and a belief in the inherent morality of the group.

The groupthink dynamic also is characterized by a pressure to conform that often leads group members with different ideas to censor themselves. But groupthink is most likely to occur when all or most members of a group already share the same views.

In that sense, it is the opposite of collective wisdom, said James Surowiecki, a financial writer for the New Yorker and author of the recent book, "The Wisdom of Crowds."

What's really striking about groupthink is not so much that dissenting opinions are crushed or shouted down, but they come to seem improbable," he said. "Everyone operates on the idea that this is true, so everyone goes out to prove that it's true."

Surowiecki, who concludes in his book that "under the right circumstances, most groups are remarkably intelligent," said it's when leaders surround themselves with like-minded people that groupthink is a danger.

"Collective wisdom," by contrast, comes when "each person in the group is offering his or her best independent forecast," he said. "It's not at all about compromise or consensus."

He said a guiding principle of the Bush administration seems to be that "everyone needs to be on the same page to reach a decision." To reach good decisions, he said, "I think it's exactly the opposite."

From *The Los Angeles Times,* July 10, 2004, pp. A17. Copyright © 2004 by The Los Angeles Times. All rights reserved. Used with permission of LA Times Reprints.

Sports Complex

The Science Behind Fanatic Behavior

SHIRLEY WANG

Only one month after April 3rd's opening day, baseball fans from Boston to Oakland are beginning to hear a familiar cry: "Yankees suck!" These words—chanted in unison, with clapping hands and stomping feet—are the mantra of many spectators who support opposing teams. Such vocal expressions of intergroup rivalry are just one facet of sports fans' fascinating and often perplexing behavior.

Husband-and-wife team Beth and Lefty (who have asked their last name not to be disclosed) learned this firsthand after they launched the Web site, Yankeessuck.com. Though established for the sake of "irony and humor," the site has many times fallen victim to crashes, threats, crude posts, and, once, hacking from a self-proclaimed Yankees fan who left an expletive-laced message in his wake.

"There's an expression I've heard," says Beth "that 'sports don't build character, they reveal it.' That's what's happening here. If they're angry people, this gives them an outlet. Where else in the world can you just pick an enemy and just hate them?"

Inflaming the Fan

While it may seem understandable that an athlete becomes attached to teammates and being part of a team, it is clear that sports spectators—those regulars sitting in the stands—can also become so passionate about their team that it becomes part of their identity and affects their well-being.

Research shows similarities between a fan's identification with a sports team and how people identify with their nationality, ethnicity, even gender. Team identification "is the extent to which a fan feels a psychological connection to a team and the team's performances are viewed as self-relevant," says Daniel Wann, professor of psychology at Murray State University, who has spent much of his career dedicated to research about sports spectators.

In watching the action, people do indeed identify with teams, and for some, team identification is both important and powerful to their sense of self.

"People are tying up a lot of who they are in their identity as fan of X-team," says Edward Hirt, associate professor of psychological and brain sciences at Indiana University-Bloomington, who has also conducted research on the psychology of sports fans. "A huge part of who they are, where they derive a lot of their positive and negative affect, is from what their team is doing."

Perhaps the most basic question—a genuine mystery for some non-sports-fans—is why people follow sports so ardently. What is it about watching sports that possesses otherwise composed individuals to scream, obsess over statistics, and paint their faces—particularly when they know that there's a very good chance that their team is going to lose?

Sports fan researchers emphasize this point: that sporting events are competitions in which it is guaranteed that one team must lose, which means that half the fans will be upset with the result. In other activities, those odds might not seem like a worthwhile investment of one's time.

"It's a voluntary activity where half of the people aren't going to like the product when they've finished consuming it," says Wann. "You wouldn't go see a movie if you thought there was a 50/50 chance you wouldn't like it."

So being a fan can't be all about a team's winning performance. "Everyone is eventually going to lose," says Hirt. "It's clear that has to be other benefits that people are accruing."

Perhaps no fans understand loyalty to a losing team better than followers of the Chicago Cubs. The Cubs have not won major league baseball's top prize, the World Series, for nearly 100 years (that's even without Bambino's Curse that plagued Boston). Yet the team cultivates an overwhelming fan base and maintains a legendary bleacher-section community.

Ask a Cubs fan why he or she likes the team and, according to Wann, they won't say because of all the championships. "They'll say, 'I love Wrigley Field, I love the bleachers and the community in the outfield bleachers,'" says Wann. "Identification is not just with the team—that might be the target or the focal field—but what draws with that is the identification that comes with it."

John McDonough, senior vice president of marketing and broadcasting for the Cubs, couldn't agree more. "We're marketing the experience more than other teams," he says. "Maybe they won the division or the World Series. Here, it's really about the unique mystique of the Chicago Cubs. What resonates the loudest with the fan base is the experience."

A Need to Belong

Although people report many reasons for following a favorite team, social connectedness is among the most frequently cited, as Wann finds in his research on college and professional sports fans.

"When we look at motivation for following a sport team, group affiliation is one of the top ones," says Wann. "Identifying strongly with a salient local team where other fans are in the environment—that's a benefit to social-psychological well-being."

In a series of studies, Wann has surveyed hundreds of undergraduate fans, who vary in their fanaticism for their college teams. After measuring levels of sports team identification and psychological well-being, he found that the results are correlational but consistent: Higher identification with a team is associated with significantly lower levels of alienation, loneliness, and higher levels of collective self-esteem and positive emotion.

Seeing another person wearing the team emblem on a shirt allows for an instant connection. This shared identity might facilitate communication among individuals or just increase a feeling among fans that they have shared values.

"If you take away the socialness, it would lose something for some people," says Wann. "Part of identifying with the sport team is not just with the team, but with the fan base."

Sports might be a particularly enticing means of fostering belongingness for several reasons.

"One reason is the way the activity lends itself to large audiences," says Wann. The venue, he says, provides an easy way of interacting with other spectators, and the vast majority of fans, about 95 percent, attend games with friends.

In addition, highly identified fans tend to be socialized to sports early and view it not just as a game but also as a nostalgic or emotional experience. Many say that they can remember going to games as a child, or that games remind them of pleasant childhood memories.

The repetition of the sports seasons may be another thing that draws fans to the game. "There's always the next season," says Hirt, repeating a mantra sports fans are fond of repeating after an unsuccessful season. "Everyone has a chance in spring training. There's always the sort of opportunity that next season it can happen."

An Extension of Self

Team identification not only fosters a sense of social belonging, but also it impacts individual self-esteem.

In a study published in the *Journal of Personality and Social Psychology* in the early 1990s, Hirt and colleagues examined the effects of team allegiance on individuals' beliefs about their own competence and self-esteem. They brought participants who reported being highly identified with their college basketball teams into the lab and showed them a tape of their teams either winning or losing. Afterwards, each participant was asked to predict how well he or she thought the team would do in the future. Participants were also asked to make seemingly unre-

lated estimates of their own performance on motor, mental, and social-skills tasks.

"The most powerful thing we found was that for highly allied fans, they really did view the team's success akin to how they would view a personal success," says Hirt.

Fans who watched their team win reported significantly higher estimates of the team's future performance, their own task performance, and personal self-esteem than did those who watched their team lose. The boost that the winning-team group received was similar to the boost that participants received when they personally succeeded or failed at a task.

"The team is an extension of the self," says Hirt.

Belonging Is More Important than Winning

Another facet of sports fandom is just how dedicated many fans are.

"The whole idea behind identification is that it's really part of how we see ourselves and that doesn't change easily," says Robert J. Fisher, professor of marketing at The University of Western Ontario, whose research emphasizes the effects of social expectations on managerial and consumer decision making. "If you see yourself as a member of a family, that role doesn't change. Those types of connections are very long-lasting and very strong."

He and colleagues published a 1998 study examining how fans of winning teams versus those of losing teams explained their allegiances. Surveying fans at hockey games, they found that for a successful team, performance was cited as a main reason for identification.

But for fans of continually losing teams, that relationship didn't exist. Instead, members of unsuccessful groups turned their attention to other aspects of their team, such as how much they liked the individual players.

"We actively choose to find people or organizations that enable us to have a certain kind of view of ourselves, to represent ourselves to others," says Fisher.

Like our choice of spouses or friends, "we want to see ourselves as making good choices and being smart and proud of being who we are," says Fisher. "We have to find ways to work around their failings to keep them close to us."

The annual Cubs Convention demonstrates how teams can capitalize on fans' desires to remain affiliated. When McDonough joined the organization in 1983, he wanted to keep the Cubs on the minds of fans year-round, so he set about making the team appear more personal to the fans.

The first of its kind in baseball, fans were invited to join players, management, and other fans for a weekend in the off season, both to celebrate the previous season and to anticipate the upcoming one. Now 22 years in the running, the convention attracts 15,000 fans in the dead of winter, and has spawned copycat events by other major-league baseball teams.

McDonough cites a breaking down of barriers as the main reason for the Convention's success.

"Previously in sports you were never able to ask the manager of your favorite team a question, former players, or current players about their experience," says McDonough. The Convention "humanized the game. It broke down those barriers of the players being unapproachable. Winning and losing was not an issue."

McDonough is right on, according to the sports-marketing literature. Winning is the best marketing tool, but beyond that, "one of the big recommendations is making the team accessible," says Ryan Zapalac, Rice University, who researches marketing to sports fans. "If you provide accessibility to the community, you make people feel as though that player is a part of the community."

In fact, marketers over the past decade have notably targeted the sports fan psyche by using relationship-building marketing strategies, says Jeff James, associate professor of sports marketing at Florida State University. Rather than exclusively trying to attract new fans, they are attempting to build longer lasting, closer relationships with existing ones.

"It's moving from 'I'm a fan of the team' to 'I'm a part of the team,'" says James.

The Los Angeles Dodgers' new "Think Blue" credit card points system allows fans to accrue points that can redeemed for batting practice on the field, Dodger equipment used in games, and the best seats in the stadium. The motto is "Earn Rewards. Live Your Dodger Dreams!"

Other strategies for increasing fans' connections to the team include player autographs and birthday announcements on scoreboards.

"Why do we allow people to make marriage proposals at the ballpark?" poses James. "That couple is coming back. It's now their anniversary."

Loyalty Benefits the Loyal

Apart from strategies that teams use to draw fans, fans themselves utilize psychological strategies to justify and maintain their passion—even when a team's performance is otherwise disappointing.

"Sports fans have perfected methods of coping," says Wann. "If they weren't able to cope, there wouldn't be any sports fans."

They may boost their self-esteem when the team wins by basking in reflected glory, wearing a team-logo shirt the next day, or talking about the game with coworkers at the office.

In a recent study published in the *Journal of Social Psychology*, Wann and Rick Grieve, professor of psychology at Western Kentucky University, surveyed 148 fans from both teams as they were leaving a sporting event and asked them to rate their agreement with statements that their team's fans has exhibited good behavior and sportsmanship. They were then asked to evaluate the opposing team's fans. The results showed that fans—particularly those of the winning team—were more likely to say that the opposing team's fans displayed worse behavior than their own team's fans, a clear case of in-group bias.

"It almost seems to me that they were using the denigration of other fans as a way to enhance self-esteem," says Grieve. "'Not only is my team better, but man, your fans stink, too.'"

When their team does poorly, however, they may also show biased perceptions against other people, such as the referees, the other team's players, or fans of the other team. Their recollection of events may also be inaccurate.

"The good times are always better than what they really were," says Grieve.

Those who are highly identified with their teams are particularly motivated to use these coping strategies when their teams perform poorly. Because the team is part of their identity, they cannot deny themselves the team's importance.

"Rather than distancing from teams," says Grieve, "They may shift expectations. They shift to cope."

Fans may choose to follow another favorite team in a different sport for a while, or reflect on past glory years, or dream of future success, according to Wann.

Emphasizing loyalty to a team is another way fans can soothe themselves.

When their sports team fails, the highly identified fan might say to him- or herself, "'I'm not like other people, I'm loyal in the face of all they've gone through,'" says Fisher. "'When they are finally successful, everyone will see that I'm really smart.'"

Alternatively, fans might use hindsight bias, according to Grieve. I knew they were going to lose, but I was so loyal I cheered for them anyway.

Superstition as a Way to Cope

Superstitions are an integral part of sports, and they may also be yet another way fans cope with their team's performance.

In ongoing research, Wann and his colleagues are exploring the role of fan superstition. Over half of his 1,000 participants can readily define a superstition or ritual they believe in. Moreover, some are truly convinced that their participation in ritual superstition impacts the outcome, says Wann. The more highly identified with a team the fans are, the more likely they are to believe that superstitions matter.

"It's a real struggle that sports fans experience," says Wann. "They so much care about the outcome of the event they have absolutely zilch control over. How do we gain control? We may develop superstitions."

Indeed, sports spectators employ an impressive number of strategies to develop and maintain their allegiance with teams. And they may have to strategize even more as it becomes increasingly rare for players to play for just one team in their careers.

"Now you can't go hating those guys too much because they might be on your team next year," says Baumeister. "All these illusory relationships become much more fleeting. That makes it harder to have that illusion."

Yet despite that illusion, team losses, bad seasons, and so on, the fans remain ardent.

"Sports fans," says Wann, "are so resilient because they can hope."

References

Fisher, R.J. & Wakefield, K. (1998). Factors leading to group identification: A field study of winners and losers. *Psychology & Marketing, 15,* 23–40.

Hirt, E.R., Zillmann, D., Erickson, G.A., & Kennedy, C. (1992). Costs and benefits of allegiance: Changes in fans' selfascribed competencies after team victory versus defeat. *Journal of Personality and Social Psychology, 63,* 724–738.

Lindstrom, W.A., & Lease, A.M. (2005). The role of athlete as contributor to peer status in school-age and adolescent females in the United States: From pre-title IX to 2000 and beyond. *Social Psychology of Education, 8,* 223–244.

Wann, D.L. (2006). Examining the potential causal relationship between sport team identification and psychological wellbeing. *Journal of Sport Behavior, 29,* 79–95.

Wann, D.L., & Grieve, F.G. (2005). Biased Evaluations of In-Group and Out-Group Spectator Behavior at Sporting Events: The Importance of Team Identification and Threats to Social Identity. *Journal of Social Psychology, 145,* 531–545.

From *APS Observer,* Vol. 19, no. 5, May 2006, pp. 28, 30-32. Copyright © 2006 by American Psychological Society. Reprinted by permission via the Copyright Clearance Center.

Test Your Knowledge Form

We encourage you to photocopy and use this page as a tool to assess how the articles in *Annual Editions* expand on the information in your textbook. By reflecting on the articles you will gain enhanced text information. You can also access this useful form on a product's book support Web site at *http://www.mhcls.com/online/*.

NAME: DATE:

_____

TITLE AND NUMBER OF ARTICLE:

_____

BRIEFLY STATE THE MAIN IDEA OF THIS ARTICLE:

_____

LIST THREE IMPORTANT FACTS THAT THE AUTHOR USES TO SUPPORT THE MAIN IDEA:

_____

WHAT INFORMATION OR IDEAS DISCUSSED IN THIS ARTICLE ARE ALSO DISCUSSED IN YOUR TEXTBOOK OR OTHER READINGS THAT YOU HAVE DONE? LIST THE TEXTBOOK CHAPTERS AND PAGE NUMBERS:

_____

LIST ANY EXAMPLES OF BIAS OR FAULTY REASONING THAT YOU FOUND IN THE ARTICLE:

_____

LIST ANY NEW TERMS/CONCEPTS THAT WERE DISCUSSED IN THE ARTICLE, AND WRITE A SHORT DEFINITION:

ANNUAL EDITIONS: SOCIAL PSYCHOLOGY, 7/E

BUSINESS REPLY MAIL
FIRST CLASS MAIL PERMIT NO. 551 DUBUQUE IA

POSTAGE WILL BE PAID BY ADDRESEE

McGraw-Hill Contemporary Learning Series
2460 KERPER BLVD
DUBUQUE, IA 52001-9902

NO POSTAGE
NECESSARY
IF MAILED
IN THE
UNITED STATES

ABOUT YOU

Name

Date

Are you a teacher? ☐   A student? ☐
Your school's name

Department

Address   City   State   Zip

School telephone #

YOUR COMMENTS ARE IMPORTANT TO US!

Please fill in the following information:
For which course did you use this book?

Did you use a text with this ANNUAL EDITION? ☐ yes ☐ no
What was the title of the text?

What are your general reactions to the *Annual Editions* concept?

Have you read any pertinent articles recently that you think should be included in the next edition? Explain.

Are there any articles that you feel should be replaced in the next edition? Why?

Are there any World Wide Web sites that you feel should be included in the next edition? Please annotate.

May we contact you for editorial input? ☐ yes ☐ no
May we quote your comments? ☐ yes ☐ no

We Want Your Advice

ANNUAL EDITIONS revisions depend on two major opinion sources: one is our Advisory Board, listed in the front of this volume, which works with us in scanning the thousands of articles published in the public press each year; the other is you—the person actually using the book. Please help us and the users of the next edition by completing the prepaid article rating form on this page and returning it to us. Thank you for your help!

ANNUAL EDITIONS: Social Psychology, 7/e

ARTICLE RATING FORM

Here is an opportunity for you to have direct input into the next revision of this volume.
We would like you to rate each of the articles listed below, using the following scale:

1. **Excellent: should definitely be retained**
2. **Above average: should probably be retained**
3. **Below average: should probably be deleted**
4. **Poor: should definitely be deleted**

Your ratings will play a vital part in the next revision.
Please mail this prepaid form to us as soon as possible.
Thanks for your help!

RATING	ARTICLE	RATING	ARTICLE
	1. How to Be a Wise Consumer of Psychological Research		21. *Brokeback Mountain*: A Gay and A Universal Love Story
	2. Ethnic and Racial Health Disparities Research: Issues and Problems		22. The Self-Protective Properties of Stigma: Evolution of a Modern Classic
	3. Self-Esteem Development Across the Lifespan		23. Leaving Race Behind
	4. Self-Concordance and Subjective Well-Being in Four Cultures		24. Lowered Expectations
	5. Mirror, Mirror: Seeing Yourself As Others See You		25. Change of Heart
	6. How Social Perception Can Automatically Influence Behavior		26. Thin Ice: "Stereotype Threat" and Black College Students
	7. Flashbulb Memories: How Psychological Research Shows That Our Most Powerful Memories May Be Untrustworthy		27. A Bicultural Perspective on Worldviews
			28. Anger on the Road
			29. Bullying: It Isn't What It Used To Be
	8. Culture Affects Reasoning, Categorization		30. Influencing, Negotiating Skills, and Conflict-Handling: Some Additional Research and Reflections
	9. The Social Nature of Perception and Action		
	10. Perception of Faces and Bodies		31. The Compassionate Instinct
	11. Implicit Discrimination		32. Gift Giving's Hidden Strings
	12. The Science and Practice of Persuasion		33. Trends in the Social Psychological Study of Justice
	13. In Search of Pro Americanism		34. Seven Transformations of Leadership
	14. "Thin Slices" of Life		35. When Followers Become Toxic
	15. Abu Ghraib Brings A Cruel Reawakening		36. To Err Is Human
	16. Persuasion: What Will It Take to Convince You?		37. Senate Intelligence Report: Groupthink Viewed as Culprit in Move to War
	17. Contagious Behavior		38. Sports Complex: The Science Behind Fanatic Behavior
	18. Competent Jerks, Lovable Fools, and the Formation of Social Networks		
	19. Isn't She Lovely?		
	20. If It's Easy Access That Really Makes You Click, Log On Here		

(Continued on next page)